PUBLIC ADMINISTRATION IN BRITAIN TODAY

PUBLIC ADMINISTRATION IN BRITAIN TODAY

JOHN GREENWOOD
DAVID WILSON

ROUTLEDGE
London and New York

First published by the academic division of Unwin Hyman Ltd 1984
Second edition 1989
Second impression 1990

Reprinted by Routledge 1993
11 New Fetter Lane, London EC4P 4EE

Typeset in 10 on 11 point Bembo by
Computatape (Pickering) Ltd, North Yorkshire

Printed and bound in Great Britain by
Biddles Ltd, Guildford and King's Lynn

British Library Cataloguing in Publication Data
A catalogue reference for this book is available from the British Library

ISBN 0-415-10914-0

Library of Congress Cataloging in Publication Data

Greenwood, John R.
Public administration in Britain today/John Greenwood and David Wilson.
p. cm.
Rev. ed. of: Public administration in Britain, 1984.
1. Administrative agencies – Great Britain.
2. Executive departments – Great Britain.
3. Great Britain – Politics and government.
4. Local government – Great Britain.
I. Wilson, David J. (David Jack) II. Title.
JN318.G73 1989
350'.000941—dc20 89-5702
CIP

ISBN 0-415-10914-0

CONTENTS

Preface xi

1 THE CONTEXT OF BRITISH PUBLIC ADMINISTRATION 1

What is public administration? 1
The policy/administration dichotomy 3
Environmental influences 4
The extent of public administration 5
Public and private administration 7
Managerialism and public administration 10
The IT revolution in public administration 15
The expansion and contraction of British public administration 16
The complexity of contemporary public administration 18

2 DEPARTMENTS AND DEPARTMENTALISM 21

What is a government department? 21
Departmental organization 23
Departmental organization and civil servants 27
Reforming departmental organization 28
The Ibbs Report: 'The next steps' 30
Advisory machinery 33
The departmental pattern 34
The dynamics of departmental work 40

3 CO-ORDINATING CENTRAL ADMINISTRATION 44

What is co-ordination? 44
Informal co-ordinating mechanisms 47
Co-ordination within departments 48
Co-ordination between departments 51
Central policy review staff (CPRS) 58
Improving central co-ordination 61

4 THE CABINET SYSTEM 63

Cabinet functions 63
Influences upon the Cabinet 66
Cabinet composition and size 69
Cabinet committees 71
The Cabinet Office 75
A Prime Minister's department? 77

5 CENTRAL ADMINISTRATION IN ACTION 84

Key personnel in central administration 84
Role and characteristics of civil servants 86
Civil servants and ministers: working relationships 89
A ruling class? 95
Towards a partisan bureaucracy? 97
Overview 99

6 THE CIVIL SERVICE: EVOLUTION AND CHANGE 101

Nineteenth-century pressure for reform 101
The Northcote–Trevelyan Report 101
The Fulton diagnosis 102
Fulton's recommendations 106
Implementing Fulton 108
Overview 109

7 MANAGERIALISM IN CENTRAL ADMINISTRATION 121

The Rayner scrutiny programme 122
Management information system for ministers (MINIS) 125
The Financial Management Initiative (FMI) 128
Implementing the FMI: Political clout or cultural change? 135
Managerialism and public administration 138
Public administration or public management? 141

8 LOCAL GOVERNMENT: THE ADMINISTRATIVE AND POLITICAL CONTEXT 142

Administrative complexity 142
Development and structure 143
The functions of local authorities 150
Inter-authority relationships 152
Local politics and democracy 154
Financing local government 159

9 INSIDE LOCAL GOVERNMENT 166

Formal structures 166
Corporate planning 167
Councillors 171
Officers 175
Officer–councillor relationships 177

10 CENTRAL–LOCAL GOVERNMENT RELATIONSHIPS 184

Analytical models 184
The formal framework 189
Working relationships 194
Changing relationships: the 1980s 198
The local state? 205
Overview and prospects 207

11 QUASI-GOVERNMENT 209

Introduction 209
Numbers and types of quangos 210
Non-departmental public bodies: rationale 212
Control and accountability 213
Patronage 217
Exit non-departmental public bodies? 218
Conclusions 220

12 ADMINISTERING PUBLIC OWNERSHIP AND PRIVATIZATION 222

Terminology and ambiguity of public ownership 222
The extent of public ownership 224
Reasons for public ownership 225
Forms of public ownership 226
Public corporations in action 232
Reforming public corporations 243
Privatizing public enterprise 245
Forms of privatization 246
Reasons for privatization 247
Administering privatized enterprises 248

13 REGIONAL ADMINISTRATION 253

The context of regional administration 253
The water industry 256
The National Health Service 260
Managing the NHS: the Griffiths Reports 269
Conclusions 271

14 PARLIAMENT AND ACCOUNTABILITY 273

Legislation 273
Parliament and public finance 279
Ministerial responsibility 283
Scrutiny and redress 292

15 PUBLIC ADMINISTRATION AND REDRESS 299

The courts 299
Inquiries 301
Administrative tribunals 303
Control of tribunals and inquiries 308
Ombudsmen 310
The Parliamentary Commissioner for Administration (PCA) 311
The Health service commissioner 317
Local Commissioners for Administration 319
Too many avenues? 322

References 325
Index 351

PREFACE

This book, as originally conceived, was intended as a second edition of *Public Administration in Britain*, first published in 1984. The idea was to provide an up-dated revision maintaining the same organizational structure and framework of analysis. Very quickly, however, it became apparent to us that this approach could not do justice to the *very* substantial changes in British public administration which had occurred since the original book was written. With local government, for example, the intervening period had witnessed not only rate-capping – barely on the horizon when the first book was written – but abolition of the 'met' counties, the Widdicombe Report, substantial privatization, and the promised replacement of domestic rates with the community charge. With central government also, as the Financial Management Initiative has worked through, profound changes have occurred since 1984; indeed, as the revised manuscript neared completion the 'Next steps' report – published in early 1988 – promised the prospect of radical and even more substantial reforms in departmental and administrative structures. Elsewhere in the public sector, too, important developments have occurred: privatization, for example, has diminished the scale of public ownership but has stimulated the development of new agencies for regulating privatized enterprises; whilst events like the Westland affair have necessitated a reassessment of the convention of ministerial responsibility and the workings of both the Cabinet system and Commons select committees. One of the themes of the original book, the dynamic nature of British public administration, has perhaps been more true of the 1980s than of any other decade, to an extent which has made the original concept of this new book – as an up-dated version of the first – quite inappropriate. Indeed at times the task facing us seemed almost impossible: as fast as one draft was written changing circumstances required a reassessment and – in many cases – a substantial rewrite.

In the event what has emerged is not simply a revision and an up-date of *Public Administration in Britain*, but an expanded analysis and a largely new assessment of the subject. Where appropriate, new sections have been introduced to cover fresh areas of interest and importance such as the computer revolution in public administration, the 'Next steps' programme, the administration of privatized enterprises, the NHS Griffiths Reports and the Westland affair. In addition a whole new chapter has been added to provide coverage of managerial developments in central administration. As far as possible these changes have been introduced within the framework and style of the original text, but all sections and chapters have been thoroughly revised to take account of new developments, up-to-date figures, and the latest research and source material. Reflecting this approach – a substantially new text following the style and format of the old – has made this book, we feel, more than just a new edition of *Public Administration in Britain*; hence, the title *Public Administration in Britain Today*.

Inevitably in a text such as this our debts to others are enormous. In particular we are indebted to numerous friends and colleagues who have read substantial parts of the original drafts. Professor Richard Chapman of Durham University gave unstintingly of his time to comment authoritatively and candidly on those chapters dealing with central administration and the civil service. Dr Christopher Pollitt (Open University) and Dr Geoffrey Fry (University of Leeds) made helpful comments which have much improved the wholly new chapter on 'Managerialism in central administration'. Peter Hennessey once again read, commented on and brought much more life to our original draft on the Cabinet system, and Dr Bob Borthwick of The University of Leicester was similarly helpful with the draft material on Parliament. Professor Howard Elcock of Newcastle Polytechnic made helpful and detailed comments on the three local government chapters, and Dr Stephen Young of The University of Manchester provided most helpful advice on public ownership and privatization. Three colleagues at Leicester Polytechnic, Clive Gray, Pat Mounfield and Merrill Clarke, allowed us to add to their busy schedules by reading and much improving our offering on regional administration, and we are similarly indebted to Ian Mcleod and Professor Neil Hawke (both also of Leicester Polytechnic) and Professor Roy Gregory of The University of Reading for help with the chapter on redress of grievance. We have also received much valuable help and assistance from practitioners who work and serve in public authorities and to these, too, we should like to acknowledge our debt.

We are both conscious that a text such as this belongs to more than just the efforts of the authors, and even of those who have kindly commented on specific parts of the original draft. A tremendous resource has been the collective knowledge of colleagues and practitioners with whom our long association with public administration courses at Leicester Polytechnic has brought us into contact. Space does not permit us to thank them all by name, but many will recognize their contribution by the cessation with the publication of this text of hurried inquiries from the authors about specific points or source material. Many students of public administration, particularly those at Leicester Polytechnic, have also made valuable suggestions about coverage and possible improvements. To numerous librarians – and particularly those in the Scraptoft branch of Leicester Polytechnic library – we also owe a very considerable debt.

Finally we should like to bear tribute to the fact that, beside the author of every published text, there usually lies a patient and long-suffering family. This has been true in both our cases. Our wives, Pam Greenwood and Sue Wilson – together with our children – suffered long periods of relative solitude (and in one case the prolonged disappearance of the front room beneath a sea of paper) to enable this work to reach fruition. To these – and to all who gave us their time freely and without complaint – we should like to give our thanks. Needless to say, responsibility for any errors or omissions remain ours and ours alone.

John R. Greenwood
David J. Wilson
September 1988

PUBLIC ADMINISTRATION IN BRITAIN TODAY

1 THE CONTEXT OF BRITISH PUBLIC ADMINISTRATION

What is public administration?

Any attempt to produce a simple definition of public administration is doomed to failure. As Waldo (1955, p. 2) observes, 'The immediate effect of all one-sentence or one-paragraph definitions of public administration is mental paralysis rather than enlightenment and stimulation'. In a similar vein Drewry (1984, p. 503) has argued that public administration is, by its very nature, 'notoriously a sprawling and untidy subject, yet it does perhaps possess a certain charm through being (as Lord Diplock once said of the common law) "a maze and not a motorway"'. The variegated nature of the subject's component parts and the complexity of the linkages between them makes coherent analysis extremely difficult, not least because there is no real consensus about what is 'public' or what is 'administration'. Is there, for example, a single 'public' or various 'publics'?

The *complexities* of the field in many ways belie simple generalizations. Whatever formal institutional descriptions might imply, there is, in reality, nothing simple about the practice of British administration. Organization charts in governmental institutions invariably present a neat, ordered universe, but nothing could be further removed from the actuality of public sector administration. It is a major theme of this book that the 'ambiguity, confusion and complexity' which Rhodes (1981, p. 28) maintains characterizes central/local government relationships in fact typifies the whole of British public administration. At a basic level misunderstandings can occur because the term 'public administration' is used in a number of different ways. Fletcher (1967, pp. 53–4) explains that it can be used to denote:

1 The *activity* of public servants.
2 The *structure* of executive government: that is the institutions and patterns of relationships through which the activity of public servants is carried on.
3 The study of 1 and 2.

Put another way, public administration is 'an activity', a set of institutions and a subject of study' (Stanyer and Smith, 1976, p. 11). As a subject it 'focuses pre-eminently on the institutions, organizational structures and decision/implementation processes of government. It is largely a "formal" field, concerned with arrangements and procedures for making decisions, rather than with the substance or impacts of these decisions' (Dunleavy, 1982, p. 215).

In recent years controversy about the nature of public administration has been fuelled by a de-emphasis upon its traditional regulatory and policy-advisory functions, and the widespread acceptance of a more managerialist approach which emphasizes the efficient use of resources and value for money in public service provision. The extent of this approach, and the questions which it raises about the nature and practice of public administration, are dealt with elsewhere in the text (especially pp. 10–15, and Ch. 7). Here, however, it can be noted that one important effect has been to emphasize the *skills* component of practical public administration, raising the question of how far public-administration teaching should be skills-based as opposed to knowledge-centred, a question highlighted recently by Kingdom (1986a, 1986b, 1987) and Chapman (1987). Kingdom sharply criticizes the emphasis on skills (which is particularly identified within BTEC, HNC and HND Public Administration course guidelines). While acknowledging that public administrators require skills, he contends that such skills as can be acquired 'in a college setting, in the absence of a rigorous study of the context of public administration, will tend to be either of a very low level, or conceived in terms too abstract to render them particularly effective' (1986b, p. 13). Along with Bellamy and Franklin (1985), he complains about the lack of recognition in some BTEC schemes of the need for knowledge-based components to support the development of skills and techniques. Chapman's rejoinder, however, emphasizes the skills training and development necessary to equip future public administrators, distinguishing (1987, p. 29) between what he describes as the 'real world in which students must operate' and the 'unreal world in which some academics seem more comfortable'. While some might criticize Chapman (and BTEC) for an over-zealous enthusiasm for skills, this is undoubtedly an element of public administration education which must not be underplayed. Public administration is a vocational study aimed at ensuring that students can operate within their working environment, and mastering skills is vital if students are to find jobs and enhance their careers.

At the same time public administration cannot be confined to a narrow emphasis on skills and techniques. Skills need to be acquired in context and if this is not properly understood the 'outputs' from public-sector administrators will be seriously deficient. Contextual knowledge is crucial if sensible judgements are to be made (see, for example, Greenwood and Woodhead, 1988). Future administrators need to know about the administrative world in which they will practise their skills, which they will inhabit, and which their joint mastery of skills and knowledge will help them to improve.

The policy/administration dichotomy

Confusion about definitions is compounded because the term 'administration' is not at all straightforward. Dunsire (1973) argues that there are at least fifteen different meanings of the word, ranging from carrying out decisions to initiating policy. A distinction is sometimes made between 'policy' and 'politics' (which it is suggested is the work of elected politicians) and 'administration' or 'execution' (which is the work of officials or administrators). Under scrutiny, however, this distinction breaks down, for two main reasons:

1 Policy and administration are largely indistinguishable. All policy decisions are to some extent predicated upon considerations about implementation. No government, for example, could realistically take a policy decision to put a man on the moon until means of implementation were known to be available. More than this, administrative decisions – about how a policy should be implemented – themselves require implementation, and as such often take the form of another policy decision. For example, a decision to reduce inflation might be implemented in a number of ways: controlling prices and incomes, tax changes, controlling money supply, etc. Assuming that the first of these is chosen, this in effect will become a policy – a prices and incomes policy – which will itself require decisions regarding implementation. Should, for example, all wages and prices be controlled or just some? Should machinery be established to monitor price and income movements? What penalties, if any, should be imposed upon unions or companies breaking the law? As these examples show, there is a 'seamless web' of policy and administration. Precisely where 'policy' ends and 'administration' begins is impossible to determine.
2 It is too simplistic to argue that the role of politicians is to determine policy while that of officials is confined to implementing political decisions. Indeed, even if 'policy' and 'administration' could be clearly defined, the respective roles of politicians and officials would still be difficult to demarcate. Because administrative considerations bulk large in policy-making, and because much policy-making requires specialist advice along with professional analysis, politicians in practice rely heavily on their officials when formulating policy. In recent years, moreover, elected politicians have shown much greater interest in the management of public bureau-

cracies, and efficiency considerations have become increasingly important as factors in decision-making. The distinction between policy determined by politicians and administration carried out by officials has little credibility in the contemporary world of British public administration.

Environmental influences

Public bodies do not exist in a vacuum but are closely related to the broader envirionment which they inhabit. They are both influenced by, and themselves influence, that environment.

ENVIRONMENTAL INFLUENCES UPON ORGANIZATIONS

A number of external influences serve to both assist and constrain public administrators. The political dimension is particularly important. As Ridley (1979, p. 3) explains, public administration

> is unavoidably a subsystem of the political system, not just related to it through inputs and outputs but dependent upon it for its basic structures and influenced by it in its values. If administrative systems cannot be understood except by reference to their political environment . . . political systems cannot be understood without study of the administration. The administration not only forms the largest part of government, it lies at the centre of the policy-making process.

The close interrelationship between politics and public administration is a practical reality whatever legal textbooks (and some of the 'skills' school) might indicate to the contrary. Public administration cannot be abstracted out of its social, political and economic environment; it needs to be considered as part of that complex environment.

Environmental factors inevitably help to determine the choices made by politicians and administrators. The prevailing social and political culture provides a framework within which administrative action occurs. Pitt and Smith (1981, p. 25) show, for example, how organizational life in government departments 'is affected by the rules and pressures generated by the political environment'. While recognizing the importance of environmental factors it is, however, unwise to ignore the role played by key personnel, especially those with strong ideological predispositions. The relationship between an organization and its environment is never purely mechanistic; the importance of choice within an organization must always be recognized.

ORGANIZATIONAL INFLUENCES UPON THE ENVIRONMENT

Public authorities are not simply passive systems upon which external forces impact; they themselves can affect the environment in which they operate. Civil servants, for example, can manipulate the environment in which they work by selecting the pressure groups which are admitted into departmental policy-making processes. Likewise, ministers can often manipulate public opinion by carefully timed 'leaks' of information to the media, or through speeches which set the subject and tone of public debate.

ORGANIZATIONAL INTERDEPENDENCE

Organizations do not simply face complex envirionments but are themselves dependent upon elements in that environment. Organizational interdependence is an important element of contemporary public administration. R. A. W. Rhodes (1981, p. 87) illustrates this in the context of central/local government relationships: 'Local authorities are not "mere agents" of central government. They are political systems in their own right with the capacity to resist central demands. Moreover, central government is dependent upon local authorities for information, for expertise and for the implementation of policy.' Similar reciprocity is replicated at all levels of public administration.

The extent of public administration

As Stanyer and Smith (1976, p. 21) observe,

> Many past studies have made the mistake of confusing public administration with the civil service and central departmental administration. Several books whose titles would lead one to expect a discussion of the whole system of public administration are found to have omitted local government, public corporations, field administration and bodies with uncertain or unusual status.

For example, one introductory text states: 'By public administration, then, we mean the machinery of central and local government, the process of implementing political decisions, and the body of people involved in that process' (Derbyshire with Patterson, 1979, p. 3). To limit public administration simply to central and local government,

Table 1.1 *Public Sector Manpower, 1986–7*

	Thousands[1]	Percentage of total public sector
Central government departments[2]	598	10.6
Armed forces	331	5.9
National Health Service	981	17.4
Local authorities[3]	2,352	41.8
Nationalized industries	1,049	18.6
Other public corporations	112	2.0
Other[4]	202	3.6
Total public sector	5,625	

Notes:

1 Actual figures, UK (rounded to nearest thousand).
2 Includes trading funds and self-financing bodies (e.g. Civil Service College).
3 Includes Northern Ireland; community programme and trading bodies.
4 Includes Northern Ireland Civil Service and Prison Service; and research councils.
Source: calculated from *The Government's Expenditure Plans 1988–89 to 1990–91*, (London, HMSO, 1988, Cm 288, Table 2.14).

however, is to omit from analysis roughly half the public sector (Wilson and Woodhead, 1982, p. 210). As Table 1.1 shows, only about half of the 5,625m public service employees in the late 1980s worked for the civil service or local authorities; the rest were employed by the National Health Service, the armed forces, nationalized industries and other public corporations.

An approach which ignores half the public sector leads, as Stanyer and Smith (1976, p. 22) comment, to a failure to appreciate that there exists a system of government, of which central administration is only part. 'The pattern of interactions and relationships between separate elements – the structure of the system – can never be studied properly from the point of view of only a small part with highly specialised characteristics.' It is important to recognize that the 'system' of public administration is linked in a variety of ways with the rest of government and with society as a whole. Public bodies are part of a complex environment.

Complexity is compounded, moreover, by the tremendous diversity within parts of the public sector. With local government, for example, Birmingham City Council (with 1,009,400 inhabitants) is worlds apart from a tiny parish council (such as Walton-on-the-Wolds in Leicestershire with an electoral roll of 214 in 1988). Statutorily, both are 'local authorities' but in practice they are very different. Similarly, central government departments vary enormously in terms of size, internal structures, and operating styles. The 'typical' government department does not exist, and this makes the administrative environment at the core of central government particularly complex. Most complex of all, perhaps, is the world of quasi-government (see Chapter 11). Contrast, for example, the United Kingdom Atomic Energy Authority, employing 13,867 staff and spending £472m in 1986/7, with the Apple and Pear Development Council employing just six staff and spending £1.067m. The presence of such diverse bodies within a single category is indicative of the complexity which characterizes British public administration both between and within the various organizational categories.

Further ambiguity and confusion stems from the blurred terminology which besets public administration. Many of Britain's political institutions have evolved slowly over long periods and although the terms used to describe them have been retained the institutions themselves have changed markedly. For example, the designation 'government department' now covers so many organizational forms that it is almost incapable of precise definition. As Hood, Dunsire and Thompson (1978, p. 22) have observed: 'Every public administration student (not to mention teachers), it might innocently be thought, ought to know what a "Government Department" is. But we came to realise that the question is a deep indeed a philosophical one, and that there is certainly no single and all-encompassing definition of such agencies'. A similar lack of clarity surrounds the term 'civil service', one consequence of which, as Wood (1981, p. 480) points out, is that 'even the question of total numbers is difficult to answer'. Apparently simple issues are invariably far from straightforward.

Public and private administration

Public administration is undertaken in a political setting, which is often highly partisan. Stated simply, its broad focus is the activity of the state. This contrasts to some extent with private sector administration where the goals are those of non-state organizations. Whereas public administration is broadly concerned with the formulation and implementation of public policy, private sector administration has a more restricted set of aims and is often motivated by practicalities such as profit margins. One difficulty, however, is that whenever comparisons are made between public and private administration the impression is frequently given that each is opposed to the other and occupies a separate and distinct field. In practice, much of what takes place in public administration is accomplished with the collaboration of numerous private groups and individuals; 'indeed, the line between "private" and "public" has now become so blurred that it is difficult to tell where government leaves off and private business begins' (Nigro and Nigro, 1973, p. 17). In reality, public and private administration are not nearly so distinct as is sometimes suggested.

Private organizations such as political parties and pressure groups, for example, are intimately involved with public administration, setting the parameters and the 'political agenda' within which public policy is formulated. No less obviously, public bodies make great use of private contractors to build offices, houses, hospitals, etc. Such contractors spend many millions of pounds of public money and employ large numbers of workers who, while technically not government employees, are in many respects a real part of its workforce. Equally, private business depends heavily upon public authorities to supply a host of services, some of them essential for economic performance (roads, postal services, etc.) and others fundamental to the maintenance of an effective workforce (health, education, social services, housing). The interdependence of the two sectors quickly becomes apparent.

As Dunsire (1973, p. 179) reminds us, it is a mistake to draw too firm a line between public and private administration. Often the internal distinctions between different public sector bodies are much more significant than contrasts with the private sector. Dunsire recommends: 'step back a pace and look at both public and business administration in the West together, in contrast to another culture . . . and they are seen as intertwined parts of the same system, inseparable from one another, the values of the one dependent upon the values of the other'. Today, in fact, it is widely argued that public sector efficiency can be adequately assessed with tools originally designed for private sector analysis. Likewise, many public sector organizations – particularly nationalized industries – produce and market products in a manner not dissimilar from private companies. Public and private enterprises, while legally distinguishable, are less clearly disentangled in practice. Did, for example, the purchase by the state of a majority shareholding in British Leyland in the 1970s transfer it overnight from the private to the public sector and turn its 'managers' into public administrators?

As Dunsire (1982, p. 15) argues, the boundary between what is 'state' and what is 'non-state' is increasingly 'seen as a distraction and an irrelevance'. In many policy areas 'the policy community', comprising not only officials but 'businessmen, academics [and] spokesmen of various interests' is involved in initiating or implementing a programme. Consultative committees and advisory councils proliferate and, as Dunsire (1982, p. 16) suggests, 'Institutionalised traffic across the state/non-state boundary is heavy'. In certain contexts it is even appropriate to recognize the 'colonisation of the private sector by government' (Pitt and Smith, 1981, p. 39). Policy communities, of both a formal and informal nature, incorporating both public and private interests, illustrate the difficulty of separating state from non-state organization and management. There must inevitably be an element of artificiality associated with any such exercise. Public administration does, nevertheless, have certain distinctive features, described in the following sections.

PUBLIC ACCOUNTABILITY

Probably the main distinguishing feature of public administration lies in its accountability to the public. As Stanyer and Smith (1976, pp. 30–1) observe: 'At its most elementary, public accountability simply requires that public bodies give an account of their activities to other people and provide a justification for what has been done in terms of other people's values, in a way that private bodies do not'. In other words, public bodies are subject to external checks and overseeing (for example, ministers are accountable to Parliament for the conduct of their departments by the convention of ministerial responsibility) from which private companies are relatively immune. The nearest analogy in the private sector is the ultimate accountability of a company board to shareholders, although this rarely involves the same degree of external checks and overseeing as in the public sector.

The *accountability* of public bodies for their actions should not be confused with the *control* of them exercised by politicians. Nevertheless, the two concepts are closely linked: ministers, for example, cannot be held accountable for their departments unless they have the means to control them. In Britain politicians have traditionally exercised constitutional control over public bureaucracies, and been held accountable for their stewardship to Parliament (in the case of central government) and to elected local councils (with local government). Of course, one effect of this is that public administrators are obliged to pursue aims determined by people other than themselves. This is fine in theory for accountability reasons, but in practice aims determined by outsiders may be vague and even contradictory. As Stanyer and Smith (1976, p. 31) conclude: 'Public bodies are expected to pursue multiple goals and meet multiple standards; hence the problem of distinguishing good and bad is particularly acute and hard to solve.'

EQUITY

Administrators are expected to treat members of the public fairly without showing partiality to one at the expense of another. While there is often ambiguity about precisely what this means, at some levels it is relatively easy to determine. With taxation, for example, where liabilities, allowances, exemptions, etc. are laid down quite precisely in law, it follows that taxpayers in identical circumstances should receive identical treatment – even though they may be dealing with different local offices. As Stanyer and Smith (1976, p. 31) comment, this has important administrative implications 'in that it puts a premium on stability, consistency and accuracy, which are less important values in many private enterprises.'

LEGALITY

Another principle of public administration is that the decision and actions of officials must never be *ultra vires* (or beyond their legal powers). Whereas private individuals and companies are generally free to perform any act not prohibited in law, public authorities can only do those things which they are specifically empowered by law to perform.

DIVERSITY

The fact that public administration takes place within the constraints of equity and legality does not mean that policy outputs and implementation are both uniform and standardized throughout Britain. Public administration must respond to diverse pressures, needs and circumstances, and most government systems are flexible enough to allow this. In Britain, for example, there are major variations in the standard of provision by local authorities (see Chapter 10). A common legal framework does not automatically produce common policy outputs and implementation patterns; hence the importance of analysing administrative processes rather than simply the formal legal/constitutional framework within which public administration occurs.

Managerialism and public administration

The distinction between private management and public administration has become even more blurred in recent years by the widespread adoption within the public sector of management tools originally designed for private sector analysis. The view that public sector efficiency can be assessed by the utilization of such techniques has, in fact, long been advocated. In 1968, for example, the Fulton Report (para. 150) recommended the establishment of accountable units within government departments – 'units where output can be measured against costs or other criteria, and where individuals can be held personally responsible for their performance'. This idea of measuring *outputs* (such as number of soldiers trained – Ministry of Defence; value of tax collected – Inland Revenue) against *inputs* (such as staff, buildings, consumables, etc.), and constructing *performance indicators or measures* (cost per soldier week training – MOD; tax collected per employee – Inland Revenue), draws heavily on the essentially private sector concept of *management accounting* (see *Efficiency and Effectiveness*, 1982, especially Appendix 3, and Annex B and C). Unlike conventional accounting, which is geared to inputs or subjects of expenditure (e.g. wages), management accounting relates to 'outputs' or objects of expenditure, enabling specific programmes or services to be costed, costs to be analysed against benefits, and some assessment of value for money to be obtained.

Fulton believed that arrangements along such lines could be applied quite extensively in central administration. The idea was to transfer to accountable units largely self-contained functions where performance could be measured in financial or quantitative terms, and managers held accountable for standards of achievement. This was expected to provide both greater efficiency and more effective accountability than orthodox departmental arrangements. Managers would be largely freed from the bureaucratic constraints inherent in departmental procedures, and agency costs could be budgeted for separately (instead of being 'lost' in wider departmental accounts). This would present the opportunity for enhanced budgetary control in line with 'output budgeting' techniques pioneered in programme, planning and budgeting (PPB) systems in the USA (see Bourn, 1979, especially ch. 3; Garrett, 1972, pp. 115–49 and 1980, pp. 88–98). Despite Fulton's enthusiasm, however, only limited progress was made during the 1970s in developing such arrangements in central government (see Chapter 2). In government departments the traditional accounting focus is geared to parliamentary supply votes, and is little concerned with outputs. Moreover, the diversity and range of departmental functions makes it difficult to isolate, let alone evaluate, separate cost centres. There are also fundamental problems in identifying the outputs of many public sector bodies (what, for example, is the output of the Prime Minister's Office?) – and problems also in measuring performance in the non-trading parts of the public sector are considerable. As Flynn (1986, p. 393) suggests, 'In these organisations where there is no "market" for the product or service, or where the notion of a market has limited applicability (e.g. in health, school education, social services), imported notions of profitability or other financial ratios will only ever be surrogate, artificial measures'.

Notwithstanding such difficulties, performance measurement in the public sector attracted renewed interest after 1979. A number of factors accounted for this: suspicion of bureaucratic inefficiency, an environment of scarce resources, the development of new technology, the failure of institutional reforms in the 1970s, and most important of all the Thatcher government's support for private sector techniques. While quite significant work on performance indicators was undertaken by a number of public sector bodies even before 1979, after Mrs

Thatcher's election their development and utilization developed apace. As Pollitt (1986b, p. 315) observes, the post-1979 period 'has seen such a proliferation of attempts at performance assessment, appraisal, evaluation, review, measurement and indicators that the difficulty is finding a public service that has not been affected'. This 'wave of performance assessment' has also been accompanied by other measures designed to produce a more 'commercial' approach within the public sector: for example, privatization, competition, the development of quasi-commercial trading organizations, the introduction of private sector managers and management techniques into public sector bodies, and so on.

The underlying object of most of these activities is the pursuit within the public sector of value for money (VFM). Particularly important in this search are what are often referred to as the 'three Es' – efficiency, effectiveness, and economy. Unfortunately, there is no universally accepted definition of these terms, and they are often incorrectly used interchangeably. *Economy* – using fewer resources (input reduction) – is perhaps the most easily understood of the three. Efficiency and effectiveness, by contrast, often give rise to confusion. According to the Treasury and Civil Service Select Committee (1982, HC 236, Appendix 1; see also HM Treasury, 1986b, Annex B), *effectiveness* is essentially concerned with objectives, and can be measured in terms of the extent to which objectives are achieved. *Efficiency*, on the other hand, is concerned with the relationship between the inputs (resources) into a particular activity and the outputs (goods or services) produced by it. Consequently an effective manager – meeting all the desired objectives – might be regarded as highly inefficient if he used more resources than was necessary. Of course, for either term to be used meaningfully it is necessary for organizations to have clear ideas not only of their inputs and outputs – which in the public sector, as we have already seen, is not always easy – but also of objectives. In the private sector, where profit is usually the main organizational objective, this is *relatively* straightforward (although there may often be very difficult decisions to make between, for example, maximizing short-term and long-term profits). In the public sector, however, defining objectives is usually *even* more difficult. Not only is there a problem in defining the objectives of say, the Cabinet Office or the Treasury, but political considerations – difficult to quantify or assess objectively – often influence public sector policy decisions and outcomes.

What, of course, can be identified and measured with *relative* ease are the total inputs (resources consumed) by public sector bodies, and for this reason (and also because managerialism in public bureaucracies has become fashionable in a climate of public expenditure restraint) all too often 'effectiveness' and 'efficiency' have been used as surrogates for 'economy'. The 'three Es', in other words, have in practice often been regarded as reducable to 'economy' or, put more simply, cost (or input) reduction.

Many of the post-1979 managerialist initiatives in British public administration are dealt with in the body of the text, but can be usefully summarized here. In addition to privatization, and the contracting-out of services, which has been carried out extensively in all parts of the public sector, the main developments have been:

a) In *central administration*, the (Rayner) Efficiency Programme, Management Information Systems for Ministers (MINIS), and the financial management initiative (FMI) (see Chapter 7).
b) In *local government*, compulsory competitive tendering has been introduced in building and maintenance work and other services (see Walsh, 1988). In addition, auditors of local authority accounts are required to certify annually that each authority has adequate arrangements for securing economy, efficiency and effectiveness in its use of resources. The Audit Commission, established in 1983 to oversee the work of local-authority auditors, has developed comparative performance indicators by which to judge authorities (see Audit Commission, 1984a and 1986).
c) The *education service* has become increasingly subject to value-for-money initiatives, including assessment of the effectiveness of education authorities, schools, colleges and universities (see CIPFA, 1984; Jarratt Report 1985; Audit Commission, 1985; Committee of Vice-Chancellors and Principals (1986); Pollitt, 1987; and Howell, 1988).
d) *Nationalized industries* since 1978 have regularly published performance indicators in their annual reports (National Consumer Council, 1981; Woodward, 1986) and have been brought within the scope of the Monopolies and Mergers Commission by the 1980 Competition Act (Garner, 1982; Wright, 1984).
e) *Quangos* have been brought within the scope of the financial management initiative (Cabinet Office (MPO)/Treasury, 1984a).
f) *The National Health Service* has made extensive use of performance measurement. Of particular note is the promulgation by the DHSS in 1983 and 1985 of performance indicators for use by health authorities (DHSS, 1983 and 1985; Pollitt, 1985; Allen, Harley and Mackinson, 1987).

In addition, during the 1980s there has been, within the public sector, an increased emphasis upon *consumerism*. As an alternative to traditional methods of expressing consumer preference – through the ballot box and elected representatives – emphasis has been placed upon what Pollitt (1988b, p. 121) describes as 'the encouragement of greater consumer responsiveness in the [public services]'. This, as Potter

(1988, p. 162) explains, 'involves more than being nice to consumers . . . It demands a searching review of the relationship between providers and those for whom services are provided'. While it can be argued that to date this has been manifested in British public administration more by rhetoric than reality, and obvious difficulties exist in identifying and measuring consumer satisfaction (Pollitt, 1988a), there are already signs of significant differences of practice and of a developing shift in organizational cultures. (For discussion see also Hambleton, 1988; Seneviratne and Cracknell, 1988; Griffiths, 1988; Morrison, 1988; Local Government Training Board, 1987; National Consumer Council, 1987).

What these developments make clear is that under the Thatcher government major emphasis has been placed upon the application in the public sector of essentially private sector management techniques or, more precisely, upon the application of a particular selection of such techniques. There has been little emphasis on, for example, the 'human relations' elements in private sector management thought, but a very great deal upon the rather mechanistic model of objective setting and performance measurement and, where possible, merit pay (to reward 'efficient' officials) and employment by contract. This, in turn, ties in with other major objectives of the present government such as privatization and contracting out. The avowed aim of all these developments is to improve efficiency and effectiveness and thereby obtain value for money. Of course the gains which these developments have brought, given the problems of applying such management techniques in the public sector, and the tendency to make the three Es in many cases reducible to economy, remains a matter of doubt. Doubt also exists about the value of some of the performance measures adopted (Flynn, 1986; Pollitt, 1986a, 1986b; Beeton, 1987), and the extent to which a more managerial culture is actually developing among public administrators (Metcalfe and Richards, 1984, 1987). Some of these issues will be developed further in subsequent chapters (particularly Chapter 7).

More fundamentally, perhaps, these developments raise important questions about the distinctiveness of the public sector. Some aspects of the new managerialism fit uneasily alongside notions of equity and accountability (see Chapter 7), and some observers suggest that the application of essentially private sector managerial techniques is inappropriate within the public sector. Woodward (1986, p. 316), for example, suggests that 'in the public sector, while much of the private sector rhetoric (efficiency, productivity, return on capital) survives, analogous . . . conditions for evaluation . . . do not obtain'. Others take the opposite view, suggesting not only that such measures have been a success but that 'managerially, there is no real alternative' (Peat Marwick, 1986, p. 6). Objectively, the evidence seems to suggest that the value of such developments has been patchy, but that important changes are nevertheless being made. Public administrators are increasingly being required to think, act and perform more like private sector managers, and to run public bodies more like private concerns. In short, the distinctive nature of the public (as opposed to the private) sector is being questioned in an acute form. Significantly, public administration is now taught quite widely in business schools, and as an option or stream on many business studies courses. Even the term 'public administration' might seem to be under threat, with terms like 'public management' (or 'public sector management') increasingly being used instead. Is public administration simply private management writ public? This question, increasingly posed in recent years, (see, for example, Chandler 1988b; Greenwood, 1988a) is also one to which we shall return later.

The information technology revolution in public administration

The managerial developments outlined above have been accompanied by the increasing use of computers and information technology in British public administration. Computers, of course, are not a new phenomenon, having been used in public bureaucracies in Britain and overseas for several decades. However, many early computers were extremely large as well as expensive, and the tendency was towards centralized installations at headquarters or regional bases. In recent years, however, the advent of small, reliable and relatively cheap mini- and micro-computers has made it possible to install computer technology on a widespread basis throughout all parts of the public sector. The effect has been to bring about what Pitt and Smith (1984) describe as a 'Computer Revolution in Public Administration'. In central government alone total spending on information technology was £1,580m in 1986–7, with around 65,000 video terminals (plus 1,000 medium/large systems and 10,000 small systems) in use, and 18,500 civil servants employed in managing, developing, implementing and running systems (Beard, 1988, p. 174 and table 13.1).

These developments have had, and will probably continue to have, a profound effect upon public bureaucracies. IT systems are today not only 'an essential support to the day-to-day work of most public service organisations' (Beard, 1988, p. 173), but have also provided a powerful stimulus to the introduction of performance measurement schemes (by providing the capacity to store, analyse and retrieve the vast quantities of data which most such schemes require). They have consequently enhanced management capability, and improved operating systems as well as planning and research functions. They have also, however, brought the prospect of significant organizational changes. For example, it is often argued (Booth and Pitt, 1984, p. 33) that the structural impact of information technology will be a diminished need for middle-level supervisory functions, and that there will be a consequent reduction in the number of hierarchical levels – which may undermine the tendency towards bureaucratic organization (see Chapter 2). A considerable debate also surrounds the impact of IT upon bureaucratic power relationships, between those who stress its centralizing potential (enhanced management information and control, etc.) and those who detect decentralizing tendencies (dispersed, multi-access information storage and retrieval and so on). Indeed the potential of IT for decentralization has implications not only for the bureaucratic pattern of organization which characterizes public administration, but also for such features as accountability and equity. For example, there is a capacity to make information available to politicians by desk-top VDUs (rather than as traditionally through officials), and to decentralize decision-making (and give greater discretion) closer to the point of contact with the public.

As these examples suggest, the impact of new technology within British public administration is likely to be far-reaching. What seems clear, however, is that the scope and form of change within a particular organization will depend upon a variety of factors: the nature and functions of the organization, the nature of the technology, and the purposes for which it was introduced. As such, diversity seems likely to remain a marked feature of public sector organizations. As Pitt and Smith (1984, p. 6) conclude, 'there are no *automatic organisational outcomes* available as the result of the importation and exploitation of IT . . . organisations – public and private – will *continue* to display a degree of *variety* after the full implementation of IT'.

The expansion and contraction of British public administration

The size and complexity of British public administration increased enormously between the late nineteenth and early twentieth centuries. Increased government intervention, particularly in economic and social provision, led to a steady expansion in the public sector. By 1979, under the aegis of the welfare state, social provision in Britain – health, social security, education and, to a large extent, housing – was largely a public sector concern. Nationalized industries – which dominated such basic fields of industrial activity as transport, energy, shipbuilding, steel and aerospace – were valued at £123.5bn and their share of the national capital stock stood at 17.7 per cent (Gretton, Harrison and Beeton, 1987, p. 23). Reflecting this expansion the number of people in public sector employment in 1978 stood at 28 per cent of the working population (compared with only 3.6 per cent in 1891). The civil service alone expanded from 16,000 in 1868 to 748,000 in 1976. Not surprisingly, by 1979 there was widespread adherence to what Gretton, Harrison and Beeton (1987, p. 17) refer to as 'a gut feeling that the State was too big, was getting bigger and ought to be smaller', an attitude which manifested itself strongly in the Thatcher government's commitment from 1979 onwards to 'rolling back the frontiers of the state'.

Since 1979, as a result, the public sector has begun to contract, a development reflected not only in the privatization of many former nationalized industries, but also in the encouragement of private sector provision in fields such as housing, education and pensions. In consequence the proportion of the working population in public sector employment began to fall (to 25.2 per cent by 1984), while civil service numbers fell from 732,000 in May 1979 to 597,000 in April 1987, on target for a drop to 590,400 by April 1988. Nevertheless, the public sector (in 1988) remains substantial, and the extent of its 'rolling back' since 1979 is somewhat less than the Thatcher government's rhetoric might suggest. Cutting public expenditure, for example, has proved elusive, and the proportion of gross domestic product absorbed by the public sector has remained consistently above the level of 1979–80. In 1988–9 public expenditure in Britain was projected at £156.8bn, and government planning totals suggested a further rise to £176.1bn by 1990–1 (1988 Public Expenditure White Paper, Cm 288, Table 2.3). According to Gretton, Harrison and Beeton (1987, pp. 25, 18) the 'dramatic changes' achieved in selling off nationalized industries largely conceal the fact that 'by international standards' the Thatcher government has not rolled back the state's frontiers very far. Whilst the 'size and shape' of the public sector 'has undoubtedly changed', this has been somewhat less than 'the protestors would have us believe or the Government's more radical supporters would have liked'. Summarizing post-1979 developments they conclude:

> As far as central government, the NHS and local government are concerned, few activities have been transferred entirely to the private sector. And where the private sector has gained, as in education, at the expense of public provision, that has not always been as the result of any specific Government policy designed to achieve that. Where, as in housing, the Government could claim substantial success, the rump public sector remains much larger than the share transferred to owner-occupation . . . Overall then, our conclusions must be that the Government have been conservative rather than radical.

As this comment suggests, 'rolling back the frontiers of the state' since 1979 has been less dramatic than might at first appear. Much of the work performed by the UK public sector is not performed within a commercial framework and is likely to prove unattractive to profit-oriented private companies. There is also, among many public sector professionals, a service ethos which does not fit easily with the profit motive, whilst among the public at large there remains a widespread commitment – particularly in welfare fields – to the concept of 'free' public provision. On this view what seems clear is that, without quite radical policy shifts, public administration in Britain – despite much political rhetoric – seems destined to remain an activity of considerable importance and extent. To quote Gretton, Harrison and Beeton (1987, p. 25) again, at the end of 1987 'there are few signs of the radical thinking that a fundamental reshaping of the public sector would require'. This is a judgement, however, which we elsewhere have challenged (Greenwood and Wilson, 1988). By the late 1980s signs were emerging that quite radical thinking was occurring within the government and among its supporters, with manifesto commitments to allow council tenants and state schools to opt out of local government control, legislation requiring councils to put important services out to competitive tender, and suggestions even for privatizing such fundamental parts of the public sector as libraries, prisons, railways, coal and even motorways.

The complexity of contemporary public administration

One feature which the post-1979 retreat from state provision cannot reverse is, of course, the *complexity* of government work. Today, public administrators frequently require a technical orientation – with appropriate skills and equipment – which was unimaginable in the nineteenth century. A hundred years ago any literate person with reasonable intelligence and education could make a competent administrator. Many of today's public administrators, however, have to perform functions (such as economic planning) and use techniques (such as cost-benefit analysis, economic model building) which were unheard of a century ago. There have also been institutional changes of unforeseen dimensions. Institutions formed to perform functions in the pre-twentieth century state, such as the Cabinet, government departments, and local authorities, have had to adapt to new and more exacting circumstances. Other institutions such as public corporations have been added and removed piecemeal as the state has acquired or lost functions. At the same time the political environment of public administration has undergone major changes. For example, the rise of disciplined parties, which has given ministers in normal circumstances the ability to control Parliament, has strengthened the position of civil servants by giving them the means, through their political 'masters', to turn their policy proposals into legislation. In other respects, however, the civil servant's position has been weakened. Not only has the development of universal adult suffrage reinforced the concept of accountable public administration, but the rise of the mass media, and the proliferation in the twentieth century of pressure group activity, has introduced new external constraints to which public administrators must respond. These important changes present two main problems:

1 The institutions, personnel and techniques of British public administration must be seen within the context of adaption to changing circumstances. Despite substantial change, much of the past has been retained. The legacy of the past cannot be ignored if we are fully to understand the institutions, techniques and personnel of contemporary British public administration.
2 At the same time new governmental forms and administrative processes have developed such as accountable units, departmental agencies and quangos. Additionally, a host of new and sometimes perplexing terms have emerged: Ombudsmen, PESC, PAR, hiving-off, and so on. British public administration has to some extent become 'jargonized', creating obvious difficulties, especially for students new to the subject.

This book sets out to examine British public administration, not from a formal, legal standpoint but by explaining what actually happens. The extent and scope of British public administration is, of course, enormous, and given the 'ambiguity, confusion and complexity' which it exhibits, the reader cannot expect to find neat, definitive conclusions. The subject, moreover, is continually changing; models or generalizations are liable to prove inaccurate or misleading within even a short passage of time.

Inevitably in a book such as this the complex administrative network has to be divided up into a number of constituent parts for the material to be manageable. While, for example, there are sections on government departments, the Cabinet, the civil service and so forth, these should not be regarded as neat, self-contained compartments operating in isolation from each other. Extensive interrelationships occur both formally and informally. Informal relationships, not easily charted, are particularly important in keeping the wheels of administration satisfactorily oiled. Common backgrounds and educational experiences between ministers and civil servants, for example, can result in working relationships which are far removed from any formal 'position statement' or chain of command. Likewise, common membership of social or professional organizations may facilitate co-ordination both within Whitehall and between Whitehall and individual local authorities. Formal hierarchies reveal little about actual working relationships, which are invariably much more ambiguous than boxes on neatly designed organizational wall charts would indicate. In the final analysis, public administration responds to many values – efficiency, rationality, equity and so forth – and thus defies neat labels.

2 DEPARTMENTS AND DEPARTMENTALISM

Although in 1988 central administration accounts for only about one-tenth of public sector employment, the British political system is highly centralized. It is largely within central administration that public policy is formulated, and although many services are provided by subordinate agencies (such as local authorities and public corporations) fundamental decisions about standards and machinery of provision are usually taken at the centre. It is to central administration, therefore, that we now turn, commencing with government departments, the main components of the central administrative machine.

What is a government department?

As used in government the word 'department' has several meanings, although in Westminster systems it is often used in association with the adjective 'ministerial' to denote a major unit of government headed by an elected minister (see Bogdanor, 1987, pp. 170–1). In practice, however, there is no clear definition of the term 'government department', and no such thing as a 'typical' department (see Hood and Dunsire, 1981, especially ch. 3). Even the term 'department' is not unambiguous, sometimes being used synonymously with other terms such as 'ministry' or 'office', at other times describing divisions within what might normally be thought of as a government department (such as the fifty-seven departments of the Foreign Office: Rose, 1987, p. 23). Disregarding nomenclature problems, however, it is possible to identify three broad types of government department:

(i) *Ministerial departments*: the key departments which operate under the direction of ministers.
(ii) *Non-ministerial departments* under non-political executives, such as the Department of Inland Revenue, Board of Customs and Excise. Although formally headed by boards, departmental administration and policy is usually answered for by ministers.
(iii) *Semi-autonomous agencies*, a miscellaneous group exhibiting some of the features normally associated with departments, but generally operating independently of ministers unless major political questions are involved. They may nevertheless be thought of as departments in their own right through being staffed by civil

servants, being in receipt of budgetary estimates, or being classified as a Crown body. Included within them are departmental agencies (such as the Defence Procurement Executive within the Ministry of Defence) and, more problematically, 'hived-off' non-departmental agencies such as the Training Agency.

This ambiguity surrounding the term 'government department' presents difficulty in delineating the boundaries of central administration. Whether, for example, the Royal Mint or the Training Agency should be seen as part of central administration depends largely upon the criteria used for defining government departments. Indeed, the position has become more confused in recent years, both by the occasional wholesale removal of departmental functions and status – in 1969, for example, the functions of the Post Office, a ministerial department, were transferred to the Post Office Corporation, a public corporation (see Chapter 12) – and by the proliferation of new organizational forms such as departmental agencies – which even in the mid-1970s employed about 26 per cent of the civil service (Pitt and Smith, 1981, p. 65) – and 'hived-off' non-departmental agencies. Bodies of these kinds now exist in quite large numbers, often performing functions similar to those previously carried out by departments. Richardson and Jordan's view in 1979 (p. 57) that there had been a 'Disintegration of the Centre' and that there was now 'no reasonable means of distinguishing between "central administration" and bodies outside' the perimeter, is even more true at the end of the 1980s.

Because of such problems even a count of government departments is difficult. As Rose (1987, pp. 22–3) shows, within government itself different official lists of departments are used. Defining the term 'ministry' as 'those organizations headed by a member of Cabinet or in the sole charge of a minister of Cabinet rank', he identifies about twenty such bodies (including the Prime Minister's Office, the Privy Council Office, and the Duchy of Lancaster Office). Hood and Dunsire (1981, especially pp. 41–51 and 157–69), by contrast, settled on the sixty-nine departments 'which accounted for a vote in the budget estimates in . . . 1976–77' (a definition inclusive of the British Museum, the National Gallery, and the Wallace Collection). These sixty-nine departments covered a multitude of functions and were organized on a variety of principles. Perhaps only two generalizations can safely be made about them: (i) most, if not all, had some links, however tenuous, with ministers; (ii) the most politically salient were usually ministerial departments (Hood and Dunsire, 1981, pp. 143–63). These ministerial departments represent the most recognizable inner core of central administration, and the most important and best known are those listed in Table 2.1.

Table 2.1 *Major Government Departments and Staff in Post*[1] *1987*

Ministry of Agriculture, Fisheries and Food (MAFF)	10,480
Ministry of Defence (MOD)	164,003
Department of Education and Science (DES)	2,429
Department of Employment	32,357[2]
Department of Energy	1,031
Department of the Environment (DOE)	6,488[3]
Department of Health	8,439[4]
Department of Social Security (DSS)	87,230[4]
Department of Trade and Industry	12,593
Department of Transport	14,350
Foreign and Commonwealth Office (FCO)	9,506
HM Treasury	3,359
Home Office	37,658
Law Officers' Department	19
Lord Chancellor's Department	10,305
Northern Ireland Office	175
Scottish Office	9,832[5]
Welsh Office	2,278

Notes:

1 Full-time equivalents including industrial civil servants.

2 Excludes Manpower Services Commission; Health and Safety Commission/Executive; Advisory, Conciliation and Arbitration Service.

3 Excludes Property Services Agency and Crown Suppliers. Includes staff providing common services with Department of Transport.

4 The former Department of Health and Social Security (DHSS) was divided into the Department of Health and the Department of Social Security (DSS) in July 1988. Staffing figures for these departments are from *The Times*, 26 July 1988.

5 Includes Royal Scottish Museum.

Source: Civil Service Statistics, 1987 (HM Treasury, 1987), Table 1.

April 1987 figures, except where indicated.

Departmental organization

Although departments vary widely in internal organization, reflecting differences in the volume and complexity of their work, three important features common to many, if not most, departments can be identified: size; decentralization; and bureaucratic organization.

SIZE

As Table 2.1 shows, departments vary markedly in size, although most major departments are large organizations. This has a bearing on the way in which departments operate. Pitt and Smith (1981, p. 63) explain: 'Larger size increases the complexity of organizations. There is greater division of labour . . . The range and frequency of repetitive occurrences increase. This requires the development of rules and procedures as an alternative to personal control by superiors of their subordinates.' In other words, the bureaucratic characteristics of government departments – written rules, codified procedures, hierarchical structures, and so on – are partly a product of size, and are usually most marked in the larger departments. Larger departments, in fact, generally present greater managerial problems than smaller ones. Internal communications are usually more formalized, effective ministerial control is more difficult, and problems of 'specialization, line management, co-ordination and planning' are more likely to be encountered.

While size is related to organizational complexity it is not, however, an indicator of departmental influence. (The Treasury, for example, is one of the smallest departments.) Essentially, size reflects the nature of departmental work: departments concerned mainly with policy formulation, or supervisory functions, are usually smaller than those providing services direct to the public. Thus the DES, with around 2,400 civil servants, is relatively small: it employs no teachers itself, its main responsibility being to advise, and to monitor, local education authorities which do. The DSS, by contrast, had some 800 local offices handling benefit claims and employed 87,000 officials in 1988.

DECENTRALIZATION

Although their precise geographical jurisdiction varies, most departments administer services over large areas. Some provide services exclusively for constituent parts of the United Kingdom (Northern Ireland, Scottish, Welsh Offices); others on a British basis (Employment); others still on a United Kingdom (Customs and Excise) or world (Foreign and Commonwealth Office) basis. To discharge functions over such wide areas many departments operate through local or regional 'field offices'. This process, known as *territorial decentralization*, is a familiar feature of British government departments. Civil servants, operating within the 'organisational structure and hierarchy' of the department, and with centrally determined 'spheres of competence' exercise delegated authority within their area (Smith, 1985, pp. 142–3). (Functional, as opposed to territorial decentralization, where the basis of delegation is not primarily areal, also occurs within government departments: see pp. 36–40).

Despite their extensive use there is little standardization in the distribution of departmental field offices. Traditionally each department has developed whatever local pattern best suited its own tasks, despite the problems of interdepartmental co-ordination which this often creates. Indeed, single departments sometimes have different field networks for different functions: for example, in 1971 the

Environment Department had fourteen 'separate out-stationed organisations', many with different boundary patterns (Draper, 1977, pp. 51–2). Likewise, there is little standardization of field office functions. Some have executive functions; others are concerned with inspection, regulation, planning, or a mixture of functions. Often, however, because effective decentralization can only be achieved by weakening central control, the amount of authority delegated is limited, inviting the description 'pseudo-decentralization'.

Decentralization should not be confused with the location in Belfast, Edinburgh and Cardiff of the headquarters of the Northern Ireland, Scottish and Welsh Offices; nor with the deconcentration from London of headquarters units of other departments, such as DSS headquarters divisions in Lytham and Newcastle. Nevertheless, the combined effect of these factors is striking, with about three-quarters of civil servants being employed outside London in 1988. Indeed in the 1980s, with increasingly high living costs in the south-east, plans were reportedly under consideration to disperse up to 90 per cent of remaining London-based civil servants to provincial locations (*The Times*, 20 August 1988).

BUREAUCRATIC ORGANIZATION

Government departments are organized according to the bureaucratic pattern familiar in large organizations, particularly public bodies. Fundamentally, bureaucratically organized bodies exhibit a hierarchical structure. Each official has clearly defined duties within specified limits, and operates under the supervision of a higher officer within a 'line' command structure. This organizational pattern is particularly appropriate for public agencies given the constraints within which they typically operate. As far as government departments are concerned three such major constraints are identifiable: (i) public accountability; (ii) equity; and (iii) specialization.

(i) *Public accountability* (see Chapter 1) requires departments to conduct their work in a manner acceptable to Parliament. In most departments – and in all ministerial departments – ministers are constitutionally responsible to Parliament for every aspect of departmental work. Consequently, departmental officials must act in accordance with ministerial instructions and statutory powers.

Bureaucratic organization, by allowing detailed control of subordinates within a hierarchic command structure, offers perhaps the only means by which large government departments can discharge their functions consistent with public accountability requirements.

(ii) *Equity* (see Chapter 1) requires departments to treat citizens equally in identical circumstances. This presents considerable managerial problems, particularly for large departments with staff widely dispersed in field offices. Once again, bureaucratic organization offers an apparent solution, enabling departmental rules to be enforced through a line management system extending from the highest departmental levels, through local controllers of field offices, down to officials in contact with the public.

(iii) *Specialization*. All departments are to some degree multi-functional: at the very least they have to perform not only 'housekeeping' functions – such as finance and personnel management – but also 'operating' functions related to the laws and policies which they administer. To perform a range of functions effectively large organizations usually allocate work to different groups and individuals according to their skills and abilities. Typically the organization is divided into segments, each being given responsibility for specialized tasks under the supervision of a director. To interrelate the work of the various segments the directors themselves are within the 'control' of the overall organizational hierarchy. In this way government departments can perform a variety of functions, without undermining either internal cohesion or their ability to provide accountable and equitable administration.

Of course, bureaucratic organization has some disadvantages (hence, the pejorative use of the term 'bureaucratic'). The limited responsibility afforded to each official, for example, may stultify initiative; the constant reference upwards and downwards through a hierarchy may cause delay; and strict application of rules may make officials inflexible and insensitive. While bureaucracy, however, is 'antithetical to some human values' it is nevertheless 'supportive of others such as accountability, rationality and equity, [which are] of central significance' to democratic governmental systems (Pitt and Smith, 1981, p. 139). For this reason it is probably unavoidable as a feature of government departments.

Bureaucratic organization is evident from even a brief glance inside government departments. Usually, the basic organizational unit is the division, each division being responsible for particular areas of departmental work. (In 1980, for example, the Department of Employment had twelve main divisions: Industrial Relations I, Industrial Relations II, Research and Planning, Economic Policy (Manpower), Overseas, Incomes I, Incomes II, Statistics, Finance, Establishments, Manpower (General), and the Solicitor's Office.) Divisions are normally broken down into branches – the Statistics Division in the above example had branches dealing with Earnings, Prices, Unemployment, Employment and Price Surveys – and branches, in turn, into sections. In larger departments related divisions may be formed into 'groups', 'units', 'directorates' and so on, precise arrangements varying between, and sometimes within, departments. Built into the departmental structure will be the minister's private office. Run by the minister's private secretary – usually a young civil service 'high flier' – the private office deals with the minister's correspondence, keeps his diary, and handles his communications with departmental officials (Hall and Green, 1984).

When full allowance is made for the internal organization of departments, the complexity of Whitehall becomes very apparent. In 1985 Cabinet ministers had beneath them 526 departmental divisions, plus 75 or so in the defence field. As Rose (1985, p. 234) comments, 'Although Whitehall appears small when viewed as . . . Cabinet Ministers . . . around a table, it appears vast when the divisions of the ministries are arrayed'. For the same reason, he adds (p. 238), 'The unity imposed upon a ministry by its metaphorical embodiment in the Secretary of State is very misleading . . . . The greater the number of the divisions within a ministry . . . the greater the potential for [fragmentation]'.

Departmental organization and civil servants

Departmental organization is closely linked with civil service career grades (which are unified throughout the service), particularly the grades of generalist civil servants who have traditionally held the key departmental posts (see Chapter 6). Each policy section is typically headed by an officer at principal level, a branch by an assistant secretary, a division by an under secretary, and a group of divisions by a deputy secretary (or in larger departments perhaps by a second permanent secretary). Finally there is the permanent secretary (or a designated permanent secretary if there is more than one) who is the senior departmental manager and the adviser and confidant of ministers. He is also the designated accounting officer for his department and the department's finance division usually operates under his personal control.

This congruence of departmental and civil service hierarchies arguably exacerbates some of the problems inherent within bureaucratic organizations. Because civil service career patterns are involved, gradings may determine the allocation of tasks within departments, rather than vice versa. For example, if departmental work does not really require an assistant secretary, an appointment will nevertheless usually be made at this level, otherwise career prospects would differ between departments, undermining the uniform grading which is the essence of civil service organization. This, of course, creates possible extra delay and inefficiency; not only may appointments and promotions not be justified by departmental work, but the number of heriarchical grades through which communications must pass is unnecessarily extended. (For discussion and examples see Wardale Report, 1981; and Elcock, 1985.)

Of course, many departments require specialist skills and employ appropriate staff (scientists, engineers, doctors and so on). Such specialists have traditionally had their own separate career and grading structures (see Chapter 6), and their own specialist branch and divisional hierarchies. Under this system of *parallel hierarchies*, a generalist policy formulator requiring technical advice would typically refer to a specialist of similar rank. This arrangement, a legacy from periods when government required less technical information, not only placed specialists in subordinate positions (as technical advisers to the generalists who formulated policy and briefed ministers) but required continual cross-referencing between specialist and generalist hierarchies. Under modern conditions this often produced confusion and delay, and led, perhaps inevitably, to demands for changes in patterns of departmental organization.

Reforming departmental organization

Until the 1980s the most authoritative demands for the reform of departmental organization came from the Fulton Report on the Civil Service (1968). This made two particularly important recommendations:

(i) Integrated hierarchies
Fulton (vol. I, para. 162) recommended the creation, 'under a single head', of 'unified hierarchies' consisting of both 'administrators and specialists'. This followed earlier experimentation within a small number of departments, notably the Ministry of Technology, part of which operated with 'a unified hierarchy incorporating . . . technical, financial, administrative and other specialist staff.'

(ii) Functional decentralization
Fulton envisaged an element of functional decentralization, a process whereby 'a special body is set up to assume responsibility for . . . [specified] functions, usually . . . on a national basis' (Steel, 1979, p. 30). Fulton recommended:

(a) the establishment of *departmental agencies* within departments. Although remaining within the department, and operating 'under the direction of a Minister . . . answerable for its activities to Parliament' (Brown and Steel, 1979, p. 301), normal lines of departmental organization would be relaxed, leaving managers considerable autonomy in managerial and budgetary matters.

(b) 'Hiving-off' departmental functions to autonomous *non-departmental agencies* established outside departments. Wholly responsible for work delegated to them, they would not normally be subject to direct ministerial control, their relationship with government and Parliament being similar to that of public corporations and other *ad hoc* agencies (see Chapters 11 and 12).

Progress with introducing these arrangements, despite strong support from the 1970–4 Conservative government, was somewhat limited in the 1970s. Most departments, for example, were reluctant to change to integrated hierarchies, and apart from minor exceptions – notably the Ministry of Public Building and Works, which merged higher professional and managerial hierarchies in 1969 – there were few significant moves in this direction. One reason is that integrated hierarchies arguably threaten the continued dominance of the generalist administrators within departments – the very officials who, ironically, were charged with effecting their introduction. Organizational structures often reflect the interests and attitudes of the staff within them. According to Garrett (1980, p. 65) 'the idea of . . . integrated hierarchies was . . . buried by the Civil Service'; consequently, most departments have retained their parallel hierarchies, even though as an organizational arrangement it is almost unique among Western bureaucracies.

With the establishment of 'hived-off' and accountable units there was, as we have seen (p. 22), rather more progress. Major departmental functions have been allocated to accountable departmental agencies within, for example, the Ministry of Defence and the Department of the Environment. Parts of the latter department in 1987 included the Property Services Agency, operating under the managerial responsibility of a chief executive and a management board; and the Crown Suppliers, a self-financing business operating as a government trading fund. (Jointly these two agencies employed 24,707 staff – 22,801 and 1,906 respectively – almost six times more than the rest of the department). Similarly, the Department of Employment was largely dismembered, with three major non-departmental bodies (the Manpower Services Commission; the Health and Safety Commission/Executive; and the Advisory, Conciliation and Arbitration Service), employing between them 28,107 staff in 1987, existing alongside the main department (with 32,357 staff). As an Efficiency Unit Report stated in 1988 (pp. 17–18), central government functions are today performed by 'a variety of different structures'.

Even so, in the short term at least, progress was probably less than Fulton might have hoped. Apart from the obvious difficulties of isolating self-contained departmental functions, there is evidence of some civil service resistance to the creation of semi-autonomous units. In 1977 the Expenditure Committee reported (HC 535, 1976/7, vol. I, para 94) 'that the Fulton proposal of accountable units [had not] been taken sufficiently seriously' by civil servants. Not only does 'hiving-off' reduce the direct control of top departmental officials over service provision but the preoccupation of such officials with policy and political work arguably diverts their attention from matters of departmental management and organization (see Efficiency Unit, 1988, for example, pp. 24–9). Moreover, the model of departmental and autonomous agencies tends to be most appropriate for those areas of public administration where work can be measured in financial or quantitative terms (as with quasi-commercial activity) or where too much political control may be undesirable (as with regulatory agencies). Much departmental work, however, is not of this kind. Few services in central administration produce profits, and cost/benefit calculations usually include political and social as well as financial factors. As Howells (1981), contrasting Marks & Spencer with the civil service, observes, the differing basic activities of public and private sector bodies, coupled with the varying requirements of external accountability, tend to produce distinctive patterns of decision-making, record keeping, management style, and organization. Significantly, even where accountable units have been formed in Whitehall, they have often been less autonomous in practice than in theory. As Pitt and Smith (1981, p. 65) observe, 'In government the practice of management . . . reflects political compromises and objectives. Degrees of managerial autonomy do not . . . correlate neatly with management structure.'

The Ibbs Report: *The Next Steps*

In the late 1980s, under the impact of Mrs Thatcher's drive for a more efficient and managerially competent civil service (see Chapter 7), the idea of substantial delegation of departmental functions to autonomous and semi-autonomous agencies attracted renewed interest. According to a 1988 Efficiency Unit Report – entitled *Improving Management in Government: The Next Steps*, but widely known as the Ibbs Report after the Head of the Efficiency Unit, Sir Robin Ibbs – two decades after Fulton there was still 'a lack of clear and accountable management responsibility' within departments (p. 7). Particular problems identified by the report were the largely uniform system of organization within departments and the many common grading, pay, and promotional structures. As different departments have different functions the work of each, it was recommended (p. 7), 'must be organised in a way which focuses on the job to be done; the systems and structures must enhance the effective delivery of policies and services'. To achieve this, Ibbs (p. 9) proposed the creation of a network of 'agencies', 'to carry out the executive functions of government within a policy and resources framework' set by departments. Headed by a chief executive, with managerial freedom over matters such as recruitment, pay, grading and structure, such agencies would be largely responsible for operational matters within broad policy objectives, budgets and performance targets set by ministers. Precise relationships with departments would vary according to the job to be done: some agencies, for example, might remain within departments, others might become non-departmental bodies whilst others still could be in a position where they are 'no longer inside the Civil Service' (p. 10).

At the time of writing the full impact of these proposals is difficult to assess. While the report was quite well received publicly, early signs are that the underlying managerial concepts have little appeal to ministers who appear generally to have remained indifferent. Thus, although Ibbs envisaged that agency-type arrangements 'could be used to cover a substantial proportion of the activities of the Civil Service' (p. 10), the government's initial commitment was merely to implement the report's proposals 'to the greatest extent practicable' (*Hansard*, VI, vol. 127, cols 1,149–1,156, 18 February 1988). Initially a mere twelve functions – including the Jobcentre Network, Passport Office, Meteorological Office, and the Driver and Vehicle Licensing Directorate – were listed as promising initial candidates for agency status, although on 25 July 1988 (*Hansard*, VI, vol. 138, cols 21–4) the government announced that the list had grown to twenty-nine, including the Companies Registration Office, DHSS Resettlement Units and the employment services. These twenty-nine activities jointly covered some 170,000 civil servants (more than a quarter of the total), and ministers were reportedly engaged in seeking out other departments suitable for transfer to agency status. (The first agency, the Vehicle Inspectorate, was established in August 1988.) According to 'The Next Steps' Project Manager, within ten years at least three-quarters of the civil service could have agency status established, a view supported officially by the government in July 1988 (ibid., col. 21).

While it seems clear that a large number, possibly a large majority, of civil servants may in future work for agencies rather than conventional departments, considerable obstacles to progress still exist. Departments, for example, may be reluctant to lose direct control of activities, and many departmental functions may be inappropriate for delegation. The real managerial independence of chief executives, moreover, may prove to be limited. Ministers (the Treasury) will set agency budgets and will also be responsible for policy – an arrangement which seemingly belies the policy/administration dichotomy (see Chapter 1) and ignores the ministerial interference which has long characterized many other public agencies (such as nationalized industries – see Chapter 12) theoretically operating at arm's length from government. Significantly, the Treasury, in evidence to the Treasury and Civil Service Select Committee (1988, HC 494–II, Memorandum submitted by HM Treasury, para. 2), has argued that, when delegating authority to agency chiefs, account must be taken of the need 'to safeguard the control of public expenditure in accordance with the Government's macro-economic policies and . . . to continue to contain the overall cost of administration. Flexibility in areas such as pay and recruitment will, therefore, have to be applied within a suitable overall framework.' In other words, so long as agencies remain within the public sector, pay and manpower controls cannot be relaxed to allow maximum flexibility to agency managers. According to *The Times* (18 July 1988), what the Treasury's evidence suggested was 'fundamental disagreements' within government about the scope of change, with the Treasury 'fighting hard against anything more than minimal changes in the way departments are managed'.

Ibbs' proposals also have important implications for accountability. While ministers would retain responsibility for budgets and broad policy, chief executives would have personal responsibility for managerial efficiency and results. As such they could be questioned by parliamentary select committees (see Chapter 14) and receive correspondence on operational matters direct from MPs. Although largely similar arrangements already pertain with existing departmental and hived-off agencies, as well as with nationalized industries, their extension across virtually the whole field of government executive operations could seriously undermine formal accountability – particularly if functions were delegated to agencies outside the civil service. As the Ibbs Report recognizes (p. 17), 'the precise form of accountability for each agency would need to be established as part of drawing up the framework for agencies'. (One possibility is that regulatory bodies and tribunals – see Chapter 15 – may increasingly be used to monitor, and hear complaints about, executive agencies.) Nevertheless, accountability, in future, could vary from agency to agency, producing overall a complex array of mechanisms confusing both to MPs and the public.

Accountability, of course, has implications for control (see p. 9). So long as ministers retain formal accountability to Parliament for the work of agencies – the position officially anticipated by government, and demanded by MPs anxious about their continued ability to redress grievances – ministers will continue to be consulted about, and in all probability intervene in, decisions about operational matters. In these circumstances the managerial independence of agency chiefs may in practice be heavily circumscribed, the more so as they are likely to be appointed by ministers on renewable contracts.

While the extent and speed of Ibbs' implementation remains to be seen, its implications for the future structure of Whitehall could be profound. What essentially it seeks is a divorce between the *executive* functions of government – which employ 95 per cent of civil servants – and the ministerial support and *policy* functions which are mainly the preserve of top civil servants. If Ibbs is fully implemented the vast majority of officials carrying out executive functions would in future work for agencies, leaving departments – collectively staffed perhaps by 20,000 or so elite policy-makers – to formulate policy, advise ministers and, increasingly, to monitor and co-ordinate the work of agencies. While departmental organization would vary – some departments might contain one agency, others several, others still (especially where functions were 'hived-off' to non-departmental agencies) none – the main instrument for delivering what are presently central government services would in future be the agency. The structure of Whitehall, in short, *could* be transformed, with the conventional Whitehall department as we know it ceasing to exist.

Advisory machinery

A further important feature of departments is the advisory committees (or councils) which enable civil servants and ministers to ascertain informed opinion before arriving at decisions. Consisting of outside 'experts' and pressure group representatives, as well as departmental officials, they are normally formed at ministerial discretion (although in a few cases Parliament has given advisory bodies statutory rights of consultation). Their existence is largely a response to two developments: a) as government work has become more technical, departments have increasingly needed advice from outside experts; b) as governments became more interventionist, departments increasingly consulted affected interests, both because they were felt to have a 'right' to consultation and because their co-operation was often essential to policy implementation. Most departments are keen to establish close relations with client groups – the Department of Health with the British Medical Association, for example – while pressure groups themselves welcome the access to departmental personnel which such relationships provide.

Although rarely 'hitting the headlines', advisory bodies are an important element in central policy-making. One survey in 1985 identified 1,069 advisory bodies attached to the main central departments (Jordan and Richardson, 1987a, table 8.1). Their value lies in enabling departmental officials and client groups to achieve consensus in private before submitting an 'agreed policy' to ministers. These formal channels, of course, are often supplemented by informal consultations and negotiations, attesting that in Britain the most influential groups have traditionally concentrated pressure upon departmental civil servants (Eckstein, 1960), and to the fact that such officials play a crucial part in government policy-making. Widely known as clientelism, negotiation and consultation between departments and groups is a marked feature of British central administration and crucially important in policy formulation. As Hogwood and Mackie (1985, p. 49) note: 'Even if the Cabinet or cabinet committees subsequently formally consider proposals from the department concerned, there may be little scope for unwinding any deal struck between the department and the group'.

The departmental pattern

While the efficient allocation of work is important in all organizations, in central administration it is especially so. Ministerial responsibility (Chapter 14) requires a designated minister to be answerable for every aspect of government work; consequently, any confusion about work distribution between departments will blur ministerial responsibility. More fundamentally, as Chapman (1988b, p. 220) observes: 'Without good organisation and structure for their execution, government policies, however attractive they may appear to politicians and the electorate, may be unachievable or undermined'. Partly because of this, ultimate decisions about the number and jurisdiction of departments – the departmental pattern – rest with the Prime Minister; indeed Pollitt (1984, p. 164) describes the view 'that the distribution of functions is a personal matter for the Prime Minister' as one of the most fundamental Whitehall beliefs. Nevertheless the Prime Minister's choice is subject to serious constraints, and the tendency at any one time is for the departmental pattern to reflect three main influences: a) the role of the state; b) political factors; c) administrative considerations.

THE ROLE OF THE STATE

The mid-nineteenth-century state had a minimalist role: the government was more concerned with foreign affairs and defence than domestic politics, and the departmental pattern reflected this. In 1851, for example, the main departments were: the Treasury, Customs and Excise, Inland Revenue, Board of Trade, Post Office, Home Office, Irish Office, Lord Chancellor's Office, Privy Council Office, Admiralty, War Office Ordnance Board, Foreign Office, and Colonial

Office. A century later the pattern was very different. The state had lost its 'caretaker' role, and was now interventionist in both social and economic fields. Technological and industrial developments had also influenced the departmental pattern, which in 1951 embraced thirty major ministries. Of the 1851 departments, the Irish Office and Ordnance Board had disappeared and the Privy Council Office was no longer of major importance. To the remaining eleven, however, had been added nineteen 'new' ones: Commonwealth Relations Office, Defence, Materials, Civil Aviation, Labour, Transport, Works, Local Government and Planning, Health, National Insurance, War Pensions, Education, Air, Supply, Scottish, Fuel and Power, Scientific and Industrial Research, Agriculture and Fisheries, and Food. Since 1951, although the state's role has remained relatively stable, governments have faced further new problems which have been reflected in the departmental pattern: technological changes (Ministry of Technology, 1964–70); decline of Empire (Colonial and Commonwealth Relations Offices merged with Foreign Office); economic decline (Department of Economic Affairs, 1964–9); inflation (Department of Prices and Consumer Protection, 1974–9); national minorities (Welsh and Northern Ireland Offices, 1964 and 1972).

As these examples show, the departmental pattern changes as governments respond to new circumstances. Nevertheless, as Rose (1987, pp. 40–4) observes, the gradualness of Britain's historical development has sustained a considerable measure of continuity within Whitehall. Although, obviously, they have adapted greatly to changing conditions, about half of today's major departments (such as the Home Office and the Treasury) pre-date modern government, and a quarter originated in Victorian times (such as Scottish, Education). As Rose concludes (1987, p. 44), 'The most appropriate way to think of ministries in British government is to recognise both persistence *and* change; the former reflects the force of inertia, and the latter the consequences of choice'.

POLITICAL FACTORS

The departmental pattern is inevitably influenced by political considerations, the main factor usually being concern to signal a new political priority (Pollitt, 1984, table 9.1; Rose, 1987, pp. 36–8). A new department, for example, may reflect a policy shift (for instance, the Northern Ireland Office was created in 1972 after the introduction of 'direct rule'); a response to new problems (such as the creation of the Energy Department in 1974 following fuel crises); an attempt to reassure the public that 'somthing is being done' about pressing problems (such as the recreation of the Department of Health, 1988); or a political appeal to important electoral or client groups (such as the creation of the Welsh Office, 1964). Again, a departmental reconstruction may be related to political tensions within government. A department might, for example, be created to accommodate a particular politician, or a departmental reconstruction used as an excuse for a ministerial reshuffle. Given, moreover, that 'administrative gains' usually 'take some time to [reach] fruition' and are 'subject to [considerable] uncertainty', prime ministers are often 'tempted to design changes that . . . maximize the shorter term benefits', such as political gains, 'rather than administrative efficiency' (Pollitt, 1980, pp. 96–7).

Because of such influences, the departmental pattern may become administratively untidy, but most prime ministers apparently feel that the 'right' political image brings greater electoral rewards than considerations of administrative efficiency. Consequently, while long-overdue administrative reforms might be 'ignored' – producing a 'freezing' of outdated departmental structures – shifts in public opinion and political circumstances may produce sudden and frequent alterations to departmental boundaries, and a consequent destabilization of the departmental pattern. As Gray and Jenkins (1985, p. 10) argue, 'administrative organisation reflects' a history of political aims and ambitions, all varying in nature and even contradictory in practice'.

ADMINISTRATIVE CONSIDERATIONS: THE ALLOCATION OF FUNCTIONS

The development of the departmental pattern has been largely haphazard. Broadly speaking, as new governmental functions have appeared, they have been allocated either to existing departments or, where existing departments were overloaded or political considerations dictated otherwise, to newly-created ones. As Hanson and Walles (1984, p. 139) put it, the departmental pattern has been shaped by 'a continuous process of creation, fission, fusion and transfer, rapid at some times, slower at others'.

Despite the primacy of political considerations, administrative efficiency is nevertheless sometimes influential in determining the departmental pattern. Moreover, beneath the surface of the main departmental contours, transfers of programmes occur between existing ministries (on average between three and four times per year, according to Rose, 1987, p. 49). As long ago as 1918 the Machinery of Government Committee (Haldane Report, 1918) identified two main principles for allocating functions between departments: 'distribution according to the persons or classes to be dealt with, and distribution according to the services to be performed'. The former, the clientele principle, was rejected. Although clientele-based agencies (such as poor law boards in Haldane's day) are not unknown in British public administration, as a guiding principle for allocating all central administrative functions the outcome would be massive duplication of provision: for example, hospitals for the old, for students, for the unemployed and so on, an arrangement described by Haldane as 'Lilliputian administration'.

The alternative, which Haldane recommended, was 'distribution according to . . . services . . . performed', with departments providing a comprehensive service to the whole community. Application of this principle, usually known as the 'functional' principle, would, Haldane argued, produce 'the minimum amount of confusion and overlapping'. Ten services, he believed, could be identified, each of which could be placed 'under separate administration': Finance, National Defence, External Affairs, Research and Information, Production, Employment, Supplies, Education, Health and Justice. This was not a plea for just ten departments to be established, because some of the services would probably need to be administered by more than one department.

Haldane's recommendations can be questioned on two main grounds:

(i) Haldane ignored two other principles of allocation: *process* and *area*. The omission of *process* (kind of work) is understandable – not until much later was it seriously considered as a possible principle for allocating functions. Moreover it is unlikely that all central administrative functions could be distributed on this basis. Although not entirely absent from the departmental pattern – the Public Record Office, and some accountable units (e.g. Defence Procurement Executive) offer examples – the comprehensive allocation of functions by process would cause innumerable administrative problems (especially interdepartmental co-ordination), and would seriously blur the policy-making process.

The omission of *area* is more surprising, for several departments with territorial responsibilities existed in Haldane's day: the Colonial, Irish, India, and Scottish Offices. The latter, together with the Welsh and Northern Ireland Offices, still exists, and the problems of constituent minorities within the UK are likely to present a continuing need for such departments into the foreseeable future. Nevertheless, the area principle could not provide a basis for allocating all central functions, for certain of them, such as defence, diplomacy, economic affairs, and transport, have a national dimension not easily divisible on an area basis.

(ii) A more serious charge against Haldane is oversimplification (see Johnson, 1971). The functional principle is not always distinguishable from process: Research and Information, and Supplies, from Haldane's list could both be regarded as processes. Likewise, the functional/clientele distinction is not always clear: a department administering the 'function' of education, for example, serves a specific clientele (pupils and students). The functional principle, moreover, does not always indicate clearly to which departments particular services should be allocated. Thus Aviation, just emerging in Haldane's day, could be placed with Research and Information on Haldane's list, with Production, or even Defence. The functional principle, in short, offers little guidance about which functions should be grouped together.

Discussion about appropriate functional groupings has usually in Britain been conducted 'by taking the then present as the starting point and proposing marginal changes – amalgamations and splitting-offs' (see Pollitt, 1980, p. 95). Consequently the Haldane Report, although commanding a measure of 'lip-service', has had 'only a low defining power with respect to the pattern of central departments' (Pollitt, 1984, p. 159). Nevertheless, while its recommendations were never consciously implemented the functional principle has 'in general prevailed in British government' (Gray and Jenkins, 1985, p. 91) and has provided the main basis of the subsequent departmental pattern. Indeed it was reaffirmed, in the White Paper entitled *Reorganisation of Central Government* (1970). This specifically endorsed (paras 8 and 11) 'the application of the functional principle as the basis for the allocation of responsibilities' and called for 'the grouping of functions together in departments with a wide span', an approach which foreshadowed the creation in 1970 of two 'giant' departments, Trade and Industry, and Environment.

GIANT DEPARTMENTS

The process of merging smaller departments with related functions into larger 'giant' departments is not new. The 1970 'giants' were, in fact, the continuation of a process which started in the 1950s, and gathered pace in the 1960s when three major mergers occurred (creating the Department of Health and Social Security, the Foreign and Commonwealth Office, and the Ministry of Defence). The rationale for such mergers was largely administrative. Sir Richard Clarke (1971, p. 3) explains:

> The 'giant' can develop its own strategy and decide its own priorities; it can settle problems itself instead of lengthy discussion in interdepartmental committees; it is big enough to have specialised services; it can support a clearer strategy at the centre.

A further advantage was a reduction in the number of departments requiring Cabinet representation, thereby limiting the Cabinet's size in accordance with administrative thinking which sees smaller Cabinets as more efficient than larger ones.

These 'giant' departments were not supposed to be federations of ministries, but were unitary departments in their own right. 'The hope was that the differentiation of these functionally related areas would be integrated into single policy structures *within* departments . . . before issues came to Cabinet committees' (Gray and Jenkins, 1985, p. 98). In practice, however, many failed to develop real cohesion. The Environment Department (DOE), according to Painter (1980, p. 142), 'resembled a conglomerate rather than an integrated coherent whole'; while the DHSS, despite having a 'common' Secretary of State and some common support services, operated essentially as two distinct wings corresponding to the separate ministries which had been merged. In 1973 each of these wings had its 'own' permanent secretary, finance division, and funds (Brown, 1975, pp. 53–4). 'Giant' departments, moreover, were difficult to manage. Teams of ministers were necessary to run them – the DOE had nine ministers at one stage – and formal machinery was often necessary to effect internal communications which previously had been conducted informally (see Draper, 1977, p. 97). Because of such problems, as well as through political expediency, during the 1970s the process of merging departments was reversed. Although the Ministry of Defence and DHSS remained unscathed, other major 'giants' all underwent some unscrambling. In 1974 Energy was detached from the Department of Trade and Industry following a fuel crisis, and a few months later the remnants were formed into three new separate departments: Trade, Industry, and Prices and Consumer Protection. In 1976, likewise, Transport was detached from the DOE. In 1983, however, the departments of Trade and Industry were yet again merged to form a single Department of Trade and Industry. In July 1988 the DHSS was split into two separate departments: Social Security and Health.

HALDANE IN THE 1980s

No one organizational principle underlies the development of the post-Haldane departmental pattern. Pollitt (1980, pp. 95–6), in fact, identifies four main influences which have been at work:

(i) General preference for organizing by 'function' . . . .
(ii) An upper limit to the number of important ('main') departments set by the traditional, political need for the ministers of all those departments to have seats in the Cabinet . . . .
(iii) A lower limit . . . set by the requirement that any given department must not be so large or so heterogeneous as to [be unmanageable] . . . .
(iv) The political need of Prime Ministers to find [senior] posts . . . for his most important party colleagues

Elsewhere Pollitt (1984, pp. 16–18) shows that changes in the departmental pattern occur frequently (with a peak following elections – the 'new broom' effect). Between 1960 and 1983 thirty-four ministerial departments disappeared and twenty-nine were born. Many of the new creations had a short existence; indeed, fifteen of them had disappeared by June 1983. As these figures show, the departmental pattern is dynamic, not static. Given the scale, complexity and political environment of public administration today, searching for one universal principle for allocating functions is doomed to failure. While Haldane's list of functions, despite its shortcomings, foreshadowed later developments quite well – reflecting a general preference for the fewest possible combinations of functionally coherent departments – political and administrative exigencies have continued to intrude. As Brown and Steel (1979, p. 291) suggest, 'departmental structures' reflect contemporary 'needs and political preferences . . . rather than abstract principles'.

The dynamics of departmental work

According to Gray and Jenkins (1985, p. 71), a major shortcoming of many studies of central administration is 'the monolithic view', often presented of 'the administrative apparatus'. While the basic Whitehall unit is the government department, departments 'are not islands' (p. 79), but exist as part of a system of interrelationships described variously as communities and networks. To understand central administration it is necessary to recognize the clash of interests and goals which occur both within and between departments, inviting as 'appropriate descriptive labels of British government' such terms as 'political administration' and 'administrative politics' (ibid., pp. 70–1).

As Hogwood and Mackie (1985, p. 7) observe:

> Most government decisions are made within the confines of government departments: departmental officials advise ministers about policy and implement ministerial decisions. Departments, however, are part of a complex policy community, embracing client groups, media correspondents, outside 'experts', informed MPs and so forth, within which many policy attitudes are generated and developed. Much policy is also initiated within departments themselves, arising from perceived defects in existing arrangements, changing circumstances and so on. Moreover, although most important policy decisions require ministerial approval, implementation is largely left to departmental officials.

As Rose (1987, p. 230) explains:

> The programmes of ministries have grown so much that they cannot be run from a minister's private office . . . . When the monolith of a ministry is viewed in programme terms, it is disaggregated into a series of discrete units, each concerned with a particular set of activities . . . . Many hundreds of hands are responsible for delivering public policies in Britain today.

Departments, as should be clear, are not monolithic: they contain a myriad of personnel hierarchies, organizational units, client groups and so forth, each with their own distinctive perspectives and influence. One important internal division is that between ministers and top departmental officials (see Chapter 5). Differences, however, can also arise between specialists and generalists, between headquarters and field offices, between one division (or group of divisions) and another, within or between advisory committees, and between departmental client groups (for instance between county and district councils in the case of the DOE). Departments, moreover, are dynamic, living organisms: officials within them each have their own perspectives, rivalries, career aspirations, values and experiences, which are all brought to bear in making decisions. Many departments, moreover, as Griffith (1966, p. 515) writes, are 'split amongst many different buildings and, as in every organization, the smaller separate groups acquire their own characteristics'. Consequently, within most departments, there is enormous heterogeneity, which manifests itself in differences over resources, structure, and policy. Thus Griffith found 'differences in the attitudes of the Ministry of Health to health services and to welfare services, in the Ministry of Housing and Local Government to housing and to planning, in the Home Office to children and to police'.

Differences within departments are sometimes related to the departmental pattern. If a department's scope is too wide it may become split by deep divisions; if it is too narrow it may be 'captured' by a client group (the Ministry of Agriculture with the National Farmers' Union is one possible example). Again, departmental size may affect the relative influence of ministers and civil servants: for example, transport was detached from the giant DOE in 1976 partly through a belief that transport policy was not adequately under ministerial control.

Just as sections within departments develop distinctive viewpoints, so might departments themselves. A former Head of the Home Civil Service, Sir Edward Bridges, explained in 1950, 'there has been built up in every department a store of knowledge and experience . . . which eventually takes shape as a practical philosophy, or . . . departmental point of view' (Chapman, 1988b, p. 285). In more recent times, too, the importance of distinctive departmental attitudes has been observed.

According to Shirley Williams (1980, pp. 92–3), 'the extent to which departments have characteristics and indeed even characters' of their own is 'often underestimated'. As an example she cites the contrast between the departments of Employment and Industry. The former – which works closely with unions, and often participates in 'urgent' talks concerning industrial disputes – has a 'twenty-four hour time-scale', and 'many' of its 'senior officials work in shirtsleeves'. In the latter – which is more concerned with industrial investment and which works closely with the CBI – senior officials 'dress differently' and have a 'slightly longer time-scale'. Departments, moreover, operate from their own buildings, and their staff interchange little (other than at top levels). Consequently, each department tends to develop what Griffith (1966, p. 515) describes as 'a philosophy, an ethos, and an atmosphere which is peculiarly its own'. Departmental officials also develop loyalty towards their department. As Crossman (1975, p. 31) observed, though 'civil servants . . . respect . . . the Minister, they have a much stronger loyalty to the Ministry'.

Out of this individualism a distinctive departmental approach to policy and administration often emerges. In Shirley Williams' (1980, p. 92) view, departmental attitudes are 'coloured . . . by the last major reform that they undertook' or by past achievements. (Thus the Department of Health instinctively tends to defend the integrity of the National Health Service.) In some cases ministers may be at odds with departmental policy. When this happens, Crossman (1975, p. 31) observed, the minister meets 'quiet resistance . . . a great deal of it'. Even if departmental policy is ignored or overturned by a minister, it may be successfully 'imposed' upon successors. To quote Crossman again, departmental 'policy goes on while Ministers come and go'.

Sometimes, inevitably, departments compete with each other. Spending departments, for example, are often in competition with one another, as well as with the Treasury, for finance. Departments also fight over 'territory' or policy space (Jordan and Richardson 1987b, pp. 167–9). Crossman (1975, pp. 24–5) observed how his permanent secretary 'waged . . . battle' for four days 'to save her Department' from losing functions to a new department. New departments, in fact, often have difficulty in establishing themselves in the face of 'suspicion and distrust' from 'elderly and well established' departments (Williams, 1980, p. 93). The Department of Economic Affairs, an innovation of Wilson's first government, survived only five years. Its first ministerial head explains: 'Our success meant a tremendous threat to half a dozen old-established departments' (Brown, 1972, p. 112). Sometimes territorial battles are fought over many years. Drewry (1983), for example, shows how the Lord Chancellor's Office and its permanent secretary throughout the interwar period (Sir Claud Schuster) successfully opposed the threatened transfer of its functions to the new Ministry of Justice proposed by the Haldane Report. More recently the Civil Service Department, established in 1968, was never popular with the Treasury. In 1981, four governments later, it was abolished. Many of its functions were then returned to the Treasury, with others following in a further transfer in 1987. Departmental competition also occurs over policy. Jordan and Richardson (1987b, pp. 164–9), describing what they call the 'sectorization of policy making', explain: 'Departments which are supposed to be serving the same government take what is a parochial view of policy'. Some departments are almost permanently in conflict. The Department of Trade, according to Williams (1980, p. 89), 'has traditionally been a free trade department' while the Industry and Employment departments 'have a considerable tendency towards protectionism'. Interdepartmental policy battles may be fought both inside and outside Whitehall. Outside signs of rivalry will be manifested in departmental briefings and 'leaks' to MPs, pressure groups, the media and so on. One of the most public conflicts in recent years was the Westland affair in 1985/6 which was, at root, 'departmental rather than personal' (Jordan and Richardson, 1987b, p. 166). Inside government, rivalry will occur within inter-departmental and Cabinet discussions, with civil servants briefing minister against minister. As Barbara Castle observed (*Sunday Times*, 10 June 1973) shortly after joining the Cabinet, 'I suddenly found I wasn't in a political caucus at all. I was faced by departmental enemies'.

Departmental influence is, therefore, considerable, but is it sinister? According to Chapman (1988b, pp. 286–90), Lord Bridges 'queried whether departmental philosophies could harden into a rigid point of view and perhaps conflict with the needs of government policy; but he decided there were safeguards to prevent this,' frequent staff changes within and between departments, the need for departments to co-operate, and Whitehall's 'collegiate approach to decision making'. Also, of course, departments may ally on one issue, but disagree or remain neutral on others. On other occasions there will be unanimity. Whatever the line-up, however, 'central policy-making' is usually the product of what Richardson and Jordan (1979, p. 26) describe as 'a process of departmental pluralism'.

This analysis, however, should not be carried too far. Many policy initiatives occur outside central administration, and even within it departmental influences are not always decisive. Not all ministers tamely endorse departmental policy, and even when they do their arguments may not prevail. In particular they may be defeated in the various supra-departmental agencies within central administration, agencies which not only resolve departmental disputes but seek to forge a collective governmental view from the disparate pressures emanating from within and without central administration. These agencies are examined in the following two chapters.

3 CO-ORDINATING CENTRAL ADMINISTRATION

The differences which often exist within and between departments can sometimes be minimized or reconciled by co-ordinating mechanisms. This chapter focuses on the most important such mechanisms operating within central administration.

What is co-ordination?

Stanyer and Smith (1976, p. 157) define co-ordination as 'the controlling of activities and decisions of individuals or agencies so that they are harmonized in the pursuit of some stated common goal or objectives'. As this definition implies, two broad aspects can be identified: (i) the co-ordination of *decisions*; and (ii) the co-ordination of *activities*.

(i) The co-ordination of 'decisions' is broadly synonymous with the co-ordination of policy-making. In central administration different sections or departments frequently have responsibility for closely related functions and, if incompatible policies are to be avoided, co-ordination has to take place at an initial stage. If compromise cannot be reached, or if initial co-ordination fails, any ensuing inconsistencies must subsequently be resolved. Co-ordination thus involves both the *avoidance* and the *resolution* of conflict.

Policy co-ordination has both a *preventative* and a *strategic* function. Preventative co-ordination primarily involves preventing (or resolving) policy conflict; strategic co-ordination is more concerned with relating particular policy decisions to overall goals, and in this sense is closely allied to planning. Although planning need not involve co-ordination – an individual may plan his own actions without reference to others – in central government, because decisions often involve several parts of the administrative machine, co-ordination is usually an integral part of effective planning. Strategic co-ordination may involve just a few organizational units, or an entire organization (as with corporate planning). It invariably also involves forward planning (either short or long-term), in which case the co-ordinator may be concerned with a variety of tasks: forecasting, budgeting, goal identification and so forth. The wider the policy range and the longer the time scale, the more difficult strategic planning is likely to be. Nevertheless, strategic co-ordination is fundamental to public administration; without it policy-making could easily become a piecemeal, incremental process conducted without reference to overall goals.

(ii) The co-ordination of 'activities' is essentially concerned with the *co-ordination of administration*. Here, too, both conflict *avoidance* and resolution can be distinguished, as well as *preventative* and *strategic* aspects. With administrative co-ordination, however, a further distinction can be made: that between *procedural* and *substantive* co-ordination. With the former the co-ordinator, usually for reasons of efficiency and consistency, seeks common administrative procedures and methods (such as accounting procedures). Substantive co-ordination, by contrast, is concerned with harmonizing the acts of individual persons or units to obtain efficient policy execution. As such it involves the allocation of functions and resources, as well as performance review and monitoring tasks.

In practice, it is often difficult to distinguish between these various forms of co-ordination. Many central administrative agencies co-ordinate both administration and policy, while the distinctions between preventative and strategic co-ordination, and between the procedural and substantive, are not always clear cut. Nevertheless, co-ordination is essential to efficient administration. As Stanyer and Smith (1976, p. 157) explain, co-ordination 'is the essence of organizational decision making and permeates the whole administrative process . . . [it is] almost . . . synonymous with management'.

While co-ordination is important in all organizations, it is particularly so in central administration – for the following four main reasons.

SIZE AND COMPLEXITY

In small organizations co-ordination is relatively simple: in a two-man shop, for example, each partner observes the other and regulates his own work accordingly. In government departments, however, the number of employees, and the diversity of functions, makes the harmonization of work difficult without formal machinery. These problems multiply when co-ordination *between* departments is involved. However carefully tasks are allocated, the possibility of functional overlap always exists. As Hogwood and Mackie (1985, pp. 49–51) observe, 'bilateral negotiation' between spending departments and the Treasury is commonplace, whilst 'multilateral' bargaining – often affecting several departments – also frequently occurs, either because of 'functional interaction, or because special arrangements [exist] for the administration of the policy in Scotland, Wales and Northern Ireland'. So wide is the scope of central administration that the most disparate units may sometimes find themselves with common interests. For example, the Sports and Recreation Unit of the Department of the Environment and the Soviet Department of the Foreign and Commonwealth Office may have largely separate interests, yet their work must be co-ordinated at any point where it impinges (such as over the proposed boycott of the 1980 Moscow Olympics). Its sheer size and diversity make central administration heavily dependent upon co-ordinating mechanisms: without them its numerous departments and divisions would be unable to work in unison at any of the almost infinite number of points at which their work overlaps.

EQUITY

The need for equity also makes co-ordination necessary within central administration. Effective co-ordination, for example, facilitates equitable treatment of clients by departmental field offices, and by different departments where several have responsibility for a particular service. (The DES, and the Welsh, Scottish and Northern Ireland Offices, for example, all have education responsibilities.)

ACCOUNTABILITY

Ministerial Responsibility (see Chapter 14) also provides a stimulus for co-ordination within central administration. In ministerial departments each minister has individual responsibility to Parliament for all his department's work. Consequently, unless all departmental divisions are working in harmony, a minister may find himself defending incompatible actions and decisions. Under the convention of *collective* responsibility ministers are responsible, not only for their own department, but also for the work of all other departments. Although today often interpreted rather loosely, this convention nevertheless requires a measure of consistency between departments, further reinforcing the importance of co-ordinating mechanisms.

POLITICAL FACTORS

As undue favouritism to one client or electoral group (unions or tenants, for example) runs the risk of alienating others (such as employers or landlords), most governments try to maintain a balanced programme. Policy co-ordination is thus important in central administration for political as well as administrative reasons.

While such factors make co-ordination important in central administration, the problems presented are considerable. Central administration is not only bigger and more multi-functional than other organizations, it also lacks coherent goals against which alternative courses of action might be assessed. (For example, in private companies, conflicts can often be resolved through profit-and-loss calculations.) As Simon, Smithburg and Thompson (1971, p. 435) observe, usually only in wartime is there an overriding goal (winning the war) sufficient to impose coherence at governmental level; consequently, in normal circumstances goal co-ordination has to be secured largely by mechanisms within central administration itself.

Informal co-ordinating mechanisms

In many organizations, particularly in small ones, co-ordination is achieved informally. Even in large organizations, however, there can be a good deal of informal co-ordination: for example, by conversation or memoranda. That this is so in central administration is explained by Pliatzky (1982, pp. 32–3): 'A great deal of business is carried out by inter-Ministerial correspondence . . . almost always [this] is copied to, say, half a dozen other Ministers, or the Cabinet. The photocopier is now . . . an essential element in the machinery of government'.

In fact, aspects of British central administration are particularly conducive to informal co-ordination, even at the highest levels. Ministers, for example, frequently have informal links with one another, usually having worked together for many years in political circles and sharing broadly similar political attitudes. Thus ministers in different departments will invariably be on the same 'political wavelength' and will feel able to contact one another informally should the need arise.

Informal co-ordinating mechanisms also exist among civil servants. As Heclo and Wildavsky (1981, p. 80) explain, 'co-operation is facilitated by the fact that, despite departmental allegiances, all officials are part of a greater civil service society'. Such co-operation is further assisted by the common grading system used throughout the service (see Chapter 6) which allows identification by officials of their 'opposite numbers' in other sections or departments. It also encourages a willingness to communicate: officials not knowing each other may nevertheless talk frankly if their grades – and hence their status and responsibilities – are similar. This tendency is reinforced by the similar social and educational backgrounds of many top civil servants, and their movement between departments (see Chapter 6). Senior civil servants develop a common 'culture' and 'language'; 'so many assumptions are shared' that discussion is often unnecessary (Kellner and Crowther-Hunt, 1980, pp. 272–3). Consequently a measure of unconscious co-ordination occurs, with civil servants tending to 'work and think in similar ways' (Baker, 1972a, p. 109).

Of course, not all 'assumptions' within the civil service are shared.

Differing perspectives, new ideas and circumstances can often divide opinion. It is helpful here to bear in mind the negotiated order model of Strauss *et al.* (1976). Co-ordination within and between groups involves a multitude of linkages between individuals and agencies, usually with a wide variety of interests and views. While largely governed by formal rules, as well as informal conventions and understandings, the actors in each linkage have considerable autonomy. Each linkage is in a sense unique, being built around individual perceptions and interests of the actors concerned. As circumstances change these actors adapt by a process of bargaining and negotiation. Sometimes one party will give way as a reward for past favours by the other, or simply to maintain a relationship which may prove valuable in future. The effect is that co-ordination within central administration – and within any large organization – does not occur between monolithic blocs, but by a process of interpersonal interaction. It is a product of a multiplicity of individual decisions, each one of which affects the overall order. As a result relations between, as well as within, departments are not static, but are an ever-changing pattern of negotiation, bargaining and compromise by individuals at many levels and points of contact. Interestingly this model is also applicable to policy-making and implementation (see Richardson and Jordan, 1979, pp. 101–3; Barrett and Fudge, 1981, especially pt 3), emphasizing the diffusion of power among a multitude of semi-autonomous individuals and agencies rather than the master/subordinate relationship often portrayed in formal organization charts.

While informal co-ordination is important, the size and complexity of central administration necessitates the existence of formal co-ordinating mechanisms – both within and between departments.

Co-ordination within departments

Nominally, at least, co-ordination within departments is the responsibility of the permanent head who acts, as necessary, in consultation with the minister. In small departments 'where all the senior staff are accommodated in close proximity and are frequently in contact with each other and with the permanent head', this function may be discharged largely without 'formal arrangements' (Walker, 1982, p. 259). While even in large departments there will be some informal co-ordination, most also need formal mechanisms. At least three such mechanisms normally exist within departments:

(i) Common service divisions, such as Finance and Establishments, whose horizontal links throughout the department usually enable them to perform a central co-ordinating role.

(ii) The hierarchic structure also assists intra-departmental co-ordination. Painter (1980, p. 137) explains:

> The conventional Whitehall department is offered as the organizational solution with its centralization of authority, upward flow of advice through regular hierarchical channels, and common frame of policy guidelines and traditions to provide coherence for policy.

(iii) The functional principle of work allocation (see pp. 36–8), which is applied widely inside departments, locates related functions within the same departmental divisions.

Despite the existence of these 'traditional' co-ordinating features in most departments, intra-departmental co-ordination frequently exhibits serious shortcomings. This is especially so with strategic co-ordination, which is often crowded out from the attention of ministers and top civil servants by immediate policy pressures. Indeed, from the 1960s there were a number of developments which, although concerned mainly with expenditure planning, policy analysis, and efficient management, if fully implemented would nevertheless have vastly improved intra-departmental co-ordination. The most significant of these are described in the following sections.

PLANNING UNITS

The Fulton Report recommended that departments should establish 'planning and research units' to be responsible 'for major long-term policy-planning' (1968, vol. I, para. 173). Fulton envisaged that such units, headed by a senior policy adviser and containing outside experts on temporary contracts as well as civil servants, should identify future needs and problems and ensure that 'day-to-day policy decisions' were taken with due recognition of 'likely implications for the future'. Ten years after Fulton, Macdonald and Fry (1980) identified 'policy planning units' or similar bodies in at least thirteen departments. While their structure and functions varied widely, most had responsibility for co-ordinating departmental policy. They concluded (pp. 421, 432):

> Policy planning units are a familiar feature of British central government . . . . What seems to be happening is that all the various elements of forward policy consideration are co-ordinated, the co-ordination produces a capacity for oversight, and the oversight makes possible a limited degree of central direction.

PESC AND PAR

The 1961 Plowden Report, *The Control of Public Expenditure*, led to the establishment of annual government reviews of public expenditure co-ordinated by the *Public Expenditure Survey Committee* (PESC). An inter-departmental committee chaired by a senior Treasury official and containing the principal finance officers of the main spending departments, PESC was intended to replace the former year-at-a-time expenditure cycle by a comprehensive medium-term planning apparatus (Pliatzky, 1982, especially pp. 48–50). Essentially it incorporated forward projections over a number of years, with each department having *relative* freedom to determine priorities within global totals agreed by the Cabinet.

One effect of this was to stimulate the development of departmental machinery for co-ordinating future policy programme and resource needs. To assist with this a system of *Programme Analysis and Review* (PAR) was established in 1970. Concerned with assessing policy objectives and the need for changes, PAR provided a mechanism for the regular review and co-ordination of departmental programmes. Thus by the early 1970s most departments had special machinery for conducting annual exercises in forward planning, programme analysis, and policy co-ordination.

The impact of these developments should not be exaggerated. The planning units, which apparently flourished in the 1970s, were not the kind envisaged by Fulton. No 'Fulton-type' senior policy advisers were appointed, and most planning units were as much concerned with short-term problems as with long-term policy co-ordination (Macdonald and Fry, 1980; Garrett 1980, pp. 101–9). A survey by Prince (1983) found that, while planning units in some departments were making a useful contribution, they did not generally enjoy free access to ministers and their value was 'frequently' limited by the need to give 'priority to survival over service' (p. 62). Hardly more successful as instruments for intra-departmental co-ordination were PESC and PAR, although the causes of their failure lie largely in factors which are examined later (see pp. 56–8). Here, however, it is sufficient to note that in 1979 PAR was wound up and that thereafter intra-departmental co-ordination became increasingly intertwined with the Thatcher government's managerialist initiatives in central administration (especially the Rayner Scrutiny Programme, and MINIS – see Chapter 7).

One point can, however, be made. Co-ordination often restricts the independence of organizational sub-units; consequently individual policy divisions and officials are often reluctant to see their freedom threatened by the introduction of departmental co-ordinating mechanisms. Some of these mechanisms, notably planning units and senior policy advisers, also conflicted with traditional Whitehall practice whereby policy divisions led by generalist civil servants monopolized policy advice at higher levels. At the best of times, therefore, one might expect new internal co-ordinating mechanisms to be coolly received by departmental officials. In a recession, however, with governments committed to retrenchment in Whitehall, they might additionally threaten civil service jobs, careers and even whole sections. It is not, therefore, surprising that attempts to improve intra-departmental co-ordination have generally had limited success, and that by the early 1980s PESC, PAR and planning units had all failed to meet initial expectations.

Co-ordination between departments

Co-ordination between departments is not unrelated to co-ordination within them. Blocks of work in one department requiring co-ordination may, following changes in the departmental pattern (see Chapter 2), be relocated in separate departments and thereafter require co-ordination by inter-departmental machinery. Indeed changes in the departmental pattern are often influenced by co-ordination considerations. For example, the creation of giant departments was partly designed to alleviate the burden upon inter-departmental machinery by transferring large amounts of work to the intra-departmental plane. In practice, however, many of the anticipated improvements failed to materialize: internal co-ordinating machinery within these larger departments frequently became overloaded, and real 'integration' often never materialized. In any event the drift back towards smaller departments after 1970 largely reversed the process, and led to much co-ordinating activity being returned to the inter-departmental sphere.

Co-ordination *between* departments generally poses greater problems than co-ordination *within* them: there are more functions, more personnel, and the co-ordinated units – government departments – are often strongly placed to challenge 'unsympathetic' co-ordinators. Moreover, the hierarchical pattern of organization which enhances vertical co-ordination within departments is usually absent at the inter-departmental plane. As no department is officially 'superior' to any other, inter-departmental co-ordination is largely conducted through horizontal channels, by a process of discussion, negotiation and adjustment between theoretically equal departments.

While much horizontal co-ordination of this kind occurs informally, considerable use is also made of formal channels. These include the following categories.

COMMON MACHINERY

Administrative co-ordination is greatly facilitated where different departments utilize common machinery. The Departments of Industry and Trade, for example, before being merged in 1983, maintained a common network of regional field offices, as well as some common headquarters service divisions. Obviously, the scope for such arrangements depends largely upon the departments' functions. (Industry and Trade worked in similar fields, had similar service needs, and similar regional client groups.) Where, however, departments have little in common, administrative alignments of this kind are less appropriate.

COMMON SERVICE ORGANIZATIONS

These have 'horizontal' links between departments, and also an important co-ordinating role, especially with regard to procedural co-ordination. The National Audit Office, for example, which audits the accounts of all departments, influences the standardization of accounting procedures throughout Whitehall. 'Common service' bodies may also co-ordinate particular governmental activities; thus the Central Office of Information supplies publicity services to government departments, and the Property Services Agency provides common services relating to government property, land, buildings and furnishings.

THE TREASURY

This is the most important 'common service' organization within central administration. It has long been recognized 'as the leading department, controlling the departments' expenditure and staff and appointments, besides its function as the central economic and financial department' (Clarke, 1975, p. 69). Particularly important is Treasury control: the Treasury's role in co-ordinating financial, manpower, and economic resources.

Financial control includes the Treasury's right to vet departmental estimates before presentation to Parliament, a right which enables the Treasury to identify any overlap of departmental functions, to ensure that departments are spending (and acting) according to agreed policies, and to influence procedural co-ordination in financial matters. Financial control also involves policy co-ordination. As Treasury control extends to virtually all government expenditure, departments wishing to embark on new policy (requiring expenditure) must first bargain with it. Lord Bridges (1964, p. 41) explains:

> One of the main tasks of the Treasury . . . is to examine the stream of proposals submitted to it so as to provide material for a judgement of their comparative merits. Given that there can never be enough money . . . which are the most deserving? And as between approved objects of expenditure, how much should be spent on each to retain right priorities?

As central departments, moreover, have increasingly provided funds for local authorities, nationalized industries, and numerous other non-departmental bodies, so the Treasury's financial control has extended beyond central administration to the wider public sector.

Manpower control involves the Treasury's responsibilities for civil service manpower, pay and superannuation. This enables the Treasury to monitor manpower throughout central administration, and requires departments to bargain with the Treasury for extra manpower resources.

Economic control, the significance of which increases with greater governmental intervention in the economy, also enhances the Treasury's co-ordinating role. This involves financial and manpower management in support of national economic targets (reducing inflation or unemployment, stimulating investment, improving productivity and so forth). As economic control involves future as well as current expenditure, the Treasury's role also extends to forward planning. Since the mid-1970s, moreover, as governments have placed increasing emphasis on cash-limited central and local government expenditure (and tighter borrowing controls on nationalized industries), so the significance of the Treasury's economic control function for public sector co-ordination has also increased.

Of course, the Treasury's co-ordinating role varies with political and economic circumstances. Its policy co-ordinating role, for example, has probably diminished since the interwar years when the Cabinet Office and Prime Minister's Office were less developed (Peden, 1983). Changes in the departmental pattern are also significant. Between 1964 and 1969 the Treasury lost, nominally at least, economic co-ordination functions to the Department of Economic Affairs, while between 1968 and 1981 manpower control was lost to the Civil Service Department. (Control over manpower, numbers, administrative costs, pay and conditions were regained by the Treasury in 1981.) For most of the postwar period, however, economic and manpower functions have been exercised by the Treasury, and even when they have not the Treasury's financial control has assured it of a central co-ordinating role. To quote Lord Bridges (1964, p. 41), the Treasury's 'business' leads it 'to concern itself with every important aspect of government policy'.

INTER-DEPARTMENTAL COMMITTEES

These further facilitate co-ordination within central administration. Some, being serviced by the Cabinet Office, are technically Cabinet committees (see pp. 71–5) although unlike the most important Cabinet committees they usually consist only of civil servants. The number of inter-departmental committees fluctuates with changing political and administrative circumstances, although one survey in the early 1950s revealed 'at least 700 interdepartmental committees, of which more than 100 were technically Cabinet commmittees' (Daalder, 1975, p. 247). Some inter-departmental committees are *ad hoc*, formed to co-ordinate specific parts of central administration as and when necessary; others are permanent. Examples are the Public Expenditure Survey Committee (chaired by a senior Treasury official and containing the principal finance officers of the main spending departments) which co-ordinates the annual PESC exercise, and the City Action Teams established in 1985 in some areas to co-ordinate the activities of DOE, DTI and MSC in dealing with inner city problems (Goddard, 1988, p. 158).

While the importance of inter-departmental committees varies enormously, at the highest level their influence is considerable. This is particularly true of those 'official' committees (usually consisting of permanent secretaries or other top departmental officials) which 'shadow' ministerial Cabinet committees. Crossman (1975, p. 198) felt that these enabled civil servants to 'pre-cook' ministerial decisions, while Haines (1977, p. 16) described the committee of 'first' permanent secretaries which meets weekly to discuss forthcoming Cabinet business as an additional 'Cabinet . . . that very few people outside Whitehall know anything about'. Such committees usually meet more frequently than, and in advance of, ministerial committees; consequently, they may 'develop inter-departmental loyalties, and even commit their departments . . . without ministerial authority' (Wilson, 1977, p. 127). While, clearly, inter-departmental committees cannot be disregarded as a source of civil service influence (see Headey, 1975, pp. 119–21), they are nevertheless indispensible to central administration. A response to the growth of government, and to the development of government activity across departmental boundaries, they provide an essential instrument for horizontal co-ordination between departments, leaving only the most intractable and politically sensitive issues to be resolved at ministerial level. Without them central administration would grind to a halt, and ministerial workloads become even more unbearable.

CO-ORDINATING MINISTERS

Where major inter-departmental co-ordination is required, special co-ordinating ministers have sometimes been appointed. In 1936, for example, a Minister for the Co-ordination of Defence was appointed to integrate the work of the three service ministries, an arrangement reinforced in 1940 when the Prime Minister, Churchill, took over the role. Churchill experimented along similar lines in 1951 by appointing a number of co-ordinating ministers (or 'Overlords'). For example,

Lord Woolton (Lord President of the Council) was made responsible for co-ordinating the Ministries of Food and Agriculture; and Lord Leathers for co-ordinating Transport, and Fuel and Power. Departmental ministers retained responsibility to Parliament for their departments, but their work was co-ordinated by the 'Overlords' who represented the departments in the Cabinet. These arrangements, however, effectively ceased in 1953, mainly because they were felt to blur accountability. While departmental ministers retained constitutional responsibility to Parliament, policy for their departments was largely determined by the 'Overlords'. (Controversy was further heightened because the main 'Overlords' were peers and could not be questioned in the House of Commons.) Consequently, prime ministers since Churchill have used co-ordinating ministers more sparingly. Unlike the 'Overlords', such ministers have rarely had powers of direction, and have usually been appointed either:

(i) To co-ordinate activities or policies cutting across several departments (such as Michael Heseltine's responsibilities for co-ordinating government action in Merseyside following the 1981 riots) (Parkinson and Duffy, 1984); or
(ii) To act as 'neutral' chairmen of Cabinet committees on which representatives of co-ordinated departments also sit.

CO-ORDINATING DEPARTMENTS

The co-ordinating department is, in theory, more sound constitutionally than the co-ordinating minister because there is usually a clearly defined 'division of responsibility' between the co-ordinating department and the departments 'which it co-ordinates' (Mackenzie and Grove, 1957, p. 346). It is also more effective administratively because, whereas 'Overlord-type' co-ordinators, having no department, usually 'operate with a small office of civil servants', often drawn from the Cabinet Office (Jones, 1975, pp. 42, 51), the ministerial head of a co-ordinating department has full departmental resources to support and advise him or her. An obvious example is the Ministry of Defence, which from 1947 to 1964 had statutory responsibility for co-ordinating the three service departments in specified areas (a task which was formerly done by an 'Overlord-type' minister). Similarly, between 1964 and 1969 the Department of Economic Affairs held responsibility for long-term economic planning, which involved co-ordinating the related activities of various departments such as the Treasury, Employment and Trade.

Despite these theoretical advantages, however, most co-ordinating departments have been barely more effective than 'Overlord-type' co-ordinators. Co-ordinating departments are no less likely to meet resistance from the departments which they co-ordinate, particularly as their respective responsibilities cannot in practice always be clearly delineated. (Those between the Treasury and the DEA, for example, were not always 'meaningful'.) Moreover, co-ordinating departments are usually dependent to some degree upon the co-ordinated departments to implement their decisions. The DEA failed, partly at least, because the 'execution' of its economic plans rested with the Treasury. Similarly Defence ministers between 1947 and 1964 were often unable to develop coherent defence policies: they could only 'negotiate compromises and allocate "fair shares" between the Services' (Clarke, 1975, pp. 70, 75). Significantly, in this case, the co-ordinating and co-ordinated departments were amalgamated in 1964 to form the 'new' Ministry of Defence – again illustrating the value of combining administrative as well as co-ordinating powers through departmental mergers. Undoubtedly this logic was not lost upon those prime ministers who between the mid-1950s and 1970 instituted numerous such mergers culminating in the creation of giant departments (see Chapter 2). This process has, of course, gone into reverse since 1970, a development which highlights an important point: valuable though co-ordination usually is, other criteria – political as well as administrative – may sometimes be more important, and necessitate organizational structures which may impede efficient co-ordination.

PESC AND PAR

PESC and PAR (see pp. 49–50) also had implications for co-ordination *between* departments. A major aim of PESC was to plan and prioritize public expenditure between departments on the assumption that collegiate decision-making by Cabinet ministers on public expenditure plans 'would lead to a willingness to forswear departmental loyalties and take a broader view' (Heald, 1983, p. 187). PAR, likewise, sought to provide a policy evaluation mechanism between as well as within departments. Gray and Jenkins (1985, p. 108) explain, 'Prior to PAR, programmes were rarely assessed together or in terms of their influence on each other. Thus a department's policy impact on other departments, as well as the whole gamut of interdepartmental initiative and the latter's consequences' were often analysed superficially if at all'. Under PAR, topics were reviewed by teams of departmental staff plus representatives from the Treasury and the Central Policy Review Staff (see pp. 58–61). These reports were intended to feed directly into PESC exercises and to relevant Cabinet committees. Co-ordinated by a representative committee, PARC, PAR thus sought to provide a 'co-ordinative and controlling capacity at the centre of government' (Gray, 1986, p. 13).

Although bold in conception, these initiatives were not a success.

Expenditure crucially affects policy, and while PESC provided machinery for national planning and allocation of resources, spending ministers inevitably fought to defend departmental budgets. Economic problems in the 1970s, moreover, made forward expenditure planning increasingly speculative and by the 1980s PESC had changed 'from a mainly planning system to one in which short-term cash control predominated' (Hood and Wright, 1981; see also, Wright, 1980; and Heclo and Wildavsky, 1981, pp. ix–lvii). Volume targets were replaced by cash figures and new machinery (a Cabinet Committee popularly known as the Star Chamber) established in 1981 to hear spending ministers' appeals against PESC allocations. (Those decisions not resolved in the Star Chamber are settled in negotiations with the Prime Minister or if still unresolved in Cabinet.)

A further factor undermining PESC was that PAR did not provide the hoped-for complementary policy evaluation. The 'initial intention of a rolling programme of annual [PAR] reviews to feed into the PESC cycle was never realised' (Gray, 1986, p. 13), and after the first few years the impact of PAR steadily waned. Prime ministers – especially those who succeeded Heath, PAR's initiator – became preoccupied with other interests, civil servants resented the 'heavy burden' which it imposed (Wass, 1984, p. 17), and departments perceived PAR reviews 'as a threat to their territories and programme survival' (Gray and Jenkins, 1985, p. 111). A further weakness was that PARC, the body established to co-ordinate PAR, had 'little important power' (Heclo and Wildavsky, 1981, p. 280); consequently there was no effective inter-departmental agency to impose PAR upon departments. Usually departments were careful not to select for review topics which might be vulnerable, inter-departmental subjects were rarely reviewed, and PAR reports were often ignored (fuelling criticisms that 'the effort seemed pointless' – Wass, 1984, p. 18). Significantly, in 1979 PAR was wound up, the Cabinet deciding it should be superseded by the Rayner Scrutiny Programme (which, unlike PAR, was to enjoy strong prime ministerial backing and, as it developed into the Financial Management Initiative, sought to create more supportive cultural attitudes within departments – see Chapter 7). PAR failed, in the final analysis, because it potentially threatened the policy territory of Whitehall departments. As Heclo and Wildavsky (1981, pp. xliii–xliv) conclude, 'The people who it was supposed to be for didn't want it . . . . [Apart] from a natural self-interest in defending what they were already doing [Whitehall] . . . was not much interested in producing critical evaluations of their own work'. Significantly, however, they add, 'Something like PAR is still needed, because the reborn annual budget process does little to disturb the inertia of existing policy. Worse it tends to displace any concern for policy contents with a pre-occupation of cash controls'.

Central Policy Review Staff (CPRS)

Another important co-ordinating mechanism introduced by Heath's government was the Central Policy Review Staff (or 'Think Tank'). Its main concern was strategic co-ordination, as the White Paper announcing its formation (*Reorganisation of Central Government*, 1970, para. 45) made clear: 'Governments are always at some risk of losing sight of the need to consider the totality of their current policies in relation to their longer term objectives; and . . . of evaluating . . . the alternative policy options and priorities open to them'. To rectify this deficiency it proposed (para. 46) the creation of a 'small multi-disciplinary central policy review staff in the Cabinet Office'. Working under prime ministerial supervision, but serving all ministers collectively, its tasks were to enable ministers

> to work out the implications of their basic strategy in terms of policies in specific areas, to establish the relative priorities to be given to the different sectors of their programme as a whole, to identify those areas of policy in which new choices can be exercised and to ensure that the underlying implications of alternative courses of action are fully analysed and considered. (para. 47).

Starting work in February 1971 the CPRS performed a major role in central government co-ordination until its disbandment in 1983. Its work during this period can be examined under several headings as follows.

COMPOSITION

The CPRS was intended to provide a counterweight to departmental interests and civil service advice; consequently, its composition was untypical of central administration. Its members were temporary, there was no internal hierarchy, and there was a mix of specialist and generalist skills. Staff were usually drawn about equally from inside and outside the civil service. Those from inside were usually 'high fliers' seconded from departments; outsiders came mainly from business, banking and universities. Usually about eighteen-strong, 'its size was almost ludicrously small' given the nature of its task, although 'one justification . . . for this was the need for tightly controlled teamwork' (Isserlis, 1984, p. 30). The diversity of membership was reflected in the backgrounds of the four CPRS directors. Lord Rothschild (1970–4) was former head of research at Shell; Sir Kenneth Berrill (1974–80) an academic economist and former Treasury official; Sir Robin Ibbs (1980–82) a former ICI director; and John Sparrow (1982–3) a merchant banker.

In other respects, however, the CPRS was more typical of British administrative practice. Members were recruited primarily for intellectual qualities and, although empowered to commission research from outside consultants, the CPRS essentially relied upon its members' intellect 'to assess the arguments of experts' (Brown and Steel, 1979, p. 334). In this respect there were close parallels with the generalist tradition inherent in British central administration.

ACTIVITIES

CPRS activities varied according to personalities, political circumstances and levels of prime ministerial support. Plowden (1981), however, identified five main activities:

(i) *Strategy discussions.* During the Heath government (1970–4) strategy discussions with ministers – at which the government's progress in attaining strategic objectives was reviewed – were regular occurrences.

(ii) *Contribution to day-to-day issues.* Housed in the Cabinet Office, the CPRS contributed to briefing documents prepared by the Cabinet Secretariat (see Chapter 4), and thereby injected strategic considerations – including views which departments might not put – into Cabinet and Cabinet committee briefs.

(iii) *In-depth studies.* The CPRS mounted numerous in-depth studies. Some, but not all, were published (Hennessy, Morrison and Townsend, 1985, p. 21, identified at least thirty-six). Most crossed departmental boundaries (such as race relations) and often, too, they had long-term relevance (such as implications of population changes).

(iv) *Co-ordinating inter-departmental activities.* The CPRS sometimes had a 'troubleshooter' role, chairing and/or providing the secretariat for sensitive inter-departmental committees.

(v) *Intra-departmental co-ordination.* The CPRS was closely involved with departmental PAR exercises (see pp. 49–50, 56–7), assisting in the choice of programmes for review, and to some extent in the conduct of reviews themselves.

By performing these tasks the CPRS, as a contemporary Cabinet Secretary (Lord Hunt of Tanworth) put it, sought to fill 'a hole at the heart of the British government' (Hennessy, Morrison and Townsend, 1985, p. 1). It attempted to offer 'a synoptic view of policy' and a means of devising 'a more rational system of decision-making between competing programmes' (ibid., p. 15).

THE CPRS: AN ASSESSMENT

When the CPRS was formed there was speculation that it might be a 'forerunner of a new Prime Minister's department taking over the co-ordinating functions of the Treasury, Civil Service Department and . . . Cabinet Office'. Others, however, felt it would be 'reduced to impotence by the unwillingness of departments to supply it with information' (Bourn, 1979, p. 35). The first possibility, although Heath reportedly favoured it, never materialized. According to James (1986, p. 431), 'the Cabinet Secretary adroitly headed off this intention, and both Mr Heath and Lord Rothschild foresaw the resentment – ministerial and official – that this would arouse'. Consequently, the basic ingredients for such a development were lacking from the start: the CPRS served all ministers collectively, had no permanent members, no executive functions, and few independent information-gathering and research resources. Heath's successors, moreover, never harboured the same ambitions for the CPRS. Indeed, Wilson and Callaghan established in Number 10 a small policy unit, headed by Dr Bernard Donoughue, which met for them 'some of the needs that the CPRS had met for Mr Heath' (Plowden, 1981, p. 81). Mrs Thatcher, likewise, relied heavily on her own policy unit, and on other personal advisers.

Since it lacked the resources to develop into a prime minister's department, civil service opposition to the CPRS was less than might otherwise have been expected. Other factors also minimized potential opposition: the high proportion of CPRS members drawn from the civil service, and the heavy dependence on departments for information. In the early years at least the CPRS enjoyed good access to departmental information and developed an 'excellent relationship with the civil service' (James, 1986, p. 434). Indeed the relationship may have been too close. After 1974 there were repeated suggestions that the CPRS had been 'captured' by the civil service, and after 1979 it 'secured the opprobrium of Mrs Thatcher . . . as another useless appendage of the civil service machine' (Gray and Jenkins, 1985, p. 96).

Nevertheless the CPRS undoubtedly improved co-ordination in central administration. According to James (1986, p. 438) it 'made some impression on most spheres of government activity . . . [and] identified serious gaps in the workings of the Cabinet system: the lack of strategic thinking, the absence of a collective briefing mechanism . . . the need for a unit to tackle long term studies'. By the late 1970s the CPRS had seemingly established itself as a strategic policy unit capable of relating departmental programmes to long-term and corporate objectives. Sir Harold Wilson's view in 1977 (p. 125) was that the CPRS had 'come to stay' as 'an integral part of the decision-making centre of government'. Six years later, however, in July 1983, Mrs

Thatcher abolished it, claiming that 'the purposes for which [it] was set up [were] now being met satisfactorily in other ways': for example, by 'the increased role for Cabinet Office secretariat in preparing issues for collective ministerial discussion, and the Prime Minister's own policy unit' (*The Times*, 17 June 1983). Undoubtedly the establishment of the policy unit in 1974 did diminish the CPRS's role and Mrs Thatcher's subsequent consolidation of personal policy advisers within Number 10 (see Chapter 4) further accelerated this trend. Whereas the CPRS served the Cabinet collectively, the Number 10 policy unit provided the Prime Minister with her own personal 'think tank'. Shutting down the CPRS, and strengthening the policy unit, enabled Mrs Thatcher to '[relocate] the central capability even more firmly under the Prime Minister' (Jordan and Richardson, 1987b, p. 131).

Other factors also influenced the CPRS's disbandment. As time went on – and particularly after 1974 with the cessation of strategy discussions – the CPRS became less concerned with overall strategy and more with policy research and advice. This role, however, inevitably produced conflicts with departments (for examples see Hennessy, Morrison and Townsend, 1985, pp. 57–68), which in turn affected ministerial and civil service perceptions. Ministers, according to James (1986, p. 429), were 'more likely to take offence at criticism from the [CPRS] than from any other government department', whilst many civil servants probably shared Wass's view (1984, pp. 38–9) that as the CPRS paid less attention to strategic issues it became 'a meddler in departmental business'. Wass also pointed to resource problems. The CPRS had insufficient expertise to comment authoritatively on the government's programme as a whole, whilst its staff were out of touch with departmental business at the working level. There were also problems of secrecy, highlighted before the 1983 election by several politically embarrassing 'leaks' from confidential CPRS reports. Analysing policy options may be a sound feature of rational decision-making but can be politically embarrassing when possible shortcomings in government policy become public knowledge. It is also likely that 'rational' policy advice became less highly regarded in the climate of 'conviction politics' which characterized the 1980s, whilst strategic planning became increasingly speculative in a period of rapid economic and technological change. Whatever the reasons, by 1983 the CPRS had lost prime ministerial support and it was disbanded without a single minister speaking in its defence (Hennessy, Morrison and Townsend, 1985, pp. 98–102).

Improving central co-ordination

That there is a need within central administration for strategic policy analysis across inter-departmental boundaries is beyond doubt. What is less clear is whether this role can be performed better by a body such as the CPRS, relatively free from departmental pressures and the everyday exigencies of government, than by other agencies more firmly rooted in the political and administrative system. The dominant view is that probably it can, but only with firm prime ministerial support. While Sir Douglas Wass (1984, p. 39) criticizes the CPRS for becoming 'the creature of the Prime Minister' – and calls for a new central analytical staff located within the Cabinet Office with 'new guidelines and safeguards' – most observers feel that a close prime ministerial relationship is inevitable. Thus one former CPRS member (quoted in Hennessy, Morrison and Townsend, 1985, p. 102) feels that any revived CPRS should function as a French-style prime ministerial Cabinet, and James (1986, pp. 439) that, while the 'natural home' for such a body should be the Cabinet Office, it might instead 'become the nucleus of an expanded Prime Minister's Office'. More fundamentally, Sir John Hoskyns (1983, p. 47), former head of Mrs Thatcher's policy unit, argues that the rightful home of a CPRS is within a small new department, responsible for the development and overseeing of the government's total strategy across all departments, integrating policy and politics into a single whole. More significantly, perhaps, Mrs Thatcher herself, before disbanding the CPRS, flirted with the idea of a merger with the policy unit 'as a kind of half-way house to a Prime Minister's Department' (Hennessy, Morrison and Townsend, 1985, p. 84).

What this seems to suggest is that the success of any future CPRS-type body is likely to be dependent upon its relationship with the Prime Minister, the Cabinet, and their various supporting agencies. As Jordan and Richardson (1987b, pp. 132, 130) observe, co-ordination is 'often just another word for coercion'. Consequently, any realistic attempt to improve central co-ordination hinges on the support likely to be forthcoming from those agencies – notably the Prime Minister and Cabinet – with power to impose solutions upon competing factions or departments. As such, the question of co-ordination in central administration is acutely linked to the operation of the Cabinet system, a subject which requires detailed treatment in a separate chapter.

4 THE CABINET SYSTEM

At the apex of central administration lies the Cabinet, consisting of the Prime Minister and twenty or so of his or her most senior ministerial colleagues. In 1867 Walter Bagehot wrote that Britain enjoyed 'Cabinet government': the Cabinet was the instrument of 'fusion' between the executive and legislative branches of government, the body which effectively ruled the nation (Bagehot, 1963 edn, pp. 65–9). Developments since then have greatly increased the Cabinet's significance. Modern Cabinets normally consist of leading members of the majority party and, so long as party discipline is maintained, can control the legislative as well as the executive branches of government. At the same time the expansion of state activity has vastly increased the significance of Cabinet decisions. It has also increased the volume and complexity of Cabinet work, necessitating changes in its composition, organization, and procedures.

Some of these changes have arguably strengthened the Prime Minister at the expense of Cabinet colleagues, leading to suggestions that Cabinet government has now been replaced by prime ministerial government. No less important to public administration students, however, is the issue of whether the Cabinet system has adapted sufficiently during the twentieth century to provide for the efficient direction of central administration. Both these issues are discussed in this chapter.

Cabinet functions

The Cabinet lies at the apex of both central administration and the wider political system. Within central administration its main task is 'to co-ordinate the work of the various departments and committees and thus ensure that the activity of the government has a certain coherence' (Mackintosh, 1977, p. 413). Within the political system it is the ultimate target of the host of extra-governmental pressures which make demands upon government. Modern Cabinets, to update Bagehot's terminology, are the final point of 'fusion' between central administration and the wider political community, their role being to ensure that the former remains aware of, and responsive to, legitimate demands of the latter.

While technically the Cabinet determines its own functions, administrative and political demands necessitate the performance of several broadly identifiable tasks. Essentially there are three main functions: policy-making; administrative control; and co-ordination and delimitation.

POLICY-MAKING

The Cabinet is the ultimate policy-making body within central administration. However, meeting as it usually does for only a few hours per week, it cannot take all government policy decisions. Less important decisions are normally taken within departments or, where several departments are involved, by inter-departmental or Cabinet committees. Urgent decisions may be taken by the Prime Mninister alone or in consultation with key ministers, or by an inner or partial Cabinet (pp. 70–1). Even when Cabinet discussion does occur, however, it may be superficial, and decisions often merely ratify conclusions reached elsewhere. The main participants in Cabinet discussions, for example, are frequently ministers with departmental interests, who speak to briefs prepared by their civil servants. Skilful timing and presentation by influential ministers, especially the Prime Minister, may also inhibit Cabinet discussion. Bruce-Gardyne and Lawson (1976, p. 28), for example, explain how, following extensive behind-the-scenes discussions, Macmillan steered the decision to build Concorde through his Cabinet:

> The Prime Minister . . . told his colleagues about his great aunt's Daimler, which had travelled at 'the sensible speed of thirty miles an hour', and was sufficiently spacious to enable one to descend from it without removing one's top hat. Nowadays, alas! people had a mania for dashing around . . . . He thought they all really agreed. No one seriously dissented. It was all over in a few minutes.

Despite these limitations, 'for the most politically important issues the Cabinet is the effective decision-making body' (Jones, 1975, p. 31). Although technically the Cabinet agenda is drawn up by the Cabinet Secretary in consultation with the Prime Minister, in practice most important issues have to be included for discussion at some point. For example, decisions concerning all, or nearly all, departments – such as a public expenditure 'package' – usually 'go direct to the Cabinet' as do those which 'are too big, too urgent or too secret' to be resolved elsewhere. Usually departmental ministers, or the Prime Minister, decide which issues come into this category, although some are 'blown on to the Cabinet by their suddenness and importance' (Gordon Walker, 1972, pp. 117–21). For example, the 1982 Argentine invasion of the Falkland Islands led to the summoning of an 'emergency Cabinet meeting', attended by the Chiefs of Staff, to decide the government's response (*The Times*, 3 April 1982). Nevertheless, prime ministerial opposition has sometimes prevented important issues from being raised in Cabinet: one instance allegedly occurred during the Westland affair when Mrs Thatcher reportedly blocked attempts by her Defence Secretary, Michael Heseltine, to have the matter discussed by Cabinet colleagues (Oliver and Austin, 1987, p. 22).

Many issues, of course, reach Cabinet as a matter of routine. Usually all important Foreign and Commonwealth items and all White Papers are automatically reported to it. The Cabinet also considers the Chancellor's budget proposals, although normally only a day or so before they are presented to Parliament. However, Cabinet disagreement over the 1981 budget led to prime ministerial assurances that, in future, budget strategy would be discussed by the full Cabinet before, and not after, the Chancellor's proposals were finalized.

Forthcoming parliamentary business also receives regular Cabinet consideration. As a major element in the initiation of legislation, the Cabinet spends much time considering Bills emanating from departments for inclusion in the government's legislative programme. As parliamentary time is a scarce resource, this involves considering not just the merits of proposed legislation, but also the priority that it should receive. Of course, in 'normal' circumstances most Cabinet legislative proposals are subsequently endorsed by Parliament; consequently, modern Cabinets usually function, not just as the final determinant of government policy, but as the ultimate determinant also of public policy and legislation.

ADMINISTRATIVE CONTROL

The Cabinet not only takes policy decisions, but also bears ultimate responsibility for their implementation. In most cases Cabinet decisions are simply communicated to the departments for implementation. Occasionally, however, the Cabinet's role is more positive. A serious breakdown in administration, for example, would most certainly be discussed by Cabinet. Sometimes in such circumstances the Cabinet may decide to maintain direct oversight and control of administrative work – for example by authorizing a Cabinet committee or group of ministers to exercise control – or it may establish new administrative procedures or machinery. Consequently, while most administrative work occurs below Cabinet level, the Cabinet bears ultimate responsibility and 'takes the lead in initiating most . . . administrative action' (Steel, 1979, p. 23).

CO-ORDINATION AND DELIMITATION

The Cabinet is 'the ultimate forum for the co-ordination of all the activities of government' (Steel, 1979, p. 23). Its primacy in policy determination gives it final responsibility for both preventative and strategic policy co-ordination (pp. 44–5). It also has an important role in administrative co-ordination. The Cabinet, writes Hennessy (1986a, p. 7) is 'a blender. It must try and reach rational, practical decisions from a most unpromising mixture of ingredients . . . a reconciliation of short-term requirements with medium-term needs and long-term strategy; and a balancing between the twin pulls . . . from administrative requirements and political imperatives'. It is also, Mackenzie and Grove (1957, p. 360) explain, 'the court of last appeal for disputes between Departments about jurisdiction' and thus bears ultimate responsibility for the departmental pattern. As they observe (p. 359), 'effective "co-ordination" requires power to decide who is to be responsible for action. The "sovereignty" of the Cabinet includes power to shape the machinery of government'.

Influences upon the Cabinet

Cabinet decisions are not taken within a vacuum. The Cabinet responds to issues, problems, and opinions emanating from within central administration, as well as to environmental influences (economic factors, social forces, international tensions, and so forth) and a host of other extra-governmental pressures. Some of the latter, like Royal Commissions and public inquiries, advisory committees, quangos, and public corporations, may have been established by central administration to perform advisory or executive functions. Other pressures will be generated independently of central administration. In addition to parliamentary influences, and pressure from foreign governments and international agencies such as the EC and NATO, such influences include: a) electoral factors, b) party pressures, c) the media, and d) pressure groups.

ELECTORAL FACTORS

The Cabinet's authority in normal circumstances stems from its electoral mandate; consequently, it will be influenced by election commitments. As these, however, are invariably broad statements of intent, often drawn up in opposition, the Cabinet still has a significant role: for example, making decisions about the details, priority, and feasibility of commitments as well as about issues unforeseen in the manifesto.

PARTY PRESSURES

Modern Cabinets are usually party Cabinets and, as Rose (1980, pp. 312–13) observes, 'rely upon a majority in . . . Parliament to sustain [their] existence'. The maintenance of a parliamentary majority is essentially the responsibility of the Government whips who, while exerting pressure upon MPs to support government proposals, also communicate backbench views to the Cabinet. Norton (1981, pp. 29–30) quotes one Conservative whip: 'if the Chief Whip comes to the conclusion, on the basis of sounding out the parliamentary party, that something cannot be done, then, as a general rule, that is that: it cannot be done'. Views are also transmitted to the Cabinet through the parties' organizations. Both main parties are highly organized in Parliament (Norton, 1979, 1983), with regional and subject committees of MPs, and regular meetings of the full parliamentary party – machinery which provides an important, and private, channel through which backbenchers can exert pressure on their party leaders.

The Cabinet must also respond to pressures from its extra-parliamentary supporters. These may be transmitted either informally, through exchanges between ministers and party members, or through formal organizational channels (party conferences, committees and so forth). While their effect will vary according to issue and circumstance, the Cabinet must nevertheless at all times seek 'to carry the party with it'. Failure to do so may not only sap party morale, with ultimate electoral repercussions, but, more immediately, may breed disaffection among backbenchers and make the work of the whips more difficult.

THE MEDIA

The Cabinet is also influenced by the media, which transmit public opinion and report, comment upon and interpret happenings of political significance. As a result the media help to 'set the agenda' of political debate. Emergence of issues through the media is an important source of public policy, and when salient issues develop the Cabinet must usually respond. At times the media may become all-important. According to Lord Boyle (Boyle and Crosland, 1971, p. 109), 'The Cabinet increasingly, as the years go on, tends to be most concerned with the agenda that the press and media are setting out as the crucial issues before the nation at any one time'.

The media, of course, transmit opinion in two directions: from ministers to the public as well as vice versa. Most departments have press offices, including Number 10. The latter is particularly significant: busy journalists often simply reproduce the material it supplies, leading to suggestions that the media is manipulated into setting the political agenda desired by the government and, particularly, by the Prime Minister (Cockerell, Hennessey and Walker, 1984). More negatively, information flowing out of central administration is restricted by the Official Secrets Acts, which prevent disclosure by civil servants of even the most trivial official information. Although difficult to enforce, the effect is to make British central administration perhaps the most secretive in the Western world (see Michael, 1982).

PRESSURE GROUPS

Pressure groups represent another major influence upon the Cabinet; indeed, their influence upon both policy-making and administration increased considerably during the twentieth century as the expansion of state activity made central administration increasingly dependent upon group co-operation and advice. Generally the most influential groups are sectional groups (like the CBI and TUC) which defend important sectional interests. Many such groups help provide essential public services or possess power to cause social and economic disruption. They often also possess other significant resources: organization, wealth, status, large or influential memberships, expertise, and so on. Often, too, they command considerable political 'muscle'. During the 1960s and 1970s this was particularly evident in fields such as industrial relations and prices and incomes, where the policy initiatives of successive governments were frustrated largely by opposition from powerful trade unions.

Not all groups, of course, possess such influence. For example, promotional groups which (like CND or the League Against Cruel Sports) promote a particular cause usually possess fewer resources: smaller memberships, less expertise and wealth, and relatively little disruptive capacity. Nevertheless, some promotional groups have campaigned with great success. Environmental groups, for example, have presented a considerable challenge to perceived threats to the environment (Kimber and Richardson, 1974; Lowe and Goyder, 1983); while CND during the early 1980s focused mounting public attention on the Cabinet's decision to site nuclear cruise missiles in Britain. Often using the media with effect, such groups usually try to force on to the 'political agenda' issues which the Cabinet might otherwise ignore.

While pressure groups, by seeking (often conflicting) concessions from government, make the work of central administration more difficult, in other respects they make it easier. They provide information essential for policy formulation, assistance with implementation and a means of consulting sections of the community about policy proposals. Indeed, since the war, Cabinets have tended increasingly to look to groups (rather than Parliament) to 'legitimize' policies. A 'voluntary' prices and income policy, for example, supported and 'policed' by the CBI and TUC, is more likely to prove effective than one imposed by legislation. So interdependent at times are key producer groups and government that some writers, particularly in the

1970s, claimed to detect in Britain the emergence of *corporatism* – a system in which, stated simply, major functional groups are incorporated into government decision-making (becoming part of the extended state) in return for policy concessions (Pahl and Winkler, 1974; Schmitter, 1979; Middlemas, 1979). Although the general inability of large peak organizations to impose deals negotiated with government on unwilling members, coupled with the emergence of large numbers of radical campaigning 'outsider' groups, makes the label 'corporatism' arguably inapplicable to Britain (particularly in the 1980s with the Thatcher government's posture of less dependence on groups), the corporatist model nevertheless emphasizes what Jordan and Richardson (1987a, p. 181) describe as the 'natural tendency for the political system in Britian to encourage the formation of stable policy communities, one of the primary purposes of which is to achieve a negotiated and stable policy environment'.

Generally, of course, the Cabinet becomes involved directly in group bargaining only when demands are too intractable to be resolved by departments, or where client groups of different departments make conflicting demands. As this implies, Cabinets frequently reject 'unacceptable' group demands, and indeed possess formidable resources – from the armed forces at one extreme, to the claim to represent the national interest at the other – with which to resist. Nevertheless, the cumulative influence of group pressures upon Cabinet decision-making is considerable. As Richardson and Jordan (1979, p. 3) observe, 'a proper understanding of the ways . . . issues arrive on the political agenda, . . . the way in which policies are decided, their actual content, and subsequent implementation, can only be reached by reference to the group system'.

As should be clear, the Cabinet is the ultimate target of pressures emanating both from within and without central administration. While the source and strength of pressure will vary from issue to issue, whenever pressures conflict the Cabinet will calculate relative costs and benefits of different courses of action. The Cabinet, in short, must try to balance incompatibles, or, as Jones (1975, p. 40) puts it, 'make unity out of diversity'.

Cabinet composition and size

The Cabinet's composition is itself a source of diversity. Although members normally belong to the same party, they are also ambitious politicians often representing different factions and 'wings' within the party. Most, moreover, are departmental ministers whose policy perspectives invariably reflect departmental attitudes. Consequently, participants in Cabinet discussions themselves reflect diversity, and their decisions often represent compromises rather than outright victory or defeat for individual competitors. 'Ministers', Jordan and Richardson (1987b, p. 126) explain, 'regularly adopt the role of departmental defender' thereby preventing the Cabinet from developing an effective policy-making or co-ordinating capacity.

Ironically, it is the need to produce unity which largely explains the Cabinet's diverse composition. Because of its co-ordinating role all major departments – as well as any co-ordinating ministers (see Chapter 3) – are usually given representation. Departments and their client groups, moreover, are likely to feel loss of prestige and influence without Cabinet representation. Patronage and party considerations also intrude: most prime ministers use Cabinet posts to reward supporters, 'neutralize' rivals, and represent all strands of party opinion. Indeed, while Cabinet composition is theoretically a matter of prime ministerial discretion, in practice administrative and political factors seriously restrict his or her choice. They also tend to exert pressure for large Cabinets, pressure which has increased over the past century as the central administrative machine has expanded. Surprisingly, in view of such pressures, the Cabinet was barely larger in October 1988 (with twenty-two members) than in 1900 (with nineteen). One reason is that large Cabinets usually take longer to reach decisions than smaller ones; more members want to speak and more views must be reconciled. Other than in wartime, most twentieth-century Cabinets have numbered about twenty: since the war, for example, most Cabinets have had between sixteen and twenty-four members. Despite the vast increase in government work, therefore, the Cabinet's size during the twentieth century has remained surprisingly stable. Prime ministers have balanced the need for Cabinets large enough to allow effective co-ordination, and adequate patronage, with the requirement to keep them below the level – just over twenty – beyond which they become too unwieldy for effective decision-making.

Even with Cabinets of around twenty, modern prime ministers have often formed inner Cabinets which they have consulted more regularly than the full Cabinet. Usually, the term 'inner Cabinet' denotes an informal grouping of 'friends or confidants of the Prime Minister drawn from members of his Cabinet' (Gordon Walker, 1972, p. 37). While they may carry considerable political weight, such bodies have no official status and their decisions do not bind the Cabinet. In 1968 Wilson, departing from this informal model, established a Parliamentary Committee of the Cabinet. Comprising senior ministers, and serviced by the Cabinet Secretariat, it functioned in some respects as a formalized inner Cabinet (Hennessy, 1986a, p. 71). However, it disappeared in 1970, and has had no lasting effect on central administration.

Different from an inner Cabinet is what Gordon Walker (1972, pp. 87–8) describes as a 'partial Cabinet' – 'a number of Ministers who constitute part only of the Cabinet but act for a time as if they were the Cabinet'. Sometimes these are technically Cabinet committees (see next section), at other times not. Usually concerned with 'matters of great moment and secrecy' they 'prepare policies . . . and . . . take decisions without prior consultation with the Cabinet' although the Cabinet 'is in due course informed and consulted'. According to Gordon Walker (pp. 89–90), partial Cabinets took the decision to manufacture the atom bomb in Attlee's government, and drafted plans to invade Suez in 1956. Similar arrangements existed during the 1982 Falklands dispute when an inner group of Cabinet ministers, chosen and chaired by the Prime Minister, was entrusted with the day-to-day handling of the crisis (Seymour-Ure, 1984).

By utilizing inner and partial Cabinets, prime ministers, with the assistance of senior colleagues, have been able to discuss issues more thoroughly, swiftly, and urgently than would otherwise be possible given the size of modern Cabinets. It is in the same vein that the establishment of a Cabinet committee system should be seen.

Cabinet committees

Cabinet committees offer a classic example of the ambiguity and complexity which characterizes public administration. Technically these comprise all committees serviced by the Cabinet Office, but as the composition, terms of reference, and number of these (at least 160 in 1985–6) vary widely this definition has little practical value. Some committees, moreover, consist of ministers, others of civil servants, and others still of both; some are permanent standing committees and others temporary or *ad hoc*. The picture is further confused because information about Cabinet committees is shrouded in official secrecy. For students of public administration, therefore, Cabinet committees present many problems. One, for example, is that a distinction between inter-departmental committees (see pp. 53–4) and Cabinet committees, and between official (civil service) and ministerial committees, cannot always be clearly drawn.

Despite occasional prior use of committees, it was not until the First World War that a Cabinet committee *system* came into being. Under war pressures vast amounts of work were delegated to newly-created Cabinet committees, of which 165 were in existence by 1918. Between the wars these committees were largely unscrambled (see Gordon Walker, 1972, p. 39). However, similar arrangements were reintroduced during the Second World War, following which Attlee's government – with a heavy programme of social and economic reconstruction – retained them as a permanent peacetime structure, as they have remained ever since. As a minute by Prime Minister Callaghan in 1978 stated, 'The Cabinet committee system grew up as the load on the Cabinet itself became too great' (Sedgemore, 1980, p. 77).

Two main types of Cabinet committee can broadly be identified: *standing committees* (which may form sub-committees) and *ad hoc committees*. In 1983 Mrs Thatcher acknowledged the existence of four main standing committees: Home and Social Affairs, Legislation, Economic Strategy, and Oversea and Defence (Hennessy, 1986a, p. 26). Consisting essentially of ministers (Cabinet Office officials also attend), chaired by senior Cabinet ministers, and each covering broad policy fields, committees of this kind are now a permanent feature of central administration.

Many *ad hoc* committees, by contrast, are either temporary – being formed to deal with particular problems – or are for long periods inactive. The temporary committees are often entitled MISC (short for miscellaneous) followed by a number, a title which conceals the influence which many of them wield. In 1981/2, for example, MISC 7, consisting of the Prime Minister and four Cabinet colleagues, was effectively responsible for the decision to replace Polaris with the Trident missile system, while in 1984/5 MISC 101, chaired by Mrs Thatcher, was responsible for day-to-day handling of the miners' strike. Of those inactive for long periods some recur: Mackintosh (1977, p. 528) cites the Agriculture Committee, revived annually for price reviews. Others are resurrected to deal with particular crises: examples are the Transition to War Committee, chaired by the Cabinet Secretary (responsible for planning mobilization in the event of war or international tension); and the Civil Contingencies Unit, chaired by the Home Secretary (responsible for maintaining essential services during industrial disputes). (For further examples see Hennessy, 1986a, table 1, pp. 27–30.)

The composition of Cabinet committees is determined by the Prime Minister, although usually representatives from all 'interested' departments are included. In 1974 Headey (p. 36) wrote that on average each Cabinet minister attended three or four committee meetings each week, and usually spent more time (four to six hours) in committee than in full Cabinet (three to five hours). Of course, since then normal Cabinet meetings have been reduced from two to one per week, and much business formerly conducted in Cabinet committees now takes place in *ad hoc* ministerial meetings (see pp. 74–5). Nevertheless the burden upon Cabinet ministers is considerable and, partly to ease this, junior ministers often represent their departments on committees, especially on less important ones. Civil servants also sit on the 'official' committees which 'shadow', and often influence, the ministerial Cabinet committees (Hennessy, 1986a, p. 31).

Cabinet committee *functions* are also technically a matter of prime ministerial discretion, although essentially they perform a twofold role: a) they enable problems to be delegated for detailed consideration and resolution on the Cabinet's behalf. This allows matters to receive the attention they require, and saves Cabinet time. b) They allow less important items to be resolved without involving the Cabinet. Normally a policy initiative emanating from a department is sent by the Cabinet Office to the appropriate standing or sub-committee for a decision. (Usually, it will also be discussed beforehand by the shadowing official committee or, if the Cabinet Office feels much more work is required, an *ad hoc* official committee may be formed.) In 1967 a ruling was introduced that appeals to Cabinet against committee decisions would not be allowed without approval from the committee chairman concerned. This arrangement, although not always rigidly applied, 'appears to encapsulate the reality of practice under most recent British governments' (Hogwood and Mackie, 1985, p. 51), and in effect gives Cabinet committee decisions virtually the same authority as the Cabinet itself. Under Mrs Thatcher their role has been further strengthened by ending the traditional practice whereby committee decisions were usually reported to Cabinet (Kavanagh, 1987a, p. 13).

Cabinet committees undoubtedly improve the efficiency of the Cabinet machine, keeping the Cabinet agenda free from all but the most important and controversial issues. Today, Hogwood and Mackie (1985, p. 54) conclude, 'the major decision-making role of cabinet is as a resolver of controversial issues that cabinet committees have been unable to resolve, or which go straight to cabinet'. Cabinet committees are the means by which the Cabinet machine has adapted to the twentieth-century increase in the volume and complexity of government business, preventing the Cabinet from becoming overloaded yet enabling – as one Cabinet Secretary described it – 'the necessary co-ordination at ministerial level' to continue, and the 'reality of collective discussion and responsibility' to be maintained (Hennessy, 1986a, p. 38). They have produced, in effect, a Cabinet *system* of government in place of the nineteenth-century 'Cabinet government' described by Bagehot.

Significantly, however, they have also altered the decision-making process within central administration in a manner which arguably strengthens the Prime Minister at the expense of his or her Cabinet colleagues. The structure, composition, remit, and chairmen of Cabinet committees are determined by the Prime Minister. Sometimes committees have been established 'to by-pass . . . a particular minister' (Mackintosh, 1977, p. 521); at other times their decisions – and even their existence – have allegedly been concealed from other Cabinet members (Benn, 1982, p. 29; Sedgemore, 1980, pp. 14–15). During the Westland affair one Cabinet sub-committee meeting was allegedly cancelled by the Prime Minister in order to deny Mr Heseltine an opportunity to report progress to sympathetic colleagues (Hennessy, 1986c, especially pp. 426–7). Several issues of fundamental importance, in fact, have allegedly been decided in committee without full Cabinet knowledge: Crossman (1963, pp. 54–6), for example, cites the Attlee government's decision to manufacture the atom bomb and Eden's decision to invade Suez in 1956. (See also Gorst, 1987; Hennessy, 1986a, especially pp. 55–8, 123–34; Seymour-Ure, 1984.) One conclusion drawn by some observers (Benn, 1982; Crossman, 1963; Mackintosh, 1977; Sedgemore, 1980) is that Cabinet committees (as well as partial and inner Cabinets) have resulted not simply in the demise of Cabinet government, but in its replacement, effectively, by prime ministerial government. As Jordan and Richardson (1987b, p. 152) conclude, 'Our main point about the Cabinet committee system is that it is an extra prime ministerial power – perhaps *the* prime ministerial power'.

Not all observers accept this analysis. Gordon Walker (1972, pp. 85–91), for example, rejects Crossman's interpretation of decisions such as manufacture of the atom bomb and Suez. Hennessy (1986a, p. 131) also argues that it was 'widely assumed that Britain was making atomic bombs' and that few ministers 'would have dissented' had Attlee taken the issue to Cabinet; and Seymour-Ure (1984, p. 184) that the Egypt Committee – which Eden formed to bypass the Cabinet and its Defence Committee in 1956 – nevertheless had a loose and fluctuating membership which reflected his 'need to carry the full Cabinet and the party with him'. As Jones (1975, p. 49) argues, committees and partial Cabinets are subordinate to the Cabinet which 'is a constant restraint on them and whose reactions they anticipate'. They also include influential ministers whose support the Prime Minister must retain. Significantly, Crossman, a leading member of the prime ministerial school, argued while a member of Wilson's Cabinet for the establishment of an inner Cabinet to restrain the Prime Minister from making policy through private consultations with departmental ministers (Jordan, 1978).

This latter practice, which undermines the role of both Cabinet and Cabinet committees, has reportedly increased sharply under Mrs Thatcher's premiership, with a growing tendency towards decision-making in *ad hoc* groups consisting of herself and ministers (and sometimes also members of the Prime Minister's Policy Unit (see p. 79) and other personal advisers) skewed towards her own policy preferences (Hennessy, 1985, p. 37). Decisions reportedly taken in this way include abolition of exchange controls, banning unions from GCHQ, and early Westland deliberations. One effect is that under Mrs Thatcher fewer Cabinet committees have been appointed, and the number of Cabinet meetings (about 45–50 per annum) has fallen to about half the post-war norm (Hennessy, 1986b, p. 141). According to Burch (1987), what we are witnessing is the 'demise of Cabinet government'. 'To a large degree', he tells us (p. 33), 'the Cabinet has become a residual institution'. Nevertheless Cabinet committees still 'perform the decisive role in the process of arriving at many government decisions' (Hogwood and Mackie, 1985, p. 53). To quote Sir Harold Wilson (1977, pp. 86, 89), Cabinet committees 'make the whole government more effective . . . . If the system had not existed, it would have had to be invented'.

The Cabinet Office

The business of the Cabinet and its committees is co-ordinated by the Cabinet Office. Formed in 1916 to enable the Cabinet to operate under war pressures, it has, during the twentieth century, developed into 'the "nerve-centre" of British Government' (Jones, 1975, p. 50). In 1988 it comprised 1,591 staff, many of whom were senior civil servants seconded from departments. Its head, the Cabinet Secretary, is the most influential figure in Whitehall, and holds the post of Head of the Home Civil Service.

In 1988 the Cabinet Office included the following main components:

(i) *The Cabinet Secretariat* is the original and most important component. Its work is closely linked with the Cabinet: it assists the Prime Minister in preparing the Cabinet agenda, keeps Cabinet minutes, transmits Cabinet decisions to departments and monitors their implementation. It performs similar functions for Cabinet committees and sub-committees, also providing a 'neutral' chairman for them where necessary. By the mid-1980s it had become, effectively, a federation of six secretariats each with its own head: Economic; Oversea and Defence; Home Affairs; Science and Technology; Security and Intelligence; and European (Hennessy, 1986a, pp. 25–6).

(ii) *The Central Statistical Office*, which prepares and interprets statistics for use in policy-making and co-ordinates governmental statistical work.

(iii) *The Historical Section*, which is responsible for the preparation of official histories.

(iv) *The Government's Chief Scientific Officer* has been housed in the Cabinet Office since 1966.

(v) *The Efficiency Unit* (see Chapter 7) has been physically located in the Cabinet Office since 1983.

(vi) *Office of the Minister for the Civil Service.* Established in 1987 following disbandment of the Management and Personnel Office. The Office of the Minister for the Civil Service operates as a Sub-Department of the Cabinet Office under the Head of the Home Civil Service (the Cabinet Secretary). Responsible for advising the Prime Minister (as Minister for the Civil Service) on duties and standards in the civil service and for recruitment, training and development policies, day-to-day charge of the office is delegated to a junior minister (in 1988, the minister of state at the Privy Council Office).

The Cabinet Office, clearly, is more than just a secretariat. It is today 'the main co-ordinating office' within central administration (Mackintosh, 1977, p. 519). As the 'general administrative co-ordinator of Government' (Jones, 1975, p. 50) it monitors the implementation of Cabinet decisions by departments and acts as a 'clearing house' for inter-departmental communications. It also has a central role in policy co-ordination, invariably being involved in important initiatives emanating from departments. Normally a department wishing to raise an item in Cabinet (or committee) produces an advance paper. Other departments with an interest may also produce papers, the Cabinet Office's minimum role being to ensure that such papers are circulated in good time and that all appropriate departments are consulted. The Office may also produce a 'neutral' steering brief for committee chairmen (Berrill, 1985, pp. 252–3). Its maximum role is to try to remove any apparent defect in proposals, and to resolve any inter-departmental differences. Vast areas of government work are co-ordinated in this way: the Oversea and Defence Secretariat, for example, 'blends foreign and defence policy-making with the output of the intelligence agencies', while the European Secretariat provides a similar function for the 'wide span of Whitehall departments' with EEC-related business (Hennessy 1986a, p. 25).

To perform this role the Cabinet Office possess considerable resources. Its prestige usually enables it to obtain advice and co-operation from departments and most Secretariat officials specialize in specific fields. Nevertheless, Berrill (1985, especially pp. 295–6) questions whether, given the secretariat's 'mixture of roles' and 'revolving team' of 'officials on secondment for a couple of years or so', its resources are really sufficient. It is also possible to question the extent of its influence. Wass (1984, p. 35) warns that while the Secretariat briefs the 'chairmen of the Cabinet and its committees, . . . it does so mainly . . . on procedural matters. Where a clearly exposed conflict has emerged, it may suggest a possible compromise to the chairman. But its advice is privy to the chairman and it is not available to the Cabinet or to the Cabinet committee as a whole'. Its influence may also have diminished in recent years with decisions being taken increasingly in *ad hoc* ministerial and other groups rather than in formal Cabinet and Cabinet committee meetings. Nevertheless, the Cabinet Office's position at the centre of government remains crucially important. Hennessy's view in 1976 (*The Times*, 8 March 1976) was that 'whether it requires fine-tuning or knocking heads together, this is where policy is invariably handled in its final stages'. It is also true that, while the Secretariat does not advise the Cabinet on policy, the Cabinet Secretary does so advise the Prime Minister and that 'in some cases the relationship' between the two 'becomes particularly close' (Rush, 1984, p. 39).

The Cabinet Office's development reflects the twentieth-century expansion of government activity and the increase in potential points of inter-departmental conflict. In the interests of co-ordination it has been necessary to strengthen the 'centre' against departments. Significantly, the Treasury – the original co-ordinating department – has long sought to absorb the Cabinet Office (see Peden, 1983). That it failed is partly because the Treasury, as a department itself, cannot be neutral in inter-departmental battles; and partly because the Prime Minister – the minister closest to the Cabinet Office – has more control over co-ordination by having important functions performed there.

Although the Cabinet Office serves the Cabinet collectively, it operates under prime ministerial direction. Its development has greatly increased the Prime Minister's administrative support: it transmits his or her views throughout central administration, warns about problems 'looming up', and provides a mechanism for bringing particularly complex problems under closer prime ministerial control. Despite this the Cabinet Office is not the Prime Minister's department. It serves the Cabinet collectively, its responsibility being to execute the wishes, not of the Prime Minister, but of the Cabinet. Indeed, not having a department leaves the Prime Minister under-resourced relative not only to departmental ministers, but possibly also to the chief executives of most other national governments. The implications of this are further discussed in the next section.

A Prime Minister's Department?

The Prime Minister is the focal point of the Cabinet. He or she summons and chairs its meetings, appoints its members, determines its agenda, sums up discussion, and supervises the Cabinet Office. Thus, while subject, like other ministers, to the final authority of the Cabinet, in practice the Prime Minister exercises considerable influence over it.

The Prime Minister is heavily involved in the policy-making, administrative, and co-ordinating work of central administration. Major policy initiatives usually come to the Prime Minister's notice before they reach the Cabinet, while subjects assuming major importance within Parliament, the media, or the party, will usually at some stage receive his or her personal attention. Once directly involved in an issue, moreover, the Prime Minister is powerfully placed to steer it through the Cabinet system. Of course, no Prime Minister can deal personally with all policy matters. His or her involvement is inevitably selective but, when it does occur, may well be crucial to the outcome.

The Prime Minister also becomes involved in major administrative issues. While departmental ministers are primarily responsible for policy implementation, the Prime Minister will usually react to 'danger signals' suggesting that departmental administration is suspect. The Prime Minister, moreover, exercises substantial control over the government machine: he or she has considerable control over the departmental pattern (see Chapter 2) while appointments to the most senior civil service posts usually require prime ministerial approval. The Prime Minister also plays a crucial co-ordinating role, having access to all ministers and – through the Cabinet Office – communications with all departments. As Rose (1980, p. 34) explains, his or hers is an ideal vantage point from which 'to scan the horizon', to see the 'interconnections among policies', and to 'steer policies toward certain broad political objectives, and away from recognizable difficulties'.

Despite these responsibilities, only limited resources are available directly to the Prime Minister (as opposed to the Cabinet collectively). These are mainly located in the *Prime Minister's Office*, which usually contains around eighty full-time staff employed in four main groups (Jones, 1980, 1985). These are:

(i) *The Private Office*, staffed by civil servants, which keeps the Prime Minister's diary, deals with correspondence, and provides briefing material. It is headed by the Prime Minister's Principal Private Secretary who leads a small team of assistant private secretaries – normally 'high fliers' seconded from departments – each covering broad policy areas.

(ii) *The Political Office*, usually consisting of political appointees chosen by the Prime Minister, has been an important feature of recent governments. It provides political advice, and help with constituency and party duties. Its members have sometimes allegedly exercised considerable influence, most notably Mrs Marcia Williams (Lady Falkender) who headed Wilson's political office (Jones, 1976, especially pp. 34–6; Williams, 1972). (See also Jones, 1985, p. 91.)

(iii) *The Prime Minister's Press Office*, which handles public relations and acts as a link between the Prime Minister and journalists. It may be headed either by a civil servant or by a journalist with sympathies close to the Prime Minister (see Jones, 1976, pp. 34–6; Haines, 1977). Since 1979 the post of chief press secretary has been held by Bernard Ingham, a civil servant and former journalist, whose vigorous role in lobby briefings and in the alleged leaking of selections of confidential ministerial correspondence during the Westland affair have occasioned much comment (Cockerell, Hennessy and Walker, 1984; Oliver and Austin, 1987).

(iv) *The Policy Unit*, created in 1974 by Wilson, operates as a policy analysis unit capable of providing advice independently of the official machine (see Willetts, 1987). Acting on its own initiative, or at the Prime Minister's request, it is usually headed by a political sympathizer of the Prime Minister. Other members may include either political appointees or civil servants seconded from departments.

Collectively these resources are meagre, and leave the Prime Minister ill-equipped 'to compete with the Cabinet Office or other departments' (Jones, 1975, p. 55). Significantly, Mrs Thatcher has sought to strengthen them. A more overtly partisan element has been introduced into the Policy Unit and its scope has been extended. Members now routinely monitor areas of departmental responsibility, assess the progress of overall government strategy, receive copies of most policy papers, and, according to some accounts, participate in committee proceedings and in *ad hoc* ministerial meetings. In 1983, following disbandment of the Central Policy Review Staff (see Chapter 3), the unit's membership was expanded, leading to suggestions that Mrs Thatcher was increasing her own support while reducing that available to Cabinet colleagues. Mrs Thatcher's advisory support, moreover, has been further reinforced by the addition to her office of (usually short-term) specialist advisers independent of the Policy Unit (such as Professor Sir Alan Walters on economics and Sir Anthony Parsons on foreign affairs). She has also drawn heavily on the advice of people who hold no position in Downing Street, particularly from within the Centre for Policy Studies (a right-wing policy research 'ginger group') (for discussion see Jones, 1985, especially pp. 88–95; Kavanagh, 1987a, p. 13, and 1987b, pp. 89–91 and 253–65; Willetts, 1987). While by no means representing wholly new departures, these developments have aroused speculation that they represent the nucleus of an emerging Prime Minister's Department; indeed, Mrs Thatcher actively considered forming such a department prior to the 1983 general election (Hennessy, Morrison and Townsend, 1985, p. 84).

The case for a Prime Minister's Department, in fact, has frequently been advanced, and rests on three main arguments:

(i) The Prime Minister requires briefing and policy options other than those presented by departments. To some extent this facility is already provided by the Policy Unit and the Prime Minister's special advisers. However, a Prime Minister's Department would be able to tap more expertise, present a wider range of options, and produce more thoroughgoing analyses than are presently available.

(ii) Prime ministers need staff commensurate with their range of functions. A former head of the CPRS (Berrill, 1985) observes that modern prime ministers are expected to answer 'for virtually every act or omission by the government' and are in increasing contact with foreign heads of government. Consequently, they need 'a support system with time to work on problems in some depth across the width of government activities'.

(iii) The need to strengthen the Prime Minister's co-ordinating role. Existing machinery for co-ordinating the work of central administration is, it is argued, inadequate. Conflicts not settled by the plethora of co-ordinating agencies described in Chapter 3 are normally passed upwards through the Cabinet system for resolution. However, while the Cabinet and its committees may arbitrate in such matters, it does so in 'day-to-day' dealing with 'issues as they come up, sorting them out on an *ad hoc* . . . not a strategic basis' (Hennessy, Morrison and Townsend, 1985, p. 102). Moreover, appeal to the Prime Minister and to *ad hoc* groups is increasingly an option available to ministers defeated in Cabinet and Cabinet committees. There is, therefore, arguably a need for machinery to enable prime ministers: a) to arbitrate in conflicts not resolved within Cabinet and Cabinet committees; and b) to develop a capacity for strategic co-ordination across the whole range of governmental activities. Jordan and Richardson (1987b, p. 162) see Mrs Thatcher's strengthening of the Prime Minister's Office as a response to what they describe as 'the co-ordination problem' within central administration. 'The co-ordination that is available via the Prime Minister, the Cabinet Office and the other No. 10 staff is conceivably inadequate – [and] the divided Cabinet is not the institution to provide for such a need'.

Common to most such arguments is an awareness that, despite presiding over a highly centralized political system, British prime ministers lack the capability for central direction possessed by most other chief executives (Rose and Suleiman, 1980; Weller, 1983, 1985). To resolve the problems various prescriptions have been advanced. Mackintosh in 1977 (p. 519) suggested that placing the Cabinet Secretariat, the former CPRS, and the public expenditure and manpower units of the Treasury and former Civil Service Department *directly* under prime ministerial control would 'make an effective equivalent of the White House Staff with the other agencies co-ordinating work for the President'. Sir John Hoskyns, who has likened Whitehall to 'a headless chicken', (*The Times*, 8 November 1982), argued in 1983 (p. 147) 'for a small department' incorporating the CPRS and 'a reconstructed Cabinet Office' capable of developing and overseeing 'the government's total strategy, across all departments'. Berrill (1985) more specifically calls for a Prime Minister's Department incorporating the CPRS, the Cabinet Secretariat, and an enhanced Prime Minister's Office. What these observers seem to be highlighting is the need for central mechanisms capable of asserting a capacity for central co-ordination and control. And while not all are strictly calling for a Prime Minister's Department this, it can be argued, is the logical outcome of their prescriptions. As Jordan and Richardson (1987b, pp. 130, 128) explain, 'Any attempt at central co-ordination ends up as being dominated by the Prime Minister . . . . The argument for a Prime Minister's Department is the argument for central co-ordination'.

There are, however, equally powerful arguments *against* establishing a Prime Minister's Department. These include:

(i) A Prime Minister's department is arguably unnecessary. Although the Cabinet Office serves the whole Cabinet, it gives considerable assistance to the Prime Minister and is 'the functional equivalent' of prime ministerial departments in other countries (N. Johnson, *The Times*, 17 November 1982). As Sir Harold Wilson (1977, p. 106) argues, a Prime Minister's Department is unnecessary as 'everything he could expect to create is there already to hand in the Cabinet Office'. In addition, Wass (1984, pp. 34–57) tells us, prime ministers requiring extra briefing about departmental business as a rule readily receive this from staff of the department concerned.

(ii) A Prime Minister's Department is not only administratively unnecessary, but arguably also undesirable. Such a department could impose serious administrative burdens upon the Prime Minister. It would also develop its own attitudes and tend to urge these upon the Prime Minister. Consequently, the Prime Minister's status as 'neutral' Cabinet chairman, and his or her ability to help Cabinet colleagues reach unified decisions, would be seriously impaired (Jones, 1985, pp. 87–8).

(iii) A Prime Minister's Department would downgrade other departments and increase the Prime Minister's capacity to impose his or her will on Cabinet colleagues. It would consequently 'set the Prime Minister apart from the Cabinet, frustrate Cabinet cohesion, and symbolise a shift from Cabinet to prime ministerial goernment' (Jones, 1983, p. 84).

To understand the force of this latter argument it should be stressed that control of the Cabinet and government machine (see previous section) forms only part of the potential for prime ministerial government. Alongside this must be seen the Prime Minister's role as *party leader*: not only does this confer influence in party manoeuvring, but the increasing focus on party leaders at elections (Seymour-Ure, 1974, pp. 202–39) enables a victorious Prime Minister to claim a personal mandate. The Prime Minister is also the most important MP, being able to dissolve Parliament and (through the whips) normally to determine how it votes. These powers are further strengthened by patronage. The Prime Minister appoints (and dismisses) ministers, and influences conferment of knighthoods, peerages, and appointments to state bodies (Benn, 1982, pp. 26–8; Sedgemore, 1980, pp. 57–63; Jordan and Richardson, 1987b, pp. 134–6) as well as, increasingly in the 1980s, the promotion of top civil servants (see Chapter 5). Hence, he or she can reward party workers, MPs, ministers and civil servants who show loyalty and overlook those who do not. The Prime Minister also hands in the government's resignation, which – like the power of dissolution – might be used or threatened to bring rebels into line (Sedgemore, 1980, pp. 66–7). He or she is also the focus of the media, and thus well-placed to set the subject and mood of public debate. This potential for prime ministerial government has evoked particular controversy during Mrs Thatcher's premiership. A particular high point was the Westland affair when Mrs Thatcher's Defence Secretary, Michael Heseltine, resigned because the Prime Minister in his view was 'behaving more like a president than "primus inter pares"' (Oliver and Austin, 1987, p. 26).

This concentration of power is, of course, counterbalanced by important constraints. One is the amount of work, which limits the time that can be devoted to all but the most important issues. Another is the need to retain party and parliamentary support which may necessitate policy compromise and limit prime ministerial freedom with ministerial appointments. Because of the political damage that the resignation of key ministers might cause, the Prime Minister must carry ministerial and party colleagues with him or her. Numerous observers (Jones, 1965; Gordon Walker, 1972; Wilson, 1977) reject the prime ministerial thesis, emphasizing the collective role of the Cabinet and the constraints which make it difficult for prime ministers to act alone. Even Mrs Thatcher has suffered policy reverses at the hands of Cabinet colleagues. Her style, writes Hennessy (1985, p. 38; 1986a, pp. 121–2) is not 'presidential': 'There genuinely is a contrast between her . . . assertion of personality and the reality of the decision-making process'.

Whichever view is most accurate, the Prime Minister's bureaucratic resources are a factor in the equation. While it is true, as Weller (1983,

p. 75) claims, that 'any concept of prime ministerial government needs to be based on far more than bureaucratic support', the establishment of a Prime Minister's Department would undoubtedly be widely seen as a further increase in prime ministerial power. The administrative gains of such a development are, moreover, also questionable. While a Prime Minister's Department would undoubtedly enhance the potential for prime ministerial direction of policy and administration, it would also leave the Prime Minister with less time and detachment to devote to inter-departmental and strategic problems. According to Rose (1980, p. 321) a Prime Minister's primary concern is 'with meta-policy, that is, relationships between the particular policies of different ministries or sub-governments'. It is an open question whether a Prime Minister's department would impair, rather than enhance, the ability to perform this role.

5 CENTRAL ADMINISTRATION IN ACTION

In advanced political systems bureaucratic influence is inevitable. In Britain such influence is checked by constitutional restraints: civil servants work under the direction of ministers who are accountable to Parliament. This constitutional bureaucracy owes much to history, having evolved during the early nineteenth century (see Parris, 1969). Since that time, as governmental workload has increased, it is frequently alleged that civil servants – not ministers – effectively run the central administration. This chapter focuses on central administration in the context of the complex relationships which exist between civil servants and ministers.

Key personnel in central administration

There are two main types of personnel: ministers and civil servants.

(i) Ministers
Ministers provide the political leadership. Normally drawn from the majority party in the House of Commons, most are MPs, although a minority – usually about 20 per cent – may be peers. During the twentieth century, as central administration has grown, so too has the number of ministers, from sixty in 1900 to 107 in October 1988 (85 MPs and 22 peers).

While the number of ministerial posts varies greatly between departments, the average is four (Rose, 1987, pp. 77–8). They comprise a small ministerial team, only one of whom – usually denoted by the title *Secretary of State* – sits in the Cabinet. Sometimes major departments, such as the Treasury, may have more than one Cabinet representative, as also, exceptionally, may other departments (see Jones, 1975, pp. 44–5).

Below Cabinet rank are two subordinate ministerial tiers. First, full ministers not in the Cabinet: sometimes these may head small departments (such as the Minister of Overseas Development) but more usually they are second-rank ministers – known as *Ministers of State* – in large departments (such as Minister of State, Home Office). Below these are *Parliamentary Under Secretaries of State*, often colloquially known as junior ministers. (These should not be confused with *Parliamentary Private Secretaries*, who are unpaid ministerial aides and not officially members of the government: see Theakston, 1987.) Although the Secretary of State remains constitutionally responsible to Parliament for the work of his or her ministerial subordinates, in practice departmental business is usually allocated between members of the ministerial team. Indeed, in many cases junior ministers take the 'final' ministerial decision, leaving the Secretary of State free to concentrate on the most important matters. Non-Cabinet ministers also frequently sit on inter-departmental and Cabinet committees, and are thus a factor in relations between, as well as within, departments.

The most important member of a department's ministerial team is the Secretary of State: he or she represents the department in Cabinet and has overall control of its affairs. According to Headey (1974, chs 9–11) three broad ministerial roles are identifiable:

(a) *Policy initiators*: ministers making a significant contribution to departmental policy.
(b) *Executive ministers* who, while regarding policy formulation as important, also attach importance to departmental management: Michael Heseltine, for example, when Secretary of State for Environment (1979–83) and Secretary of State for Defence (1983–6) paid great attention to the development of departmental organization and information systems.
(c) *Ambassador ministers* who, like Tony Benn as Minister of Technology (1966–70) and Secretary of State for Industry (1974–5), attach priority to publicizing the policies and services of their department. While most devote some attention to all these roles, as a rule their routine is so demanding that there is insufficient time to pursue all three simultaneously with any great effect.

Prior to taking office, most Cabinet ministers have served a long 'apprenticeship', both in Parliament and in different departments, working their way up the ministerial hierarchy. Few, however, have specialized knowledge of their department's work (which can inhibit the policy-initiator role) or have prior experience of running large organizations (thereby inhibiting the 'executive minister' role). The background of British ministers, in fact, differs dramatically from their equivalents in many other countries: for example, Dutch ministers tend to be specialists in the work of their departments, while in the USA they are often experienced business executives (Headey, 1974, pp. 249–69; Rose 1987, pp. 80–4). It is at least arguable whether the ministerial contribution to departmental policy-making and management would be greater if a different pattern of ministerial recruitment and career development was adopted in Britain.

(ii) Civil servants

The term 'civil servant' lacks precise definition, an ambiguity which is not just of academic significance. As the Expenditure Committee observed in 1977 (HC, 535, I, p. lxxvii), 'the vagueness of definition has given scope for a fruitless juggling of statistics in which numbers of "civil servants" are bandied about which are really almost meaningless'. Thus, in 1974, officials in the Manpower Services Commission and associated agencies were excluded from civil service statistics, but two years later were included in them. This imprecision, while sometimes politically convenient for ministers and civil servants, makes any attempt to interpret civil service statistics fraught with difficulty.

Notwithstanding such difficulties, the most authoritative definition is that used in the annual *Civil Service Statistics*. This essentially defines a civil servant as:

> A servant of the Crown working in a civil capacity who is not: the holder of a political (or judicial) office; the holder of certain other offices in respect of whose tenure of office special provision has been made; a servant of the Crown in a personal capacity paid from the Civil List. (*Civil Service Statistics*, HMSO, 1987, p. 11).

This definition, while leaving ambiguity as to whom precisely it includes, nevertheless excludes ministers, judges, members of the armed forces, and employees of nationalized industries, local government, and the NHS. In April 1987 some 597,800 full-time equivalent civil servants were officially in post, of which 507,800 were non-industrials, and 90,000 industrials (*Civil Service Statistics*, 1987, p. 4).

As government work expanded during the twentieth century, civil servant numbers increased sharply. In 1976, although the total subsequently began to fall, there were 748,000 civil servants in post. This twentieth century increase was at a vastly greater rate than has occurred with ministers. Kellner and Crowther-Hunt (1980, p. 220) have observed: 'In 1900, we had 50,000 civil servants controlled by about 60 ministers. Today we have some 700,000 civil servants with just over 100 ministers.' This relatively faster growth rate is not without significance for minister/civil service relationships.

Role and characteristics of civil servants

In theory there is a clear distinction between the *political* role of ministers, and the *administrative* role of civil servants. The minister is politically accountable for departmental policy and administrative efficiency, while the civil servant serves the minister and implements policy on his minister's behalf. Several characteristics of the British civil service stem from this distinction between political and administrative roles, the most important being: (i) permanence, (ii) political neutrality, and (iii) anonymity.

(i) *Permanence.* Britain, unlike some countries (such as the USA) does not have a 'spoils system', where administrative posts are in the gift of politicians and the occupants usually change with each new government. British civil servants are permanent career officials who work with governments of all political complexions.
(ii) *Political neutrality.* Because British civil servants must serve ministers with differing views, they must observe strict political neutrality. This requires some restrictions on civil servants' freedom: for example, they must avoid partisan political activity, and the expression of views contrary to those of ministers.
(iii) *Anonymity.* Because too close an identification with particular policies or ministers might compromise political neutrality, British civil servants have traditionally enjoyed anonymity. Their relations with, and advice to, ministers, are confidential; and the convention of 'individual responsibility' (Chapter 14) normally ensures that ministers answer for their actions in public and in Parliament.

In recent years some of these traditional characteristics have been weakened as civil servants and their actions have become more open to the public gaze. Senior officials now frequently give evidence to parliamentary select committees (Chapter 14) and the actions of almost any civil servant can be investigated by the Ombudsman (Chapter 15). The Financial Management Initiative (FMI), as it works through (see Chapter 7) should also make it easier to pinpoint responsibility to specific civil servants. Some civil servants now even appear at press conferences and on television as departmental spokesman. Some have also identified closely with particular ministers. Sir William Armstrong, when Head of the Home Civil Service, had such a close relationship with Heath that he was nicknamed the 'deputy Prime Minister'. Again, the use in recent years of specialist advisers – political appointees who act as temporary departmental officials – has blurred the traditional concept of a permanent, politically-neutral, and anonymous civil service. Likewise 'the growing phenomenon of inward secondments' into the service is increasingly giving rise to questions and concerns about the fundamental characteristics of the service (see Chapman, 1988a).

Particular controversy has come to surround the nature of political neutrality in recent years. As Ridley (1986, p. 23) observes, there are two different aspects to civil service political neutrality: (a) Civil servants must provide impartial advice to ministers, providing them with various possible solutions to a policy issue and then letting ministers make the choice in the light of their political programme; (b) Because senior civil servants collaborate closely with ministers they must also work out measures that are in the spirit of the government and advise ministers on their likely political consequences. Thus the British civil servant 'is expected to be a chameleon, changing colour as governments change'.

These notions of neutrality received particularly severe jolts via the Tisdall and Ponting cases in 1984 and 1985 which saw these two civil servants leaking information to third parties (see Benyon 1988, pp. 132, 133; Jordan and Richardson 1987b, p. 177). These and similar cases raised major questions about the alleged 'neutrality' of civil servants. One school of thought argues that, as politics has become more polarized with the breakdown of postwar consensus, it has become 'harder to accept the comfortable tradition that civil servants can serve whatever king may rule and remain honourable men' (Ridley 1985, p. 41). In other words, is political neutrality possible in an era of radical politics? (See Ridley, 1987.)

The government's reaction to the 'not guilty' verdict in the Ponting case was to issue in Feburary 1985, through the Cabinet Secretary, Sir Robert Armstrong, some notes of guidance on the 'Duties and responsibilities of civil servants in relation to ministers' (for text see *Social Studies Review*, vol. 1, no. 4, March 1986, p. 26). This memorandum asserted that civil servants were the servants of the Crown and, that for all practical purposes, this meant the government of the day. It outlined the relative positions of ministers and civil servants and emphasized that the duty of a civil servant is first and foremost to his or her minister and when their minister has made a decision 'it is the duty of civil servants loyally to carry out that decision with precisely the same energy and good will, whether they agree with it or not'.

Relationships between ministers and civil servants were again under scrutiny in 1986 during the Westland affair (see Chapter 14). A subsequent report from the Select Committee on Defence (1985–6) was critical of both Leon Brittan and the civil servants involved and, in the light of this and other observations, Sir Robert Armstrong issued a new version of his memorandum, in December 1987 (*Hansard*, VI, vol. 123, cols 572–5, 2 December 1987).

This 1987 memorandum reaffirmed the traditional view that ministers are answerable to Parliament for the conduct of their departments, while civil servants are responsible to their ministers, whom it is their duty to serve loyally. While the memorandum does refer to issues of conscience, 'many of the critical questions essentially remain unanswered' (Benyon, 1988, p. 133). Indeed, in many respects the traditional model simply does not accord with contemporary practice such as civil servants having to appear before select committees or being obliged to answer to the Ombudsmen. The notion of neutral, anonymous bureaucrats answerable only to their political masters is quite clearly difficult to apply in practice under modern circumstances.

Mrs Thatcher's personal involvement in the promotion of top civil servants has also raised questions about neutrality. As Drewry and Butcher note (1988, p. 169), the 1980s coincided with the retirement of a large number of permanent secretaries, and Mrs Thatcher has shown a close personal interest in senior appointments. In 1983 some eight new permanent secretaries were appointed. 'Particularly controversial were the appointments of Peter Middleton, aged 48, only a third-ranking deputy secretary, to Permanent Secretary to the Treasury, and Clive Whitmore, Mrs Thatcher's former Principal Private Secretary, as Permanent Secretary to the Ministry of Defence'. Yet there is no evidence that the party-political orientation of civil servants is the critical factor in accounting for promotions. Rather, their effectiveness as managers and implementors appears to be paramount. Again, though, the concepts of neutrality and impartiality are perceived to be under threat, thereby bringing the danger that civil servants will 'trim' their advice to what they know ministers want to hear, in order to climb in the promotion stakes.

Under modern conditions, of course, the distinction between political and administrative roles is far from clear. It is blurred not only by the policy/administration dichotomy, but also because today ministers have to recognize the administrative implications of their policy decisions. Indeed, much ministerial time is devoted to discussions about resources (finance, manpower and so on) necessary to implement policy. Conversely, under modern conditions, civil servants not only take policy decisions but – as the size of the administrative machine makes detailed ministerial control impossible – they must also bear some responsibility for administrative efficiency. In addition they must develop an awareness of their minister's political position – anticipating party reaction, parliamentary questioning/criticism, public opinion and so forth. According to Chapman (1988b, pp. 290, 291), the 'clear demarcation between policy formation and execution is now to be seen only in the most elementary textbooks and superficial statements of individuals who have little conception of political reality'.

Civil servants and ministers: working relationships

The constitutional distinction – between ministers who make policy, and civil servants who advise upon and administer it – bears little relationship to what actually happens. In practice, civil servants are far more influential than their constitutional position suggests. Their relationship with ministers, however, as Brown and Steel (1979, p. 127) observe, 'is a complex and subtle one, varying with different personalities and circumstances'. For convenience it can be explored in relation to six key factors.

TENURE OF OFFICE

Civil servants, once appointed, have tenure and cannot easily be removed. Although they frequently change jobs they are nevertheless 'able to develop an expertise within a particular area of policy and administration which the minister will find difficult if not impossible to emulate' (Pitt and Smith, 1981, p. 51). This permanence contrasts with the transitory nature of ministers, who spend a *relatively* short time in government and rarely remain in the same department for more than a few years before being moved on. In Conservative governments from 1951 to 1964 the median tenure of departmental ministers was twenty-eight months (Headey, 1974, p. 96). Under Harold Wilson's administration from 1964 to 1970 the median tenure for Cabinet ministers was one year and thirty-two weeks, while from 1974 to 1979 the median tenure was two years and five weeks (Alderman and Cross, 1981, p. 428). The effect of frequent ministerial 'reshuffles' – usually dictated by political rather than administrative considerations – is often to leave ministers with insufficient time to acquire adequate expertise to enable them to formulate and implement key policies. As Anthony Crosland commented, 'I reckon it takes you six months to get your head properly above water, a year to get the general drift of most of the field, and two years really to master the whole of a Department' (Boyle and Crosland, 1971, p. 43). Between 1944 and 1986, for example, there were twenty-one ministerial heads at the DES – with an average tenure of about two years. The irony is, of course, that just as ministers begin to master their departmental work they are invariably transferred to another post. Consequently, as Kellner and Crowther-Hunt (1980, p. 213) observe, when ministers and civil servants disagree 'it is not an equal contest between two temporary incumbents, but an unequal match between a temporary minister and the permanence of the accumulated experience and policy of the department itself'. As Rose (1987, p. 83) has observed, 'even when a minister is not reshuffled, the prospect of being posted to another ministry . . . discourages a politician from identifying with the long-term concerns of the ministry'.

EXPERTISE

Lack of specialist preparation for ministers is compounded by the absence of planned career development. Ministers move from department to department, often for pragmatic political reasons, as the Prime Minister directs, rarely having relevant expertise in their new policy areas. Headey (1974, p. 94) shows that in only twelve out of ninety-three Cabinet appointments between October 1964 and April 1971 was a minister appointed who had previous experience in the same department or in the same general policy area.

In this vein, Richard Crossman (1975, p. 23) – although he had previously been a leader of Oxford City Council – ventilated his own anxiety on his appointment to the Ministry of Housing and Local Government in October 1964: 'It's amazing how in politics one concentrates on a few subjects. For years I've been a specialist on social security and I know enough about it. Science and education I had picked up in the months when I was Shadow Minister. But I've always left out of account this field of town and country planning . . . all this is utterly remote to me and it's all unlike what I expected.' In this context, the initial dominance of the permanent secretary, Dame Evelyn Sharp, was hardly surprising. Initially at least 'a minister's lack of any specialist knowledge of his ministry . . . discourages him from initiating policies' (Rose, 1987, p. 83).

Anthony Crosland's career provides a good example of the difficulties facing ministers attempting to acquire and develop expertise in specific policy areas:

1964–5:	Minister of State, Economic Affairs
1965–7:	Secretary of State for Education and Science
1967–9:	President of the Board of Trade
1969–70:	Secretary of State for Local Government and Regional Planning
1974–6:	Secretary of State for the Environment
1976–7:	Foreign Secretary

In nine years as a minister Crosland held six different posts with little logical progression from an expertise standpoint. 'Ministers do not serve a long apprenticeship in their departments in a junior position as do many managing directors in industry, but instead are catapulted into their offices with minimal preparation. Thus it is the rare exception to find a minister . . . who has prepared himself for the burdens of the office which he assumes' (Pitt and Smith, 1981, p. 52).

Some ministers do, of course, stay in a single policy area/department for several years; Denis Healey, for instance, was Minister of Defence (1964–70) and from 1974 to 1979 was Chancellor of the Exchequer. Additionally, of course, some departments are less specialized and technical than others, so at least some ministers can be expected to pick up departmental threads fairly quickly. Nevertheless, given the increase during this century in both the scope and complexity of government, many policy decisions are inevitably made in areas where ministers are unlikely to have any expertise. The lack of career development for ministers plays directly into the hands of senior administrators who often have 'a near monopoly of knowledge relevant to policy-formation' (Smith, 1976, p. 102). Hence 'while our civil servants are often criticized as policy amateurs, they are often likely to be much more expert than the ministers who, on average, spend only twenty months in any one post' (Jordan and Richardson, 1987b, p. 177).

Of course, while expertise is a major civil service resource, there is always the possibility that civil servants may themselves disagree and be unable to reach an agreed compromise on a particular subject. Chandler (1988a, p. 57) argues that Crossman's account of civil service power is insensitive to these possibilities. In his view in 'the context of policy making towards local government, arguments promoting the idea that the civil service has a major role in determining policy seem rather thin'. For Chandler, civil servants are not (as Sedgemore suggests) politicians writ large, but politicians writ small. Most ministers, he concludes, 'will have no small measure of faith in their own ideas and these will usually only be deflected by officials who can forward an extremely convincing case against them' (1988a, p. 58).

DEPARTMENTAL SIZE

The growth of government, and the disproportionate increase in civil servants relative to ministers, has further tilted 'the balance of Whitehall power more in favour of civil servants and away from ministers' (Kellner and Crowther-Hunt, 1980, p. 220). Departmental management is theoretically the province of ministers, (and increasingly so given the Thatcher emphasis on ministers 'managing' departments) but the size and functional range of many modern departments – particularly those which came into being following mergers in the 1960s and 1970s – in practice makes this impossible. A massive department like Social Security, for example, with over 87,000 civil servants, cannot be effectively controlled by a single Secretary of State, two ministers of state, and three under secretaries. The growth of government, in short, has largely outstripped the capacity of ministers to control their departments. As Pitt and Smith (1981, p. 53) put it, 'increase in the size of organizational units has inevitably led to officials having the power to decide what issues will be referred to ministers and what can be resolved without ministerial intervention'. Nevertheless, the size of some departments also creates problems for the major policy advisers, the permanent secretaries. 'If power accrues to officials as a result of the complexities of the department it is acquired only in discrete areas by middle-ranking officials whose actions may be overlooked by overworked ministers and high-ranking officials' (Chandler 1988a, p. 56).

WORKLOAD

Just as the size and complexity of departments often strengthens the hand of civil servants, so likewise workload prevents ministers from dealing personally with more than a limited number of issues. As Jordan and Richardson (1987b, p. 177) explain, 'Ministers are quite simply too busy to be involved in all but a tiny proportion of a department's business'. Not only does the bulk of departmental work continue without ministerial involvement, but ministers have a wide range of duties *outside* their departments. Between 1964 and 1974, one survey found, ministers spent a minimum of sixty hours each week working: of this at least forty-five hours were spent in Cabinet and Cabinet committees, Parliament, interviews and discussions outside the department, receptions and lunches, official visits, as well as constituency responsibilities. 'In other words, every minister has a strenuous full-time job as politician and as ambassador for his department *before* he can deal with the direct task of running his department' (Kellner and Crowther-Hunt, 1980, p. 216). In these circumstances ministers inevitably become very dependent on civil service briefing papers presenting clear recommendations. As Smith (1976, pp. 105–6) explains, 'a minister's policy-making responsibilities are outnumbered by other tasks . . . policy matters often appear to be dealt with in whatever time is left over from other commitments'.

Pressure upon time can sometimes be played on by civil servants: for example, by briefing ministers at the 'last minute' when there is insufficient time to search for alternatives to options recommended by officials; and by requesting 'urgent' approval of complex decisions when the minister is short of time (for example, see Crossman, 1975, especially p. 79). As Norton (1982, p. 77) explains, 'A minister with a crowded diary, one organised for him by his officials, is not in the best position to maintain effective supervision of the empire under his nominal control'.

INFORMATIONAL RESOURCES

Ministers depend heavily on civil servants for information. Issues working their way up through the Whitehall hierarchy are documented at every level in reports and minutes drafted by civil servants. Civil servants, likewise, filter the demands of client groups and determine the options to be presented to ministers. As a result, ministers on most issues take 'their' decisions on the basis of civil service briefs containing carefully sifted background information and official recommendations. 'Ministers', as Kellner and Crowther-Hunt (1980, p. 237) put it, 'confront problems on the basis of papers written by officials'.

The way information is presented, of course, may help to shape both the decision and its implementation. Benn (1980, p. 68) cites one interesting example of alleged bureaucratic manipulation of information. A draft Defence White Paper presented to one Cabinet meeting showed such a gap in the military balance between East and West as to arouse questioning:

> It turned out that in calculating the military strength of the West the Ministry of Defence had left out the French armed forces. When questioned the reason given was that NATO did not exercise the same operational control over the French forces as applied to the rest of the alliance . . . . [This] crude misinformation was designed to win public support for a bigger defence budget by suggesting a more serious imbalance than existed.

IMPLEMENTATION

The implementation or execution of policy is an area where civil servants are particularly important. To a great extent politicians, once policy has been decided, leave implementation to the bureaucracy. Ministerial decisions, however, do not automatically take effect. Occasionally ministerial instructions will be unwittingly overlooked in the welter of departmental work, or will be nullified by the discretion allowed to departmental officials. (The discretion allowed to DSS counter staff to deal with individual cases, for example, is sometimes considerable.) In addition, however, there are various tactics civil servants may deliberately employ to thwart implementation of policies about which they are sceptical: procrastination, 'discovering' insurmountable obstacles, effecting unworkable solutions, even – according to Shirley Williams – 'losing things' (Norton, 1982, p. 87).

There are several well-documented examples of bureaucratic inertia successfully frustrating the expressed intentions of ministers. One is the 'implementation' of the Fulton Committee's proposals for civil service reform (see Chapter 6). Another concerns the 1974–6 Labour government's education policy. Page (1979) has shown how Labour's 1974 election manifesto undertook to 'withdraw tax relief and charitable status from public schools'. The permanent secretary at the Department of Education and Science, Sir William Pile, was 'wholly committed to the private sector' of education, and in 1975 he dispatched a memorandum to the Education Secretary displaying all the classic signs of delay: the term 'public school' could not be defined adequately, redefining charitable status was a matter for other departments, withdrawal of tax concessions was the Treasury's responsibility, and so on. Pile concluded:

> these nine words from the manifesto raise technical problems to which at present nobody knows the answers . . . action in relation to them lies primarily not with you but with the Home Secretary, the Chancellor of the Exchequer and the Secretary of State for the Environment . . . I cannot think of anything that we ourselves can usefully do in the interim.

Needless to say, the government's election commitment was never implemented.

A ruling class?

Senior civil servants, it seems, can on occasions thwart ministers; their permanence, expertise, numbers, and the ability to manipulate informational and implementation processes equip them to challenge even the most forceful minister in defence of departmental priorities. That these powers are used, moreover, seems clear from the memoirs of ex-ministers and others with inside knowledge. Marcia Williams (1972), Wilson's political secretary, maintained that the civil service obstructed the policies of the 1964–70 Labour administration, while Benn (1980), Haines (1977), and Castle (1980) make similar points about Labour governments in the 1970s. Furthermore, criticisms have not come solely from the left: Mrs Thatcher, for example, was reported in 1980 to be 'highly critical of the influence wielded by officials over both ministers and the choice of where expenditure cuts were to fall' (Norton, 1982, p. 83). Indeed, as Shirley Williams (1980, pp. 92–3) argues, it has become almost standard for Labour politicians to allege that the civil service is Tory, and for the Tories to allege that it is tinged with leftist views. Whatever the true picture, many knowledgeable observers clearly feel that the civil service is not politically neutral, and that public policy is determined at least as much by civil servants as by ministers. Thus Brian Sedgemore depicts civil servants as 'politicians writ large' (Expenditure Committee (1977), I, p. lxxix); while Fry (1985, p. 21) refers to civil servants as a 'permanent government'. Indeed, according to Chapman (1988b), civil service advice to ministers has often touched on the most sensitive political matters, even down to recommendations about the size of the Cabinet and who, by name, should be in it. One example will suffice. After Churchill resigned in May 1945 and was asked to form a new administration, Edward Bridges, Secretary to the Cabinet, advised the Prime Minister on the size of the new Cabinet. Bridges ended his note to Churchill, 'Attached as a cockshy is a suggestion as to who might be in a Cabinet of, say 12 . . . ' (pp. 271–2).

Despite the above material, several factors caution against too ready an acceptance of the 'dictatorship of the official' thesis. Much of the evidence on which it is based is anecdotal which, as Goodin (1982, pp. 37–8) observes, proves nothing. Allowance must be made, he argues, 'for the possibility that disparate intentions of the various political actions' recorded by 'memoir-mongers . . . may aggregate into collective actions in a way that none of them properly understand themselves'. There is also the possibility that bureaucratic hostility may be a scapegoat for ministerial incompetence. Benn's criticism of the civil service, for example, is dismissed by Heseltine (Young and Sloman, 1982, p. 29) as 'one of the classic rationalisations of personal failure'. Benn himself (1980, p. 75), perhaps significantly, quotes a former senior civil servant, Lord (William) Armstrong, who, while admitting that he 'had a great deal of influence', felt that this was partly because 'most ministers were not interested [and] were just prepared to take the questions as we offered them'. Even Sedgemore (1980, p. 103), an arch-critic of civil service influence, concedes that 'most Ministers could do more to help themselves' and that their relative lack of influence is largely 'their own fault'.

A further factor is that not all ex-ministers accept the 'dictatorship of the official' thesis. In evidence to the Expenditure Committee (1977, II.2, para. 1877), Edward Heath observed that in his experience 'civil servants were . . . clearly and definitely . . . under Ministerial control'. Harold Wilson told the same committee (para. 1942) 'that if a Minister cannot control his civil servants, he ought to go'. During the Attlee government's massive nationalization programme the civil service, according to Morrison (1959, pp. 335–6), was 'loyal to the Government of the day'. There is, in fact, convincing evidence (Headey, 1974, pp. 131–5) that most officials welcome ministers who are capable of taking decisions and who give a firm lead which they can follow. Even where civil servants have been sceptical of ministerial policy, some ministers have nevertheless successfully imposed their will. Barbara Castle, for example, overcame objections in the Ministry of Transport (1965–8) to her integrated transport plan (Pitt and Smith, 1981, p. 53), while Benn scored a 'personal victory' (Sedgemore, 1980, p. 122) against his Energy Department officials over the future development of nuclear power. Benn's victory, however, was short-lived, for the new government returned in 1979 provided civil servants with an opportunity to re-fight 'the battle' and ultimately to win 'the war' (Norton, 1982, p. 88).

If the evidence about civil service power is inconclusive, this is probably because the 'evidence' is 'patchy', and also because the minister/civil service relationship cannot easily be measured. As Smith

(1976, p. 108) observes, the 'personalities, ideologies, and circumstances' around which the relationship is built vary considerably. Strong ministers, or strong ideological commitments to policies, inevitably reduce the influence of civil servants: the Thatcher administration, for example, appeared to secure a marked shift towards monetarist policies despite the Keynesian orthodoxy of many Treasury officials. Relationships will also vary with circumstances: for example, a radical policy change is more likely to be effected if ministerial and civil service attitudes coalesce than if they do not. Likewise, a minister is likely to encounter more resistance if his or her proposals threaten conventional departmental wisdom – or departmental ambitions over territory and resources – than if they do not. Civil servants and ministers, moreover, are not monolithic groupings. Sometimes civil servants will disagree and ministers will be caught up in the battle, perhaps being briefed against one another. At other times ministers may be in disagreement. According to Heseltine (Young and Sloman, 1982, p. 29), Benn achieved so little as a minister not because of civil service obstruction, but because the Prime Minister 'disagreed with Benn [and] stopped him pursuing his ideas'.

As these examples indicate, the minister/civil service dichotomy is too simplistic. That civil servants have more influence, and ministers less, than constitutional theory suggests is undeniable. But where the boundary is drawn is impossible to determine. As Norton (1982, p. 90) concludes,

> the argument . . . is not . . . necessarily an argument of extremes . . . . The extent to which officials will or will not enjoy a certain mastery over their minister's decisions will vary from minister to minister, depending upon the minister himself, his permanent secretary and other senior officials, the ethos of the department . . . and the political conditions then prevailing.

Towards a partisan bureaucracy?

As a tentative response to the growing awareness of civil service power, ministers since 1964 have adopted the practice of appointing special advisers to complement the advice supplied by their civil servants. From 1964 to 1970 advisers such as Thomas Balogh at Number 10 were much involved in policy-making. The 1974–9 Labour governments agreed that any Cabinet minister could appoint up to two political advisers, and at one time there were thirty-eight such advisers, some working in a special policy unit in the Prime Minister's Office and the rest in other departments. Under Mrs Thatcher special advisers have also been employed, albeit on a slightly reduced scale (eighteen were in post in 1985: Drewry and Butcher, 1988, p. 163). Most such advisers (whether full- or part-time) have been paid from public funds as civil servants on period appointment (Williams Report, 1987, p. 33).

Special advisers are chosen by the minister and serve ministerial interests in a variety of ways. 'They act as the personal confidants of ministers; they brief the minister on non-departmental Cabinet matters; they assist in the political presentation of policies and act as a channel of communication between the minister and his party; and they play a role in departmental policy-making by commenting on civil service recommendations and extending the range of options and ideas available to the minister' (Drewry and Butcher, 1988, pp. 163, 164).

Views about the impact of special advisers vary a good deal. Lord Donoughue sees them as 'the most important development in modern government in Britain. The machine is now so powerful and the career civil service so big and so influential, and with the capacity effectively to control many ministers, that ministers need an alternative source of advice and information' (Young and Sloman, 1982, p. 88). Brown and Steel (1979, p. 130) suggest, however, that they have always been appointed on too small a scale 'for the basic relationship between a minister and his career officials to be altered' (Brown and Steel, 1979, p. 130).

Nevertheless, there remains a substantial groundswell for the introduction of more 'partisan advice' at the higher levels of the civil service. One of the main advocates of the approach, Sir John Hoskyns, former head of Mrs Thatcher's policy unit, calls for the partial politicization of the higher civil service. In his view, civil servants – being required to maintain political neutrality – lack the total commitment to implement radical policies, and develop an attitude of passive detachment which does not produce the enthusiasm needed to tackle problems effectively. Up to twenty senior posts in each department, he suggests, should be political appointees who would come from private industry and commerce. Such outsiders might initially serve with an opposition party and would move into departments when the party won office (see Hoskyns, 1983).

Predictably, perhaps, these proposals have been criticized from sources close to the civil service establishment. Pliatzky (1984, pp. 23–8), a former permanent secretary, defends the civil service against Hoskyns' criticisms, arguing that his proposals would 'undermine . . . the Rolls Royce support which ministers get from the civil service machine'. Sir Douglas Wass, former Head of the Home Civil Service, also rejects Hoskyns' analysis (Wass, 1983) which, he argues, overlooks the civil servant's duty to ensure that ministers are informed of all the problems associated with their initiatives. This, Wass claims, is the value of a politically neutral civil service. Again, if service posts ceased being filled by career officials, ministers would lose much of the departments' 'collective and historical knowledge' (1983, p. 13). Wass further suggests that the procedures and methods of governments are different from business administration: 'businessmen . . . cannot be expected to know how to run a government department any more than a civil servant can be expected to manage an industrial concern without a lot of training and experience' (Wass, 1984, p. 56). There are also practical problems associated with the Hoskyns 'solution'. For example,

> does British business possess the talented personnel to provide up to 400 politically committed outsiders, and would such individuals be prepared to interrupt their business careers for a lengthy spell, first as part of a shadow team in opposition and then for up to five years in government, especially on present civil service salaries? (Drewry and Butcher, 1988, p. 168).

In 1986 the debate was carried a stage further by the Treasury and Civil Service Select Committee (1986, HC 92, paras 5–32) which recommended the introduction of ministerial policy units, based in ministers' private offices, and consisting of career civil servants together with temporary appointees from outside the service. Such arrangements, reminiscent of the French 'Cabinet' system would, the committee suggested, complement rather than replace the higher levels of the civil service. An even more radical way forward would be the adoption of the pattern in the USA, replacing wholesale one government's top officials by others supportive of the incoming government. This would provide ministers with senior personnel inside their departments to formulate and administer policies in line with the minister's own sympathies. At the same time, however, it would reduce continuity and, probably, administrative expertise. Brown and Steel (1979, p. 332) add that a further difficulty in this context is that Britain 'has no "inner-and-outer" tradition and a much less flexible career structure, both in government and in the universities'. One danger with politicization is, of course, that civil servants would gear their advice to what they know ministers will want to hear. Awkward questions will always need to be asked.

Overview

As this chapter has shown, there are major difficulties in determining the relative influence of ministers and civil servants. Measuring 'power' and 'influence' in any meaningful way is a difficult exercise. With ministers and civil servants, confidentiality presents added difficulties for researchers, as does the fact that relationships vary over time, and with issues, personalities, and circumstances. As Kellner and Crowther-Hunt (1980, p. 239) conclude, 'The exact balance between ministerial and civil service power will very much depend on what is being decided, the political circumstances surrounding it, and the relative abilities of civil servants and ministers'.

While the relative influence of ministers and civil servants is difficult to determine, collectively they wield considerable power. Indeed, it is unwise to distinguish too starkly between their respective roles. Ministers and senior civil servants are part of a relatively small 'Whitehall universe'; they work together, dine together, sit together on committees, and so on. In Neustadt's view (1966, p. 57) there is an intimate collaboration between civil servants and ministers 'grounded in the interests and traditions of both sides. Indeed, it binds others into a Society for Mutual Benefit: what they succeed in sharing with each other they need share with almost no one else, and governing in England is a virtual duopoly.' However, despite this view, it needs to be remembered that ministers and civil servants are only two out of many constituent elements in the various policy networks which characterize both national and sub-national government. Most policy proposals in central government also involve, for example:

(a) discussions with interested pressure groups, often presenting conflicting demands to civil servants;
(b) discussions with backbench party groups, particularly on contentious issues;
(c) where appropriate, discussions with external bodies such as the EEC, NATO, IMF, and so forth.

Lord Crowther-Hunt emphasized the complexity of policy-making and the difficulty of determining which particular sectors of the policy community have been influential: 'In the web of pressures, policies are refined and modified, sometimes even rejected, compromises have to be made, public opinion satisfied. So when policies eventually emerge from the government machine it is hardly ever possible to determine relative responsibilities for what has or has not happened' (Kellner and Crowther-Hunt, 1980, p. 397). Ministers and civil servants are invariably central actors in the policy-making process but it is important to see their contribution alongside that of other groupings inhabiting the policy networks. Once again, complexity is the order of the day.

6 THE CIVIL SERVICE: EVOLUTION AND CHANGE

As administrative and political roles have become blurred under modern conditions, the recruitment, training and management of civil servants has become increasingly significant. Such factors affect not only the policy outputs and efficiency of central administration, but also its capacity to respond to ministerial directions and to wider environmental pressures. Dissatisfaction with the bureaucracy and pressure for reform is, however, nothing new.

Nineteenth-century pressure for reform

Until the nineteenth century there was no clear distinction between political and administrative roles. Recruitment was largely by patronage, and promotion by seniority. Although not conducive to efficiency, contemporary administration was relatively simple: specialized techniques were unnecessary, workload was relatively light, and departments generally were small. Nevertheless, from the late eighteenth century demands for reform began to appear, gathering momentum during the early nineteenth century as the state acquired new functions and administrative costs began to rise.

As the evolution of the civil service receives detailed coverage elsewhere (see, for instance, Brown and Steel, 1979, ch. 1; Parris, 1969; Drewry and Butcher, 1988, ch. 2) this chapter concentrates mainly upon two major official investigations into the civil service which produced a) the Northcote-Trevelyan Report, 1854, and b) the Fulton Report, 1968.

The Northcote-Trevelyan Report

This made four main recommendations: a) recruitment by open competitive examination; b) promotion by merit; c) unification of the service; d) a division between intellectual work to be performed by graduates, and mechanical work to be allocated to those of lesser ability. These were radical proposals for the nineteenth century and were implemented only slowly. In 1855, following administrative shortcomings during the Crimean War, the Civil Service Commission was established to test candidates for recruitment, but not until the early twentieth century were all Northcote-Trevelyan's recommendations implemented.

Of Northcote-Trevelyan's recommendations, the last listed above was probably the most significant, for it influenced the creation of hierarchical class divisions and entrenched the concept of the generalist administrator. In the 1850s, understandably, the efficient performance of administrative work was seen in terms of general ability. Specialist skills were unnecessary because – apart from surveyors and inspectors – there was little need for them. Hence, the argument ran, any able intellectual could meet the demands of the service even at the highest levels. While the Northcote-Trevelyan Report itself noted the advantages of recruiting graduates in 'relevant' subjects – such as political economy – as time passed this was seemingly forgotten. As the Fulton Report (1968, 1, para. 3) observed a century later, 'There emerged the tradition of the "all rounder" . . . or "amateur"'. At lower levels this tradition became equally entrenched: for more routine mechanical tasks – copying, keeping diaries and so forth – specialist qualifications were considered even less necessary.

Of course, with the subsequent increase in the volume and complexity of government work, the demands upon civil servants changed substantially. By 1968, when Fulton reported, the civil service was twenty times bigger than in 1854, departments were larger, and work immeasurably greater and more complex. Senior civil servants advised ministers on major policy, took many policy decisions themselves, implemented and co-ordinated complex administrative schemes, and managed large departments. Such tasks required not only high administrative skills, but also managerial ability. They also necessitated employment of a wide range of specialist personnel such as economists, engineers, and statisticians. Even at lower levels within the service mere 'intelligence' was no longer sufficient. Today, relatively routine tasks (such as information retrieval or data processing) may require competence in computer handling and quantitative techniques. Since the 1850s, then, the civil service has come to require vastly different skills. And yet, as Fulton observed (1968, 1, para. 6), Northcote-Trevelyan's influence, a century later, was still profound: 'The basic principles and philosophy of the Northcote-Trevelyan Report have prevailed: the essential features of their structure have remained'.

The Fulton diagnosis

The Fulton Report (1968), the most significant inquiry into the civil service since Northcote-Trevelyan, contained both a detailed analysis of the civil service in the 1960s and major recommendations for improvement. Fulton's analysis clearly revealed the continuing influence of the Northcote-Trevelyan philosophy. Six main defects were outlined in the report:

'GENERALIST' DOMINANCE

> The Service is still essentially based on the philosophy of the amateur (or 'generalist' or 'all-rounder'). This is most evident in the Administrative Class which holds the dominant position in the Service. (1, para. 15).

By a 'generalist', Fulton meant 'the gifted layman' who was capable of taking 'a practical view of any problem, irrespective of subject-matter'. Largely a product of historical development, the virtual monopoly of major policy and administrative work held by generalists was still widely justified within the service by the breadth of outlook – as opposed to the 'narrow' approach of specialists – which they arguably brought to the problems of government. They could also arguably communicate more easily with ministers who were themselves usually laymen in departmental matters.

THE 'CLASS' SYSTEM

> The system of classes in the Service seriously impedes its work. (1, para. 16).

Northcote-Trevelyan's division of the service into 'mechanicals' and 'intellectuals' developed during the twentieth century into a hierarchy of *general service* (or *Treasury*) *classes*. In 1966, when the Fulton Committee was appointed, these comprised three main classes containing 138,700 members (clerical class, 89,500; executive class, 46,800; and administrative class, 2,400), and each with its own internal grading structure. Found throughout central administration, and staffed essentially by generalists, members of these classes largely monopolized senior policy and administrative work. The most important was the administrative class: working closely with ministers, its members' primary function was to examine policy options, prepare advice for ministers, and to take responsibility, on behalf of ministers, 'for the administration and control of government departments' (Kellner and Crowther-Hunt, 1980, p. 33).

In addition there was an extensive network of *departmental and specialist classes*. Some departments, because of their specialized work, developed their own variant of the general service classes (for example, Customs and Excise, Inland Revenue). Some also employed staff with specialist skills, although until 1939 their numbers were so small that each department individually recruited and employed such specialists as it needed. After the war, however, a number of separate 'service-wide' specialist hierarchies were created (such as accountants, scientists, economists, statisticians). By the 1960s, as a result, a chaotic structure existed. The service was divided vertically into different specialist, departmental and general service classes; and usually also horizontally between higher and lower levels within each class. Altogether Fulton identified '47 general classes' and 'over 1,400 departmental classes', an arrangement which produced a 'rigid and prolific compartmentalism' and artificially limited 'the range of jobs' on which any individual official could be employed (1, para. 16).

SPECIALIST SKILLS UNDERVALUED

> Many scientists, engineers and members of other specialist classes get neither the full responsibilities . . . nor the opportunities they ought to have. (1, para. 17).

The corollary of generalist dominance was that specialists had a subordinate position within the service. Unlike many other countries (such as the USA, France and West Germany), where higher civil servants generally have expertise in fields relevant to their work, specialists in Britain were largely excluded from the top departmental posts. Traditionally organized in separate hierarchies parallel to those of generalists, their role was to give technical advice to generalists who made the final policy recommendations to ministers. Critics of this arrangement argue that ministers, being isolated from specialist knowledge, may be 'kept in ignorance of the range of options available, while the transmission of expert advice through a generalist hierarchy may result in that advice being distorted' (Drewry and Butcher, 1988, pp. 141–3).

LACK OF MANAGEMENT SKILLS

> Too few civil servants are skilled managers. (1, para. 18).

Although the major managerial role within departments fell to the administrative class, most of its members saw themselves as policy advisors rather than departmental managers. Partly, Fulton felt, this stemmed from inadequate training in management. Indeed, training generally within the service had a low priority. The generalist ethos saw practical experience of departmental work as the best way of 'learning' the job; consequently, formal training usually involved only short departmental induction courses. Following the Assheton Report

(1944), the Treasury was made responsible for co-ordinating training throughout Whitehall, and in 1963 a Centre for Administrative Studies was established. Nevertheless, 'many administrators and specialists . . . received inadequate training (or none at all) in techniques of modern management' while training in policy fields was devalued because of the frequent job changes inherent in generalist career patterns (1, para.97).

AN ISOLATED AND EXCLUSIVE SERVICE

> There is not enough contact between the Service and the rest of the community. (1, para. 19).

Fulton feared that civil servants, particularly at higher levels, suffered from 'exclusiveness or isolation' from the outside world. Partly this was because a career service allowed little opportunity for familiarization with other walks of life, but partly also because recruitment to the administrative class had 'not produced the widening of its social and educational base that might have been expected'.

Recruitment to the highest administrative levels has since 1870 been mainly by open competition. Although opportunities existed for recruitment to the administrative class by transfer or promotion from other classes – about two-fifths of its members in 1967 had formerly belonged to other classes (Brown, 1970, p. 46) – those reaching the top posts (of under secretary, deputy secretary, permanent secretary) were overwhelmingly graduates recruited direct from university. Many of these came from a relative narrow social spectrum (59 per cent of 1968 recruits had been educated at independent or other fee-paying schools, and 59 per cent also were Oxbridge graduates). Many, too, had studied arts subjects (54 per cent in 1968), producing at the top of the service a graduate elite drawn mainly from arts backgrounds (all figures from Brown and Steel, 1979, p. 77). The causes of these trends have been a matter of controversy. Partly they may suggest a greater tendency for persons from such backgrounds to consider civil service careers, whilst the arts dominance may also have reflected the paucity of university coverage of social science teaching before the 1960s. Equally, however, there might be an element of social and educational bias in civil service selection methods. Although recruitment is the responsibility of the independent Civil Service Commission, former or serving administrative class officials are prominent upon it. They also figure prominently in selection procedures conducted by the Civil Service Selection Board (CIZBEE), while some of the tests and interviews used may favour certain types of candidate. (For discussion see Kellner and Crowther-Hunt, 1980, ch. 6; Chapman, 1984a.)

Whatever the reasons, the higher civil service in the 1960s was not thought to be sufficiently socially representative. What is less clear is whether this had any effect upon its efficiency and performance. It can be argued that a relatively homogeneous higher civil service promotes informal co-ordination, and that the recruitment of successive generations of officials from similar backgrounds is conducive to continuity and stability within central administration. On the other hand, social composition cannot easily be divorced from attitudes. In Miliband's view (1973, p. 115), the civil service in advanced capitalist societies 'by virtue of its ideological dispositions, reinforced by its own interests . . . is a crucially important and committed element in the maintenance and defence of the structure of power and privilege in advanced capitalism', a view arguably reinforced in Britain by the increasing tendency of top civil servants to take up business appointments on retirement (Richardson and Jordan, 1979, pp. 61–70; Sedgemore, 1980, pp. 154–61). Whichever analysis one accepts, today's higher civil servants are concerned increasingly with administering and making policy for sections of society – welfare recipients, racial minorities, manual workers, and so on – with whom usually they have little direct experience.

POOR PERSONNEL MANAGEMENT

Serious criticisms of personnel management. (1, para. 20).

Personnel management deficiencies identified by Fulton stemmed partly from the rigidity of the class structure. While mobility across class lines was possible – and was increasingly encouraged – for the majority of officials transfer to another class was unlikely to happen; and, even when it did, transferees usually faced competition for subsequent promotion from younger and better educated candidates who had entered the higher class direct.

While it should be remembered that promotion within many organizational hierarchies may reflect similar patterns, Fulton attributed many of the deficiencies in civil service personnel management to the Treasury which, since the beginning of the century, had generally been responsible for civil service matters. The Treasury's handling of personnel management could not easily be divorced from financial and economic considerations, while its Pay and Management Group had 'too few staff and too little expertise' to perform an effective 'central management role'.

Fulton's recommendations

Fulton made 158 recommendations. Some were mainly concerned with departmental organization and are discussed elsewhere (see

Chapter 2). Others, however, were more specific to the civil service, notably the following:

(a) 'All classes should be abolished and replaced by a single, unified grading structure covering all civil servants from top to bottom.'
(b) 'The service should develop greater professionalism both among specialists . . . and administrators . . . . For the former this means more training in management, and opportunities for greater responsibility and wider careers.'
(c) '[When recruiting graduates] more account should be taken of the relevance of their university courses to the job they are being recruited to do.'
(d) 'A Civil Service College should be set up . . . [to] provide major training courses in administration and management and a wide range of shorter courses. It should also have important research functions.'
(e) 'A new Civil Service Department be set up . . . under the control of the Prime Minister . . . . The Permanent Secretary of the Civil Service Department should be designated Head of the Home Civil Service.'
(f) '[More attention to] career management.'
(g) 'Greater mobility [between the civil service] and other employments.' (1. pp. 104–6).

The significance of these proposals should not be exaggerated. Many – on career structure, training, administrative specialization – would probably have occurred anyway, whilst recruitment trends during the 1960s were already showing diminished intakes from Oxbridge graduates. Moreover, in concentrating primarily on the higher civil service, the needs of the service at lower levels were largely ignored. Nevertheless, the Fulton Report – with its recommendations for relevant degrees, training courses, and unified grading – represented a fundamental attack on the generalist philosophy. While in retrospect, from the vantage point of the late 1980s, the proposed reforms can be seen to have had much less impact than Fulton would have hoped, his report nevertheless stimulated a debate, and set in train a series of developments, which were to permeate thinking about civil service reform over the following decade or more. As such, attempts to implement Fulton's recommendations provide a useful vehicle for examining developments in civil service management during the intervening years, and also reveal wider lessons about the problems of reforming bureaucracies.

Implementing Fulton

In 1968 Fulton's main recommendations were officially accepted by the government – with one significant exception: the proposal that preference be given to graduate applicants with relevant degrees was rejected. Even for those proposals which were officially accepted, however, implementation was in many cases destined to prove problematical.

Implementation focused upon four major areas: (a) the creation of a Civil Service Department, (b) the abolition of classes, (c) the establishment of a Civil Service College, and (d) recruitment reforms.

CREATION OF A CIVIL SERVICE DEPARTMENT (CSD)

This was the first recommendation to be implemented; necessarily so, for it was to provide the spearhead for implementing the other proposed reforms. Its first permanent secretary was designated Head of the Home Civil Service – as Fulton suggested – and ultimate ministerial control vested in the Prime Minister (although day-to-day responsibility was usually delegated to another minister). Its functions encompassed the work of the former Treasury Pay and Management Group, as well as that of the Civil Service Commission. These arrangements gave the CSD responsibility for civil service pay and management, administrative and managerial efficiency, and the recruitment functions of the Civil Service Commission (which formed an independent unit within it).

From a wider perspective the CSD can be seen as an attempt to strengthen 'the centre' of British government, providing a central management capability within Whitehall on manpower, management techniques, and efficiency matters. Its permanent secretary, as Drewry and Butcher (1988, p. 92) explain, was expected to become one of 'a triumvirate of "super permanent secretaries" sharing responsibility for economic policy, the running of the Cabinet and the operation of the civil service, all with access to the Prime Minister'.

In practice the CSD failed to develop this 'central management' capability. Several factors explain this failure:

(i) Fulton's view (1, para. 255) was that the CSD should not be 'predominantly staffed' by former Treasury officials; instead, he recommended a mixture of short and long-term appointments, including staff seconded from other departments and persons with management experience from outside. In the event, however, while some senior officials from other departments were brought in, the CSD was formed largely from the old Pay and Management Group of the Treasury, and its key personnel overwhelmingly had generalist backgrounds (Expenditure Committee (1977), III, pp. 1105–6).

(ii) The CSD 'had no real power to impose its will on departments' being able to enter departments only by invitation and its views having only advisory status (Chapman, 1983, pp. 52, 60; Expenditure Committee, 1977, III, pp. 1105–6).

(iii) The CSD had an uneasy relationship with the Treasury, which resented its loss of functions. As time went on difficulties arose through separation of the Treasury's public expenditure responsibilities from those of the CSD for manpower costs. This not only created co-ordination problems, but increasingly identified the CSD, particularly in prime ministerial circles, with the defence of civil service pay and conditions. According to Fry (1985, pp. 91, 93), the 'CSD's apparent inclination to appease the unions during the civil service strike of 1981 ensured its death later that year'. He adds, 'If there was to be central control of civil service manpower it had to go with control of money in the Treasury, or risk duplication at the centre'.

(iv) Successive prime ministers, although designated Minister for the Civil Service, took little interest in CSD affairs, while 'few of the junior ministers they nominated to take charge of the CSD carried weight in Cabinet or found their political reputations enhanced by promoting the CSD's normal run of business' (Lee, 1982, p. 6).

(v) Successive permanent secretaries found the CSD a limited base from which to exert influence within Whitehall. Generally, they delegated managerial problems to deputies within the department, and although formally designated 'Head of the Home Civil Service', holders of the office found it increasingly difficult to 'strengthen' their 'position in the confidence and trust of the prime minister' (ibid., pp. 6–7).

It is important, as Chapman (1983, especially pp. 59–60) reminds us, to see the CSD within the context of an episodic twentieth-century debate within Whitehall about a more professional management approach. Although Fulton's 'rather ideological reformist approach' helped to create the CSD, the department never quite took the form he envisaged. After the first few years 'with the passing of the Fulton boom' its *raison d'être* was largely removed (Fry, 1985, pp. 88–90) which further undermined its position. In 1981 it was disbanded, the Treasury regaining responsibility for manpower, pay, allowances, and pensions, and a new unit within the Cabinet Office, the Management and Personnel Office, absorbed the CSD's other functions (personnel, management, recruitment, and training). The designation 'Head of the Home Civil Service' was conferred jointly upon the Permanent Secretary of the Treasury and the Cabinet Secretary and, after 1983, upon the latter alone. Thus 'the triumvirate was reduced to two once more, and the Treasury re-acquired much of its lost territory' (Drewry and Butcher, 1988, p. 95). In 1986 the Treasury and Civil Service Select Committee (1986, I, para. 5.44) recommended separation of the posts of Cabinet Secretary and Head of the Home Civil Service on the grounds of workload and potential conflict of interest, but the arrangement survived the retirement of Sir Robert Armstrong and his replacement by Sir Robin Butler in January 1988.

In 1987 the Treasury acquired other former CSD functions when the Management and Personnel Office was disbanded. Responsibilities for civil service pay and conditions were restored to the Treasury, while the MPO's residual functions – notably civil service selection and career development – were transferred to a new unit within the Cabinet Office, the Office of the Minister for the Civil Service. Responsibility for this new unit was retained by the Prime Minister as the Minister for the Civil Service, although day-to-day matters were devolved upon a junior minister.

THE ABOLITION OF CLASSES

Fulton's answer to the chaotic class system was to abolish the vertical and horizontal barriers within the service and to replace them with a single unified grading structure similar to that in many large firms and in 'the Civil Service in the United States' (1, para. 218). What Fulton envisaged was 'some twenty grades' containing 'all the jobs from top to bottom in the non-industrial part of the Service' (1, para. 218). While recruitment at different levels, depending on qualifications and experience, would be possible, promotion would be governed not by an official's class but by his or her suitability for the vacant job. This was to apply even at the highest levels – in what Fulton described as the 'Senior Policy and Management Group', embracing the grades from under secretary to permanent secretary – where the only criterion for appointment was to be 'range of experience, and personal qualities and qualifications' (I, para. 222). Through these arrangements any individual would become eligible for consideration for any job on the sole basis of job suitability.

Single unified grading structures are not unknown in the public sector in Britain: they exist, for example, in the police and the armed forces, in both of which promotion from the lowest to the highest grade (rank) is technically possible. Of course, introducing such arrangements in the civil service would have presented considerable difficulties. Every job in the service, for example, would have required evaluation and grading. Moreover, unified grading, if implemented in an organization as large and diverse as the civil service, may well have presented major managerial anomalies (a view now reflected in the Ibbs Report – see Chapter 2) and could even have exacerbated recruitment difficulties (particularly in highly paid occupations such as actuaries and lawyers). It is also claimed that unified grading aroused widespread opposition from within the service, particularly from the administrative class whose continued monopoly of major policy and administrative work it most threatened (see Kellner and Crowther-Hunt, 1980, especially ch. 4). For whatever reason, however, only very tentative steps were made to reform civil service structure along lines recommended by Fulton.

The essence of the post-Fulton structure is that horizontal barriers within the service have largely been removed, facilitating upward promotion within particular classes (or similar groupings). This has been achieved by merging many former classes into new entities known as 'groups' and 'categories'. The most important of these is the *administration group*, formed in 1971 by merging the lower rung of the administrative class with the clerical and executive classes. This – together with the economist, information officer, librarian and statistician groups – now forms part of the general category, the largest category within the service, employing 232,915 officials in 1987 (*Civil Service Statistics*, 1987, p. 21). Many of the vertical barriers within the service, however, have not been removed. These exist not only between the new categories and groups but also between the many departmental (such as Inland Revenue grades, Home Office Prison Service grades) and specialist (medical officers, actuaries) classes.

Only in what is known as the *open structure*, in fact, is there a unified grading structure. Set up in 1972, the open structure initially consisted of only the top three grades (permanent secretary, deputy secretary, under secretary), and despite authoritative calls in the 1970s for its extension (Expenditure Committee, 1977, I, para. 34) this was still the position in 1981 when the CSD was disbanded. In 1984, however, a further three grades (down to senior principal) were unified and a further extension (to principal and equivalent grades) occurred in 1986.

The creation and subsequent extension of the open structure is essentially in the spirit of Fulton. Promotion to it is technically open to staff from any category or group, and within it there are no formal barriers to movement. Its effect has been not only to open access to the highest levels to persons from any background within the service but also to create a more rational structure at the top. For example, the 1984 open structure extension encompassed some 5,600 staff previously organized within 100 different grades, while the 1986 measure involved a further 5,500 staff previously organized in about 60 grades (*Civil Service Statistics*, 1984, p. 6; 1986, p. 6). In 1987 the open structure embraced the 18,568 officials on the numbered scale illustrated in Figure 6.1.

Even so the open structure's impact is limited by the small number of posts it embraces (less than 3.7 per cent of service posts in 1987), whilst at other levels the service remains far from unified. Within the

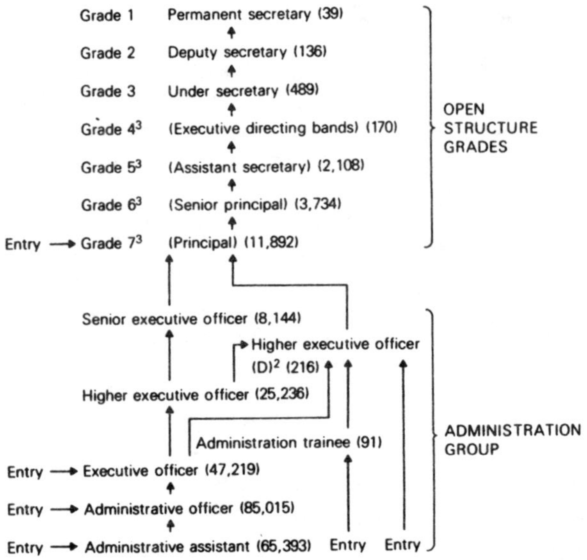

Figure 6.1 Open structure and administrative group: grades, staff numbers, main career paths, 1987.[1]

Notes:
1. Full-time equivalents (all staff) in post, 1st January 1987.
2. Higher Executive Officer (D) posts are mainly recruited
   a) by competition from in-service candidates (of any grade) nominated by departments
   b) successful external applicants to the AT/HEO(D) competition over 25 years of age.
3. Includes corresponding professional and scientific grades.

administration group – the largest group within the service employing 231,404 staff in 1987 – there has, as Fry (1988a, p. 14) notes, been 'little sign of radicalism' regarding structure, although there has been an element of grade renaming (in 1987 clerical assistants and clerical officers were renamed administrative assistants and administrative officers) arousing 'suspicion that a classic pseudo-restructuring exercise was engaged in'. Elsewhere, the plethora of categories and groups remains, as Drewry and Butcher (1988, pp. 63–7) explain:

> The civil service remains afflicted with numerous horizontal subdivisions . . . the multiplicity of grades is considerable. . . . Separate but parallel hierarchies exist for the various specialist groups . . . and separate departmental classes have not disappeared . . . . [Some of] the broad categories . . . often cover a huge variety of jobs ('science category', for example, covers almost every conceivable science

> discipline) . . . . Any prospect of achieving a straightforward organization chart . . . onto which all groups and grades of personnel could be fitted, remains a utopian dream.

Despite some rationalization, the single unified grading structure recommended by Fulton has not appeared. One corollary of this is especially significant: the vast bulk of generalists are still organized separately within the administration group whilst most specialists continue to be employed within their own classes (or categories or groups). Although higher and senior executive officers within the administration group seeking promotion to the open structure now face competition from specialists in other groups and categories, the extra experience in administration and policy work which employment in the administration group provides gives them an advantage. Thus while a substantial proportion of open structure posts are filled by staff with specialist backgrounds – the Expenditure Committee in 1977 (vol. II(I), p. 21) put the figure at almost 40 per cent – most of these are appointed to posts within their own specialist area (for example, an engineer as Chief Water Engineer in DOE). Very few are found in grades 1 to 3 (under secretary and above). As Drewry and Butcher (1988, pp. 143, 220–1) conclude, 'Despite the Fulton proposals, the dominance of the generalist in the departmental hierarchy has not really changed . . . the impact of remedial devices like the open structure . . . has been more symbolic than real.'

Perhaps too it should be noted that, while the Thatcher government has extended the open structure, the concept of a unified civil service has been at odds with other aspects of its approach towards the civil service. The Ibbs Report (1988, p. 4; see also Chapter 2), for example, stated:

> The Civil Service is too big and too diverse to manage as a single entity . . . . A single organisation of this size . . . is bound to develop in a way which fits no single operation effectively . . . . The advantages of an all-embracing pay structure are breaking down . . . the uniformity of grading frequently inhibits effective management and . . . the concept of a career in a unified Civil Service has little relevance for most civil servants whose horizons are bounded by their local office or, at most, by their department.

Certainly the unified service ideal does not adhere well with Ibbs' own proposals for extensive delegation to executive agencies (see Chapter 2) nor with those aspects of the Thatcher government's managerialist approach which emphasize budgetary decentralization and managerial freedom (see Chapter 7). As Fry (1988b, p. 105) concludes, the Thatcher government's 'steps towards greater conformity at the top of the Home Civil Service' seems at odds with the 'wish to encourage individual initiative in the Service. For they effected a form of rationalisation whereas other approaches seemed aimed at obtaining greater differentiation.'

THE ESTABLISHMENT OF A CIVIL SERVICE COLLEGE

The Civil Service College was intended to expand central training in three main ways: i) providing post-entry training for administrative recruits in economic, financial or social areas of government; ii) providing courses in administration and management for specialists; iii) conducting research into administrative problems. In addition the college was to provide 'a wide range of shorter training courses for a much larger body of staff', including staff in local government, industry, and the lower rungs of the civil service.

While these proposals largely built on earlier 1960s developments in training, they nevertheless represented a departure from the traditional 'generalist' view that 'training' was best achieved by practical experience of departmental work. Although the college opened in 1970 – with centres at Sunningdale, London, and in Edinburgh – it never really functioned as Fulton had intended. Several factors illustrate this.

(i) Fulton proposed an independent governing body drawn from both civil servants and 'a wide range of interests outside the Service' (1, para. 114). This was never implemented; from the outset the college was effectively controlled by the CSD and operated as a civil service institution. Although some staff are recruited from universities, polytechnics and business, most are civil servants on loan from departments. In 1976 the college became part of the training group of the then CSD and the post of principal was effectively downgraded from deputy secretary to under secretary (Drewry and Butcher, 1988, p. 112).

(ii) Serious resource constraints 'virtually wiped out' any capacity for 'expansion' in the early 1970s (Mair, 1977, p. 41). In 1976 the Edinburgh centre closed for financial reasons, and in the 1980s the free provision of training to departments ceased. Under the new regime departments have to pay for staff trained at the college. Financial arrangements are likely to become even tighter when the college – as is anticipated at the time of writing (1988) – acquires agency status under the Ibbs-inspired Next Steps programme (see Chapter 2).

(iii) Relations between the college and departments were cool, mainly perhaps because civil service culture has always held 'establishment work', including training, in low esteem (Chapman and Greenaway, 1980, especially ch. 3; Chapman, 1988b, especially ch. 2). Departments generally did not make promotion dependent upon completing college studies, and consequently course dropout rates were often high, and morale among college staff and students low.

Although these various factors all inhibited the college's development, its intended role was admittedly daunting. As an early review (Heaton/Williams Report, 1974, para. 5.3) observed, it was expected 'to combine the roles of All Souls and an adult education centre, with some elements of technical education and teacher training thrown in for good measure'. In fact, it is neither a staff college – in the sense of catering just for an elite – nor a management college providing purely management training (see Moore, 1984, p. 96). In practice the range of courses provided is extremely wide. In 1986–7, for example, it ran 1,337 courses for 21,535 students, embracing 82,000 student days (*Principal's Annual Report, 1986–87*). Courses are provided for both junior and senior staff in a variety of fields (the main ones in 1986–7 being in Systems, Management Studies, Public Administration and Social Policy, and Accounting and Internal Audit). Nevertheless, the college provides only a fraction of total civil service training (around 5 per cent), the vast bulk (around 75 per cent) – including virtually all induction training – being provided by departments themselves. As Drewry and Butcher (1988, p. 113) comment, departments 'have been slow to relinquish their traditional predominance in this field'.

Much disquiet has in particular been expressed about the Administration Trainee (AT) course introduced in 1971 following Fulton's criticisms of the training of administrative class recruits. Initially planned as two fifteen-week multi-disciplinary blocks, by the early 1980s the scheme had been reduced to two block-release eight-week courses. In 1981, largely because changing conditions 'began to make it difficult to release staff for long courses' a new modular system was introduced (Thompson, 1984). This now comprises twelve separate modules of mostly one to three weeks' duration, offering twenty-two weeks' training over about five years. Building on induction modules – typically comprising communication skills, information technology, public expenditure, Parliament and government and so on – later modules cover such fields as quantitative skills, economics, principles of accounts, government and industry (which involves attachment to a private company), and resource allocation. Attendance at any or all of the courses is not mandatory and withdrawals due to the demands of departmental work are high (for details see Thompson 1984; Fry 1985). While arguably an improvement on pre-Fulton arrangements, the programme has been widely criticized. Twenty-two weeks of formal training is inadequate either to impart real understanding of the public sector or to inculcate essential skills, and the scheme falls far short of the equivalent scheme in France (which greatly impressed the Fulton Committee). There, higher civil service recruits – most of which, unlike Britain, have job-relevant degrees – undergo a thirty-month course at the Ecole Nationale D'Administration (ENA). Approximately half the course is college-based, the rest comprises mainly practical work experience in both public and private sectors. Students are stringently assessed and performance has a direct bearing on career prospects (see Stevens, 1978). While the ENA system can be criticized as elitist, it nevertheless produces civil servants of remarkable quality, and graphically illustrates how higher civil service training in Britain could be developed.

While post-entry training has undoubtedly expanded since its formulation, the college has nevertheless not become the catalyst envisaged by Fulton for promoting change within the service. Underlying its failure it is possible to detect both a reluctance by departments to relinquish their own training role, and the continuing cultural view within the service that 'training [is] the icing on the cake of experience' (Drewry and Butcher, 1988, p. 111). Perhaps also one can sense a more fundamental problem: whether public administration is an art, to be perfected by practical experience, or a science, to be learned and applied by trained practitioners. The generalist administrator has traditionally accepted the former view; Fulton inclined to the latter. The Civil Service College's halting progress thus probably reflects, partly at least, underlying uncertainty about the nature of public administration itself.

RECRUITMENT REFORMS

While Fulton dealt with recruitment problems within the whole service, its main focus was upon recruitment at the highest levels. The Report had three main recommendations:

(i) preference to be given to graduates whose university courses were relevant 'to their future work' (1, paras 75–7);
(ii) 'Late entry should be considerably expanded' to enable 'people in business, the professions, nationalised industry, local government and the universities' to bring their 'experience into "the Service"' (1, para. 124);
(iii) the social and educational base of top civil servants was to be widened, both by recruitment changes, and the enhanced opportunities for internal promotion throughout the service expected to flow from the introduction of a single unified grading structure.

Some of these proposals, of course, never materialized: preference for relevance was rejected, and single unified grading abandoned. The proposed expansion of late entry also was disappointing although during the 1980s – as a result both of the difficulty of recruiting and retaining able staff on normal career pay scales, and of the Thatcher government's emphasis on tapping private sector expertise – there was a considerable inflow of appointments and secondments from outside. About seventy such appointments were made at grade 3 (under secretary) level or above between 1979 and 1985 alone (*Civil Servants and Ministers*, Cmnd 9841, para. 28), arousing comment that the 'career concept' of the service was being undermined (Chapman, 1988a; Fry, 1986a, pp. 275–6; 1986b, p. 554). Even so, 'permanent or temporary recruitment at senior levels . . . [of] individuals with outside experience or particular skills . . . has been only small scale' (Williams Report, 1987, para. 3.23). For example, only 13 out of 670 senior open structure personnel in post in January 1985 were on period appointments or on loan from outside organizations.

Perhaps more disturbing, the AT scheme did not significantly broaden the social base of post-Fulton administrative recruits. From the outset the AT scheme drew recruits from two main sources: i) external applicants with degrees; and ii) serving officers (or those of equivalent grades) with a degree or at least two years' service. Initially it was expected that there would be 250–300 ATs per year, 175 from external sources and the remainder from internal candidates. In practice in-service recruits have been fewer than expected – the highest annual total was 53, in 1971 and 1974 – and, to compensate, more than 175 external applications were recruited in some years. Although after 1975 the number of AT vacancies began to fall, numbers of internal recruits have remained low. This in-service shortfall has occurred, moreover, despite possible bias against external candidates in AT selection procedures (Chapman, 1982), one factor being reluctance by serving executive officers to relocate to London where most AT posts were based. As a result AT recruits have been drawn overwhelmingly from external candidates, with 79 per cent coming from this source between 1971 and 1985 (calculated from Drewry and Butcher, 1988, table 3.8).

An additional factor is that internally selected ATs usually performed less well than external recruits. Until 1982 ATs were 'streamed' within two to four years and those with most potential given promotion. Based essentially on departmental performance 'on the job' the Expenditure Committee (1977, II, ii, p. 506) heard that almost all external recruits were 'fast'-streamed compared with only 50 per cent of internal recruits. The Expenditure Committee itself recommended replacement of the AT scheme by a more intensive higher-management-training course which, coupled with the findings of an internal committee (CSD 1978), possibly influenced limited changes introduced in 1982. A new scheme (AT/HEOD) was established whereby trainees, drawn as before from graduates and serving executive officers, after training entered a new Higher Executive Officer (Development) (D) grade. Common standards were applied for both internal and external applicants, and streaming disappeared. In 1985 automatic appointment to HEO(D) was offered to all successful candidates over 25 years old. These changes, however, failed to improve the flow of in-service candidates. A sharp cut-back in AT vacancies after 1980 – to a low of only forty-four in 1982 – coupled with the change to 'fast stream only' entry in 1982 – probably disadvantaged them further. After 1982, numbers of successful internal candidates were always in single figures even though the Commission consistently failed – partly owing to uncompetitive salaries – to fill all AT vacancies. In 1986, significantly, the internal element of the scheme was discontinued (Civil Service Commission, *Annual Report 1986*, p. 47). A parallel scheme, enabling in-service candidates nominated by departments to compete for appointment direct to HEO(D) grade, has also had little effect – partly through departmental reluctance to make nominations – producing only 20 HEO(D)s (plus two grade 7 – Principal – appointments) in 1987. As in pre-Fulton times, future generations of top civil servants seem likely to be drawn disproportionally from externally recruited graduates.

In other ways, too, pre-Fulton patterns have survived. The AT scheme, by providing selected generalists with unique experience in policy and administration – experience which specialists, still largely compartmentalized within their own groups and categories, are largely denied – and accelerated promotion thereafter to the fringes of the open structure, virtually guarantees generalist leadership into the foreseeable future. In addition a preponderance of arts and Oxbridge graduates is still discernible among external recruits, partly because 'preference for relevance' was rejected but possibly also because of what the Expenditure Committee (1977, III, p. 1,093) described as 'bias in favour of Arts and Humanities' within the Civil Service Commission. Commenting on this, the committee concluded (I, para. 13) that 'there may be something wrong, with the constitution of the Commission' and with aspects of the selection process. Among its recommendations (I, paras 13, 14, 20) were: i) an enlargement of the Civil Service Commission by the addition of 'a majority of . . . part-time outside Commissioners', which was subsequently acted upon to the extent of adding one or two (but not a majority) of part-time outsiders; and ii) broadening the final selection board (which comprised three civil servants and two outsiders), an arrangement which remained largely unchanged (see Atkinson Report, 1983, pp. 31–3). Most significantly, however, the committee's allegation of bias was rejected, a subsequent Civil Service Commission review (1979) specifically praising 'the inherent fairness' of AT selection procedures. In 1983 another internal review dismissed as a 'myth' the view 'that Oxbridge candidates have an unfair advantage' (Atkinson Report, 1983, para. 92) and proposed only minor reforms designed to attract more graduate applicants from redbrick universities and polytechnics. Even so, in 1987, 54 per cent of AT/HEO entrants were Oxbridge graduates (compared with 59 per cent in 1968), and 60 per cent had degrees in arts (compared with 'only' 54 per cent in 1968) (*Civil Service Commission Annual Report*, 1987, p. 46; Brown and Steel, 1979, p. 77). While there are risks in over-simplifying lessons drawn from complicated statistics, Chapman's conclusion in 1982 (p. 13) that 'the higher civil service in 20–30 years' time is likely to be even more elitist than . . . today' seems unlikely to be wide of the mark.

Overview

Fulton's proposals, while producing a more rational structure and a greater awareness of central training needs, had nothing like the impact that their advocates hoped. Major administrative reforms are usually difficult to bring about in large organizations, and clearly complex problems and pressures inhibited full implementation of Fulton's recommendations. One factor was tension between departmental independence and the 'pull' of the centre. Fulton's recommendations ignored aspirations for greater autonomy within departments which, as Chapman (1983, p. 56) notes, 'in the last century . . . were virtually independent, with their own recruitment procedures and departmental traditions'. Gray and Jenkins' (1985, p. 97) view, that the CSD lacked 'fit with the realities of power in Whitehall', in some respects encapsulates the weakness of Fulton's strategy as a whole.

A second interpretation is that implementation suffered because the task was entrusted to mandarins who – determined to defend generalist traditions – decided for themselves 'which recommendations to carry out and which to ignore' (Kellner and Crowther-Hunt, 1980, p. 98). In Fry's view the existence of the CSD, which symbolized 'the Civil Service being treated as an interest in its own right', had by 1981 itself become an obstacle to radical reform of the service. Its disbandment, he claims, and return of its main functions to the Treasury, not only emphasized the Thatcher government's concern with 'financial considerations' but also reaffirmed 'political primacy over the Service'. Of course, it can be argued that ministers in the late 1960s and 1970s themselves bear much blame for the post-Fulton failures. Not only did Fulton fade from ministerial agendas, and governments change, but political impetus to achieve reform was absent. According to Craig (1984, pp.68–9) Fulton, prevented by its remit from examining minister–civil service relationships, 'was forced down the fashionable but politically naive road of managerial recommendations' in which ministers were simply not interested; indeed, the genesis of Fulton's Report, he argues, 'was merely a device to deflect the growing public disquiet of the [1960s] regarding British administrative and political institutions'.

In the 1980s, arguably, there have been signs of change. Following abolition of the CSD there has been a more assertive stance against civil service unions, a new pay system (related more to market conditions and the taxpayers' ability to pay: Megaw Report, 1982), and an attempt to 'deprivilege' the career civil service. To some extent these developments have built on Fulton; notably, the extension of the open structure and renewed emphasis on accountable management. In other ways, however, the Thatcher government has rejected Fulton's approach, abolishing the CSD, stressing the need for cultural change within the service and – particularly if the Ibbs *Next Steps* approach (see Chapter 2) is followed – recognizing that the service is too big and diverse to be managed as a single entity.

A final point is that changes of the scale envisaged by Fulton cannot be implemented overnight; and circumstances may change before reforms are carried through. As Johnson (1985, pp. 421–2) reminds us, Fulton's reforms were passed on the assumption that the state's functions 'would remain more or less the same, that the overall responsibility of the government would remain unchallenged, and that resources would continue to be available on a steadily increasing scale'. These assumptions all turned out to be ill-founded, and while 'the administrative system *was* changing under the impact of the post-1968 reforms', it was clear by the late 1970s that the pace, and arguably the direction, of change was out of tune with political and economic realities. After 1979 the question of civil service reform became increasingly and inextricably intertwined with the Thatcher government's political priorities: public expenditure restraint, a more limited concept of government, and a greater emphasis upon efficient and effective resource management within the public services. By the 1980s what remained of the Fulton reforms had largely been overtaken – on the Prime Minister's part at least – by a more managerialist concept of civil service functions. It is this concept, and its implications for central government, which forms the subject of the following chapter.

7 MANAGERIALISM IN CENTRAL ADMINISTRATION

The inability of the Fulton initiative to produce radical changes was only one of a number of administrative reforms which by 1979 were generally adjudged to have failed. PESC, PAR and the CPRS had not lived up to initial expectations, and changes in the departmental pattern had failed to produce either significant administrative gains or organizational stability. Consequently the Thatcher government elected in 1979 turned away from what Pollitt (1984, p. 121) describes as 'the classic [Machinery of Goverment] issues' – the macro-structure of departments and policy appraisal and planning mechanisms – towards one concentrating primarily on resource use and constraints. In this way the logic of Whitehall reform effectively coincided with Thatcherism's emphasis on the use of business techniques within the public sector generally.

As observed in Chapter 1, the Thatcher government's general approach has been to couple the application within the public sector of those private managerial techniques perceived as most conducive to value for money – notably objective setting and performance measurement – with an increasing encouragement to greater consumer responsiveness. The philosophy underlying this approach has been aptly summarized by Gray and Jenkins (1986, p. 171):

> The guiding principles are the pursuit of efficiency, effectiveness and value for money: responsibility is to be decentralised, lower level operatives made aware of and accountable for the costs of their operations, targets are to be established and individuals assessed according to their ability to achieve them. In brief we are offered a world where bureaucrats (and ministers) are redefined as *accountable managers*, public sector operations sub-divided into *businesses*, and the public seen as the *customer*.

The post-1979 managerial emphasis in central administration was not wholly new: indeed, it started from much the same principle as Fulton – that civil servants needed to adopt a more business-like approach – and drew upon a number of Fulton's ideas about departmental organization (see Chapters 1 and 2). What was new, however, is what Gray and Jenkins (1985, p. 127) call 'organisational learning': acting on experience gained from earlier failed attempts at administrative reform. For example, whereas Fulton suffered heavily from lack of civil service support, advocates of the new managerialism have emphasized the need to change the Whitehall culture in order to generate reform from within. In order, moreover, to minimize departmental opposition – which had been instrumental in neutralizing the impact of PAR and the CPRS – departments have been given discretion in determining the pace and nature of managerial change. In similar vein, recognizing departmental sensitivity about policy territories, the post-1979 initiatives have focused on efficient administration rather than policy. To quote Gray and Jenkins (1985, p. 165) again: 'The moves beyond Rayner to the FMI represent attempts to work within the political and organisation system, rather than against it and to couch debate in terms of means rather than ends'.

A further important contextual difference has been provided by ministerial attitudes. Whereas momentum behind Fulton's reforms dissipated once they faded from ministerial agendas, post-1979 managerialism has derived considerable support from the Thatcher government. Not only does it draw from what Pollitt (1986a, p. 159) describes as the 'belief-system of the incoming Conservative government of 1979' – the crusade against bureaucratic waste, belief in the superiority of private sector managerial techniques and drive towards increased value for money – but it shares the same ideological roots as privatization and contracting out. Indeed, improved managerial efficiency can be seen as the Thatcher government's alternative solution 'for those parts of the public sector that could not be privatised or subjected to the sanitizing forces of the market'. This ideological underpinning has been particularly significant, vesting the post-1979 managerialist reforms with what Metcalfe and Richards (1984, 1987) describe as 'political clout', a strong measure of personal support from the Prime Minister and her closest advisers.

Despite this political and ideological underpinning it is unlikely that the Thatcher government entered office with any grand strategy for the civil service. Rather, developments have proceeded incrementally with early initiatives such as the Rayner Scrutiny Programme leading subsequently to the introduction of departmental management information systems and the Financial Management Initiative. Collectively these three initiatives encompass the main thrust of the post-1979 managerial approach in central government, each of which will now be examined in turn.

The Rayner Scrutiny Programme

In 1979 Mrs Thatcher appointed Sir (now Lord) Derek Rayner, of Marks & Spencer, as an adviser on administrative efficiency. Supported by a small 'efficiency unit' – composed of both civil servants and outside consultants – and originally established as part of the Prime Minister's Office, Rayner's job was to stimulate improvements in administrative efficiency within Whitehall. Subsequently the efficiency unit was relocated in the Management and Personnel Office, but in 1983 – when Sir Robin Ibbs (a former head of the CPRS and executive director of ICI) succeeded Rayner as the Prime Minister's Special Adviser on Efficiency – it was located physically in the Cabinet Office. Throughout, both Rayner and Ibbs have enjoyed strong prime ministerial backing, ensuring 'that civil servants (and ministers) in departments continued to take the Efficiency Unit's work seriously' (Metcalfe and Richards, 1987, p. 9).

One of Rayner's first acts was to set in train a series of efficiency scrutinies within Whitehall. According to Rayner the objectives of the scrutiny programme were:

i) to examine a specific policy or activity, questioning all aspects of work normally taken for granted;
ii) to propose solutions to problems and to make recommendations to achieve savings and increase efficiency and effectiveness;
iii) to implement agreed solutions, or to begin their implementation within 12 months of the start of a scrutiny (Rayner, 1982, para. 2.2).

Although these objectives refer to 'efficiency' and 'effectiveness', in practice the scrutiny programme has been mainly concerned with the third 'E', 'economy' (for definitions see Chapter 1), focusing mainly on cost reduction through streamlining administrative procedures. As several authoritative inquiries (such as National Audit Office, 1986a, para. 2; Public Accounts Committee, 1985–6, para. 8) have observed, few scrutinies – particularly in the period to 1983 – addressed effectiveness issues or those with major policy content.

Basically each efficiency scrutiny encompasses the following five main stages:

1 *Setting up a strategy*: All departments regularly suggest topics for scrutiny. Most reviews concern departmental activities, although some have examined cross-departmental work (such as government forms and property management).
2 *Investigation*: Usually carried out by departmental staff, with reports submitted to the minister within ninety working days.
3 *Action plan*: Summarizing plans for implementing savings. To be approved within three months of receipt of report.
4 *Implementation*: The responsibility of the departmental permanent secretary.

5 *Implementation report*: Summarizing action, savings and so forth achieved. Produced within two years of start of scrutiny. (*Making Things Happen*, 1985).

As the above indicates, the scrutiny process emphasizes action and implementation within a specified timetable. The 'key elements are radical questioning, direct observation, proposals based firmly on factual evidence and a sense of urgency' (ibid.). According to Bray (1988) the underlying aim is to serve departmental needs. Indeed, 'Rayner had no right of entry into departments. He could investigate by invitation only, and even then only in areas selected by the departments themselves' (quoted in Fry, 1988a, p. 6). A crucial role in the scrutiny process is assigned to what is described as 'top management' – the permanent secretary and deputy secretaries 'acting as the top board of the department' – who are involved at every stage in the process. Ministers also carry major responsibility, approving scrutiny topics, deciding action plans, and receiving implementation reports. As Beesley (1983, p. 31) emphasizes, reviews rely 'heavily on self-examination' reflecting the belief 'that Ministers and their officials are better equipped than anyone to examine the use of resources for which they are responsible'.

In the first six years a total of 266 reviews were conducted, identifying annual savings of £600m with an additional £67m of one-off savings (*Making Things Happen*, 1985, p. 9). Most reviews have identified administrative deficiencies – one scrutiny found it cost £90 to administer £100 of woodland grant – and some have led to major changes (such as the establishment of a non-Defence central purchasing unit: see *Government Purchasing: A Review of Government Contract and Procurement Procedures*, 1984). By 1986 total savings were estimated at £950m against scrutiny costs of only £5m (Public Accounts Committee, 1985–6, para. 15). By any standards these are impressive results.

Nevertheless, while many administrative shortcomings have been identified, the scrutiny technique does have inherent limitations. Inevitably there is a tendency for departments to select 'safe' scrutiny topics and ignore findings they dislike. The scrutiny approach is also arguably unsuitable where quick decisions are needed or where inefficiency arises from the inability of departmental staff rather than deficient procedures or systems (see Bray, 1988, p. 21). Critics, moreover, argue that sacrifices in service quality have sometimes been necessary to obtain savings. Many identified savings, furthermore, have not been realized: of the £600m annual savings identified by 1985, for example, only £295m had actually been implemented. Of the shortfall, departments had assessed £80m as being unobtainable, and £65m had been rejected for political and other reasons (*Making Things Happen*, 1985). Many scrutinies, moreover, are not completed within the two-year time span, and departments have frequently been criticized for delays in implementation.

Although the scrutiny programme has received most publicity, Rayner also emphasized the need for 'lasting reforms' which would help remove the underlying causes of Whitehall inefficiency. Broadly he identified two categories of reform: those relating to people (designed to produce changes in civil service culture), and those relating to institutions (designed to clarify arrangements for resource management). While as Collins (1987, p. 14) observes, 'few, if any of the scrutinies have borne directly on any of these concerns, a surprisingly large number . . . have led, directly or indirectly, to widespread changes in the management of central government'. Two scrutinies, in particular, were crucially important: the first in 1979 led to the decision to implement a management information system for ministers (MINIS) in the Department of the Environment (DOE). The second in 1981, known as the Joubert Study (after the official conducting it), devised a structure which divided the DOE into 120 cost centres as a basis for a financial management system (Collins, 1987, p. 15; Fry, 1984, p. 332). These two scrutinies led directly to the two other major planks of the Thatcher government's managerial approach within central government; namely, MINIS and the Financial Management Initiative (FMI).

Management information system for ministers (MINIS)

In 1980, following a Rayner scrutiny, MINIS was introduced into the DOE. Essentially a management tool, MINIS was strongly associated with Michael Heseltine who, as Secretary of State for the Environment, introduced MINIS into the DOE and subsequently, as Defence Secretary, into the Ministry of Defence (MOD). As he explains (1987, pp. 19–20) the essential objective was to 'find out what was happening in my department and who was responsible for making it happen, who had set the targets, what the targets were and whether they were being monitored. Nobody could recall [these questions] being asked before'.

MINIS, at its simplest, represents 'an . . . attempt to collect information about a Department's activities and to place responsibility for using this information with the Department's top management, Ministerial and official' (Richards, 1987, p. 26). It enables departmental 'top management' to ascertain within their departments who does what, why and at what cost. As initially developed in the DOE (Likierman, 1982; Whitbread, 1987) and later in the MOD (Omand, 1983) it involved three main stages:

1 Each section head prepares a statement of activities, staff numbers, achievements, and so forth; developing where possible perform-

ance indicators (such as average time spent on each planning appeal).

2 These statements are considered by ministers and top management. Section heads can be questioned about performance, objectives and so on.

3 Implementation of ministers' decisions arising from stage 2.

The process above is conducted annually – each cycle in MINIS parlance being known as a 'round' – enabling performance to be analysed against plans, and information to be updated. The effect is to bring 'Ministers into the management structure of the Department' (Whitbread, 1987, p. 95), providing 'a comprehensive grasp of the activities of the Department, with information presented in a much more systematic way than was normally available through briefing by officials on particular issues or in response to particular requests' (Likierman, 1982, p. 130). This, in turn, enables ministers and senior officials to review progress of departmental activities, monitor the effectiveness of policies, and to take resource allocation decisions 'in accordance with ministerial priorities and objectives' (Bradley, 1983, p. 41). It also offers a potential for assessing more accurately the effects of projected staffing or expenditure cuts and to identify any mismatch between departmental functions and ministerial objectives. Significantly, following the introduction of MINIS into the DOE, directorates were reorganized and within four years departmental manpower fell by 15,000 (29 per cent) (Heseltine, 1987, p. 18). As the government acknowledged (*Efficiency and Effectiveness*, 1982, para. 27), MINIS provided ministers 'with a most valuable instrument to assist resource allocation'.

MINIS, it should be stressed, was not totally new. A number of departments, prior to its introduction into the DOE, possessed systems for obtaining information about departmental activities, although the 'more rigorous' and comprehensive analysis offered by MINIS did represent a 'real departure' (Likierman, 1982, p. 135). MINIS, moreover, was an ongoing system capable of having refinements added over time. In its early stages in the DOE, for example, it focused mainly on departmental structure, activities, and administrative expenditure, whilst by 1985–6 the system had been improved to include performance review reports and programme expenditure (Whitbread, 1987, p. 96). Of course, such arrangements were not introduced without criticism. Association with expenditure cuts, particularly at the DOE, aroused criticism among lower-level staff and public sector unions. In the DOE it also tended to overburden top management, producing large amounts of detailed information about costs whilst ignoring both wider policy judgements (which perhaps offer greater scope for savings) and day-to-day political issues (which usually preoccupy top civil servants and ministers). Nevertheless, as McGill (1984, p. 25) notes, by the early 1980s MINIS-type arrangements were being seen in the UK public sector as something of a 'management panacea', with similar developments occurring beyond Whitehall within, for example, water authorities and local government.

Ultimately the attractiveness of MINIS-type systems to public sector managers lies in the comprehensive picture which they can provide of organizational activities, and also in the potential which they hold for decentralization within departments. As Metcalfe and Richards (1987, p. 24) observe, departmental decentralization was a key theme to emerge from early Rayner scrutinies, the object being to push responsibility down the departmental hierarchy to where costs were being incurred. MINIS, when properly developed, could identify and measure the performance of departmental cost centres, and thereby provide a potential for the comprehensive reorganization of departments based upon the principle of decentralization to managerially autonomous accountable units.

By no means a new concept – Fulton had strongly advocated the development of units of accountable management – such arrangements had previously proved difficult to introduce on a widespread scale owing largely to the difficulty of isolating discrete elements of departmental work. MINIS, however, by dividing departmental work into discrete blocks, and summarizing the costs/objectives/achievements and so on of each, provided the basis for such a reorganization within the DOE. Following the Joubert Study (see pp. 125) a computerized budget system (MAXIS) was installed into the DOE in 1983 and a network of 120 cost centres established, each controlled by a manager with budgetary responsibility for running costs including staff (Fry, 1984, p. 332; *Financial Management in Government Departments*, 1983, pp. 50–2). Final budgets for each centre were then integrated into each MINIS round, and the Treasury and Civil Service Select Committee (1982, vol. 1, p. xl) – perceiving the implications for other departments – recommended the extension of MINIS 'or its equivalent' to all main central departments.

Although initially there was considerable opposition in Whitehall to such arrangements (Heseltine, 1987, pp. 22–3), the government was anxious to develop similar systems throughout Whitehall. Accordingly in 1982 it announced that, while varying systems could be established to reflect differing departmental roles, all departments were to introduce 'management systems like MINIS' together with 'a structure of organization' in which identifiable functions could be assigned to 'responsibility centres' (*Efficiency and Effectiveness*, 1982, para. 29 and annex C). The MINIS and Joubert systems, with due allowance for departmental differences, were to be universalized throughout Whitehall, and it was this which provided the impetus for the launch of the Financial Management Initiative (FMI) in 1982.

The Financial Management Initiative (FMI)

The FMI, launched in May 1982, has been described by Gray and Jenkins (1986, p. 173; 1985, p. 124) as 'a general approach rather than a single strategy', and as 'an umbrella under which a new management philosophy is being developed'. It draws not only on the experience of Rayner scrutinies and MINIS, but also on the concept of management accounting (see pp. 11). All departments were recommended on the launching of the FMI to establish a 'management accounting system' to be integrated as far as possible with 'existing systems for the public expenditure survey, estimates, and appropriation accounts' (*Efficiency and Effectiveness*, 1982, app. 3).

Officially the aims of the FMI were to promote in each department an organization in which managers at all levels would have:

i a clear view of their objectives and means to assess and, wherever possible, measure outputs or performance in relation to those objectives;
ii well-defined responsibility for making the best use of resources including a critical scrutiny of output and value for money; and
iii the information (particularly about costs), the training and access to expert advice that they need to exercise their responsibilities effectively (ibid., para. 13).

In keeping with these objectives departments were 'called upon to examine the way they managed all aspects of their programmes and to work out the best pattern of managerial responsibility, financial accounting and control' (ibid., para. 14). The initiative was co-ordinated by a specially created unit – comprising both civil servants and management consultants – known as the Financial Management Unit of the Cabinet Office (MPO) and the Treasury, which was replaced in 1985 by the Treasury/Cabinet Office Joint Management Unit. In accordance with allowance for departmental variations, each department was left to formulate its own plans for implementing the FMI (see *Financial Management in Government Departments*, 1983 and *Progress in Financial Management in Government Departments*, 1984), producing a variety of patterns of implementation. While these variations need to be borne in mind, four distinctive features of the FMI can be identified:

1 TOP MANAGEMENT SYSTEMS

The White Paper launching the FMI (*Efficiency and Effectiveness*, 1982, para. 15) 'expected' each department to establish 'an information system that not only provides higher management with aggregated information needed for estimating and control, but managers at successive levels down the line with the information they need to do their job properly'. In essence, what was envisaged was the construction of internal management systems around the hierarchical command structures characteristic of government departments (see Chapter 2). By 1984 every department had reportedly 'taken steps to introduce a top management system for Ministers and senior managers', enabling these 'to review regularly the department's aims, examine its "businesses" and the "customers" they serve, set objectives, and establish priorities' (*Progress in Financial Management in Government Departments*, 1984, p. 3). Although features varied between departments, most required each identifiable unit to report regularly to 'top management' on their structure, activities, and resources consumed. Initially most systems concentrated on reviewing administrative activities and costs but subsequent refinements enabled them also to review programmes (that is, activities and costs covering a policy objective or a group of related policy objectives). By 1985 many departments were reportedly using such systems to conduct annual reviews of departmental programmes and administrative work, and feeding results directly into public expenditure and parliamentary estimates exercises (Cabinet Office (MPO)/Treasury (FMU), 1985a, p. 1).

In practice, of course, the development of information systems presents considerable difficulties. As Plowden (1985, p. 401) observes, 'almost any information system exploiting modern technology is likely to generate too much information'. In the DOE, for example, senior officials often became involved in lengthy discussions on minor matters at the expense of strategic discussion and analysis. Many lower-level managers found MINIS time-consuming and unhelpful, while some also found it difficult to depict their work accurately. There may also be a tendency, as the Public Accounts Committee (1986–7c, para. 23) has warned, for 'top management systems . . . to be regarded as a substitute for FMI, rather than an integral part of it'. While monitoring and refinements should bring improvements over time, clearly serious difficulties have been experienced with the development and utilization of departmental information systems.

2 STATEMENT OF OBJECTIVES

Underlying the FMI is a belief that better use of resources requires a clearer definition of the objectives of expenditure, and as a first step all departments were obliged to specify their objectives as a basis for determining priorities and measuring achievement. On paper all have done so, although in reality most statements of departmental objectives have tended to be rather vague and generalized, describing functions or responsibilities rather than underlying goals or objectives (*Financial Management in Government Departments*, 1983; Gray and Jenkins, 1985, pp. 84–7). Departments have also generally found it easier to establish objectives for administrative costs (which account for only 13 per cent of departmental expenditure) than for programme costs (87 per cent of departmental expenditure and, therefore, offering potentially much greater scope for savings) (*Public Accounts Committee*, 1986–7c, para. 30).

This relative lack of progress, of course, largely reflects the problems of goal-setting in the (generally) non-profit-oriented public sector. In the absence of profit, objectives are usually more difficult to define, whilst many government departments and public agencies – and many of the programmes they administer – have multiple objectives. Goal identification, moreover, is often inseparable in Whitehall from questions of policy, which gives rise to frequent conflict both within and between departments. For these reasons goal-setting by departments has been fraught with problems, creating for those seeking to implement the FMI continual 'difficulties created by imprecise, broad, policy objectives' (National Audit Office, 1986b, para. 13).

3 DECENTRALIZATION AND DELEGATION

A key feature of the FMI is delegated budgeting, a process requiring each department to 'examine the scope for breaking its structure down into cost-centres or responsibility-centres to which resource costs can be allocated and for which, where appropriate, measures of output can be devised and monitored' (*Efficiency and Effectiveness*, 1982, Appendix 3). The underlying idea is that cost-centre managers should become budget holders responsible for cost management and results, an arrangement contrasting with traditional departmental practice whereby finance and staffing are controlled by specialist establishment and finance divisions. As Richards (1987, p. 29) observes, such central divisions 'must be willing to . . . stand back and let the . . . [cost centre] manager succeed or fail, according to his or her own lights'. Budgetary decentralization also has important personnel implications, requiring training initiatives to familiarize line managers with the accounting and other skills required to perform their new responsibilities.

In practice, progress in developing decentralized budgeting has varied considerably between departments. Although most departments have drawn up plans, many areas of departmental work cannot easily be broken down into discrete cost centres. Generally the scope for such arrangements is least in departments dominated by HQ units engaged in policy work, and greatest in those with extensive local networks (such as the DHSS which had developed 800 cost centres by 1984, with individual managers having 'to bid for their requirements' and enjoying flexibility to switch funds between budget heads) (*Progress in Financial Management in Government Departments*, 1984, pp. 62–3). Where this has happened, middle-level managers, according to Richards (1987, p. 27) 'for the first time in their working lives' have been able 'to see a connection between the activity they were authorising and the cost of carrying it out'. This, coupled with cognate developments such as the dispersion of departmental functions to semi-autonomous agencies, has done much to extend cost-consciousness and value-for-money considerations down the management line in accordance with the FMI's underlying principles. Indeed, in April 1988 civil service manpower targets were dropped and a new regime of running-costs control imposed upon departments. In future all department running costs will be cash limited with the intention of giving 'individual civil service managers greater flexibility to make best uses of the resources available to them' (*Hansard*, H.C., VI, vol. 110, cols 933–4, 18 February 1987).

Nevertheless, while some impact has been made, overall progress has been limited. Budgetary decentralization not only undermines the primacy of central establishments and finance divisions within departments, but also conflicts with the hierarchical command structure typically found in bureaucratic organizations. Consequently in some departments the effective delegation of responsibility to lower-level managers has not always been pursued with enthusiasm by senior departmental officials. Even where decentralized budgeting projects have been introduced, these have often taken the form of pilot projects or trials (*Progress in Financial Management in Government Departments*, 1984, especially Appendix 2), whilst the authority delegated to budget holders has often been severely constrained (not least by centrally determined manpower ceilings and pay scales). Problems have also been experienced with providing cost-centre managers with sufficient incentives to manage resources economically, efficiently and effectively. For such reasons overall progress with budgetary decentralization was described by the Public Accounts Committee (1986–7c, paras 34–8) as having been so slow as to threaten 'the [very] success of the FMI'.

4 PERFORMANCE MEASUREMENT

Essentially concerned with a comparative evaluation of inputs and outputs (see Chapter 1), performance measurement has long been recognized as important within Whitehall. Until the 1980s, however, its development was limited to executive functions where inputs and outputs could be most easily identified and aligned (see Treasury and Civil Service Committee, 1982, vol. III, Appendix 9). With the subsequent adoption of top management systems, however, departments acquired enhanced capacity to identify costs, tasks, achievements and so on, and from the outset performance measurement was seen as an integral feature of the FMI, offering a tool for assessing progress with the attainment of departmental objectives and – since the Treasury's multi-departmental review of budgeting (HM Treasury, 1985; 1986a) – for linking cost-centre managers' budgets to output and achievement.

Performance measures are usually most helpful when used for comparisons: for example, between units performing similar tasks, or over time. Measures can be of efficiency, effectiveness, economy or any other aspect of performance. Initially under the FMI emphasis was placed upon measuring *administrative functions*. Most departments have quantifiable running cost inputs (postage, staff, travel and so on) and outputs (such as payments, collections, caseloads) which can be used to develop performance measures such as accuracy (proportion of errors), timeliness (such as response time), throughput (such as number of cases dealt with) and unit cost (such as average cost per case/client). Such measures in turn can be used to identify underperformance, set targets, appraise staff and reallocate resources (for examples see H.M. Treasury 1986b, and 1987). At a later stage the emphasis was switched from administrative to *programme measurement* (which – as costs may be spread amongst numerous departmental sections as well as outside agencies such as local authorities or quangos – is usually much more difficult). In the DTI, for example, resource inputs into financial assistance schemes were measured against outputs (such as jobs created/safeguarded) enabling the cost-effectiveness of the programme to be assessed, and targets set for furture schemes (*Progress in Financial Management in Government Departments*, 1984, p. 103). By 1985 according to the Financial Management Unit (Cabinet Office (MPO)/ Treasury (FMU), 1985a, p. 4) 'most departments [were] developing new (or strengthening existing) arrangements for reviewing programmes systematically each year', and all departments were being urged to adopt similar procedures. As a result, by the mid-1980s a wave of performance measures had been adopted. The 1986 Public Expenditure White Paper, for example, referred to over 1,200 such measures – the majority in Whitehall departments – and by 1987 the figure had increased to 1,810. Undoubtedly performance measurement was being widely used as a tool for measuring value for money not only in Whitehall but also in outside agencies (such as quangos) involved in implementing departmental programmes (Cabinet Office (MPO)/Treasury (FMU), 1984a).

At the same time problems have been much in evidence. Assessment is costly in manpower and time, and much government work is difficult to measure: consultancy, inspection, and review activities, for example, pose special problems, while as Beeton (1987, p. 78) observes, 'by 1986 no department had begun to measure performance of its policy makers, finding the quality and effectiveness of advice too difficult to quantify'. Moreover, inputs and particularly outputs are often difficult to quantify, and sometimes even to identify. Too often in the public sector *final* outputs become reducible to vague and unquantifiable notions of public good, which leads in many cases to the measurement instead of more easily quantified – but possibly misleading – *intermediate* outputs. For example an advance factory programme should ideally be measured by additional benefit to a region's economy, but in practice intermediate measures such as jobs created may be used instead (National Audit Office, 1986b, para. 13). Sometimes performance measures obscure, or even undermine, policy objectives. A target for reduced hospital waiting lists, for example, may – by reducing hospital stays – actually impair patients' health.

Partly because of such difficulties the development of meaningful and quantifiable output measures has not occurred for many areas of departmental activity. One Treasury review (1985, p. 19) candidly admitted, 'What has been achieved so far amounts to an impressive array of intermediate indicators . . . there are, as yet, relatively few links . . . between inputs and outputs which show managers how changes in resources and priorities can lead to changes in output . . . . Performance measures still impact only slightly on resource allocation decisions'. Certainly the measurement of *programme* expenditure has lagged far behind that of *administrative* expenditure (National Audit Office, 1986b, para 12), while 'little progress' has also apparently been made with integrating performance measurement with the public expenditure survey and parliamentary supply procedures (Richards, 1987, pp. 28–9) – a development much sought after by the Financial Management Unit. As Beeton (1987, pp. 88–9) concludes, the government was unable to 'master a comprehensive range across all their spending programmes. Particularly striking [was] the failure to find, or agree on, measures or acceptable proxies of final output . . . . Some measures used [were] ambiguous, misleading or open to manipulation by managers'. This latter difficulty, possible manipulation by managers, is found with practically all performance indicators, with gaming often being practised both to meet targets and to downgrade aspects of performance not specifically measured.

A further charge is that, being introduced in an era of expenditure restraint, performance measurement has focused largely on measuring, and minimizing, inputs (costs and manpower). Gray (1986, pp. 11, 16) sees 'little evidence of genuine assessment beyond the establishment of a few input indicators', and suggests that we are witnessing 'the ascendancy of economy and efficiency over effectiveness and efficacy'. The emphasis is upon input cost minimization, with wider questions of quality, customer satisfaction, and policy outcomes being largely ignored. Similarly, Plowden (1985, p. 407) complains that the focus is 'almost entirely on the costs of governmental activities rather than on their quality'. How far, he asks (p. 399),

> are the relatively simple techniques relating to the facts about costs and outputs – numbers of staff, numbers of applications dealt with – capable of being developed to deal with far more complex questions about outcomes: what did this activity actually achieve, in terms of modernizing British industry . . . improving the nation's health, or educating it for the 21st century?

Pollitt (1986a, pp. 168–9) draws attention to one further problem: namely that performance measurement in the public sector is 'at root a . . . political question'. Performance criteria are often 'value-laden' and raise 'perennially awkward, political question[s]'. There is also 'the problem of how to aggregate different judgements of performance' which presents 'formidable difficulties of principle and practice'. In 1985 a Financial Management Unit report (Cabinet Office (MPO)/Treasury (FMU) 1985b, p. 1) admitted that as a policy-analysis tool the FMI left 'scope for very considerable further improvement'. It particularly noted the setting of imprecise goals, hidden assumptions underlying policies, and a failure to test the link between policy and impacts on the outside world. A further point is that departmental officials (and client groups) might feel threatened by the policy implications of performance measurement, as might 'a Cabinet of ministers committed to a party programme and to ways of winning the next general election' (Lee, 1984, p. 5).

In part, as Gray and Jenkins (1985, p. 165) suggest, these problems are the price paid for departmental acceptance of the FMI. The effect, however, has been to produce what they describe (1984, p. 425) as 'managerial myopia', a fixation with short-term managerial innovation at the expense 'of that long-term focus which is essential for achieving programme and policy effectiveness'. Can the FMI realistically be extended to the study of policy effects without alienating those within the administrative and political community – ministers, departmental policy makers, and client groups – whom such developments might threaten? This (as yet unresolved) dilemma is not only crucial to the FMI's future. It also raises important questions about the role of civil servants in effecting managerial change, and about the FMI's compatibility with concepts of fundamental importance to public administration.

Implementing the FMI: political clout or cultural change?

The FMI was not intended to be implemented immediately, but was to develop over time, and at a different pace in different departments. Consequently in the first six years implementation was patchy. Progress was greater, for example, with developing management systems than with defining objectives, decentralization was developed more readily in field offices than in headquarters and policy divisions, and performance measurement applied more easily to inputs than outputs, and to administrative rather than programme expenditure.

Part of the explanation for this patchy development may lie in what Richards (1987, p. 36) calls the 'fragmentation of the institutional arrangements within central government for guiding the changes'. These include, according to Gray (1986, p. 18), 'the Treasury (in a number of guises), the [former] Management and Personnel Office (especially the Management Efficiency Division), the Efficiency Unit, the Joint Management Unit, and even (in the wings) the National Audit Office'. Some of these overlap, and their respective roles are a mystery to spending departments.

Nevertheless, progress has been made. Several studies, for example, suggest that departmental productivity, in so far as it can be measured, has improved significantly in recent years. The FMI, some claim, is now 'a question of internal management rather than political initiative', and future governments will maintain it to secure 'the best possible value from limited resources' (Peat Marwick, 1986, p. 15). Johnson, (1985, pp. 428, 432) feels 'that the priority given to effective and efficient management by the civil service will endure'; and Greenaway (1987, p. 53) sees it as 'inconceivable . . . that recent developments in these areas will simply be reversed following a change of Government'.

Even so, a cautionary note must be sounded. The FMI's emphasis upon managerial efficiency as opposed to policy, and the obstacles – political as well as technical – to developing effective performance measures of programme (as opposed to administrative) expenditure, inevitably limits achievable savings. As Fry (1988a, p. 10) notes, 'The running costs of government departments . . . are dwarfed by programme expenditure, the sheer scale of which . . . make the savings obtained from cash limits, staff reductions, the Rayner scrutinies and the FMI seem relatively unimportant'. Progress within departments in implementing the FMI, moreover, has sometimes been limited. For example, in 1987, a Public Accounts Committee report (1986–7c, paras 20, 44) claimed that 'a major effort' was needed to speed up implementation of the FMI. For 'some' departments 'full implementation [was] still many years away'. The committee was 'particularly concerned about the relatively slow progress of the Home Office' and felt that it would be 'a long period of years' before systems in the Ministry of Defence could be relied on. Five years after the FMI's launch, in other words, full implementation was still a long way off and ultimate success was far from assured.

While recognizing the difficulties inherent in implementing the FMI, the slow progress recorded suggests at least some lack of consensus within Whitehall. Gray and Jenkins (1984, p. 425) point to intra-organizational tensions created by the FMI: for example, between service departments on the one hand and the Treasury (and formerly also the Management and Personnel Office) on the other, with the latter fearing loss of control over departmental expenditure and manpower. Within departments, too, strains may be caused as establishment and finance responsibilities are decentralized from headquarters to new responsibility centres. As Fry (1988a, p. 17) observes, without 'devolved powers' for managers 'to decide the terms and conditions . . . of officials in their cost centre' – powers which central departments and departmental top management have been reluctant to concede – 'the impact of the FMI seems bound to be . . . relatively restricted'. Again, FMI developments have aroused tensions among middle- and lower-management grades, not only through fears about jobs and increased central monitoring, but concern also that financial strigency could impact on staff development and training 'with longer term consequences for an efficient and effective Civil Service' (Public Accounts Committee, 1986–7c, para. 39). Tensions may also arise through departmental clients perceiving the FMI as a threat to service provision. Intra-organizational tensions within Whitehall, in other words, compounded by the concerns of civil service unions and public sector consumers, may have impeded development of consensus about the FMI.

A further obstacle concerns the skills needed to implement the FMI. As Plowden (1985, p. 407) comments, 'few ministers know the first thing about running large organisations' whilst civil servants are generally not trained in financial and management skills. Since the FMI's launch some attempt has been made to address these problems through courses at the Civil Service College, and more generally through what Tyson (1987, p. 70) describes 'as a long-term process of personal development and change' (see also *Financial Management in Government Departments*, 1983, pp. 7–8). In addition, following the Cassels Report (1983) a Personnel Work Action Programme was launched, key elements of which included more effective staff appraisal and incentives such as merit pay (see *Progress in Financial Management in Government Departments*, 1984, p. 7; *The Times*, 26 November 1986, and Fry, 1988a, pp. 13–14). At lower levels, too, cost-centre managers have been given more flexibility with personnel management providing a greater link between performance and promotion (Thorpe-

Tracey, 1987, pp. 334–5). Johnson (1985, pp. 424–5) also cites prime ministerial intervention in promoting top civil servants, and the increasing frequency of appointments to senior posts from outside the service (such as Peter Levene recruited from the private sector to head the Defence Procurement Executive in 1985) as evidence of 'a more active personnel policy' designed to enhance managerial competence.

While such developments *may* herald profound changes for the future, their full effects must take time to work through. The civil service provides its staff with fewer incentives to encourage efficiency than in the private sector (where bonus, commissions, 'perks' etc. are often widespread), a position unlikely to be altered much by limited experimentation with merit pay and the like. Fry (1984, p. 334) claims to detect 'little obvious sign of . . . change' from the traditionally 'comfortable world of established pay scales . . . routine career expectations, and security of tenure'. Indeed, introduced as they have been in a climate of manpower cuts by an allegedly insensitive senior management, the main effects of these developments may be to produce 'not just disgruntled employees' but also 'ineffective organisation' (Plowden, 1985, p. 410).

More fundamentally, cultural changes of the kind envisaged by the FMI's sponsors may not have been forthcoming. As Richards (1987, p. 27) observes 'the fundamental, if unstated objective of the [FMI] was to transform the culture of Whitehall, supplementing the primarily administrative values . . . with other values . . . directed at managerial effectiveness'. Some observers suggest that important changes have already occurred. Cassels (1985, p. 36), for example, feels that the FMI 'has changed the culture in departments a lot already', and Johnson (1985, p. 432) that 'a gradual transformation in ethos' has occurred which will produce 'by the end of the century a civil service qualitatively different in decisive respects from that . . . created by the great reforms of the last century'. If these observers are correct then the FMI's future development will presumably be secured from within by a civil service committed to bringing about 'lasting reforms'.

These developments of course (and herein lies the difficulty of gauging progress), may be more apparent than real. As Pollitt notes (1986a, p. 165) 'a government can force its employees to go through the motions, but it cannot mandate enthusiasm and commitment'. Metcalfe and Richards (1984, p. 451) also emphasize the 'impoverished concept of management' within the service, and its cultural bias towards defensiveness and risk avoidance. They point also (1987, pp. 18–19) to an entrenched 'disbelief system' which includes scepticism about attempted reforms and a belief – far from groundless – that such reforms often fail. Chapman (1984b, pp. 1–2) points similarly to the downgrading of 'management' within 'the administrative culture of the British Civil Service', and Howells (1981) to the contrast with attitudes in the private sector where managerial work generally carries much higher prestige than in Whitehall. There is also the point that the civil service will continue to require officials who are not primarily good managers but whose ability lies in policy work, drafting papers and sensitivity to ministerial needs. This, too, must present a barrier to cultural changes of the kind required by the FMI.

While cultural attitudes within the service, under the impact of the FMI, may be changing, Metcalfe and Richards' view (1984, p. 452) is that the initial impact of the FMI probably owes more to 'political clout . . . the repeated confirmation of Prime Ministerial backing' than to genuine cultural change. If this conclusion is correct then either *much* more may need to be done to force changes in the underlying culture of Whitehall, or the FMI may be laid 'to rest as soon as the architect [Mrs Thatcher] is removed' (Gray and Jenkins, 1984, p. 427).

Managerialism and public administration

The managerialist initiatives described above represent an attempt to implant into central government selected managerial practices and cultural attitudes derived from the private sector. The focus is upon better management and greater resource consciousness, emphases which are undoubtedly valuable in themselves, but which pose fundamental problems given the nature and distinctiveness of the public sector. In particular there are implications for the policy/administration dichotomy, equity and accountability (see Chapter 1).

i) THE POLICY/ADMINISTRATION DICHOTOMY

The focus of the efficiency strategy and FMI is premised on the view that 'maximizing the effectiveness and efficiency of government-delivered services' lies basically, with 'better management' (Pollitt, 1986a, p. 157). The emphasis, in other words, is upon good management rather than policy, an approach influenced partly by the need to minimize opposition from policy-conscious Whitehall departments, and partly because in the private sector – from which the managerial approach has largely been adopted – decision-making usually has only a limited policy content. However, in the public sector, resource-management considerations are usually much more difficult to disentangle from policy. Thus Likierman (1985, p. 18) warns against efforts to mark a divide between 'policy and implementation'. It is too simplistic, he suggests, to attempt 'to put the value-laden issues of politics to one side . . . and focus on the more limited issues of how to perform tasks more efficiently'.

This point is of more than theoretical significance. As already observed, allocating resources in the public sector is often a highly political exercise. Thus, 'responsible managers' seeking value for money under the FMI might find themselves confronting policy issues. (For example, they may wish to increase staff at a time when government is committed to reducing civil service numbers.) In government, in other words, ends cannot be divorced from means, nor policy from management. To quote Lee (1984, p. 5), behind the FMI 'lie many unanswered questions . . . . [The] political function [of ministers and departments] cannot be easily translated into the language of financial management'.

ii) EQUITY

The managerial approach also has important implications for the concept of equitable administration. The idea of decentralization to departmental units of accountable management not only undermines the hierarchical authority structure traditionally used in bureaucracies to enforce equitable application of departmental rules (see p. 26), but its underlying aim, as Gray and Jenkins (1985, p. 157) warn, 'may be to downgrade . . . the search for fairness and equity of treatment . . . since such practices may not be *value for money*'. In the private sector, where equity is less important (and in some cases absent), the search for value for money conflicts with no particular value systems, but in the public sector it does.

iii) ACCOUNTABILITY

The concept of accountability – especially external accountability – is also much more pronounced in the public than in the private sector (see p. 9), and the FMI, by delegating responsibilities to line managers and accountable units, conflicts sharply with the traditional pattern of accountability in central administration. Whereas the convention of ministerial responsibility holds ministers accountable for all departmental work (see Chapter 14), the FMI assigns to departmental cost-centre managers responsibility for securing value for money. As Lee (1984, p. 5) suggests, 'on the face of it, the [FMI] should mean that ministers cannot be held responsible for actions taken by their officials under the new delegated responsibilities'.

These developments, it can be argued, far from weakening Whitehall accountability may strengthen it. The FMI not only provides ministers (through management information systems) with increased knowledge about departmental activities, but also reinforces what Gray and Jenkins (1985, ch. 6) describe as the traditional legal rational code of accountability with a primarily financial code stressing effective and efficient accountability. There has also, theoretically at least, been a shift from ministerial to civil service accountability, arguably mirroring the fact that ministers today rarely accept personal responsibility for their officials' mistakes (see Chapter 14). This development, when seen alongside the now routine questioning of civil servants by 'Commons select committees (see Chapter 14), presents the possibility of 'responsible' departmental managers answering directly to MPs for their stewardship. As Robinson (1985, p. 42) puts it, 'the FMI merely adds a new twist to the whole question of . . . civil servants' answerability to Parliament'.

Nevertheless, constitutionally, ministerial responsibility is incompatible with the FMI. While those taking a 'realistic' view (believing that the convention no longer applies in true form) do not regard this as a problem, adherents to the 'traditional' view (mainly academics and some senior civil servants) argue that it is (Robinson *et al.*, 1987, especially pp. 62–8). One academic, Jones (ibid., p. 65), argues that, because of the implications for ministerial responsibility, the FMI should be 'terminated', while Gray and Jenkins (1985, p. 161) feel that the weakening of the convention, together with increased reliance upon professional codes – such as the values of auditors and accountants – may lead to 'the disintegration of. . . accountability itself'. These views stress the difficulty of harmonizing essentially private sector norms with traditional public sector concepts and constitutional requirements.

Perhaps the likeliest outcome, however, is that little will change. Metcalfe and Richards (1984, p. 51) suggest that continuing attachment to constitutional norms will make civil servants reluctant to exercise managerial discretion. Plowden (1985, p. 400) foresees a similar possibility, that ministers' constitutional responsibility, coupled with sophisticated information systems, will produce increased ministerial intervention, 'frustrating the intentions to give officials the discretion they need to manage effectively'. Again, while the idea that officials exercising delegated authority should be directly accountable to Parliament may seem logical, it ignores the political reality of government domination which has traditionally characterized executive/legislative relationships in Britain. Significantly, the government, when launching the FMI, rejected recommendations of the Treasury and Civil Service Committee (1982) designed to strengthen Parliament's role (for example, by enabling departmental select committees to request the Comptroller and Auditor General to review departmental efficiency and effectiveness). While, therefore, the FMI might provide a potential for developing greater, or at least different, accountability, it seems unlikely, at least in the short term, to bring significantly increased accountability to Parliament for the work of central administration. As Gray and Jenkins (1985, p. 165) put it, the FMI 'might allow a change in the public image of accountability without much affecting its practice'.

Public administration or public management?

At root the managerialist approach assumes that private sector managerial techniques can be smoothly implanted into the public sector. But is this the case? Certainly, on the evidence to date, the savings achieved by efficiency scrutinies, the enhanced departmental knowledge available to ministers through information systems, and the increased resource consciousness among civil servants brought about by the FMI, would suggest that the public sector has much to gain by the introduction of managerial techniques originated in the private sector. What has also emerged, however, is that private sector attitudes and techniques cannot *easily* be transplanted into central administration. The policy implications of resource management and the administrative culture of Whitehall, departmental policy interests and the political orientations of ministers, concerns about equity and accountability, and the technical difficulties of effective performance measurement, all stand as obstacles to further progress, obstacles which may not be removed easily in the absence of a powerful central authority to co-ordinate and force the pace of future change. Of course, some of these difficulties *may* be surmounted if the structure of Whitehall is itself radically altered, with departmental policy-making effectively separated from executive functions carried out by semi-autonomous agencies as proposed in the 1988 Ibbs *Next Steps* Report (see Chapter 2).

What perhaps all this suggests is that public administration is more than private management writ public. The public sector has a political environment, theoretical foundations, an ethos, a culture and a sheer diversity which makes it distinctive from the private sector. Perhaps, also, civil service culture can only be truly changed by changing the civil service itself, not through retraining and re-educating existing officials, but by wholesale – albeit inevitably long-term – changes in personnel through new recruitment practices and procedures. Failure to recognize and to allow for this may explain why, even after nine years of Thatcherite 'political clout', doubt still exists about the extent of real cultural change within Whitehall and whether 'lasting reforms' have, or ever will be, achieved.

8 LOCAL GOVERNMENT: THE ADMINISTRATIVE AND POLITICAL CONTEXT

Administrative complexity

British local government superficially appears straightforward with its neat pattern of elected local authorities. In practice, however, government at the local level is particularly confusing because of the variety of agencies which help to shape and administer local services. This complex web includes: a) local and regional offices of central government departments, such as the DSS and DOE (see Young, 1982); b) non-departmental public bodies usually dealing with a single specialized function, such as health and water authorities; c) decentralized units of public corporations, such as electricity boards; d) innumerable autonomous and semi-autonomous official and quasi-official organizations, each with its part to play in the policy-making process, such as tenants' liaison committees and youth service advisory councils (see Cousins, 1982, 1983); e) elected local government (see Figure 8.2). Complexity is compounded because of the large number of non-governmental agencies operating locally; these include local political parties, local pressure groups, professional bodies, and industrial and commercial concerns. All of these can, on occasions, be important elements in local policy-making (Dunleavy and Rhodes, 1987).

The main focus of this chapter is elected local government, but this in itself is organizationally far from simple. There are 514 principal local authorities in Great Britain: 404 authorities in England, 65 in Scotland and 45 in Wales. Throughout the 'shire' areas of England, the whole of Wales and mainland Scotland there are two tiers of multi-purpose local authorities. Between 1974 and 1986 there had also been two tiers in Greater London and the six metropolitan counties in England, but this position was changed from 1 April 1986, when the upper-tier authorities were abolished. Their functions were transferred partly to lower-tier authorities, partly to new single-purpose joint authorities and in part to the Secretary of State.

Outside the metropolitan areas, complex *vertical* relationships (such as those between county councils and district councils) co-exist alongside *horizontal* relationships (such as those between different district councils within the same county). Additionally, there are invariably complicated networks of relationships between different departments *within* a single local authority. As Stanyer (1976, ch. 1) reminds us, it is important to see each locality as a miniature political and administrative system in its own right, a point reinforced by the Widdicombe Report (1986, p. 22) when the committee emphasized that 'some of the commonly held assumptions about local government are valid only in a minority of authorities'. Generalizing about local government can be hazardous.

Development and structure

Elected local government is big business. In Great Britain there are some 20,650 district and borough councillors and some 4,100 county, regional and islands councillors. This averages out at one councillor for every 2,200 members of the population although as Widdicombe (1986, paras 213–16) notes there are major disparities. In Birmingham, for example, there is one councillor for every 8,600 people. In Powys, on the other hand, there is one for every 590 people. These authorities employ some 2.35m staff (1987) and, collectively, they are responsible for providing over fifty different services. Their scale is demonstrated by the fact that just over 25 per cent of all public sector spending in Britain is accounted for by local authorities. Indeed, if local authorities were listed in terms of expenditure, 89 authorities would appear amongst the top 500 British companies. Quite clearly, local government deserves a major place in any study of British public administration.

THE TRADITIONAL PATTERN

The major features of local government in England and Wales were laid down by the 1835 Municipal Corporations Act and by three statutes at the end of the nineteenth century: the Local Government Acts of 1888 and 1894, and the London Government Act, 1899. These Acts created a comprehensive pattern of local authorities throughout England and Wales providing a wide range of services. With some modifications the structure lasted until the 1972 Local Government Act ushered in a new pattern of elected local administration which became operative from 1 April 1974, although this was further amended by the 1985 Local Government Act. Figure 8.1 outlines the structure of local government in England and Wales immediately prior to 1 April 1974. There were, however, a number of weaknesses in the traditional pattern, notably:

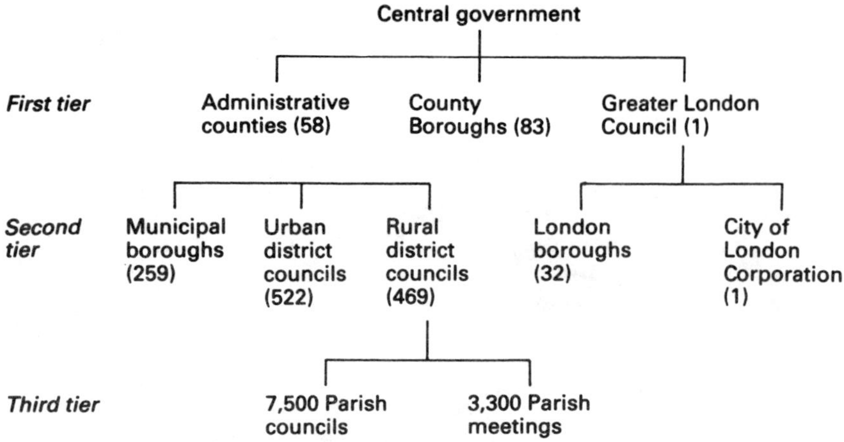

Figure 8.1 The pre-April 1974 structure of local government in England and Wales (as at March 1974).

(i) *Outdated structure.* When the local government map was laid down at the end of the nineteenth century, many of the administrative units – for example, Anglo-Saxon shires and medieval boroughs – were already outdated. During the twentieth century, as the residential pattern of communities changed, the local government structure became increasingly irrational.

(ii) *Disparities of size.* The above factors also produced wide disparities between local authorities of the same type, often producing a mismatch between resources and functions. In particular, many authorities were too small to provide an efficient standard of service (for example, the smallest housing authority, Tintwistle RDC, had a population of only 1,490).

(iii) *Administrative confusion.* There were nine different types of elected local authority. In the more built-up areas services were often provided by all-purpose county boroughs; however, in rural areas services were split between the county council and urban/rural district/municipal borough authorities. County councils, moreover, frequently subdivided their territory for administrative purposes. Education and social services, for example, were invariably administered from decentralized 'area' offices as well as from County Hall. From the consumer's standpoint, in particular, the 'old' system was therefore frequently extremely complex.

(iv) *Fragmentation of responsibility.* In many areas local services were provided by numerous different authorities, which often gave rise to acute co-ordination problems. Imagine, for example, the difficulties of community-wide planning on Merseyside where there were twenty-three local authorities (excluding parishes).

REORGANIZATION

Structural change always needs to be seen in its environmental context. As society evolved from the end of the nineteenth century, so pressure for local government reorganization increased. In London, population movement from inner London to the suburbs meant that the old London County Council's administrative network had largely outlived its usefulness and in 1957 the Royal Commission on Local Government in Greater London was established to examine the London conurbation, including the Home Counties. This reported in 1960 (the Herbert Report), and in 1963 the London Government Act set a broad boundary to the London area and gave shared responsibilty for its local services to the Greater London Council (GLC), and to thirty-two London boroughs and the City of London. Until its abolition on 31 March 1986 strategic planning functions resided with the top tier (GLC), while more personal services were administered by the boroughs. In addition, some services were shared under special arrangements (for example, education in inner London was made the responsibility of the Inner London Education Authority which initially consisted of members of the GLC from inner London plus a representative from each of the inner London boroughs), while others continue to be the sole responsibility of special agencies (the Metropolitan Police, for instance, answers directly to the Home Secretary). In 1990 ILEA is scheduled to be abolished with the relevant boroughs taking the education function back to themselves.

In 1966 two separate Royal Commissions were established to investigate local government in England (excluding London) and Scotland. When the Redcliffe-Maud Commission (on England) reported in 1969 it recommended the abolition of the old structure and the establishment of a new pattern of local authorities. Its solution, outside the urban conurbations, was unitary multi-purpose authorities (with from 250,000 to 1m inhabitants). The existing two-tier system, it recommended, should be replaced by fifty-eight unitary authorities which would cover most of the country, but in three metropolitan areas there was to be a two-tier arrangement with responsibilities divided between a metropolitan county council and large district authorities (along lines similar to those then operating in Greater London).

While the Labour government basically accepted these proposals (see *Local Government Reform in England*, 1970) the Conservatives, who came to power in 1970, produced alternative ideas which were ultimately incorporated into the 1972 Local Government Act. The concept of unitary authorities was rejected in favour of a rationalized two-tier system.

The Conservatives argued that the size of authority recommended by Redcliffe-Maud (serving populations between 250,000 and 1m) was too large; hence the need for a division of responsibilities between county and districts. Interestingly, the Wheatley Commission on Scotland also favoured a two-tier system. Likewise Derek Senior's minority report to the Royal Commission on Local Government in England favoured a two-tier system, although one based on the concept of the city region. The Conservative government's proposals divided the whole of England and Wales into two major tiers (plus parish councils as a third tier). The first tier was to be based largely on existing counties; the major changes were destined to take place in the second tier, the district level. Parish councils (community councils in Wales) made up the third tier which had both minor service and advisory functions at grass-roots level.

THE NEW SYSTEM IN ENGLAND AND WALES

Outside Greater London, a reorganized local government system was created by a series of Acts of Parliament passed during the period 1972–4. The 1985 and 1988 Local Government Acts further modified structures both inside and outside London (see below), p. 148.

The 1972 Local Government Act abolished the eighty-three county boroughs in England and Wales and reduced the fifty-eight county councils to forty-seven, ranging from populations of 110,000 (Powys) to 1.5m (Hampshire). Within these counties, 1,250 municipal boroughs, urban and rural district councils were replaced by 333 district councils with populations ranging from 396,000 (Bristol) to 21,500 (Radnor).

In the major urban conurbations six metropolitan counties (Greater Manchester, Merseyside, West Midlands, Tyne and Wear, South Yorkshire and West Yorkshire) were created containing thirty-six metropolitan districts with populations ranging from 158,000 (South Tyneside) to almost 1.1m (Birmingham). As noted above, however, on 31 March 1986 these six metropolitan counties along with the GLC were abolished and their functions largely relocated to metropolitan district councils (boroughs in London) or to non-directly elected joint boards. A significant proportion of urban England, therefore, now has only one tier of elected local government.

As a third tier, parish councils have been retained in England (known as community councils in Wales). There are some 10,204 parish councils in England and 808 community councils in Wales. Small parishes (with under 200 electors) may instead hold parish meetings which all local electors can attend. Additionally, in some urban areas neighbourhood councils have been formed but these have no statutory functions and merely provide a sounding board for local opinion. Figure 8.2 provides a summary of the present pattern of local government in England and Wales.

	England A	England B	Wales
Top tier (county councils)	39	0	8
Second tier (district councils)	296	69	37

A: Non-Metropolitan areas
B: Metropolitan areas (that is, areas covered by the former GLC and six Metropolitan county areas). Since 1986 there is no top tier in these areas.

Figure 8.2 Local authorities in England and Wales, 1988.

THE NEW SYSTEM IN SCOTLAND

In Scotland 'modern' local government was established by Acts of 1889, which created county councils, and 1900, which regularized town government. At the third tier, parish councils were created in 1894 and charged with administering poor relief. Just as the development of Scottish local government closely paralleled that in England so, too, its 'reform' followed closely on the heels of English and Welsh reorganization.

The (Wheatley) Royal Commission on Local Government in Scotland (1966–9) saw its proposals (1969) largely adopted by the Conservative government in the Local Government (Scotland) Act, 1973, which became effective in May 1975. As in England, the Scottish Commission identified large numbers of small authorities as a major weakness of the old system. The 'new' pattern saw fewer, larger authorities. There are now nine regional councils (ranging from Strathclyde with 2.3m inhabitants down to the Borders with 101,000) and fifty-three district councils (ranging from 744,000 in Glasgow to 10,000 in Badenoch and Strathspey). In addition, three island authorities were given virtually all-purpose status. At the third-tier level are some 1,350 community councils. Figure 8.3 presents the contemporary Scottish structure in diagrammatic form.

First tier	Regional councils (9)	Island councils (3)
Second tier	District councils (53)	
Third tier	Community councils (1,350)	

Figure 8.3 Local government in Scotland since May 1975.

The post-1974 pattern of local government throughout Britain appears substantially different from that which it replaced. But to what extent did the changes constitute 'reform'? A major objective of the reform movement was the rationalization of geographical areas with the aim of producing more efficient services, yet some very small organizational units still provide crucial services (such as housing, education, social services). With reorganization, moreover, local government lost some important services to other agencies. Under the Water Act (1973) the powers hitherto exercised by English and Welsh local authorities in water supply and sewage disposal were transferred to ten new regional water authorities. Likewise, in 1974 local authority health powers in England and Wales were transferred to newly created, non-elected health authorities (see Chapter 13).

ABOLITION OF THE GLC AND THE 'MET' COUNTIES

As noted above there was further structural change in the 1980s. The 1983 Conservative Party manifesto argued (p. 37) that the six metropolitan county councils and the GLC had 'been shown to be a wasteful and unnecessary tier of government'. In a White Paper, *Streamlining the Cities* (1983), the Conservative government set out its case for further structural change. The government argued that the six 'mets' and the GLC were a superfluous tier of government, very much junior partners to their constituent district (borough) councils in terms of service provision. Additionally it was maintained that the GLC and the six 'mets' had sought an outlet for their energies by developing a general strategic role which had led to conflict with lower-tier authorities (such as on land use planning) and to duplication (such as on economic development). There was also conflict with central government as authorities assumed a 'mandate' on issues such as defence and foreign policy. With their large rate base and relative remoteness from ratepayers the White Paper argued that they had pursued unrealistic spending policies.

The government anticipated a financial saving of at least £120m a year with abolition, but denied that the change would undermine local democracy. Indeed, the White Paper maintained that there would, in fact, be enhanced local accountability as the more accessible boroughs and districts would be responsible for a fuller range of services.

After what was often an acrimonious debate the 1985 Local Government Act ultimately emerged. It abolished the six 'mets' and the GLC with effect from 31 March 1986. These seven authorities had constantly exceeded government expenditure targets and had frequently engaged in 'socialist' policies which hardly endeared them to the Thatcher government.

One of the most controversial aspects of the 1985 Act was the way in which crucially important services hitherto provided by the GLC and the six 'mets' were transferred not to elected second-tier authorities but to non-directly elected joint boards. The major spending services of the Metropolitan counties (police, fire, public transport and probation), which accounted for some 70 per cent of their expenditure, were transferred to such joint boards (notably Fire and Civil Defence Boards, Police Boards, Transport Boards). These are composed largely of local councillors indirectly *appointed* by their local authority but *not directly elected* to these bodies. Some commentators see such developments as further evidence of the erosion of local democracy.

In London the post-April 1986 picture became particularly complex. By 1987 there were some seventy-seven successor bodies to the GLC – some statutory such as the Fire, Civil Defence and Waste Disposal boards, but mostly voluntary with boroughs co-operating in groups such as the Greater London Ecology Unit and the London Boroughs Grant Scheme (with leading boroughs operating on an agency basis). Other former GLC functions went to the Thames Water Authority, Arts Council, Historic Buildings and Monuments Commission, and English Heritage. Still others went to the Department of Transport and the Department of the Environment. About a dozen services were transferred to the directly elected London boroughs.

From 1986, when the GLC was abolished, the Inner London Education Authority (ILEA) became a directly elected body although the 1988 Local Government Act abolished ILEA with effect from April 1990, the educational function being transferred to the relevant Inner London boroughs.

It seems clear that, despite the Conservative government's emphasis on decentralization and accountability as objectives of abolition in London, the net result has been an increase in centralization and a reduction of both financial and democratic accountability. There were seventeen precepting bodies operating in the first year of the new system and a larger number of *ad hoc* bodies which could levy funds. This fragmentation following the 1986 restructuring produced a lack of co-ordination and an absence of overall control. Additionally, of course, such a diverse distribution of services amongst so many bodies is a potential nightmare for the ordinary consumer. From the 'street-level bureaucracy' standpoint there appeared to be little sense in the new arrangements and they were frequently viewed as the product of political pragmatism rather than administrative reasoning.

The post-1972 period has thus witnessed important *structural* changes in British local administration. But, as Stanyer (1976, p. 55) has observed: 'It is necessary to understand what a local authority is in legal terms in a particular governmental system only as a prelude to understanding what all local authorities are in behavioural terms'. The structures created between 1963 and 1988 provided a new administra-

Metropolitan districts (excluding London)		*Responsible for*
		Education Housing Personal social services Planning Environmental health Leisure services
	via joint boards	Transport Police Fire Civil Defence
Non-metropolitan counties		Police, Fire, Refuse disposal (districts in Wales) Consumer protection (districts in Wales) Major roads, planning (structure) Education, Social Services Libraries, Transport Parks and recreation Museums and galleries Baths
Non-metropolitan districts		As metropolitan districts *minus* education and personal social services (and police, fire and civil defence).
London London boroughs		Housing, Social Services Leisure, Public Health Education (Outer London boroughs currently; Inner London boroughs also from 1990)
	via joint boards	Fire Civil Defence

Figure 8.4 Local government: who does what in England and Wales, 1988.

tive framework for local government but such structures in themselves reveal relatively little about the *practice* of local administration.

The functions of local authorities

Local government is both a provider of services to a local authority and an instrument of democratic self-government. On pp. 154–6 we examine the 'democratic' dimension of local government; this section delineates local authority services.

Protective	*Environmental*	*Personal*	*Social/ Recreation*	*Trading*
Fire	Highways	Education	Sporting facilities	Markets
Police	Environmental health	Housing	Museums	Smallholdings
Consumer protection		Careers	Art galleries	Transport undertakings
Animal disease	Planning	Social services	Theatres	
Licensing (e.g. cinemas)	Strategic Planning		Camp sites	

Figure 8.5 Classification of local government services.

Local authorities can only do what the law explicitly allows; all council powers come from Acts of Parliament. Indeed, local government itself exists only by courtesy of Parliament and Parliament frequently alters its powers and functions. Should any local authority provide a service not specifically permitted by Parliament it would be acting illegally, or *ultra vires* (see Chapter 15). Nevertheless, despite the advent of 'contracting out', local authorities still carry out over fifty functions; indeed, the average British citizen probably has more contact with the state through the services provided by local government than through the outputs of any other level of public administration.

The diversity of services outlined in Figure 8.4 makes any classification somewhat arbitrary. However, Figure 8.5 offers a useful starting point for discussion. As this shows, local authorities provide services in five major fields, although with many of them (such as education, housing, social services) other agencies such as government departments, *ad hoc* authorities and voluntary associations may also play some part in implementation.

Services are not, of course, provided uniformly throughout the country. Slum clearance, for example, is only a major problem in some areas. Again, standards of service may vary; beyond the minimum standards which are usually laid down by law there is, in practice, often a wide area of discretion. Not all functions, moreover, are mandatory upon local authorities; some, like the provision of leisure centres, art galleries and playing fields are permissive (which means the authority has a choice whether or not to provide them). It is open to any authority, moreover, to promote a private Bill in order to extend its powers. Although a complex and costly procedure, over the years many authorities have acquired powers by this means to perform particular functions in their localities: for example, to maintain the external decoration of listed buildings (Kensington and Chelsea), and to operate a municipal bank (Birmingham). As this latter example suggests, there is also a wide and varied range of trading activities carried out by local authorities (see Chapter 12).

Additionally, since the Local Government Act, 1972 (section 137), local authorities have had general power to spend up to the product of a 2p rate on purposes not specifically authorized by statute. Consequently, while local authorities in Britain do not have a 'general competence' to do whatever they wish in their local areas, the variation in functions and standards between one authority and another may be considerable – to an extent which seemingly belies the simplicity of lists of services such as those contained in Figures 8.4 and 8.5. For example, there have been a large number of initiatives by local authorities in recent years intended to improve the local economy, many of which have been undertaken under section 137 of the Local Government Act 1972, to incur expenditure which in the authority's opinion is in the interests of their area. 'Local authorities are playing a part in the promotion of co-operatives, in training schemes, in business advice centres, in the development of new technology and in support for individual firms through rent subsidies, grants and guarantees' (Widdicombe 1986, para. 288). Neat organization charts simply belie reality.

The Government's White Paper responding to Widdicombe (Department of Environment *et al.*, 1988) proposes to give councils a new specific power outside S137 (S83 in Scotland) to carry out economic development. The financial limit for S137/83, currently the product of a 2p rate, will become £5 per head of population for London boroughs and metropolitan districts and £2.50 in areas with two tiers of principal councils. The powers to vary this by order will remain. This approximately halves the amount of money available for discretionary spending, even though the White Paper accepts that only twenty-one English councils were spending up to 80 per cent of their S137 limit and two-thirds of S137 spending was an economic development.

Inter-authority relationships

Further complexity in the pattern of service provision stems from the two-tier nature of much of contemporary local government, especially with services (such as planning) where responsibility is shared between districts and counties. Close liaison between authorities is obviously important in such cases, as well as in those where different authorities provide related services (such as social services and housing). This problem is particularly acute in the area of homelessness – a 'social services' condition with a housing 'remedy' (Alexander, 1982b, p. 59). Of course, co-ordination is invariably more difficult to achieve between organizations than within a single organization.

At reorganization in 1974 the functions of local government were split between four main organizational units – counties, districts, health authorities and water authorities – and relatively sophisticated consultative machinery had to be established in many areas in order to obtain local co-ordinated action. In practice, however, such arrangements have often tended to cause further confusion (particularly for consumers), as well as to create acrimony between the authorities concerned. Such acrimony has often been exacerbated, moreover, because of the tendency since the 1974 reorganization for authorities 'to view the relationship between the tiers as an adversary one' (Alexander, 1982a, p. 65); and also because of the problem of 'competing mandates' (Alexander, 1982b, p. 54) where authorities at different levels in an area pursuing different policies (and often controlled by different parties) both claim to be acting in the local interest.

One way in which liaison (and confusion) has been institutionalized is by use of agency agreements between authorities. Section 101 of the Local Government Act, 1972, makes it possible for one authority to appoint another as its agent to carry out its statutory duties – this applies to all functions except education, social services and emergency services. In practice the major use of such agreements has been in the sphere of highway maintenance and construction, where old county boroughs and large urban districts have invaribly continued to provide the service on behalf of their county council. They have not infrequently been a source of acrimony between the authorities involved, as well as of wider problems. As Alexander (1982, p. 30) notes, agency agreements, superimposed 'on an already complicated allocation' of local authority functions, have added to the confusion experienced by consumers in service provision and 'ensured that the processes of public accountability and democratic control would be so convoluted as to raise serious doubts about their effectiveness'.

A further source of friction and confusion is found where authorities have concurrent powers; that is, an equal share in providing services. The best example is planning, of which the White Paper on Reorganization (*Local Government in England*, 1971, para. 17) observed: 'All planning applications should be made to district councils . . . . Responsibility for broad planning policies and for the development of both structure and local plans must, however, rest with the county councils.' In practice these arrangements, like agency agreements, have given rise to confusion and friction, as well as in some cases to delay in determining applications. Ultimately the position was rationalized by the Local Government, Planning and Land Act, 1980, which restricted the definition of a 'county matter' and specified that all planning applications would be initially handled by district councils.

Liaison between authorities is facilitated by the establishment of forums for different authorities to discuss matters of mutual concern. Some of these (such as the East Midlands Forum of County Councils) operate on a regional basis, others on a county basis. Following the 1974 reorganization most counties established county liaison committees representing the county council and all the district councils within it, although these have generally proved ineffective and some have been abandoned. Inter-district liaison, however, has proved more successful, being facilitated either by specially formed joint consultative committees or through county branches of the Association of District Councils (Alexander, 1982, especially ch. 3). (The latter association, along with the other two major local authority associations – the Association of Metropolitan Associations and the Association of County Councils – and professional bodies such as SOLACE (Society of Local Authority Chief Executives) also provide opportunities for liaison at national level.) While forums such as these can take a community-wide approach, they rarely have executive power, being largely bodies for debate and comment. Councillor bodies are often paralleled at officer level and it is not uncommon to see different outlooks prevail – a further dimension of complexity.

The *formal* relationships outlined above need to be complemented by an appreciation of *informal* linkages, such as the sharing of knowledge and experience through the regional branches of professional associations. *Policy networks* (such as local government professionals, 'interested' councillors, local pressure groups, local/specialist journalists, and so on) are also generally of far more practical importance than is often realized. Likewise, Rotary, Round Table, and similar organizations can be important integrative tools. Liaison is often further facilitated by overlapping membership between county and district councils: Widdicombe (1986, vol. 2, Table 4.2) shows that some 13 per cent of all councillors are on two (or more) authorities.

Such structures and networks, however, have generally failed to offset the inherent fragmentation of the post-1986 local government system or the inbuilt suspicions which have accompanied recent reorganizations. In what is invariably an increasingly highly charged party political arena the goal of co-ordinated local action is often difficult to sustain.

Local politics and democracy

Some observers, like Sharpe (1970), argue that the strongest justification for elected local government is its claim to be an efficient provider of services. Because different communities have different needs, the system of government needs to be flexible; local government allegedly provides this by enabling local councillors, drawn from and accountable to the local electorate, to determine local priorities. While such claims are today being challenged by the proponents of privatization, it is as an efficient provider of services that the claims of local government mainly seem to rest.

Local government, however, is also widely regarded as an instrument of democratic self-government. The Redcliffe-Maud Commission, for example, was required to have regard to the need 'to sustain a viable system of local democracy', the assumption being that it was already democratic. What, then, are the grounds upon which local government can be said to promote democracy?

THEORIES OF LOCAL DEMOCRACY

Democratic government does not necessarily entail locally elected councils. Indeed, one strand of continental thinking argues that democracy is essentially concerned with the nation-state and with majority rule, equality and uniformity. From such a perspective local government is seen as parochial, concerned with inequalities and differences between localities. This stance, however, contrasts with the traditional British view that local government enhances democracy, both by providing a vehicle of political education and as a means of increasing the liberty of the citizen by breaking down the power of the centralized state. This view emphasizes that democracy is not simply concerned with national majority rule, social and political equality, and uniformity of standards but is, rather, an essential means of enabling individuals and local communities to voice their needs. (For discussion, see Sharpe, 1970; Smith, 1969.)

PARTICIPATION

Participation, it is often held, can be more widely achieved at the local than the national level. Elected local government enables 'ordinary' people to participate in the work of government without the disruption to their careers and domestic life that national office usually involves. Moving from theory to practice, however, it is clear that public interest in British local government is low, with turnout in local elections much lower than in most European countries. Only about 40 per cent of the electorate vote in local elections (the turnout in the 1985 English shire county elections, for example, was 41 per cent) but such a figure can be highly misleading. Stanyer (1976, pp. 271–2), for example, points out that in 1967 the turnout in Maidstone Rural District was 14.7 per cent while that in Knighton Rural District was 89.6 per cent. The dangers of generalizing about 'apathy' on the basis of aggregate data can be further highlighted by variation in turnout between different wards in the same authority. For example, in the 1986 District Council elections turnout in wards in Leicester City ranged from 28 per cent to 61 per cent. Patterns of participation, even at this minimal level of voting, cannot be divorced from the local social and political environment.

POLITICAL PARTIES

Party politics is now an established part of contemporary local government. In 1972, before reorganization, only 53 per cent of local authorities were run on party lines. By 1985 the proportion of councils in party political control had risen to 84 per cent (Widdicombe, 1986, vol. 1, Table 2.1). The 16 per cent of authorities where Independents are dominant are mostly in the more rural parts of Scotland, England and Wales, but as Widdicombe notes (1986, vol. 1, p. 23) 'the overall figure does perhaps represent a stronger resilience of the Independent tradition in an era of increasing party politicisation than might have been anticipated'. Partisan local administration has, however, quite clearly arrived in the bulk of British local authorities. This development is not uncontroversial. The view is still quite widespread that local government is about local issues and that party politics should not intrude. However, this view is somewhat idealistic, particularly given the increased size of local authority units following reorganization.

According to Dunsire (1956, p. 87), political parties are the 'indispensable element in the conversion of local councils into responsible governments'. Compared with shifting coalitions of Independent councillors, party groupings can make for coherent policy planning and administration. To some extent, of course, local party politics is simply national party politics writ small – the electorate frequently votes on the basis of non-local factors, something well illustrated in 1982 when the local elections were, as Crewe remarked (*The Times*, 8 May 1982, p. 2), 'a referendum' on the central government's 'handling of the Falklands crisis' – a far cry from the local population choosing its local decision-makers on the basis of local political issues.

In his study of Wolverhampton, Jones (1969, pp. 348–9) maintained that 'the parties have enabled individuals to devise a programme of policies and to implement it, and they have presented these programmes to the public in a dramatic and comprehensive way, enabling the public to judge a team of men and measures; thus the accountability of government to the electorate has been strengthened'. This situation is, of course, only one of an infinite number of models but while it is clearly impossible to generalize about the impact of party politics, any attempt to understand local public administration without reference to the party-political dimension is doomed to failure.

While public administration in most localities is now firmly entrenched within a party political environment, precise management styles vary considerably. Two adjacent Labour-controlled authorities, for example, may operate quite differently. Bulpitt (1967) found that in Manchester Labour group discipline was looser than in Salford. In Rochdale, where the Liberals held the balance of power, there was loose discipline and little formal party organization in the council chamber. Some contemporary Labour groups have very open decision-making structures; others are dominated by the party leader. The Conservative party's belief in hierarchy generally gives their leaderships considerable leverage, but again generalization is dangerous. Research volume 1 of the Widdicombe Report (1986) provides a wealth of information about the extent and nature of party policies in local government.

The government's 1988 White Paper (Department of Environment *et al.*, 1988) rejected as too extensive Widdicombe's proposal that all principal officers and above be banned from being members of other main councils or being active politically. The White Paper instead proposed that prohibition would apply to chief executives, chief officers, deputies and others who regularly advise or act on behalf of their councils – a concerted attempt to reduce the impact of 'twin tracking' in local politics.

PRESSURE GROUPS

Pressure group activity at the local level is considerable. Partly because of the diverse interests within local communities but also because of the ineffectiveness in many areas of more institutionalized channels – bureaucratic officials, unresponsive councillors, decaying parties, and so on – their role in local politics has tended to increase. In Birmingham, Newton (1976, chs 3 and 4) identified over 4,000 organized groups and estimated that there were probably about twice that number in total. Other studies have shown similarly extensive local group activity but in Birmingham, only about one-third were politcally active and most of these (63 per cent) were involved only with a single issue. Many groups have very specific and limited demands (such as over local amenities) and when the particular issue has been resolved they disband.

Dearlove's study (1973, ch. 8) of Kensington and Chelsea showed that the council's response to groups revolved largely around councillor assessment of them. Some groups were not favourably received, partly because they had little to offer the council but also because they were seen as making 'unreasonable' demands on the local authority –

that is, demands which did not square with the councillors' own policy predispositions. Other groups (such as the WRVS and housing associations) were seen as 'helpful', since they had something to contribute (cheap welfare provision or extra housing). Likewise, Newton's 'established' groups built up a 'close set' of relationships with public officials in Birmingham (1976, p. 85), while his poorly established groups found it difficult to gain access to decision-makers and thereby had to resort to demonstrations, petitions and so on which only served to make them even more unacceptable.

The local pressure group world does not provide equal access to all. Ethnic minority groupings, squatters and welfare rights workers, for example, usually fare badly in comparison with *status quo* middle-class groups. Again, though, generalization is dangerous since some 'radical' socialist councils may respond favourably to groups challenging traditional norms (see Stoker, 1988). Equally, of course, as Dearlove (1979, p. 49) emphasizes, the inactivity of a particular section of the local population (such as the National Union of Mineworkers in some mining areas) 'may occur precisely because that interest is built into the very heart of the council itself'. While pressure-group influence varies over time and from issue to issue, such groupings must now be seen as an integral part of local public administration.

NON-LOCAL INFLUENCES

Dunleavy argues that too frequently local policy-making is explained purely in terms of factors internal to specific localities. He maintains (1980a, p. 163) that far greater attention should be paid to non-local influences, asserting that 'local political studies have fundamentally failed to explain the observed regularity of urban policy change across many decentralized authorities'. In the educational sphere, for example, he points to the uniformity of local education authorities in adopting a tripartite system of secondary education following the 1944 Education Act. Then, from the late 1960s, most LEAs reorganized on comprehensive lines. In this and other cited areas (such as the development of high-rise flats and the commercial redevelopment of numerous town centres since the 1950s), central government did more than simply exhort – it provided financial incentives to help secure compliance.

Local authorities do not generally make policy decisions in isolation. 'In particular, over and above their local roles, councils are located and locate themselves in what may be termed the "national local government system"' (Dunleavy, 1980a, p. 105). Local authority associations, national party organizations, public service trade unions, professional bodies and the innumerable journals, conferences and publications help the nationalizing of innovations in local services.

Local public administration clearly needs to be seen in the context of the broader political, social and economic system.

Two points about Dunleavy's framework can usefully be raised: (a) He tends to assume that what applies in the case of high-rise flats or town-centre redevelopment applies in other areas of policy-making; (b) He places a heavy emphasis on the nationalizing of urban policy change, arguing (1980a, p. 98) that within 'broad limits the decentralised authorities implementing policies have moved in step with a precision that cries out for explanation'. Surely this is an exaggeration. It is possible to provide examples of policy patterns (such as provision for the disabled) varying considerably across the country. Further, the cited examples from education and planning stretch Dunleavy's 'broad limits' to breaking point. Although nationwide policy changes are observable, this should not obscure the fact that there remains considerable variety in the policy and practice of local authorities.

Financing local government

Local government finance is important both economically and politically: *economically* because about one quarter of all public expenditure is spent by local authorities; *politically* because the finance available to local government largely determines the level of services which it can provide. Whilst it is theoretically true at the time of writing that local authorities, through the rates, currently have a source of finance independent of central government, finance which can be spent on any object within their statutory jurisdiction, this is not the whole story. In reality the picture is far more complex than that.

Understanding local government finance is not easy (see Greenwood, 1988b). As a starting point, however, it is helpful to make a distinction (although the two do interconnect) between *current* (or *revenue*) finance and *capital* finance.

CURRENT (OR REVENUE) FINANCE

In 1984/5 local authorities in England incurred a total of £39.6bn revenue account expenditure. Such expenditure is used to pay for items of a relatively short-term nature (such as wages and postage). The *income* to finance that expenditure (£41.8bn in 1984/5) was raised from three main sources: 1) rates, £11.3bn (27 per cent); 2) government grants, £16.4bn (39.2 per cent); 3) charges and miscellaneous £14.1bn (33.8 per cent) (all figures from Travers, 1986. Tables App. 2, 3 and 7). While the proportion received from the various sources will obviously vary from authority to authority, virtually all will receive some revenue from all three.

(1) Rates

Local rates have long been a controversial source of local authority income. They are a form of taxation levied on local property, and are calculated on the basis of the rent at which the property might reasonably be let. Each year the rating authority fixes a rate in the pound and the occupier is obliged to pay rates at that poundage. For example, if a property has a rateable value of £100 and the local authority sets its rate at 54.5p the full rates payable would be £54.50p per annum. The crucial elements, therefore, are rateable value and rate poundage. Each year local authorities produce estimates of likely expenditure for the coming year. From this figure they deduct their estimated income from charges and central government grants together with any cash balances available for the purpose. This leaves a balance which then has to be financed through locally levied rates. In 1966 rate rebates were introduced for those householders unable to pay the full amount and by 1977/8 rebates went to 15 per cent of all households in England and Wales. In addition some properties (such as government buildings, agricultural land and buildings, churches) are exempt from rates.

What are the major objections to the rates?

(i) They are said to be 'regressive': they bear most heavily on those with low incomes since the key element is the value of the property not the occupier's ability to pay. The availability of rebates has, however, gone a long way to meeting this objection.

(ii) They are said to be unfair. Rate resources are unevenly distributed among local authorities and are not necessarily related to their different needs. Government grants, however, can be used to smooth out this unevenness.

(iii) Their basis (annual rental value) is not adequate. Calculating a notional rental value is fraught with difficulties; hence, the frequently canvassed alternative of capital values for domestic property rating, or site values, as a basis for payment.

(iv) Local accountability is undermined as (a) more than half of rate income comes from the non-voting business sector and (b) some electors (such as lodgers, young adults living with parents) do not pay rates. Of 35m local electors in England and Wales, only 18m are directly liable to pay rates, and rate rebates reduce the number paying the full rates to 12m. Thus many electors can vote for extra spending knowing the cost will fall elsewhere.

Against these objections must be set the *advantages* of the rating system: payment is difficult to avoid, income is predictable, and collection is cheap and easy.

Reform of the rating system has long been on the political agenda. In

1976 the Layfield Report, *Local Government Finance*, suggested that a local income tax should supplement the rates, although it listed many difficulties associated with such a venture. However, a government Green Paper, *Local Government Finance* (1977), issued in response, rejected this suggestion. In 1981 the Thatcher government issued a further Green Paper, *Alternatives to Domestic Rates*. This did not advocate a particular option but commented on specific alternatives (for example, local sales tax, local income tax, poll tax, an assigned share of national taxes) while ruling out others (for example, local duties on petrol, alcohol or tobacco; local vehicle excise duty; charges for licences for sale of alcohol or petrol; and a local payroll tax). Two years later, however, in a further White Paper, *Rates: Proposals for Rate Limitation and Reform of the Rating System* (1983), the government recognized that wide consultation had failed to find any consensus for an alternative local tax, and conceded that rates should remain for the foreseeable future as the main source of local government revenue. However, the issue was not settled and following a rating revaluation in Scotland, which caused much unrest, a further inquiry (the fourth in fifteen years) began, which resulted in the 1986 Green Paper, *Paying for Local Government*. This heralded the possibility of major changes, notably:

(i) A uniform business rate set by government with the proceeds distributed to all local authorities in proportion to the number of adults in their areas;
(ii) a much simplified grant system;
(iii) the replacement of domestic rates by a community charge which each authority would set and which would be paid by every adult (not just householders) resident in its area. (Subsequently, the government proposed exempting the mentally ill and elderly people living in homes and hospitals; and also allowing a discount for students and the less well off; see *Paying for Local Government – the Community Charge*, 1986.)

These new arrangements will be introduced in one stage in Scotland and Wales, in 1989 and 1990 respectively. In England there was to have been a four-year transitional period, commencing in 1990, during which the community charge would have been gradually introduced and rates phased out, but the Secretary of State, in response to pressure from his own party, agreed late in 1987 that with the exception of a handful of London boroughs (where some flexibility remains) the community charge should be introduced throughout England in 1990 without any phasing-in period. These proposals were enshrined in the 1988 Local Government Finance Act.

These changes put forward by the government are extremely

controversial. In their favour it can be stated that the consultation process which followed the publication of *Paying for Local Government* showed twice as many people wanting to abolish the rates as wishing to keep them. The community charge, which received most support as a replacement, would arguably be more fair and enhance local accountability by ensuring that all local electors contributed towards the cost of local services. However, critics point to the regressive nature of the community charge – apart from specified categories who will receive exemption or discounts (for example, students) everyone in an area will pay the same regardless of income – and the difficulties and expense of administration and collection. The retention of the business rate, moreover, will perpetuate many of the inherent problems of the rating system, and – in so far as this will be set by Whitehall – will increase the potential for central control of local finances. In Wilson's view (1986, p. 64) what is proposed does not form the basis 'for a generally acceptable . . . durable system' and 'there seems no escape from the conclusion that another attempt will have to be made to review these issues and make fresh recommendations'. If this view is correct the debate about reforming the rating system may continue well beyond the enactment of the Local Government Finance Act, 1988.

(2) Grants

Grants can be paid to support both capital and revenue expenditure, although today capital grants are relatively unimportant. About a quarter of exchequer support is paid over in the form of *specific or supplementary grants*. These are tied to particular services and in most cases reimburse individual authorities for a fixed percentage of their expenditure on the service concerned. Most important, however, is the rate support grant, which accounts for around 75 per cent of the total grant paid to local authorities and is paid over to individual authorities as a block sum. It consists of two elements: (i) *domestic rate relief*, paid to enable authorities to relieve domestic ratepayers of a certain proportion of their rates (currently 18.5p in the £); (ii) *block grant*, intended to supplement an authority's own finances so that, irrespective of individual local needs and resources, it can provide a similar standard of service for a similar rate poundage to other authorities of the same class. It can be spent on any service(s), as an authority wishes.

Each year following discussions in the Consultative Council on Local Government Finance, central government calculates a) the total amount of revenue spending it will accept for grant purposes (relevant expenditure); and b) the percentage of relevant expenditure to be financed by grant. After climbing steadily over the years, the percentage supported by government reached a peak in England and Wales of 66.5 per cent in 1975/6. Subsequently, however, it was reduced as part of central government public expenditure restraint policies and by

Table 8.1 National Rate Support Grant Settlement 1987/8[1]

	£m
Relevant expenditure	27,746
Grant at 46.3 per cent	12,842
less Specific grants	3,106
Supplementary grants	187+
Domestic rate relief	717+
Total	4,010
Block grant	8,832

1 England only

1987/8 had fallen to 47.5 per cent (46.3 per cent for England; and 66.7 per cent for Wales). Following these calculations the government deducts the value of specific and supplementary grants (including domestic rate relief grant) and distributes the remainder as block grant (see Table 8.1). In practice, as 'over-spending' authorities lose grant (see pp. 199–200), the amount distributed is less than this. From 1987/8 this money returns to the Treasury (formerly it went into a national pool for recycling to authorities).

Government grants to local authorities have now been paid for well over a century. The *justification* for them is well established: many local government services are required by national legislation, local variations in needs and resources can be equalized by grant adjustments, the impact of the regressive rating system can be reduced, and so on. Politically, however, their main effect during the twentieth century has been to make local government financially dependent upon the centre. From the Second World War the percentage of local government income derived from grants increased steadily and although the proportion began to fall during the 1980s (as a result of public expenditure restraint policies) it is still sufficient to provide central government with a powerful instrument for influencing local authorities. In recent years, moreover, a growing proportion of total grant has been contributed by specific grants (17.6 per cent in England, 1981/2; 25.6 per cent in 1987/8), which – being tied, unlike block grant, to specific services – leave authorities with less discretion to determine spending priorities.

(3) Charges

Income from charges is derived from fees, rents, tolls, fares, interest, etc. Obviously, the amounts received by individual authorities vary widely, according to the type and range of chargeable services provided, and the levels at which charges are set. The latter is in some cases subject to statutory regulation, in others it is a matter of local discretion.

CAPITAL FINANCE

Capital account *expenditure* by local authorities (£6.9bn in England 1984/5) is usually spent on longer-term items such as the purchase, construction or improvement of land, property, equipment and so forth. The *capital income* used to finance that income (£7.0bn in 1984/5) can be raised from several sources including 1) *capital grants* from the government or, occasionally, other bodies (such as the Sports Council); 2) *sales* of land, property, equipment and so on; and 3) *loans*. Both because of the long-term nature of the investments and the large sums involved, most capital expenditure has traditionally been financed through borrowing. There are, however, central government controls on what councils may borrow, and loan sanctions must usually be obtained from ministers.

Because of tightening central government controls on borrowing, the proportion of local authority capital income derived from borrowing fell sharply during the 1970s and 1980s (from 83.7 per cent in 1974/5 to 48.4 per cent in 1984/5) (all figures for England are calculated from Travers, 1986, tables, App. 4 and 5). In order to compensate, local authorities increasingly financed capital (expenditure) out of current revenues (rates and charges) and – particularly after 1980 with the Thatcher government's emphasis on council housing and land sales – with capital receipts from disposal of assets. While revenue contributions inevitably increased burdens upon ratepayers, and asset sales produced a 'once only' financial benefit (as well as being politically unpalatable to many, notably Labour-controlled, authorities) this was the perhaps inevitable response of local authorities seeking to free themselves from centrally-imposed borrowing restrictions (as well as the high cost of borrowing after the mid-1970s).

Even so, total local authority borrowing is enormous. In 1985 local authorities (England and Wales) had a gross loan debt outstanding of £42.3bn and total loan charges for the year serviced from revenue account amounted to £5.03bn (far more than revenue expenditure on major services such as police (£3.3bn) and social services (£2.98bn). (*Annual Abstract of Statistics*, 1987 edn, CSO, tables 16.13, 16.15.) The level of loan charges, moreover, is largely beyond local government's control, varying according to interest rates. As debt must be serviced to avoid defaulting on creditors, planned 'cuts' in local expenditure – particularly in periods of rising interest rates – invariably have to fall on other revenue items, such as salaries, running costs and services. By the early 1980s the combined effect of several years of high interest rates, tight centrally-imposed borrowing limits and progressive sharp falls in the level of revenue expenditure borne by block grant, were placing increasingly onerous burdens on ratepayers. In some areas rate levels were already beyond the limits which were regarded as socially and politically acceptable. It is in this context that the debate about rating reform, and the controversy surrounding increased central control of local expenditure, should be seen.

9 INSIDE LOCAL GOVERNMENT

The apparently straightforward pattern depicted on formal committee and management charts massively oversimplifies the internal working of local authorities. At a basic level *informal* as well as *formal* relationships must be considered, as must *political* as well as *administrative* dimensions. Widdicombe (1986, vol. 1, table 2.1) revealed that in 1985 the proportion of councils in party political control had risen to 84 per cent, hence in 'many, perhaps most . . . councils the party group' – which rarely figures on organization charts – 'has become the *focus* of political decision' (Alexander, 1982a, p. 97). This chapter looks inside local government at internal authority organization, at officer–councillor relationships and at the distribution of power inside the town hall.

Formal structures

While the administrative style of local authorities varies enormously, all conduct their work through: a) meetings of the council, consisting of all elected members; and b) committees and sub-committees consisting of small groups of members whose numbers and designations differ from authority to authority. (Some committees also include non-councillors; notably police committees, one-third of whose members are drawn from non-elected local magistrates.) Some committees focus on single services (such as housing or education) and are frequently called vertical committees; others, usually known as horizontal committees, deal with a single aspect of all services (such as personnel, finance). The trend in recent years has been towards establishing more horizontal committees in the interests of greater internal co-ordination. Even so, the committee system – where political control of policy and administration for each service is vested collectively in a group of councillors – offers a sharp contrast with the ministerial system in central administration. As Alexander (1982a, p. 121) puts it, 'the committee system of decision-making which predominates in British local government makes no provision for a political executive, either individual or collective'.

The committee system generally ensures detailed coverage of council business. Different items can be dealt with concurrently in different committees and the relative informality of proceedings encourages frank discussion by councillors and officers alike. Indeed, by enabling them to work together in committee – often over many years – the system facilitates contact between officers and councillors. Likewise, because committees usually contain members of different parties with different degrees of seniority and influence, contact is also facilitated between councillors of different political standing and party affiliation. One danger, however, is that committee loyalties might become too strong, causing members to become isolationist or even antagonistic to other service areas, thereby making an integrated authority-wide approach more difficult to obtain.

Just as committee systems vary between authorities, so too do departmental patterns. As in central government, the functional principle of allocation (see Chapter 2) is widely used, with departments having responsibility for particular services (education, housing, social services, and so forth); however, in local government allocation by process is also quite widespread, with departments of engineers or architects, for example, providing specialist services throughout their authority. Although invariably fewer, smaller, and less multifunctional than central governmental departments, the differences are relative and problems of co-ordination both *within* and *between* departments are nevertheless frequently found within local authorities.

While formal management and committee structures require study, informal relationships are also crucially important. At the local level, where departments are often housed in the same buildings, and where officers and councillors – as well as prominent local interest group officials, journalists, council 'clients' (headmasters, businessmen, builders, and so on) – live in the same locality, the informal dimension is especially important and should not be obscured by undue emphasis on formal hierarchies.

Corporate planning

The fragmentation of council functions between different departments and committees produced in many authorities prior to the 1970s 'a loose confederation of disparate activities' which, in the view of the Maud Committee on the Management of Local Government (Maud Report, 1967, vol. 1), dispersed 'responsibilities and scatter[ed] the taking of decisions'. In some of the larger authorities, the committee found (vol. 5) that there were thirty or more committees and forty or more sub-committees, while in local government generally 'there [was] hardly any systematic attempt at committee level to . . . co-ordinate policy as a whole'. Sometimes finance committees exerted some degree of co-ordination but they were usually ill-equipped for the task, being primarily concerned with financial implications. Consequently, Maud recommended each authority to establish 'a management board' of between five and nine members to co-ordinate council work. Committees would only be *deliberative*, making recommendations to the management board, which would perform functions similar to those of the Cabinet in central government.

The Maud Report provoked considerable hostility, particularly on the grounds of dividing councillors into first-class members (sitting on the management board) and second-class (backbench) members. Not a single authority implemented Maud's 'Cabinet style' solution in its entirety; nevertheless, many streamlined their committee structures and some even established policy co-ordinating committees. More generally, Maud generated a climate for greater integration, something which became particularly appropriate during the preparations for reorganization when two major committees (Bains for England and Wales, and Paterson for Scotland) were established to advise on management structures for the new local authorities.

The Bains Report (1972) and its Scottish equivalent, the Paterson Report (1973), both recommended a corporate approach to internal council management and policy-making. At *councillor level* a Policy and Resources Committee was proposed to prioritize resources, co-ordinate policy, and control programme implementation throughout the authority. To assist with these tasks each policy and resources committee was recommended to have four sub-committees: finance, land, personnel, and performance review. At *officer level* there was to be a chief executive (in place of the former town clerk) whose role was to advise the Policy and Resources Committee and head a small management team (consisting mainly of chief departmental officers) which would prepare plans and programmes as well as co-ordinate policy implementation. Bains also favoured committees based on broad programme areas and 'serviced by several different departments and disciplines' in place of the 'traditional separatist structures' (Haynes, 1980, p. 54) whereby each service committee had tended to be associated with the appropriate functional department and its principal officer.

In the post-Bains era corporate *structures* have been widely adopted. According to Greenwood *et al.* (1980, p. 50), 95 per cent of authorities established policy committees and 98 per cent appointed chief executives and management teams. Nevertheless, whether corporate *planning* has become a reality is a separate issue. Powerful programme committees, and influential members serving on them, have sometimes been reluctant to defer to policy committees (particularly as many councillors still cling to the traditional view that co-ordination is the role of the full council).

Similarly, there has often been a reluctance by specialist departmental officers to accept the decisions of non-specialist chief executives and management teams. Consequently it has sometimes been difficult for the new patterns to establish themselves in the face of combined resistance from programme committees, established departments, and professional senior officers. It also needs to be recognized that in some authorities – particularly small district councils where there are fewer personnel, resources and programmes – much co-ordinating work occurs informally and the elaborate corporate structures advocated by Bains are perhaps less appropriate. Managerialist attitudes have also had an impact, with a few authorities (particularly on the radical right) preferring a managing director model, which downgrades corporate management and has sometimes undermined Bains-type arrangements even where they formally continue in existence.

Changes in attitude conducive to the development of a corporate approach would have been difficult to effect at any time. During the post-reorganization climate of economic and financial stringency, however, where departmental and committee defences rise easily, it has been especially difficult. Consequently, while corporate *structures* have developed apace since reorganization, it is questionable whether the corporate *ethos* has become deeply rooted. Indeed, a few authorities have retreated from corporate structures – management teams have been disbanded and some chief executives dismissed. The reason normally given is economy but the real cause is frequently a reassertion of anti-corporate attitudes. The Widdicombe Report (1986, pp. 142–5), arguing from the standpoint that the 'need for a more corporate approach to the officer structure had strengthened rather than weakened' since Bains, recommended that all local authorities should be statutorily required to appoint a Chief Executive with considerably enhanced powers.

Other factors, of course, contribute to the difficulty of effecting a corporate approach. Statutory obligations inhibit what is structurally possible; for example, non-metropolitan county councils must have education and social services committees. There is also a fragmentary approach by central government to local authorities. As the Central Policy Review Staff (1977, p. 22) noted, most circulars 'relate to a single service and are drafted and circulated by the single department responsible'. Corporate planning must also be seen in the context of party politics. While decisions in a formal sense are taken corporately by, or on behalf of, the full council, in many authorities decisions are taken in practice on party lines. Indeed, in its White Paper response to the Widdicombe Report (Department of Environment *et al.*, 1988) the government agreed in principle that officers' terms of service should be altered to allow them to attend party group meetings, subject to procedural safeguards. This largely reflected the fact that in a significant minority of authorities – about 11 per cent – one-party policy and resources (or similar) committees are found, whilst in 64 per cent an informal 'inner circle' of the majority leadership meets regularly, usually in the presence of officers (Widdicombe, 1986, paras 5.56; 5.57). Such arrangements perhaps offer the closest local government parallel to the Cabinet system enabling majority party leaders to formulate policy with the advice of officers. Formally, however, most policy and resources committees are politically representative which – coupled with access by press and public – often prevents frank discussion by controlling group members of planning, prioritization, and co-ordination in politically sensitive fields. As a result, policy and resources committee proceedings have in many authorities become either duplicates of, or substitutes for, the work of the full council and the function of policy co-ordination has shifted to the party political groups, or to the chief executive and management team, or . . . both' (Alexander, 1982a, p. 91).

The 1988 White Paper (Department of Environment *et al.*, 1988) also asserts that membership of decision-taking committees should reflect proportionately the political composition of the full council. This provision will be implemented by law, not standing orders, and will effectively see the end of one-party committees in the vast majority of local authorities. The government also agrees that there should be a ban on co-option with voting rights to decision-taking committees, but this will not apply to magistrates appointed to police committees, church representatives on education committees, or local committees managing specific council facilities. Councils will be allowed to appoint non-voting advisers to committees who must have relevant expertise or experience and not be disqualified from council membership – except in the case of teachers on education or library committees.

It should be stressed that a local authority's corporate planning is only one variable in securing efficient management within a local community. There are a range of bodies other than local councils responsible for the provision of local services which, coupled with the tiered nature of much of elected local government, makes a community-wide approach to management almost impossible. Developing inter-governmental as well as inter-authority networks is crucial if *real* co-ordination of local services is to be effected.

While an authority's management style is usually affected by environmental factors there always remains an element of choice. There can never be a purely mechanistic relationship between an organization and its environment. Party political factors, professionalism and the dispositions of key personalities all usually have some bearing on internal management structures. The advocates of 'rational administration' remain just one voice amongst many.

Councillors

SOCIAL CHARACTERISTICS

While councillors are *representative* of their local communities they are certainly not *socially representative* of the population. Widdicombe (1986, vol. 2), found 81 per cent of councillors were male and only 19 per cent female; the report showed that 59 per cent of councillors came from three socio-economic groups (professional, employers and managers, intermediate non-manual) who contribute 23 per cent of the population. Some 22 per cent of councillors had a degree or equivalent qualification compared to only 5 per cent of the general population. The majority of councillors were aged 45 or over with none under 24, the oldest being 85. As these figures suggest, councillors are predominantly male, middle-aged, and middle-class to a far greater extent than the population as a whole. To a large extent this social unrepresentativeness reflects some of the structural inequalities of contemporary society. For example, the constraints of women's lifestyles and their domestic and family responsibilities often mean that they are effectively discriminated against in terms of availability for election and service. Similarly, the pattern of afternoon meetings, still found in many authorities, discourages certain sections of the community, including all those with 'normal' working hours and, again, women with family responsibilities, from offering themselves as candidates.

Council work is currently essentially unpaid and the heavy workload involved makes service less attractive for people with young families, who are also building careers. Widdicombe found that councillors spent, *on average*, seventy-four hours per month on council duties. Party leaders and committee chairmen spent a good deal more. The middle-class skills – such as public speaking – required to be an effective councillor may also discourage many manual workers. It must nevertheless be stressed that the figure above is an average; individual localities often have distinctive patterns, and many Labour-dominated authorities do have a high proportion of working-class councillors.

Do the trends revealed above have any significance for the outputs and conduct of local government? In one sense it can be argued that generalizations are of little use. Councillors are not a homogeneous, undifferentiated grouping; their interests, outlooks and backgrounds vary enormously. There are disagreements between councillors of the same party just as there are disagreements between those of opposing parties. Such disagreements may stem from a variety of causes: ideological perspectives, ward and area considerations, seniority (old v. young), status (chairmen/spokesmen v. backbenchers), committee and pressure-group loyalties, or simply politicking or 'bloody mindedness'. As Newton (1979, p. 112) observes, there are also varying ability levels. While some of the 'ordinary members' may accurately be depicted as ignorant and unintelligent, 'council leaders are more usually of a much higher calibre'. Increasingly, moreover, in the larger authorities council leaders and key committee chairmen effectively work full time – a development given some impetus by the introduction of Special Responsibility Allowances (SRAs) for senior councillors in 1980 (Skelcher, 1983; Widdicombe 1986, vol. 2).

Compositional trends, however, should not be dismissed too easily. As Byrne (1986, p. 127) asks, 'does the lack of women councillors explain the apparent inadequacy of nursery provision, while there is an arguably ample supply of municipal golfing facilities?' Social elitism, it is frequently asserted, effectively squeezes out working-class interests. Indeed Dearlove (1979, p. 245) maintains that part of the case for reorganizing local government in 1972 and creating larger units was 'to make local government more functional for dominant interests' (that is, less accessible to working-class representation).

Social elitism, however, needs to be distinguished from political elitism: Labour and Conservative councillors on a local authority could easily have relatively similar (and relatively elitist) social backgrounds but very different political priorities. The political/ideological dimension is perhaps a more crucial factor than social background in determining policy priorities, although the two can never be entirely disentangled. Perhaps, ultimately, the issue is this: there is nothing amiss with manual workers (or any other grouping) being councillors, provided they can control their officers. If they cannot, councillors develop policy only in so far as the bureaucracy permits. Training for new councillors might, in this context, be a useful resource but, as Greenwood and Wilson (1987a and 1987b) show, most training is lamentably inadequate, not least because chief officers and senior councillors are often unenthusiastic about new councillors being too well briefed. Payment for councillors might also persuade more working-class representatives to come forward. Indeed, the attendance allowance system has made it possible for councillors from a broader social range to serve on local authorities but this is far removed from receiving a salary.

REPRESENTATIONAL ROLES

The literature often focuses excessively upon officer–councillor relationships, thereby overlooking the very different roles which councillors themselves adopt. As Jennings (1982, p. 67) has observed, most councillors are backbenchers, not policy-makers, and about the only vital service they see themselves doing is casework for their constituents. This generalization, however, needs refining. Jones (1973, pp. 135–46) provides a useful quantification of roles, arguing that three broad categories are identifiable: (i) 75 per cent are mainly concerned with representing ward and constituents' interests; (ii) 5 per cent serve as general policymakers; (iii) 20 per cent serve as policymakers in specific service areas. Newton (1976, ch. 6) offers an even more detailed classification of councillors, based on his study of Birmingham:

(i) *parochials* – whose world is largely bounded by the ward, individual constituents and their problems (15 per cent of sample were in this group);
(ii) *people's agents* – similar to the above, but for this group ideology is more important. They see themselves as protecting citizens' interests rather than as delegates (18 per cent);
(iii) *policy advocates* – a preference for policy matters on a city-wide not a ward perspective. Strong ideological orientations (24 per cent);
(iv) *policy brokers* – similar to policy advocates but essentially moderates, compromisers and bargainers (20 per cent);
(v) *policy spokesmen* – concerned with broad policy matters but also seeing themselves as delegates. By speaking on behalf of their constituents they occasionally thereby disagree with aspects of party policy (8 per cent).

Such classifications inevitably simplify reality, but it is clear that different members may hold very different views about the role of local councillors.

PARTY GROUPS

The Widdicombe Report (1986, para. 6.57) showed that 85 per cent of councillors are elected in the name of a political party. In some authorities this party dominance has been reflected in formal structures by the formulation of one-party committees or sub-committees, although this remains the exception rather than the rule (Widdicombe, 1986, vol. 1, p. 34). More usually formal committees have remained politically representative, with the main focus of organized party activity being reflected in party groups. Groups are now an integral part of most local authorities although operational styles vary enormously. Overall, 4 per cent of groups meet weekly, 38 per cent every two to four weeks, and 58 per cent less often. Labour groups meet significantly more frequently than Conservative groups (Widdicombe, 1986, para. 6.59). In authorities where there are party groups it is almost universal practice for the group to meet before meetings of full council and for group decisions to be binding on members at full council meetings, although there is often (but not always) a more relaxed attitude to voting discipline in committees (see Widdicombe, 1986, vol. 1, tables 2.3–2.6).

Although party politics, particularly in urban areas, has long been a feature of local government, its extension after 1974 – mainly a product of the larger authority areas created by reorganization – has helped to transform the operating style of many authorities. Today many decisions are taken in private party meetings, only very occasionally with officers in attendance and then normally only for specific items. Even so it is possible to exaggerate the contributon of party groups to the policy-making process. Alexander (1982a, p. 198), for example, argues that this 'is more often than not reactive rather than initiative. Except where the controlling group comes to power with a programme worked out in detail, the relationship between professional expertise and political organisation will ensure that much of the business of the authority will be generated by officers'. In conformity with this view Green (1981, p. 62) saw Newcastle's ruling Labour group as 'a receiving shop, serving to legitimate decisions taken elsewhere'. Neither Jones (1969) in his study of Wolverhampton, nor Bulpitt (1967) in his analysis of a number of north-west Labour parties, could find evidence of party groups undertaking a successful policy formulation role. On the other hand Wiseman (1963) found a highly influential Labour group in Leeds City Council.

It is clearly a mistake to generalize from a few examples. Every party group is unique, not only in terms of composition but also in its conventions and working practices. For example, while most meet in the absence of officers, Widdicombe (1986, paras 6.173–77) found that the chief executive 'always' attended in 1 per cent of authorities and was present occasionally in 27 per cent. Again, in 72 per cent of cases non-councillors attend group meetings and in 11 per cent these may include council employees who are also party members. The Government's 1988 White Paper (Department of Environment *et al.*, 1988) backed Widdicombe's call that national political parties should ensure that only councillors vote at party group meetings and a public list of all attending is made available.

In some groups backbenchers may be largely unimportant; in others they may be able to play a decisive role in promoting policy initiatives. Davies (1979 and 1981), in a study of Wandsworth, describes how a small number of newly elected backbench councillors in the controlling Labour group crucially developed a whole range of new planning and industrial policies. They persuaded party leaders and the party group to adopt the initiative and subsequently took an important role in the process of implementation. Clearly group decisions can be decisive in some authorities and on some issues. As Stoker and Wilson note (1986, p. 292) while 'over many issues and for much of the time the group may simply endorse decisions taken elsewhere, at the very least senior councillors and officers must be careful not to offend the core political values and commitments of backbenchers'.

Officers

Unlike civil servants, local authority employees are not part of a single unified service: each council employs its own staff. Altogether, in 1987 some 2.35m people were employed by English, Welsh and Scottish local authorities, engaged in a range of occupations from architects, engineers and accountants to labourers, dustmen and park attendants. Although local authorities have considerable discretion in staffing matters, some officers must statutorily be appointed. For example, non-metropolitan counties and metropolitan districts are required to appoint chief education officers and directors of social services. Traditionally, local authority employees are categorized into *officers* (20 per cent of all employees: professional, technical and clerical staff) and *servants* (50 per cent, incorporating manual workers such as cleaners and road labourers). Additionally, some 30 per cent of local authority employees (teachers, firemen and police) form a third category. It is, however, the first category, officers, who form what is known as the local government service: it is these who have most contact with councillors and who perform primary policy advisory and managerial roles.

As with civil servants, officers in local government have both a managerial role – being responsible for the efficient running of their department – and a policy-advisory function. However, unlike their counterparts in central government, where top civil servants are usually generalists, chief officers in local government are normally specialists. Generally at the head of each department is a chief officer with appropriate technical qualifications who advises councillors and implements policy in fields relating to his specialism. In local government it is extremely difficult for a non-specialist to reach chief officer status. As Poole (1978, p. 43) observes, the local government administrator typically works 'as a subordinate of the specialist, relieving him of those tasks which have not called for specialist experience and qualifications'. In one other respect, too, local government officers offer a contrast with central government. While they are politically neutral they are not anonymous; they may speak in public at committee and other meetings, and often acquire public prominence within their locality.

The distinctiveness of localities and the relative freedom which authorities now enjoy in staffing means that generalizations are dangerous. Nevertheless, specialist officers invariably have loyalties to their profession as well as to their employing authority and this further weakens the concept of a unified service. It can also lead to narrowness, in that staff may have technical and specialist information in a single field but little concern or understanding about the work of other departments. Narrowness not only increases co-ordination difficulties between departments but is not conducive to corporate planning. Specialists, moreover, often build their careers by moving from one authority to another rather than by climbing within one authority. This, at times, can cause instability within an authority, although, equally, mobility can bring new ideas. The mobility of specialists, moreover, needs to be seen against the 'localist' orientations of councillors and administrators.

Since Bains an increasing amount of chief officers' time has been devoted to liaison with other departmental heads to formulate corporate strategies. In this context working relationships are extremely important. Whatever management structures are created in the interest of co-ordination, 'personality' remains an important variable. While academic literature is full of material on officer–councillor relationships, relatively little is known about relationships between departmental chiefs within the same authority, but these, obviously, can be of crucial significance.

Chief officers also liaise with other administrative units operating in the locality (such as the field offices of central government departments along with health and water authorities) and there are also important linkages with other councils, members of the public, and local pressure groups (such as ratepayers' action groups, local trade union branches, tenants' associations). The work of a senior local-government officer is, therefore, far broader than the confines of a single department or even a single local authority.

The government's 1988 White Paper in response to Widdicombe rejected Widdicombe's central recommendation of a powerful chief executive with statutory powers and protection to ensure the council's legal probity and managerial effectiveness. Instead the government called for each council to appoint an officer responsible for reviewing the propriety and legality of council business who would be under statutory duty to report if an action or decision was likely to be improper or unlawful. It also called for an officer to be designated as responsible for advising on management of council services (Department of Environment, *et al.*, 1988). It appears that the Widdicombe recommendation to give statutory powers to chief executives was rejected because most chief executives did not want them and politicians were cautious of such powers in the hands of one officer (see *Local Government Chronicle*, 29 July 1988, pp. 8, 9).

Officer–councillor relationships

VARYING PERSPECTIVES

One particularly crucial relationship at local authority level is that between officers and councillors, but there is no uniform pattern. Relationships vary between as well as within local authorities. There are also varying relationships between different policy fields. Chief Constables, for example, are in a different position from other chief officers by holding executive authority in their own right (and not derived from councillors), an arrangement which lies at the heart of suggestions that the police are less accountable for their actions than other local-authority employees (Oliver, 1987). Relationships in a single policy area also vary over time according to the issues and personalities involved. One must, therefore, beware of generalizations. As Newton (1976, p. 147) notes, the literature 'includes case studies of powerful officers, and powerless ones, as well as the conclusion that it all depends on the department'.

Two distinctive themes have, however, been dominant in recent years: (i) the 'formal' stance, that councillors make policy and officers simply implement it; (ii) the 'dictatorship of the official' thesis which holds that officials, with their technical expertise, are dominant in policy formulation. Such dichotomous standpoints are, however, somewhat misleading since *both* groups are involved in policy formulation. As Collins, Hinings and Walsh note (1978, p. 34), 'The evidence of the various case studies in local government leads not to the question of whether officers or members control but rather *in what ways both are involved in the process of developing and administering policy*?'

FORMAL AND INFORMAL RELATIONSHIPS

Recent studies have suggested that the 'formal' stance outlined above is largely redundant, although the reassertion of political control, particularly by the 'new urban left', perhaps suggests that it would be premature to ignore it totally. Given the technical, specialist nature of much contemporary local government activity, officers are clearly often very important. Yet, as Newton (1976, p. 148) reminds us, while the 'dictatorship of the official' thesis has 'a certain commonsense plausibility . . . it has very little empirical evidence to support it . . . because little research has been done on the subject'. At a formal level the council and its committees meet, with officers in attendance, to consider reports prepared by officers usually incorporating recommendations for action, but precise working relationships vary enormously. In some authorities officers intervene in discussions at will whereas in others more formal rules apply. At an informal level officers and councillors meet frequently at civic functions, receptions and so forth as well as before and after official meetings, and this too, serves to blur the formal relationship between them.

OFFICER–COUNCILLOR RESOURCES

(i) The *professionalism* of officers provides a level of technical expertise which councillors frequently lack. Nevertheless, councillors, through lengthy service on committees, may acquire considerable knowledge of certain subject areas. Many councillors, moreover, are builders, businessmen, transport workers, accountants and so forth who may have appropriate specialist knowledge. Councillors can also be advantaged by their knowledge of local circumstances and because the mobility of senior officers often exceeds that of senior councillors. Indeed in many authorities permanence may be characteristic more of councillors and committee chairmen than the nominally 'permanent' officials who advise them.

(ii) The officers' *control of information* is particularly important. Officers collect and present material both to committees and to the whole council. There are obvious dangers of distortion, omission or misrepresentation, not necessarily for sinister reasons but more likely because of subconscious or professional bias. Moreover, as Gyford notes (1976, p. 45), 'officers may also be able to participate in . . . decision taking by suggesting the appropriate wording of resolutions or amendments and . . . by . . . drafting' minutes of meetings. Nevertheless, councillors do have access (via pressure groups, the media, party research departments and so on) to alternative sources of information which can, in certain circumstances, enable them to challenge officers successfully. Likewise, the accumulated experience of councillors in specific functional areas, coupled with their local knowledge, means that, on occasions, they are a force to be reckoned with.

(iii) Considerable influence accrues to officers in *implementing council policy*. Typically, councillors are part-time and serve on only a few committees. They therefore rarely see 'the complete picture' and tend to lose track of an issue once discussion of it has been concluded. Usually they have few opportunities to check that their instructions are being pursued and almost none to supervise their execution at first hand. On key issues, or those with important constituency 'angles', assiduous councillors will take every opportunity to ascertain progress. On less important issues, however, not only councillors but sometimes whole committees may 'lose track' of implementation, particularly in larger authorities where there are frequently many pressing problems. Consequently, not only may inadvertent delay or failure to implement decisions go undetected but officers may attempt to 'amend' or 'shelve' decisions which they dislike (see Greenwood and Wilson, 1982).

CHIEF OFFICER – CHAIRMAN RELATIONSHIPS

The most crucial relationship is that between committee chairman and chief officer. This in many ways resembles the minister–civil service relationship (see Chapter 5) with the chairman performing a quasi-ministerial role. The specialism of chief officers and the part-time nature of council service, however, makes the chairman's role arguably more difficult than that of ministers. On the other hand, policy-making is *relatively* less complex at the local level, and in many authorities a committee chairman may have acquired considerable specialist knowledge by holding the chairmanship – or serving on the committee concerned – for many years. Frequently, at pre-committee 'agenda meetings' the chief officer goes through recommendations pointing out difficulties and likely contentious items. A close working relationship is crucial if policy is to develop smoothly and clearly. Informal linkages often develop because of the frequency of their meetings and the closeness of their working relationship, something fraught both with dangers and opportunities (see Elcock, 1986, ch. 4).

In Birmingham, Lambeth and Croydon the relationship between officers and councillors certainly appears to have been more equal than the 'dictatorship of the official' thesis would suggest. As we have seen, councillors sometimes do have resources (such as experience or local knowledge) to call upon when they confront experts. These resources are not, by any means, negligible and 'they are least negligible for the members who generally fill the most important positions' (Newton, 1976, p. 164).

One change which, if implemented, could increase the influence of councillors, would be some form of payment. As already observed, many councils have members who are effectively full-time (pensioners, housewives, and so forth). Since 1974 councillors have been entitled to claim an attendance allowance for approved duties (up to a maximum £16.70 per day in 1987). The average payment made in 1985 was £852 although this obviously concealed considerable variations. Almost all who commented to the Widdicombe Committee regarded the remuneration of councillors as 'unsatisfactory both in terms of the basis of payment and the level of payment' (Widdicombe 1986, para. 6.94) and the Committee recommended a basic flat-rate payment and a special responsibility allowance. Both should vary, it argued, according to the size of authority, with the flat rate ranging from

£1,500 p.a. in the smallest to £4,000 p.a. in the largest authorities (Widdicombe, 1986, para. 6.113). In its 1988 White Paper in response to Widdicombe (Department of Environment *et al.*, 1988) the government agreed that attendance and financial-loss allowances should be replaced by a basic flat-rate allowance, but not at rates proposed by Widdicombe. Total expenditure on the scheme should not exceed current expenditure on allowances. Additionally, the new flat rate should vary by types of authority, not by population. Whether such sums are sufficient to enable councillors to spend more time becoming more involved in local policy-making is open to question especially given the 'career building' problem outlined earlier.

The 1980 Local Government Planning and Land Act gave local authorities the power to pay 'special responsibility allowances' (SRAs) to their leading members (usually party leaders and committee chairmen). Widdicombe (1986, para. 6.92) showed that only 43 per cent of local authorities paid special responsibility allowances. The average payment was £518 p.a., (£1,402 for leaders, £572 for opposition leaders and £501 for committee chairmen). Widdicombe proposed (para. 6.109) that SRAs should continue but that local authorities should not have the discretion to opt out. Each local authority, it was suggested, should statutorily be required to draw up a scheme for the disbursement of special responsibility allowances. This should specify the amounts payable for particular posts and all councillors holding posts stipulated in the scheme should be entitled to claim the amount specified. The principle seems to be that those people exercising substantial responsibility in local government should be paid accordingly. In this context neither the attendance allowances nor the SRAs are sufficiently realistic.

A CHANGING ROLE FOR CHIEF OFFICERS: PROFESSIONAL ADVISORS OR PROFESSIONAL BUREAUCRATS?

The relationship between officers and councillors, like that between ministers and civil servants, is of crucial importance. However, whereas civil servants work exclusively for ministers – and are not usually available to assist the opposition or backbench MPs – local government officers, in keeping with the corporate nature of council decision-making, serve the council as a whole. Constitutionally chief officers are not responsible to the ruling group or committee chairmen, but to the whole council which they are obliged to keep informed of facts, law and all other considerations relevant to decision-making. As such they will normally give advice to individual councillors and parties, as well as the full council and committees.

In practice, of course, these constitutional norms fit uneasily alongside the realities of political life, especially in those authorities divided on party lines. As Laffin and Young (1985) observe, the break up of the post-war consensus, coupled with the passing of the earlier period of growth and the increased politicization of local government, has made the officer's professional stance increasingly difficult to sustain. A majority group inevitably feels, politically if not constitutionally, that it has prior claim on officer advice and loyalty, and a right to expect that professional judgements should be subordinated to party policy. In some of the more highly politicized authorities 'an unhealthy atmosphere of suspicion' has developed, with some officers – even some chief executives – 'being labelled as political appointees' (Widdicombe, 1986, para. 6.191). Even in 'hung' councils, where no party has control, senior officers, as Greenwood and Wilson (1986, p. 5) observe, 'find it difficult to avoid being drawn into the political process'. Compromises and deals have to be hatched and officers become the main repository of the views and demands of competing factions. The position may be complicated still further in cases where an officer of one authority is a councillor in another. In recent years the officers' freedom to divorce professional judgement from political calculation has, in many authorities, diminished sharply, and today's chief officers are increasingly coming 'to see their role as less than that of a neutral professional or technocrat and more that of a bureaucratic politician' (Laffin and Young, 1985, p. 51).

The Widdicombe Committee's response (1986, ch. 6) to these developments was firmly to assert the need for officers to remain neutral and to serve the council collectively. While accepting that officers must adapt to political reality – by, for example, being prepared when invited to attend party groups subject to certain safeguards – it rejected any move towards a 'spoils system' in local government, and recommended that principal officers should be prohibited from engaging in political activity, including standing for council office. At the same time it recommended enhanced powers for chief executives to arbitrate in sensitive political matters: for example, applying the rules for party balance on committees, determining whether an individual council has a need to inspect a document or attend a meeting, and deciding which chief officers should attend party group meetings. Significantly, however, it also recommended safeguards against the dismissal of chief officers including a proposal to prevent dismissal of a chief executive except on the vote of two-thirds of council membership.

As noted earlier, Widdicombe's proposals for a far more powerful chief executive were rejected by the government's 1988 White Paper (Department of Environment *et al.*, 1988). Additionally, only the most senior officers in an authority (not all principal officers and above as Widdicombe proposed) will be banned from being members of other main councils or being active politically. Prohibition will apply to chief executives, chief officers, deputies and others who regularly advise or act on behalf of their councils. The government estimates that at least 10,000 people will be prohibited from political activity – such individuals will also be prevented from speaking or writing on controversial issues unless the council deems it part of their job. Employees of joint boards and joint committees will, if the White Paper is implemented, be allowed to be councillors in constituent authorities provided they are not nominated for board or committee membership, or are prohibited by their job. Council employees will be restricted to twenty-six days' paid leave for duties as councillors. Political advisers on the rates will not be allowed despite the committee's recommendation they should be available to all party groups.

Despite the changes outlined in the 1988 White Paper, chief officers in many authorities remain likely to experience continuing tensions between the professional requirements of neutrality and the political demands of councillors. As Laffin and Young (1985, p. 59) conclude, 'it is quite clear that chief officers are going to have to live with an increasingly uncertain and tempestuous political environment and any new ground rules will be of limited value'.

A FALSE DICHOTOMY?

To what extent is it realistic to see local political relationships in officer–council terms? One of the underlying themes of corporate planning is the notion of *partnership* between officers and councillors. Elected members and officers are now *increasingly working together* on council activities. As Collins *et al.* (1978, p. 42) observe, what frequently happens is that 'a joint councillor–officer elite arises, often in a very visible form, as the major power centre of the local authority'. According to this school of thought there is neither the domination of an officer nor a member elite but rather the domination of an officer–member elite (see Saunders, 1980) but this joint-elite model can be criticized because it often assumes that, important as leading officers and councillors are, they have a monopoly of decision-making influence. In other words, this model excludes from consideration the influences on policy-making which come from outside this officer–councillor elite (Wilson, 1988). Any realistic model should incorporate more elements than simply the relative importance of leading officers and councillors, otherwise a distorted and simplistic picture of power inside local authorities will emerge.

Too often the literature gives the impression of leading councillors and officers being a united, cohesive group. In practice, relationships are frequently characterized by tensions and conflicts. Politicians *do* frequently reject plans presented to them by officers. Additionally, it is important to recognize that there are various other influences upon policy-making within the town hall. On occasion the ruling party group *as a whole*, not just its leading councillors, can be crucial in decision-making (Stoker and Wilson, 1986). Likewise tensions *between* departments and *within* specific departments can have important effects on policy. In a 'hung council' deals hammered out *between* rival party groups can often have either a direct or indirect effect on local policy-making. It is, therefore, necessary to move beyond the narrow officer–councillor confines and recognize that the internal world of local authorities is highly complex and diverse.

The above approach to the distribution of power *inside* local authorities leaves out of account the increasing influence of central government departments upon local authorities in crucial areas, notably finance (see Dunleavy and Rhodes, 1987). Nevertheless, even given the increasing constraints imposed by the centre upon local authorities (see Chapter 10) it is still important to recognize that the centre only narrows the scope of decision-making – it does not determine it. Internal administrative routines and power relationships affect local policy processes by modifying and mediating external influences, and they can also provide an independent dynamic of their own.

Perhaps local politics needs to be seen as a series of shifting alliances, varying over time and from issue to issue. To distinguish too sharply between officers and councillors is frequently to distort reality (Laffin and Young, 1985; Laffin, 1986). Senior elected and non-elected personnel might be dominant in some authorities on some issues but this is only one possible alliance; second-tier officers and party activists might combine effectively in other policy areas – the permutations are infinite. While networks and alliances vary enormously, one conclusion is clear: there is far more to local authority decision-making than simply the officer–councillor dimension.

10 CENTRAL–LOCAL GOVERNMENT RELATIONSHIPS

Although local authorities are accountable to the local electorate, their powers and a significant proportion of their finance are derived ultimately from Parliament (which in practice is invariably dominated by government). For local councillors this sometimes presents a stark dilemma: whether to put first the perceived interests of local people, or the directives and requests of central government. Central–local relations, in fact, are crucial to understanding the way local government works and to recognizing its role within the wider administrative system. Unfortunately the relationship is far from simple, being characterized, according to Rhodes (1981, p. 28), by 'ambiguity, confusion and complexity'. Relationships vary over time, from authority to authority and from service to service.

At one level, the scale of central intervention in local authorities can be measured; between 1979 and 1988 some fifty Bills having a direct effect on local government were laid before Parliament. Some see such intervention as heralding the end of elected local government but, as Goldsmith (1986, p. xiv) observes: 'Britain has not become a totally centralized state, nor is central government's control over local authorities' activities yet total . . . . British local authorities still retain considerable discretion over the way in which they run their services and the level of service they provide'. Central direction has increased since 1979 but local authorities are far more than simply field agents of central government departments. There is a diversity and vitality that makes the study of central–local government relationships particularly fascinating.

This chapter begins by examining three analytical models and discusses their usefulness as tools for analysis. Formal relationships are then examined, followed by a discussion of what happens in practice. There is an account of the changing nature of central–local relations in the 1980s and, finally, some radical literature is examined and alternative analytical perspectives presented.

Analytical models

Until relatively recently central–local relationships were viewed rather simplistically in legal, institutional and financial terms. This approach not only ignored wider political and administrative factors but, as Regan (1983, p. 45) observes, was too limiting: it was unable to encompass the 'variability, ambiguity, complexity and reciprocity' that subsequent studies have suggested obtain in central–local relations.

Broadly speaking, three major models which attempt to offer insights into central–local relations can be identified, and these are discussed below.

THE AGENCY MODEL

This model sees local authorities as having a subordinate relationship to central government with little or no discretion in the task of implementing national policies. This was the traditional view which held sway for many years. Local authorities were subject not only to central government-initiated legislative changes, but financially were seen as increasingly dependent on central government grants. As late as 1966 W. A. Robson wrote: 'Local authorities have become subservient to the central government, mainly but not entirely because of their excessive dependence on central grants' (p. 149). While Robson's view is, today, largely rejected by academic observers, the agency model is still widely adhered to by many practitioners at local level – both councillors and officers – who in the second half of the 1980s see central controls inhibiting their freedom to act in what they regard as the local interest.

The difficulty with the agency model is that it produces a somewhat 'blinkered' analysis of what is a highly complex relationship. While local government, like all public authorities, is subject to Parliament, its relationship with government is not purely legalistic; political and administrative factors are also involved. Likewise, the proportion of local government revenue income derived from central government has fluctuated sharply. Between 1958/9 and 1979/80 it rose sharply (in England from 36.1 per cent to 48.5 per cent), but this did not automatically mean more central control, any more than the subsequent fall by 1984/5 to 39.2 per cent meant increased local freedom (all figures from Travers, 1986, table app. 7). There is, furthermore, substantial empirical evidence of variations in local policy outputs. In some areas the agency model holds good (for example, county councils serve as agents of the Department of Transport in constructing motorways and trunk roads) but in general it conveys an exaggerated picture of central domination, particularly as there is a great deal of evidence of continued local discretion in service provision. Several studies, for example, show that policy outputs vary from authority to authority in a manner which is not simply related to differing resources or needs. According to Boaden (1971), party control clearly affects

Table 10.1 Variations in Expenditure in Greater Manchester, 1987/88 (£)

	Education[1]	Housing Maintenance[2]	Social Services[3]	Environmental Health[4]
Bolton	293	252	57	7
Bury	309	361	56	7
Manchester	383	**	129	21
Oldham	297	320	65	9
Rochdale	326	273	84	10
Salford	288	142	74	11
Stockport	278	343	49	6
Tameside	293	317	75	10
Trafford	280	384	51	4
Wigan	319	323	56	7
Range	278–383	142–384	49–129	4–21

Source: Local Government Comparative Statistics (1988) (CIPFA Information Service, London, 1988)

1 Cost per head of total population
2 Cost per dwelling
3 Net cost per capita
4 Net cost per capita
** Information not available.

Note: These figures are estimates. Actual expenditure may be different.

expenditure patterns. He found that Labour councils spent more on education and built more council houses than Conservative councils. Labour councils also paid higher subsidies in the housing field than other councils, irrespective of needs or resource availability. Conservative councils, by contrast, spent more on police than Labour. Alt (1971, p. 60) has likewise shown that before Health Service reorganization in 1974 there was a 'consistent, positive and generally significant correlation between Labour representation and spending on local health services'. Davies (1968 and 1972) develops similar themes in the context of social services. Likewise, Duke and Edgell (1981), in a study of two northern cities, demonstrate the importance of local political control with reference to spending cuts.

Distinguishing between a multiplicity of variables in accounting for policy variations is, of course, a hazardous exercise, but despite the methodological difficulties it seems clear that a simple agency model, with local authorities implementing national policies with little or no discretion, is far from accurate. Table 10.1 illustrates this with reference to revenue expenditure on basic services by the ten district councils in the Greater Manchester area in 1987/8. Similar variations are evident on a national scale. For example, in 1987/8 Bexley planned to spend £408 per head of its population on education while East Sussex budgeted only £213 (Source: *Local Government Comparative Statistics 1988*, CIPFA, 1988).

Case studies also reveal evidence of local discretion in other respects. In numerous policy areas (such as smoke control, comprehensive education, selling council houses) central government has often been frustrated by local authorities. Dearlove (1973, p. 20), for example, observed that the Royal Borough of Kensington and Chelsea frequently ignored or resisted central government 'advice and direction'. He concluded: 'The impact of central government upon day-to-day decisions of local authorities often depends on local responsiveness, and the preparedness of local authorities to accept advice or guidance'. Distinctiveness, albeit within a framework established by the centre, appears to be an unmistakable feature of local policy-making.

THE PARTNERSHIP MODEL

A second model, often regarded as the 'ideal' at the local level, sees authorities as more or less co-equal partners of central government in providing services. Traditional writers – noting the increased central constraints upon local government which have undoubtedly occurred during the twentieth century – often depicted a move from an earlier period of partnership to one of agent. In fact, the partnership model, as Regan (1983, p. 46) puts it, 'is so loose as to be almost vacuous'. He continues:

> Only in a formal constitutional sense are the government departments and the local authorities equal. In the sense of working together on common tasks partnership is a banal truism – of course both central and local government are involved in education, housing, transport, social services etc. but having said that there is little else one can say under the umbrella of partnership.

For Regan, then, the partnership model is too imprecise to be a useful analytical tool; hence the need for an alternative insight.

THE POWER–DEPENDENCE MODEL

This model postulates that both central departments and local authorities have resources which each can use against the other and against other organizations. In a sense this is a sophisticated variant of the partnership model, in that dependence is reciprocal. However, the relationship is far more complex and varied than that postulated by the partnership model. Resources other than the legal/constitutional and financial are built into the model: for example, political, informational and implementational resources. While there are likely to be inequalities in the distribution of the resources, these are not necessarily cumulative. Rhodes (1979, pp. 29–31) observes:

> The fact that a local authority or a central department lacks one resource does not mean that it lacks others. One resource could be substituted for another. For example, a central department lacking the constitutional/legal resources to prevent (or encourage) a specific local initiative can attempt to get its way by withholding (or supplying) financial resources. Conversely, a local authority which has been refused financial resources can attempt to reverse this state of affairs by embarrassing the central department. Press and television reports on the adverse consequences of the centre's decision may lead to the decision being reconsidered.

In this model power is seen in relative terms, hinging upon a process of bargaining and exchange.

The power–dependence model undoubtedly offers a useful analytical tool for exploring central–local relationships. It reveals clearly that neither central nor local government should be seen as monolithic blocs and that the relationship varies according to the agencies, personnel, policy areas and goals involved. For all its sophistication, however, it fails to place central–local relationships in the wider political and economic setting. The focus is upon inter-organizational relationships, and changing political and economic circumstances receive insufficient emphasis. As Dunsire (1982, p. 21) has written, 'the bargaining network model has been made to look a little shop-soiled . . . . See how fiscal crisis and a streak of Thatcherite obduracy fills one's mind again with the "reality" of the power of the state, when a government chooses to use it'.

In further reflection on his own model Rhodes (1986, p. 28) moves away from a concern with inter-organizational analysis to a focus upon policy communities. He argues that the very phrase 'central–local relationships' suggests a bias towards the analysis of *institutional* relationships. Such analysis, Rhodes maintains, 'does not always provide an adequate account of policy systems . . . Intergovernmental theory with its emphasis on fragmentation, professionalisation and policy network is more appropriate'.

Dissatisfaction with the models outlined above has led Chandler (1988a, p. 185) to put forward what he calls the *stewardship* model. He regards the stewardship metaphor as useful in the sense that a steward is delegated considerable authority by his master to order his estates. Chandler observes that the steward will on occasions consult with his employer on how best he should manage his estate and may often wish to suggest new policies or point out deficiencies in existing strategies. Chandler continues (p. 186):

> A capable landlord will listen to the advice of his expert manager and may often be persuaded by his arguments. The master, nevertheless, will always retain the power either to accept or reject the advice. Should the steward fail to obey these orders he will be compelled to change his conduct or, like the councillors of Lambeth, Liverpool and Clay Cross, be removed from office.

The central–local relationship is dynamic and multi-dimensional, and no one model seems capable of portraying it in its entirety. Of course, analysing any relationship depends upon the angle from which it is viewed. Saunders (1982, p. 55) illustrates this with reference to a Conservative government committed to a monetarist economic strategy. For the government, he writes,

> the problem is how to develop and enforce policies involving cuts in services and reductions in the public sector workforce in the face of local resistance and antagonism on the part of Labour local authorities, public sector unions, organised groups of consumers of state services, and so on. From the point of view of local Labour-controlled councils, on the other hand, the problem is how best to counter central government policies and directives in order to fulfil election pledges and principled commitments to a 'no cuts/no redundancies' platform.

The 'top-down' view of central–local relationships can be very different from the 'bottom-up' view; both perspectives require recognition.

The formal framework

This section examines *formal* relationships between central government and local authorities, an essential prerequisite to the analysis of *actual* working relationships on pp. 194–98.

LEGISLATION

The sovereignty of Parliament means that it can create, abolish or amend the powers of local authorities as it determines. For example, the 1985 Local Government Act abolished the GLC and the six metropolitan counties with effect from 1 April 1986 and the 1988 Local Government Act abolished ILEA with effect from 1990. While legislation is, therefore, an obvious means of central control of local authorities, statute also serves to restrict the role of central government, as the Tameside dispute (1976) demonstrated.

Following reorganization the Labour-controlled Tameside Metropolitan District made arrangements for the introduction of comprehensive education, but in May 1976, shortly before the changeover was scheduled, the Conservatives won control of the local authority and they were pledged to retain some grammar schools. In June 1976 the Labour Secretary of State for Education and Science issued Tameside a directive to proceed with comprehensive reorganization on the grounds that to do otherwise at such a late stage would be unreasonable. This intervention was under Section 68 of the Education Act, 1944, which states that when a local authority is deemed by the minister to be acting unreasonably, intervention by the minister is appropriate. Tameside resisted, and when the matter came before the courts the House of Lords determined that the minister's decision was invalid, holding that there was no basis upon which the Secretary of State could say that Tameside was acting unreasonably. Legislation, as this case suggests, is not simply an instrument of central control; it can also protect local authorities against central direction which is not backed by statutory powers.

Goldsmith (1986, p. xv) observes that concern with legislation as a means of controlling central–local government relations and the parallel use of the courts to enforce government intentions has been a feature of post-1979 Conservative governments. 'This rather formal approach contrasts neatly with the more informal approach generally adopted by central governments in their relations with local authorities in the years up to 1979'. There is, perhaps, something of a different operating style to the pre-1979 era.

CIRCULARS

Circulars, issued by government departments to appropriate local authorities, are a major instrument of central–local communications. (In the year ending April 1981, according to the DOE, 1,873 circulars and similar communications were issued to local authorities; however, in the following year the figure was only 592.) Although they are often cited as an instrument of central control, their effectiveness is difficult to determine because individual local authorities – and sometimes even different departments within the same authority – react differently to them. Indeed, many circulars do not contain central directives, and do not have statutory force, being issued simply for guidance and advice. Moreover, as Richardson and Jordan (1979, p. 107) observe, circulars often follow exhaustive discussion 'in the labyrinth of central/local consultative machinery'. Consequently, it can be misleading to see circulars as evidence of central departments attempting to regulate local authorities.

JUDICIAL CONTROL

Local authorities have no powers except those conferred upon them by statute, and when they take action which is not sanctioned by the law they are said to be acting *ultra vires* (beyond the powers). Any councillors (or others) who support expenditure on *ultra vires* acts resulting in loss may be made financially responsible. They might also be banned from holding public office for a period determined by the courts.

Ultra vires is obviously a restrictive doctrine (although local authorities are permitted to raise a 2p rate to finance functions not specifically authorized by statute). Its effect is to expose to restraining action in the courts any local authority activity not backed by statutory authority. One controversial instance of this occurred in 1981 when the Greater London Council's 'Fare's Fair' policy – which introduced heavy subsidization of London Transport fares from the rates – was declared illegal by the House of Lords. In January 1983, however, the High Court ruled that the GLC had power to launch a similar plan designed to reduce London Transport fares by 25 per cent. As this example suggests the use of the courts is highly controversial: the 1981 decision led to accusations that an 'undemocratic' court ruling had substituted the views of judges for those of councillors whose policies had been endorsed by the local electorate. Grant (1986, p. 203) argues that the spillover into the courts of cases such as that cited above is 'the direct and inevitable product of the worsening state of central–local relations'.

DEFAULT POWERS

These powers, granting a minister default powers over local authorities which, in his view, fail to provide a satisfactory service, are very rarely used. A minister may temporarily remove a particular service from a local authority and administer it himself (or authorize someone else to act) if he is dissatisfied with a local authority's performance. Two cases, Clay Cross (1972) and Norwich (1981–2), are particularly interesting: here, as with the GLC 'Fare's Fair' issue, the party-political dimension was very much in evidence.

(i) Clay Cross (1972)

This dispute arose when the Labour-controlled Clay Cross Urban District Council refused to operate provisions in the Housing Finance Act, 1972, requiring council house rents to be raised to the 'fair rent' level defined by the Act. The Conservative government ultimately appointed a Housing Commissioner to take over responsibility for the housing function but in 1974 the local authority ceased to exist as a result of local government reorganization. Eleven Clay Cross councillors were surcharged for the money which would have been obtained had the Act been implemented and they were also disqualified from holding public office for a period. In practice, however, the commissioner found it difficult to operate because of non-cooperation by the council: the use of default powers may be clear in statute but implementation can be more problematic. Rhodes (1981, p. 17) observes that 'although central government has an impressive list of controls at its disposal they constitute only a *potential* for control'.

(ii) Norwich (1981–2)

One important default power is that contained in the Housing Act, 1980, which can be brought into effect whenever the minister considers that tenants are having difficulty in exercising their right to buy a council property 'effectively and expeditiously'. In December 1981 the Secretary of State for the Environment threatened to activate these default powers in Norwich, where the Labour-controlled city council had sold only 250 properties in the first year of the Act. The minister's position was ultimately upheld by the Court of Appeal in February 1982. In his judgment Lord Denning suggested that if Norwich would 'get a move on' in processing applications to buy there might be no need for the minister to act. This in fact happened. Norwich agreed to take on an extra twelve staff and to clear the backlog of applications.

DEPARTMENTAL INSPECTORS

The use of inspectors as a form of central supervision goes back to the Poor Law reform of 1834. Basically only four local authority services are subject to oversight by inspectors: education, child care, police and fire. While such inspectors are usually required to satisfy their departments that local services are provided efficiently and that minimum standards are being met, their role has increasingly been educative rather than coercive. As Stanyer (1976, p. 223) observes, they 'both educate and learn . . . and . . . can carry knowledge of best practice directly from one authority to another'.

APPELLATE FUNCTIONS OF MINISTERS

Some statutes require local authorities to submit schemes or orders to the relevant minister for approval (for example, structure plans) or confirmation (for example, compulsory purchase orders). Likewise, ministers exercise various appellate functions in adjudicating between citizens and local authorities (such as appeals against a local authority's refusal of planning permission). Despite the quasi-judicial character of the process it is likely that his appellate functions serve to 'heighten a minister's perception of his supervisory role' (Boynton, 1982, p. 205).

FINANCE

Central government attempts to control local authorities by: a) carefully regulating the amount of money which they can spend locally, and b) scrutinizing the way in which money is actually spent. The increasing dependence of local government on financial support from the centre has already been noted, and through a variety of devices central government now restricts local-authority revenue and capital expenditure (see pp. 198–205). Although empirical research (for example, Boaden, 1971) suggests 'that the financial relationship has [not] decreased the decision-making autonomy of *individual* authorities, it is generally believed in local government that it has led to increased, and increasing control over local government *as a whole*' (Alexander 1982a, p. 148). This section, however, only examines the *scrutiny* of local-authority expenditure.

Traditionally, government-appointed district auditors have been responsible for examining most local authority accounts. The Local Government Act, 1972, allowed local authorities to choose between district auditors and private auditors (who needed to be approved by the secretary of state) but the Local Government Finance Act, 1982, removed an authority's right to choose its own auditor. The Act also established an Audit Commission for Local Authorities in England and Wales which became operational in 1983. Auditors are no longer employed by the Secretary of State, although the commission itself is appointed by the Secretary of State after consultation with local authority associations and professional accountancy bodies, and he is empowered to issue directions which the commission must observe. The commission has responsibility for appointing auditors for local authorities using either the District Auditor service or auditors from the private sector. Widely seen as part of the Thatcher government's policy of 'privatization', the 1982 Act effectively allows specific private auditors to be imposed upon local government. It also requires auditors to satisfy themselves that the local authority concerned 'has made proper arrangements for securing economy, efficiency and effectiveness in its use of resources'. Once the proposals in the 1988 post-Widdicombe White Paper (Department of Environment *et al.*, 1988) are implemented councils will be required to circulate auditors' reports to all members and make them public.

Far from being the lap-dog of central government, however, the Audit Commission has often flexed its muscles against the centre as well as against local authorities. Its 1986 report on community care, for example, criticized not only under-funding but the pattern of organizational fragmentation and confusion that began in central departments and worked its way down. Likewise in the area of council housing the commission (1986) pointed to the crises of management and finance resulting partly from central government's tighter restrictions on capital expenditure (Gray and Jenkins, 1987, pp. 312–13). The Audit Commission can, therefore, be something of a two-edged sword in the context of central–local relationships.

Working relationships

The formal legal framework of central–local relations needs to be set against actual working relationships. These relationships are extremely complex and varied. Griffith (1966), for example, showed that government departments varied enormously in the extent to which they sought to exercise control over local authorities. However, three major types of relationship could be identified:

1 *laissez-faire* – in 1966 Griffith cited the Ministry of Health as a department which exercised minimum intervention.
2 *regulatory* – ensuring that minimum standards of service provision are maintained and occasionally enforcing national policies on local authorities (for example, the Home Office);
3 *promotional* – here the central department either persuades or forces local authorities to adopt and implement national policies (for example, the DES).

Developing this theme further, Regan (1977, p. 34) shows that there can also be markedly different outlooks in different parts of the same government department – for example, the 'DES is not as promotional in the youth service as in primary education'. This further reinforces the view that central government is not a monolith. As Rhodes (1981, p. 18) observes, 'it is misleading to talk of central control. Rather there are different types and degrees of control exerted by the various constituent units of central government'. This point has been reinforced further by the findings of Goldsmith and Newton (1986) who show that, while the Thatcher government has been very directive towards local authorities on council house sales, by contrast it hardly involves itself in matters of environmental health (a reflection of the much lower priority the Thatcher government gives to this policy area). 'Consequently, local authorities have somewhat greater discretion in the environmental health area than they do in relation to council house sales' (p. 103).

In 1977, in similar vein, a report by the Central Policy Review Staff (1977) highlighted the great *complexity* which existed in channels of communication between central government departments and local authorities. It showed that central government departments, in making and implementing policies, acted largely in isolation from each other and conducted their relationships with local authorities accordingly. The CPRS recommended that central government should deal with local authorities more on an interdepartmental programme basis than on a separate service-by-service basis.

Regan has argued that there is an even more fundamental quality to be added to the variability, ambiguity, confusion and complexity outlined above, namely *reciprocity*. He remarks (1983, p. 45) that Friend, Power and Yewlett (1974) in their study on the expansion of Droitwich 'revealed government departments and local authorities closely involved on a common task. The process was marked by negotiation and bargaining and in these circumstances the hierarchical central–local relationship broke down and constraints were imposed mutually on all sides'. It is clearly naive to talk in general terms about 'central government control' over local authorities, or indeed to generalize about the relationship at all. As Rhodes (1981, p. 27) observes, in future 'the starting point must be the complexity of interactions and the constraints imposed thereby on *both* levels of government'.

LOCAL AUTHORITY ASSOCIATIONS AND PROFESSIONAL BODIES

Griffith (1966, p. 23) suggests that:

> Any description of central and local public authorities in Britain would be incomplete without some mention of the role of the local authority associations. It is difficult to exaggerate their importance in influencing legislation, government policies and administration and in acting as coordinators and channels of local authority opinion.

In 1973 three major local authority associations were established: the Association of County Councils (ACC), the Association of Metropolitan Authorities (AMA) and the Association of District Councils (ADC). The extensive consultation which takes place between central government and these associations should not be seen as a generous concession by government but as 'the inevitable response in a situation where the centre lacks detailed control. The associations act as filters, ranking matters according to importance, aggregating individual cases so that wider implications can be recognised' (Richardson and Jordan, 1979, pp. 105–6).

All three associations are firmly divided along party-political lines (Isaac-Henry, 1984); there is thus no single united voice of local government which further reduces local government's impact upon Whitehall. Nevertheless, against this backcloth, the associations have regular and detailed consultation with government departments, both formal and informal. It is the associations rather than individual local authorities which are invariably the point of contact between centre and localities.

There is also a range of specialist bodies which similarly represent aspects of local government at national level – for example, the Society of Local Authority Chief Executives (SOLACE). Others, like the Chartered Institute of Public Finance and Accounting (CIPFA), are professional associations with large numbers of members at officer level within local government (and sometimes also within central government as well). Such professional links also cross the public/private sector divide.

Policy statements which emanate from government departments are often, in practice, the product of prior consultation and negotiation between the centre and one or more of the many associations – not least the professional bodies, which on occasions serve to 'unite' civil servants and local authority employees. One effect of this, of course, as Goldsmith and Newton (1986, p. 103) observe, is that each policy arena involves different networks (or policy communities) of central and local actors. They show, for example, how the full range of local authority associations, together with such professional bodies as SOLACE or CIPFA, have been deeply involved in financial matters but that their involvement is less apparent in other policy areas such as fire, education, housing and transport which are marked by their own configuration of interests (such as the Institute of Housing Managers) all of which have their own style of central–local relations. Indeed Goldsmith and Newton (1986, p. 104) argue that there is a sense in which 'the phrase central–local government relations is a misnomer; what the term really refers to is a set of London-based relations between central government and the national local government community'.

What seems clear from the above analysis is that local authorities operate within a wider political system incorporating a range of national organizations and institutions, all of which can have a direct effect upon local government. Political parties, professional associations and local authority associations are frequently the major actors in what is often referred to as the 'national local government system' (see Rhodes 1988). Such networks are extremely complex and diverse but interrelationships between central government agencies and the localities via the above organizations need to be acknowledged in any realistic model of central–local relationships. Chandler, however, (1988a, p. 186) provides a timely reminder when he concludes that it 'is a frequent but pathetic fallacy in political analysis to believe that power necessarily accrues to those who habitually walk with the great'.

THE CONSULTATIVE COUNCIL ON LOCAL GOVERNMENT FINANCE (CCLGF)

In some instances formal committees and similar bodies are established to provide a mechanism for the exchange of information and views between central government and the various interests within the national local government community. One such body, formed in 1975, is the Consultative Council on Local Government Finance (CCLGF). However, as Alexander (1982a, p. 158) observes, 'The creation of this body was announced' in a way which 'suggested that the council was intended more to facilitate central control of the economy than to increase local government's capacity to protect its position and to maximise its influence on the government and on individual departments'.

The CCLGF meets six or seven times a year and is chaired by the Secretary of State for the Environment. Meetings are attended by ministers and senior officials from the DOE, Treasury and other interested departments, along with elected members and officers of the local authority associations. Although it has no formal terms of reference, its discussions principally concern grants and expenditure levels. According to Binder (1982, p. 36) 'the great significance of financial issues in the central/local relationship has led to the CCLGF attaining a predominant status in the hierarchy of Central Government/Local Authority consultation bodies'.

CCLGF business is first discussed in a body known as the Official Steering Group (OSG) which consists of senior officials of the associations and their advisers on the one side, and of senior government officials on the other:

> Ostensibly the main purpose of the OSG is to filter out and deal with items of lesser importance and to clarify issues for the 'political' side. Of course, in practice, matters of substance can be dealt with in the technical setting. A second tier of officers' groups have specialised remits and report to the Consultative Council through the OSG (Richardson and Jordan, 1979, p. 108).

Furthermore, as Binder (1982, p. 38) notes, discussions of CCLGF issues between leading association members and ministers often take place on a party political level outside the formal council. On some issues such discussions 'have had a very substantial influence on government policy – indeed an influence far in excess of that of the CCLGF'.

The development of the CCLGF has been mirrored in other policy fields (such as housing) by the creation of similar consultative bodies together with various working parties, specialist groups and so forth. Such channels provide important mechanisms for the exchange of information and influence and, together with the predominance of the associations in the central–local consultative process, have possibly resulted in a reduction of direct discussions on policy between individual local authorities and individual central departments. While bodies like the CCLGF may 'not greatly' have 'increased the power of local government' (Alexander, 1982a, p. 163) they enable local authorities (increasingly through their association representatives) to obtain access to, and collaborate with, departmental ministers and officials. Whatever the centre's theoretical potential for power might be, in practice the realities of policy formulation demand some collaboration between both levels of government.

Changing relationships: the 1980s

During the 1970s and 1980s overt tensions in central–local relationships became increasingly evident. One of the roots of the problem was the sharp cutback of financial resources provided by the centre, but this needs to be seen alongside the emergence of strongly ideological politics at both central and local levels.

The Thatcher government came to power in 1979 deeply suspicious of the size of the public sector and the levels of public expenditure. Local authorities (especially 'high-spending' Labour-controlled councils) were prime targets, particularly since local government accounted for a quarter of public expenditure in 1979/80. Consequently the period after 1979 witnessed a number of major developments with important repercussions for central–local relations. This section focuses on three of these: a) the Local Government, Planning and Land Act, 1980; b) the Local Government Finance Act, 1982; c) the Rates Act, 1984.

THE LOCAL GOVERNMENT, PLANNING AND LAND ACT, 1980

Prior to this Act the traditional approach of central government had been to view local expenditure in global terms; hence, as long as local government spending as a whole remained on target, individual authorities spending above the norm were not penalized. The 1980

Act, however, which introduced the block grant (see p. 162), allowed the government to assess how much each authority needs to spend and to allocate grant in terms of how far those assessments were breached. As Greenwood (1982, p. 259) noted, 'The Conservative Government's attempts to extract deeper cuts from higher rather than the lower-spending authorities represent a movement away' from the former 'philosophy'. This new 'philosophy', enshrined in the 1980 Act, was to lead to increasing central–local tensions during the 1980s as central government sought to impose, and reinforce where necessary, controls over the expenditure of *individual* local authorities.

Under the former 'rate support grant' (RSG) arrangement, as a local authority increased its expenditure, government grant met a constant percentage of the additional expenditure. Since 1981, however, as an authority's total spending rises above a standard level, set by central government for each individual authority, the proportion of additional expenditure met by the centre drops, thereby placing a heavier burden on local rates and deterring increased expenditure. Each authority is set a 'grant related expenditure assessment' (GREA) based on computation by the Department of the Environment of how much each authority needs to spend to achieve a common level of services with other authorities of the same type. Expenditure above the GREA level results in a reduction of block grant, with a 'steepening' effect built in above a certain threshold to penalize the high spenders. As Rhodes (1984, p. 270) comments, following the 1980 Act 'for the first time . . . central government has direct (rather than indirect) controls over the levels of expenditure of the individual local authority'.

Soon after the introduction of GREAs the government recognized a danger that some authorities might use them as targets, with the consequence that some authorities spending below their GREAs might be encouraged to spend more, while those spending far above them might find the task of cutting back to GREA level too difficult. Fearing that this might produce an aggregate increase in local government spending the government responded by introducing a second expenditure-control mechanism known as targets. Based on inflation increases and previous authority expenditure patterns, each authority was set a volume expenditure target by the Department of the Environment. Authorities exceeding their target incurred a penalty which involved loss of grant for each additional pound of expenditure per head of population above target.

Essentially the GREA and target mechanisms were two separate systems. The former assessed need to spend by an authority as a basis for calculating entitlement to block grant; the latter was a system of expenditure controls based around the progressive removal of grant above the 'target' expenditure level set for each authority. The effect, however, was that authorities had to live with both a GREA and a target and authorities spending above their target suffered a penalty even if their expenditure was within the GREA figure. The superimposition of targets and penalties upon the GREA-based block-grant mechanism made the system very complex, whilst the uncertainties engendered by fluctuations in targets, penalties, GREAs and the like inhibited financial planning and encouraged a tendency for authorities to protect themselves by building up reserves (Audit Commission, 1984b; Comptroller and Auditor General, 1985). Because quite modest increases in spending above target were also liable to result in considerable amounts of lost grant the system was also very unpopular among authorities, especially in the Conservative dominated shires where penalties fell with particular severity.

In order to meet some of these criticisms penalities and targets were abolished in 1986. However, the same block grant system was retained, and the GREA formulae tightened to produce at the local level deductions of grant for *all levels of expenditure*. The practical effect of this for most authorities is that grant decreases as spending rises and vice versa, with some authorities spending so far above GREA that they receive no block grant whatsoever. Indeed in some cases, where needs and resource assessments (upon which GREAs are calculated) are particularly severe, authorities lose all grant entitlement even before their expenditure reaches GREA. As the government's own Green Paper, *Paying for Local Government*, acknowledges (p. 33), the block-grant system remains 'highly complex and difficult to understand . . . it distorts and obscures the relationship between changes in expenditure and changes in local taxes'.

In 1986, as part of its wider proposals for the reform of local government finance, the government declared its intention to introduce a new grant system. In essence it proposes to replace block grant by a new *needs* grant (based on a simplified GREA) and a standard grant (consisting of a fixed sum per adult). Specific grants will also be reviewed. Such an arrangement, if introduced, will not only simplify the grant system but should also be more neutral in effect (by neither penalizing nor rewarding authorities for expenditure above or below GREA – see Wilson, 1986, p. 52). However, the new GREAs, as well as the level of standard grant, will continue to be determined by central government. After the repeated attempts by central government in the 1980s to control local authority spending through grant manipulations, local government anxieties are hardly likely to be quelled by the new proposals.

The 1980 Act also considerably tightened central controls upon *capital expenditure*. Government approvals now mainly apply to programmes rather than individual projects and relate to only one year at a time. Local authorities receive allocations for capital expenditure under five blocks: housing, education, transport, personal social services and other services. Allocations can be transferred between authorities and, to a limited extent (currently 10 per cent), between years. They can also be supplemented by capital receipts and trading profits. Authorities can also switch expenditure between services to a greater extent than hitherto, as virement (transfer) between blocks is permitted. These new found freedoms, however, are somewhat illusory. The main effect of the 1980 Act has been to reinforce earlier borrowing controls by expenditure controls, thereby bringing 'all capital spending [by local authorities] within the scope of control' (Travers, 1986, p. 142). Allocations relate not only to borrowing but also to expenditure (that is, loan sanction is given in line with expenditure allocations) and are determined nationally to meet government public expenditure targets. Individual authorities overspending their allocations are likely to suffer consequent reductions in subsequent years; indeed, those deliberately overspending supplemented allocations can be prevented from letting new contracts by ministerial order. As, moreover, deficiencies have appeared in the capital control mechanisms, so refinements have been introduced. Thus as the sale of council houses in the early 1980s produced sizeable capital receipts, and led to substantial capital 'overspending', the proportion which could be used to supplement capital receipts was reduced (standing at 20 per cent by 1987). As with attempts to control revenue, these capital controls were widely unpopular in local government, and authoritatively criticized as uncertain, inefficient and wasteful (Audit Commission, 1985b). While by 1986 the government itself conceded some of these criticisms, it flatly rejected calls for the abolition of capital controls and put forward proposals which, if introduced, seem likely to maintain these for the foreseeable future (*Paying for Local Government*, ch. 6).

THE LOCAL GOVERNMENT FINANCE ACT, 1982

This measure strengthened still further the expenditure controls over local authorities imposed by the 1980 Local Government, Planning and Land Act. It contained two main provisions. First, it legitimized retrospectively the grant penalties associated with targets set in 1981/2 and 1982/3 and set out the context in which expenditure guidance or targets could be issued in future years. Secondly, it prohibited local authorities from levying supplementary rates. This latter provision effectively requires rate precepts to be made or issued for complete financial years. Although intended to further curtail local government expenditure – by requiring authorities to meet any unforeseen expenditure from existing budgets – the effect may well have been to persuade local authorities to set high initial rates (to provide adequate balances to meet unexpected contingencies or loss of income). However, as

Greenwood (1982, p. 263) emphasizes, the Act also enables the Secretary of State to withdraw 'grant during the middle of the financial year from any authority which in his view is overspending'. He adds, 'it is difficult to escape the conclusion that the government has taken power: (a) to set for each authority what is to be regarded as the "needed" level of spending, (b) to enforce that level of spending by manipulation of grant'. To avoid the prospect of local authorities, whose rate fund becomes overdrawn within a year, from 'going bankrupt', the Act provides that authorities concerned may be given permission to borrow temporarily on revenue account, but only on such terms as the Secretary of State may impose.

THE RATES ACT, 1984

Despite the 1980 and 1982 Acts local government in 1983/4 was still, according to government estimates, overspending by £770m. In a White Paper (*Rates: Proposals for Rate Limitation and the Reform of the Rating System*, 1983) blame for this was placed mainly on excessive spending by a small number of authorities, which the government proposed to curtail by a new control mechanism: rate-capping. The White Paper's proposals were broadly enshrined in the Rates Act, 1984, which empowers the Secretary of State for Environment: (i) to limit the rates of named authorities (selective rate-capping) (authorities spending less than £10m, or below their GREA, are excluded from the selective scheme); (ii) to cap the rates of all local authorities in England and Wales subject to an affirmative resolution of both Houses of Parliament. (In Scotland, the Secretary of State already possessed similar, although not identical, powers to control local authority expenditure under the Local Government (Miscellaneous Provisions) (Scotland) Act, 1981.) The 1984 Rates Act also requires councils to consult with representatives of 'commercial and industrial' ratepayers before setting a rate, a measure reflecting the government's concern about the impact of rates upon business costs.

In 1985/6 the selective powers were used to cap the rates of eighteen councils; in 1987/8, twenty councils were rate-capped (plus ILEA and nineteen joint boards created following the abolition of the GLC and the metropolitan county councils). Although clear criteria for selection must be laid down (for example, expenditure 20 per cent above GREA and 4 per cent above 1984/5 target) almost all selected councils have been Labour-controlled. Machinery does exist for selected authorities to appeal to the Secretary of State, and in 1986/7 several ratecapped councils appealed for and obtained redetermined spending levels. This followed assurances that no authority seeking a redetermination should suffer a reduced spending level, fear of which had prevented any of the selected authorities from appealing in the first year of operation.

The Rates Act has been widely interpreted as a threat to local-government independence. Byrne (1986, p. 299) sees it as a constititional change such that 'central government, in relation to local government has come to resemble the Big Brother of George Orwell's *Nineteen Eighty Four*', while Newton and Karran (1985, ch. 8) compare it to 'Knee-Capping Local Government'. In the long term, they argue (p. 121) 'the constitutional issues' outweigh 'the disorganisation of local finances, and the breakdown of central–local relations . . . . The British system of government . . . was already highly centralised in 1979, and subsequent legislation has produced a quantum jump towards a more powerful and centralised state'. In the past individual authorities could always escape centrally imposed financial constraints by raising extra income from the rates without penalty (so long as it was prepared to risk the 'political' reaction from local ratepayers). That option, however, has now largely been closed.

Whilst the general power to cap the rates of all authorities has not yet been used, the switch in emphasis from concern with local *government* spending to local *authority* spending has nevertheless been marked. Almost all the selected authorities (despite loud protests) set legal rates within the limits set by ministers; and councillors in Lambeth – who delayed setting a rate to try and avoid compliance – were subsequently surcharged by the district auditor and disqualified as councillors. A similar fate befell councillors in Liverpool who, although not rate-capped at the time, delayed setting a rate on the grounds that they would otherwise have to make large spending cuts or impose rate rises (contrary to the ruling Labour group's manifesto commitments) to maintain expenditure within the block-grant regime (Parkinson, 1985; Travers, 1986, especially 164–77). Both in Lambeth and Liverpool councillors were seeking to exploit a legal loophole – the absence of any statutory date for setting a rate – subsequently removed by the Local Government Act 1986 (which requires a legal rate to be set by 1 April). Elsewhere councillors were seemingly unwilling to risk illegality. Although local government generally remained firmly opposed to the principle of rate limitation, few concessions were wrung from the government, and non-compliance petered out.

Nevertheless, while the government might successfully have enacted and implemented its rate-capping proposals, this was not achieved without considerable political cost. All the local authority associations (including those with a Conservative majority) opposed rate-capping in principle, the local government press, and the media generally were hostile, while the Bill's passage through Parliament led to strenuous opposition from senior Conservative MPs and sizeable backbench revolts in some votes. These political costs, moreover, produced only marginal gains in terms of localgovernment expenditure control. The exemption from the selective scheme of authorities spending less than GREA or £10m – a provision intended to reduce political opposition from the Conservative-dominated shire districts – removed an estimated 309 of the 333 English and Welsh non-metropolitan district councils from the scheme at the outset. Ministerial reassurances that the selective scheme would only encompass between about twelve and twenty authorities, and that the general scheme was a reserve power which ministers hoped never to use, served – although not written into the Bill – further to limit politically the scope of the measure. The combined effect of these concessions was virtually to remove from threat of rate-capping all but about 20 (4.4 per cent) of the 456 principal local authorities then existing in England and Wales. Clearly, so long as ministerial assurances are honoured, rate-capping can deliver only very limited reductions in total local authority expenditure.

Other constraints have also, in practice, limited the impact of rate-capping. As Travers (1986, p. 168) notes, the government had to set rate limits high enough to prevent legal challenges that income was insufficient to meet statutory obligations. It also had to keep the numbers of capped authorities to manageable proportions to prevent civil servants from being overloaded by the administrative burden of determining – and redetermining in the event of appeal – rate levels under the selective scheme. There were also political complications, in so far as the government wished to avoid criteria for rate-capping which might include Conservative-controlled authorities. (In the event one Conservative authority, Portsmouth, was rate-capped in 1985/6.)

For all these reasons the apparently draconian central powers contained in the 1984 Rates Act had a surprisingly limited effect in terms not only of the numbers of authorities rate-capped but also in terms of the capping limits actually imposed. According to Travers (1986, pp. 164–77) many of the rate limits were 'relatively generous', 'no significant inroads' were made into the spending of selected councils and some were able even to make 'a large rate increase'. A number of authorities also resorted to *creative accountancy* – technical accounting adjustments which maximize financial benefits in the authority's favour – as a means of 'spending above the rate-capping spending level'. For similar reasons, even in Scotland, where the Scottish Office had power to control the rates in all authorities, 'rate-capping produced few selective cuts in spending' (Dunleavy and Rhodes, 1988, p. 123).

Not only did rate-capping legislation have relatively little impact on spending patterns in selected authorities, it is questionable even whether overall local government spending was actually reduced. As Dunleavy and Rhodes (1988, p. 123) observe, 'high-spending' authorities not rate-capped tended to increase rates in order to build reserves against possible rate-capping in the future; hence, 'it is difficult to say whether selective rate-capping has marginally decreased total local government taxation . . . or substantially increased it (by encouraging many more councils to raise (taxes) as an insurance'. What is clear, however, is that rate-capping failed to produce the curbs in local spending which the government desired and in 1987 the Department of Environment, armed with the full battery of post-1979 legislation, had to concede that English local authorities were on course to exceed government expenditure targets by at least £500m (*The Times*, 28 October 1987). Indeed, at almost every turn, as central government has imposed new financial controls, local authorities have discovered loopholes and managed largely to avoid the intended consequences. Observing the statute book alone might appear to depict a massive reinforcement of the agency model of central–local financial relationships but practical outcomes are perhaps more suggestive of power-dependency.

What, of course, the failure to achieve the desired curbs in local spending did produce was an inevitable increase in the burden upon the ratepayer. As the percentage of revenue income derived from grant fell (from 46.7 per cent in England in 1976/7 to 39.2 per cent in 1984/5) so the percentage borne by local ratepayers increased (from 23 per cent to 27 per cent). This, in turn, focused attention upon the anomalies of the rating system (see p. 160–62) and increased pressure for the wholesale reform of local government finance. Of course, the climate of central-local government relationships in which these reforms were unveiled was hardly propitious. Shifting the burden from taxpayers to ratepayers, and introducing a plethora of complex and continually changing central financial controls, inevitably soured relationships even where party political and ideological differences did not intrude. While the Thatcher government has had a major policy aim of controlling public expenditure and has used the block-grant regime and rate-capping to that end, centrally imposed financial controls not only infringe the rights of elected councillors to determine local spending needs and priorities but also undermine accountability to local ratepayers. What from the central perspective might be seen as an instrument of public expenditure control, from the local level might be seen as a threat to the fabric of local government itself. Consequently, the 'bitter rancour' and 'strident tension' which Greenwood (1982, p. 254) characterized as underlying central–local government relationships has, if anything, intensified as the decade has progressed.

The local state?

On pp. 184–89 several 'models' of central–local relations were discussed. There are, however, alternative approaches. One such is provided in recent Marxist literature. In her study of Lambeth,

Cockburn (1977) provides one of the best known examples of this perspective which assumes that local government is simply one arm of the capitalist state, providing the conditions for continued capital accumulation and the maintenance of social order. In other words, a general theory of the capitalist state is applied with little modification to what has become known as the 'local state'.

Saunders (1981), however, suggests that this approach is inadequate. He argues that the 'local state' is not simply the national state writ small, and that a general theory of the state cannot be applied to the local level. He criticizes Cockburn's as 'a surprisingly crass agency model' which reduces local government to a mere agent of central government. In Saunders's view, the 'local state' cannot simply be reduced to a functioning part of a national capitalist state, for within certain constraints 'non-capitalist interests can win at the local level in a way that is becoming increasingly difficult at national level' (pp. 4, 11). In 1983, for example, there were 'radical' authorities of the 'Left' (such as the GLC), as well as of the 'Right' (such as Wandsworth), which operated with particular local distinctiveness.

As a basis for understanding 'the current crisis of central–local relations in Britain' (p. 10) Saunders offers an alternative analytical framework encompassing four main dimensions: organizational, economic, political, and ideological. Each dimension can be observed from both the central and local perspective.

From the perspective of a right-wing central government these four dimensions can be seen thus:

1 the *organizational* problem of how to impose central controls against the demand for local self-determination, especially on the part of radical Labour councils claiming a mandate for opposing government policies;
2 the *economic* problem of how to enforce reductions in local social consumption expenditure;
3 the *political* problem of how to reconcile local democratic accountability with the pursuit of a long-term economic strategy;
4 the *ideological* problem of how to break down popular expectations regarding social provisions which became established during the postwar years of Keynesian consensus politics.

From the perspective of radical Labour councils (seeking to oppose Conservative central government cuts) Saunders puts forward the same four dimensions:

1 the *organizational* problem of how to fight central government policies through local authorities which are subordinate to central departments;

2 the *economic* problem of how to finance and defend services while at the same time transforming their character in a socialist direction;
3 the *political* problem of how to mobilize alliances among different consumption sectors and between these and class-based producer movements;
4 the *ideological* problem of how to assert the principle of need in the face of central government's desire to trim welfare services.

Saunders's analysis of central–local relations goes beyond the inter-organizational focus of the power-dependence model. Rightly, he stresses economic, political and ideological dimensions as well as 'top-down' and 'bottom-up' perspectives. His approach is particularly helpful in understanding the relationship between central governments and local authorities which are opposed on political and ideological grounds. It is less helpful, however, where there is little or no political or ideological distinctiveness – in technical fields, for example, or where there is sustained political consensus between individual authorities and the centre. Perhaps, as Dunleavy (1980b, p. 131) suggests, future research into central–local relations needs to adopt a variety of analytical perspectives. Organizational issues are only one dimension of inter-governmental relations.

Overview and prospects

R. Rhodes, (1984, p. 355), observing the increased assertiveness of the Thatcher government, has characterized the changes in relationship between central and local government during the 1970s as shifting from bargaining through incorporation to direction and centralization in the 1980s. However, direction and centralization, as Dunleavy and Rhodes (1987, p. 26) warn, is not synonymous with control, as is well illustrated in the financial sphere where interventions have often been met by the development of evasion strategies by local authorities. In practice 'the degree of control has been limited: intentions and achievements have diverged markedly'.

Even if its intentions have not always been realized, the second half of the 1980s has nevertheless witnessed renewed determination by central government to exercise greater direction over local authorities. The 1986 Local Government Act, for example, limited the ability of local authorities to spend money on publicity, while the 1988 Local Government Act imposed further restrictions professedly designed to stop the use of rates for party political propaganda. The 1988 Local Government Act also sought to extend the privatization or contracting-out of local authority services by empowering the Secretary of State to specify by regulation local services which must be put out to tender. Services initially specified included refuse collection, cleaning buildings, street sweeping, school meals and catering, and ground and vehicle maintenance. Under the Act the Secretary of State can differentiate between authorities in drawing up the timetable for tendering and has powers to extend tendering to other services. First contracts are scheduled to start in April 1989. This measure effectively makes competitive tendering compulsory for designated services, replacing the former (largely discretionary) powers which had been used by relatively few authorities in specific areas (Ascher, 1987, especially ch. 7; Stoker, 1988).

These enactments, particularly when seen alongside pledges in the Conservative Party's 1987 general election manifesto (and subsequently presented to Parliament) to allow schools and council tenants to 'opt out' of local authority control, would seem to envisage a diminished role for elected local government. Indeed the abolition of the GLC and metropolitan county councils, coupled with the recent development in inner-city areas of enterprise zones, city task forces and urban development corporations, has already meant in some localities a reduced role for elected councils in local service provision. Nevertheless, despite these trends, local government retains a substantial political and administrative role in Britain, and central–local relationships remain in a continuous state of flux. As Shell (1987, p. 295) observes, 'Because Britain lacks a codified constitution, the relationship between central and local government is nowhere precisely defined'. And whilst in a formal sense local authorities are entirely subordinate to Parliament, in practice working relationships are tremendously diverse.

In 1981 Sharpe (p. 5) pointed to an 'unresolved tension' in central–local relationships arising from the ambiguous status of local government, which is subordinate to Parliament, but at the same time 'has the potential for independent power' through being elected and by having the capacity to raise at least some of its revenue by local taxation. Political, economic and social priorities can vary enormously between central government and local authorities, as well as between local authorities themselves, and over time. Interestingly, in the light of increasing central 'controls' during the late 1970s and the 1980s, Alexander (1982b, p. ix), in what could be interpreted as a swing back towards an agency model approach, argues that there has been a 'decline in the autonomy and independence of local government . . . [which] constitutes a threat to the nature of our democracy and to the sensitivity and effectiveness of our public services'. Clearly, however, the infinite number of variables prohibits the formulation of any 'rule of thumb'; complexity and ambiguity remain the order of the day, hence the inappropriateness of generalizations.

11 QUASI-GOVERNMENT

Introduction

The term 'quasi-government' refers to both the government-created and semi-private organizations which are both distinct from, but usually relate to, either central departments or local authorities. As a field of study quasi-government is both complex and confusing, being partly public and partly private, voluntary or commercial. So great is the number and variety of organizations included within it that generalizations, definitions and classifications are fraught with difficulties. Even terminology is a problem. The organizations comprising quasi-government are referred to by a variety of terms: 'fringe bodies', 'non-departmental public bodies', 'semi-autonomous authorities' and 'quangos', to name but a few. The latter term, usually an acronym for 'quasi-autonomous non-governmental organization', has now entered popular usage, indicating the interest which quasi-government has recently begun to attract.

The word 'quango', however, is essentially an umbrella beneath which a tremendous variety of organizations shelter. Compare, for example, a local association for the disabled, the Apple and Pear Development Council, the UK Atomic Energy Authority, and the Arts Council of Great Britain – all are 'quangos' but their diversity in terms of finance, organization, objectives and accountability is enormous. Generalizing about 'quangos' can be hazardous – even their origins are remarkably diverse as Barker (1982, pp. 7–8) observes:

> Many are statutory, under an Act itself (for example, Manpower Services Commission or Health and Safety Commission). . . . The founding instrument may be a royal charter (BBC or the research councils); a Treasury Minute (University Grants Committee); the articles of a non-profit company (National Consumer Council); or, more humbly, but apparently almost as effectively, a mere Answer in the House, a memorandum from the Minister to himself, a wave of the hand, or whatever else may signify a decision to establish a new body (Schools Council, Technician and Business Education Councils and that unusual 'central–local government voluntary' body, the Womens Royal Voluntary Service).

The problem of discussing quasi-government is further complicated, as Doig (1979, p. 311) notes, 'by the fact that there is no one characteristic, or lack of characteristic, that distinguishes quangos or non-departmental public bodies from other organisations in the structure of government'. Nevertheless, most, if not all, of the organizations concerned carry out their work at arm's length from central government departments and/or local authorities. Indeed, quasi-government is sometimes presented as part of a public/private continuum: from government (G), such as central departments; through quasi-governmental organizations (QG), such as nationalized industries; to quasi-non-governmental organizations (QNG), such as the National Research Development Organization; to non-government (NG), such as private companies (see Hague, Mackenzie and Barker, 1975). This is obviously a simplified and inevitably imprecise scheme but it is helpful in placing quasi-government within the broader administrative and political context.

While the rationale for the arm's length approach, as well as the length of the arm, varies widely from organization to organization, the desire to distance important areas of public administration from direct political control has been a major factor in the twentieth-century growth of quasi-government. Of course, where politicians are denied control, they cannot normally be expected to assume accountability, thus undermining the principle that public administration should be publicly accountable. As Sir Norman Chester (1979, p. 54) has observed:

> The growth of fringe bodies is a retreat from the simple democratic principle evolved in the nineteenth century that those who perform a public duty should be fully responsible to an electorate – by way either of a minister responsible to Parliament or of a locally elected council. The essence of the fringe body is that it is not so responsible for some or all of its actions.

Numbers and types of quangos

In 1987 there were, according to official figures (Cabinet Office, 1987, p. iv) some 1,643 Non-Departmental Public Bodies (NDPBs) operating in Britain, spending between them £9,100m and employing 148,700 staff. Although in 1979, when the Conservative election manifesto pledged a purge on quangos, the number had been much larger (2,167 bodies, employing 217,000 staff) quangos are clearly far from dead. Indeed, although there were fifteen fewer quangos overall than in the previous year, the twelve months ending April 1987 still saw sixty-six new bodies set up, the Ministry of Agriculture leading the way with twenty-eight.

Nevertheless, while quangos have clearly survived the first two Thatcher administrations, a precise head count is less easy than official figures might suggest. Indeed there remains much disagreement about precisely (or even roughly) how many organizations exist within the field of quasi-government. This is partly because of the difficulty in deciding where boundaries should be drawn, a difficulty which has increased in recent years with the development of new organizational forms (such as 'hived-off' agencies) and with the increasing interpenetration of the public and private sectors. As Hood (1979, p. 9) asks, 'Does one include advisory committees as "government bodies"? Contracting firms? Grant-aided bodies? Firms in which public money is invested?' Quasi-government is a grey area between not only government departments and local authorities, but also frequently beteween the public and the private sectors.

Another analytical difficulty is that organizational units are often not clear-cut. For example, it is always problematic whether or not to count Scottish and Welsh divisions of an agency as separate units or as part of a single organization. Because of these various difficulties a count of quangos is beset with problems. In 1978 the Civil Service Department reported that there were 252 non-departmental public bodies, compared with 196 in 1971, 103 in 1959 and only ten before 1900 (Bowen, 1978). The definition the CSD used for its survey was: 'organisations which have been set up or adopted by Departments and provided with funds to perform some function which the Government wish to have performed but which it did not wish to be the direct responsibility of a Minister or Department'. The CSD survey excluded non-permanent bodies, advisory committees and working parties. Other sources, using broader definitions, produce far higher figures. For example, Anderson lists almost 1,000 official organizations, many of them advisory and consultative (cited in Hood, 1979, p. 8). Philip Holland (1979) produced a list of 3,068 quangos but this was because he defined a quango as an official body to which ministers appoint directly members other than civil servants. He thereby included hundreds of advisory committees and hundreds of judicial tribunals and many more bodies with no governmental function at all (several public schools, for example). The Outer Circle Policy Unit (1979a) included 603 bodies in its list, having excluded departmental advisory committees and organizations whose function was primarily judicial.

'Head counts' of quangos are the more difficult because, as Hood (1979, pp. 9–10) observes, 'the "heads" involved are of enormously differing size and importance – on a scale more like the difference between the head of an ant and an elephant than the difference between one human head and another'. Quangos, in fact, are analogous to pressure groups; both involve tiny, relatively insignificant groupings, as well as massive and extremely powerful organizations. Indeed quangos are frequently the target of pressure group activity, and may at times themselves behave like pressure groups exerting pressure on other parts of the government machine.

The volume and variety of quangos also make any attempt at meaningful classification difficult. However, the Pliatzky Report (1980, pp. 1–2) delineated three distinctive types – executive bodies, advisory bodies, and tribunals – which offers a useful basis for categorization. In 1987 the Cabinet Office (1987, p. iv) identified within each of these categories the following numbers:

1 Executive bodies: 396
2 Advisory bodies: 1057
3 Tribunals: 64

The number of quangos in this classification, large though it is, nevertheless excludes important areas of quasi-government. It ignores, for example, the 'innumerable autonomous and semi-autonomous, official and quasi-official organizations, each with its own part to play in the policy-making process' of local government (Cousins, 1982, p. 152). It also excludes various administrative agencies connected with the National Health Service and the nationalized industries. The size, diversity, and importance of quasi-government is vast; one is dealing with a genus rather than a species. All that can really be said with certainty is that quasi-governmental bodies generally operate in narrower, more specific areas than government departments or local authorities.

Inevitably, any classification of such bodies must be arbitrary; clear boundaries between quasi-government and more orthodox areas of public administration cannot always be drawn. For presentational purposes, however, this chapter will follow Pliatzky and focus upon the major forms of quasi-government at national level, namely, *executive and advisory non-departmental public bodies*. The other major form of non-departmental body, *the public corporation*, will be discussed in Chapter 12 within the wider context of the nationalized industries. *Health and water authorities*, while part of quasi-government, have a strong regional network, and are discussed in Chapter 13 along with other forms of regional administration. *Administrative tribunals*, although included within Pliatzky's survey, are most appropriately considered alongside other channels of redress, and are therefore dealt with in detail in Chapter 15. Space does not allow consideration of quasi-government at the local level (for details of which see Cousins, 1982 and 1983; Rhodes, 1988).

Non-departmental public bodies: rationale

Quasi-government is not new although its scale is new. The Crown Agents, for example, date from the mid-nineteenth century, the

Development Commission was set up in 1909 and the Horserace Totalisator Board (the Tote) goes back to 1928. As Hood notes, however, they came into 'high fashion in the 1940s and again in the 1960s when the Fulton Committee endorsed the idea of government growth outside Whitehall by "hiving-off" units from civil service departments to non-departmental bodies' (1981, p. 100). Pliatzky (1980, pp. 2–3) presents the rationale for non-departmental bodies in the following terms.

EXECUTIVE BODIES

These include the Hops Marketing Board and the Nature Conservancy Council, for example, and are justified with the argument that certain functions can best be carried out at arm's length from central government:

(i) because the work is of an executive nature which does not require ministers to be involved in day-to-day management;
(ii) because the work is more effectively carried out by a single-purpose organization rather than by a government department with a wide range of functions;
(iii) to involve people from outside government in the direction of the organization; and
(iv) to put the performance of particular functions outside direct party political control.

ADVISORY BODIES

These include the China Clay Council and the Advisory Committee on Pesticides, for example. The major reasons for advisory committees (incorporating outside representation) are:

(i) that the department's own staff are unable to provide the necessary advice by themselves; and
(ii) that it may be desirable to enlist participation by outside interests in order to develop publicly acceptable proposals.

Control and accountability

These two concepts (see Chapter 1) are central to any discussion of quasi-government:

CONTROL

The arm's length approach usually associated with quangos means that normal departmental patterns of ministerial control do not apply.

Indeed, a minister may even 'expressly desire to keep out of the affairs of quangos within the ambit of his department, arguing that to behave otherwise is merely to frustrate the whole purpose of this way of organising public services' (Johnson, 1979, p. 389). On day-to-day matters most ministers and departments 'maintain an arm's-length relationship' from the organization which they sponsor, although considerable pressure may be brought to bear upon them on 'broader policy and resource' matters (Johnson, 1982, p. 213).

The precise way in which many quangos are controlled is difficult to determine. Obtaining even basic information can be problematical. For example, while annual reports usually name the chairman and board members they do not always reveal their salaries. Likewise the breakdown of expenses between board members and staff, and between different types of expenses, is relatively detailed in some cases but not in others. A further problem is that the governing authority of quangos often consists of a board or council. Often the only paid member is the chairman, suggesting that he may really be in charge. However, generalizations are dangerous: some chairmen are only part-time and some councils are large while others are small and highly specialized. While the staff running some are technical specialists, this is far from universal. Sometimes the relationship with the parent department is close; sometimes it is not. The permutations are infinite.

ACCOUNTABILITY

Three aspects of the accountability of non-departmental bodies require consideration:

(i) Relations with ministers

With non-departmental bodies, as Johnson (1982, p. 213) observes, 'accountability of Ministers' must remain 'attenuated', for 'otherwise there would be little point in having this form of administrative organisation'. Usually ministers are formally answerable to Parliament only for discharging their own responsibilities relating to sponsored bodies (such as in terms of broad policy and general oversight), while responsibility for efficiency and day-to-day matters normally rests with the organizations' own management. In practice, however, the precise boundaries of ministerial responsibility are often difficult to define. Not only is the borderline between ministers' policy and oversight responsibilities, and those of boards for efficiency and day-to-day administration, often blurred, but in practice there is considerable variation in relationships between ministers and boards. (The Public Accounts Committee (1986–7a, para. 32), for example, contrasted the Welsh Office's 'arm's length and detached' attitude to 'sponsorship' of NDPBs, with the Environment Department's 'involved, positive and disciplined' approach). In any event the sheer volume and variety of bodies under departmental sponsorship often makes ministerial responsibility something of a myth. In recent years the size and complexity of departmental work has seriously eroded the concept of ministerial responsibility even for their own departments (Chapter 14). How much more tenuous must it therefore be for non-departmental bodies operating at arm's length from ministers, and which 'for most of the time . . . rub along without much awareness of the Minister and his officials' (Johnson, 1982, p. 213).

(ii) Relations with Parliament

Because non-departmental bodies operate at arm's length from government, and ministers are not constitutionally responsible to Parliament for all of their work, accountability to Parliament is limited. Johnson (1982, p. 213) observes that MPs 'may attempt ingeniously to get at the activities of governmental bodies through the questioning of Ministers, but . . . it is not something attempted very regularly and, when it is, the attack focuses on policy and resources rather than on particular decisions'. The dilemma, he adds, is that 'reinforcement of the parliamentary accountability of these organisations would also entail a strengthening of ministerial control over them', so destroying the arm's length relationship with all its attendant advantages.

Nevertheless, some important instruments of accountability to Parliament can be identified, although most apply to some quangos and not all. For example, some come within the jurisdiction of the Ombudsman (Chapter 15), some have their accounts audited by the Comptroller and Auditor General and reported to the Public Accounts Committee (Chapter 14), some present annual reports to Parliament, and so on. In fact, no general pattern is discernible, except that almost all stop short of full accountability to Parliament. In 1979, however, accountability was strengthened with the advent of the fourteen new Commons select committees, each of which has power to examine the expenditure, administration and policy of the main government departments 'and associated public bodies'. While this represents an important development in Parliament's powers of scrutiny, non-departmental bodies account for only a small part of the work of these committees which are quite unable to exercise anything like detailed oversight.

(iii) Relations with the courts

The legal accountability of quangos also poses considerable difficulty. Because their legal status and powers are confused, judicial control of their activities lacks coherence. For example, remedies available against one body may not be available against another; procedures or standards applied by one quango may be legally sound but if utilized by another they may not, and so on. In Johnson's view (1982, p. 215), 'The confusions affecting legal accountability and the availability of enforceable remedies are one of the most serious aspects of the haphazard development of governmental bodies'.

While accountability problems are found throughout British public administration, with non-departmental bodies they are particularly acute. Clearly, orthodox ministerial responsibility could not be extended to them without undermining the arm's length principle. Several changes short of this, however, have been proposed: requiring greater disclosure of information; extending jurisdiction of the Comptroller and Auditor General and Public Accounts Committee to more bodies; and clarifying the authority, powers and legal status of all such organizations (see, for example, Outer Circle Policy Unit, 1979a; and Pliatzky Report, 1980, pp. 18–23). Changes of this kind would standardize and strengthen accountability without destroying the arm's length arrangement. In view of the importance and extent of quasi-government they perhaps deserve serious consideration.

In 1981 a tentative move in this direction occurred with the publication of a government guide (*Non-Departmental Public Bodies: A Guide for Departments*) laying down ground rules on the future nature of quangos and their relationships with departments. A revised edition of this document was produced in 1985 (Cabinet Office (MPO)/Treasury, 1985c) which reflected developments in policy and practice since the 1981 edition, particularly the government's drive to strengthen financial management. Departments are now obliged to review from time to time the bodies they sponsor, and have received instructions that – whatever the precise degree of independence – the minister is answerable to Parliament for whether the body is working efficiently and economically. They have also since 1984 been brought within the framework of the Financial Management Initiative (see Chapter 7; Cabinet Office (MPO)/Treasury (FMU), 1984a). Greater financial accountability, particularly for bodies utilizing government funds at a level of 50 per cent or more, was also envisaged and the establishment of new non-departmental bodies would, it was promised, involve negotiating more hurdles than hitherto.

Not surprisingly, the financial position of fringe bodies is almost infinitely varied. Some are funded by grants-in-aid (such as the Training Agency); some by statutory levy (such as the Horserace Betting Levy Board); some by annual grant (such as the Health Education Council); some by departmental vote (such as the Central Council for Education and Training in Social Work); some by drawing on the National Loan Fund (such as New Town Corporations); and some by charges for services (such as the Agricultural Marketing Boards) (Rhodes, 1988, p. 129). In each of these financial relationships the government has considerable power. Despite the diversity, therefore, central direction is marked.

Patronage

Considerable concern about non-departmental bodies has focused on patronage – the number of appointments in the gift of ministers. Promotion by merit rather than political influence has long characterized the British civil service, but outside the civil service ministers still exercise considerable patronage. In November 1978, for example, 'seventeen ministers had within their gift over 8,000 paid appointments and 25,000 unpaid ones at a total cost of £5m. a year' (Outer Circle Policy Unit, 1979a, p. 47). One department alone was responsible for nearly 1,000 appointments. Parliamentary influence over these appointments is minimal, the matter being almost entirely one of ministerial discretion. Party political factors are frequently to the fore; indeed, 'many people . . . have claimed to perceive a resurgence of eighteenth-century jobbery' (Hood, 1978, p. 40).

Whether or not patronage is used in a party political manner, the non-departmental sector nevertheless 'affords the opportunity for government by co-option rather than by election or by merit appointment' (Hood, 1978, p. 41). Additionally, once a person is appointed, not only need the minister never account for the choice, but the likelihood is that he or she will never have to justify it on performance grounds.

The Outer Circle Policy Unit study (1979a, p. 48) emphasized three major areas for concern about appointments of this kind:

(i) efficiency – does patronage result in the best available people being appointed?
(ii) power – does patronage give ministers too much power to influence supposedly independent organizations?
(iii) privilege – does it enable elite groups to dominate patronage jobs?

Although these are legitimate grounds for unease, solutions are far from straightforward because of the diversity of quangos. Some appointments could be on a representative basis where there are sectional interests, but in other cases the wider public interest would need to be safeguarded.

Holland and Fallon (1978, p. 25) argue that several reforms are necessary

(i) nomination should be much more open, with ministers more accountable to Parliament for each appointment;

(ii) the number of paid public appointments that can be held by a single individual should be limited;
(iii) all full-time paid appointments should be advertised and the appointment confirmed by a relevant parliamentary committee;
(iv) appointments on solely political grounds should cease.

In summary, any reforms to the system of ministerial patronage should aim to reduce secrecy, encourage competition, control the power of ministers, introduce accountability for appointments made, and provide for assessment of performance. It is important, however, not to underplay the political dimension of patronage; it offers a means of securing the co-operation of key pressure groups and ensuring party discipline – hence ministerial 'resistance' to drastic pruning.

Exit non-departmental public bodies?

The Conservative government elected in 1979 promised a drastic purge of quasi-governmental organizations as part of its wider strategy of reducing public expenditure. Immediately following the 1980 Pliatzky Report the government decided to reduce: a) the number of executive bodies by thirty; b) the number of advisory bodies by 211; c) the number of individual tribunals by six. In December 1980 the government announced that a further 192 non-departmental bodies were to be wound up by 1983, bringing the total savings up to about £23m a year by 1983. In February 1982 the Prime Minister announced a third round of cuts: the abolition of 112 executive non-departmental bodies and 500 advisory ones. Philip Holland, MP, observed: 'That nearly one-quarter of the executive quangos and nearly one-third of the very large number of advisory bodies, as defined by Pliatzky and inherited by this Government, are scheduled for abolition after only 2½ years is a quite remarkable achievement by any standards' (*Daily Telegraph*, 11 March 1982).

By November 1984 the Prime Minister reported that 700 bodies had either been wound up or had their expenditure reduced, giving a total saving of £118m per year (see Hood, 1988, p. 89 for further elaboration on alleged reductions). However, as Table 11.1 shows, spending on fringe bodies still remains high. In 1986–7, for example, a single executive body, the Manpower Services Commission, spent £3,129.1m (see Cabinet Office, 1987, p. 14).

Why has the promised purge of quangos proved so difficult to achieve? According to Rhodes (1988, p. 130) one main reason is that the Thatcher government has developed quangos as a convenient vehicle for bypassing what it perceived (particularly in urban areas) as a hostile and recalcitrant local government system. Quangos have provided a

Table 11.1 Non-Departmental Public Bodies 1979–87

	Number of bodies						
	Executive	*Advisory*	*Tribunals*	*Others*	*Total*	*Number of staff*	*Total expenditure* £m[2]
1979	492	1,485	70	120	2,167	217,000	6,150
1982	450	1,173	64	123	1,810	205,500	8,330
1983	431	1,074	65	121	1,691	196,700	9,940
1984[1]	402	1,087	71	121	1,681	141,200	7,280
1985	399	1,069	65	121	1,654	138,300	7,700
1986	406	1,062	64	126	1,658	146,300	8,240
1987	396	1,057	64	126	1,643	148,700	9,100

Notes:
1 Staff and expenditure figures from 1984 exclude the English and Welsh Water Authorities which were reclassified as Nationalised Industries. Water Authority staff in 1983 numbered approx. 58,000; expenditure approx. £2,600m.
2 current prices
Source: Cabinet Office, 1987, p. iv.

means of developing an administrative network at grass roots level without the uncertainty (and possible political hostility) associated with provision by elected local authorities. At the local level recent years have seen considerable central intervention via 'fringe' agencies. As Dunleavy and Rhodes (1987, p. 23) argue, the government 'has presided over the proliferation of single-function quasi-government agencies'. Recent years have seen the establishment of 'enterprise zones', Urban Development Corporations and a range of similar organizations, operating at local level but bypassing inner-city councils.

In similar vein the abolition of the metropolitan county councils and the Greater London Council in 1986 also 'produced a whole new crop of non-departmental bodies' (Dunleavy and Rhodes, 1987, p. 23). (A precursor was the London Regional Transport Board established in 1984, when London Transport was removed from the GLC.) The new bodies created to provide services in the former GLC and metropolitan county areas include numerous joint boards of councillors or QUELGOs (quasi-elected local government organizations). Consisting mainly of councillors indirectly elected by district councils in the locality such bodies are now responsible in these areas for fire, waste disposal services, and many other functions. In London responsibility for around two-thirds of GLC spending, and in the former metropolitan county areas about half, was transferred to non-departmental bodies or central departments (Dunleavy and Rhodes, 1987, p. 23). Non-departmental public bodies are far from dead!

Quangos, clearly, have been advantageous to government in allowing elected local authorities to be bypassed (and in some cases even replaced altogether). Indeed it is possible, at the time of writing, to foresee major expansion of quango-type bodies for similar reasons at national level. The 'agencies' proposed in the Ibbs *Next Steps* Report (see Chapter 2), for example, are seen as an alternative to government departments for the delivery of a wide range of executive functions in line with the Thatcher government's emphasis on 'value for money'. Significantly, they seem likely to bear many of the problems (such as accountability) already associated with non-departmental public bodies, as well as many of the hallmarks: the delegation of functions to specialist agencies, broad policy determined by government; and an arm's length relationship with departments. How far these proposals will reach fruition remains to be seen, but one thing is clear: as Hood (1981, pp. 120–1) argues, non-departmental bodies are too useful for politicians to abolish them too readily. There are, he adds, at least four potential political uses which make them unlikely to disappear:

(i) government will presumably always need bodies from which it can distance itself in sensitive areas;
(ii) there will presumably always be value in having temporary organizations outside the permanent government service that can be scrapped when chances permit;
(iii) the use of such bodies as an administrative means of bypassing other public organizations, along with the patronage dimension, continues to attract politicians;
(iv) advisory committees are useful as political 'window dressing'.

For these reasons, if for no others, quangos seem unlikely to become extinct.

Conclusions

Non-departmental public bodies have, for the most part, restricted authority, a limited arsenal of political resources, and a lack of independent finance. They do, however, have organizational and informational resources aplenty (Rhodes, 1988, p. 171). Although essentially concerned with adapting centrally determined policy to local circumstances, and interfacing with relevant consumers, the professional expertise embedded in such bodies nevertheless provides opportunities to shape decision-making in some areas of public policy.

Non-departmental public bodies have arisen to no pattern or plan. They display a variety of structures, powers, modes of finance, methods of selection, degrees of discretion and types of staff. The main problems they pose are the excessive patronage they confer on the politicians and officials who establish them and make appointments to them, 'their frustration of the implementation of public policies, their financial irresponsibility and their erosion of democratic accountability and control' (Jones, 1982a, p. 924). Jones further argues that if central government believes it cannot or should not perform a particular public function, 'it would be better if it decentralised not to technocratic quangos but to directly elected local governments'. Less radically, Johnson (1979, pp. 393–4) argues that some order could be introduced into chaos by the creation of a Standing Advisory Commission on Administrative Organization (another quango?). This would conduct a continuing survey of administrative structures with two purposes in mind: a) to produce information and thereby increase openness; b) to carry out inquiries and offer advice to central government and other public authorities.

Whatever the merits of such reform proposals it is a mistake to see quangos as wholly self-contained. As Hood (1979, p. 20) points out, government agencies are increasingly operating 'in multiple and dense networks of cross-cutting territorial, functional and hierarchical relationships, and within an overall context of . . . government by grants and by indirect administration rather than by the older pattern of directly hired bureaucrats at the centre'. Inter-organizational and inter-agency relationships have become increasingly complex; quangos (with their organizational and informational resources) are only part of this complex administrative and political environment – an environment which the operations of quangos themselves influence (see Moore and Booth, 1987).

In recent years the discrediting of quangos has become a popular political pastime. According to Dunsire (1982, p. 15), 'quango-hunting' has since 1979 'become a Conservative blood-sport, under the illusion that they are nothing but wasteful "empire-building"'. In practice, however, quangos often deal with specialized tasks in a way which both central government departments and local authorities would find difficult. They are also incredibly diverse; there is little justification for derogatory generalizations. Without denying the accountability/control/patronage problems which accompany this form of governmental organization, the survival of the species suggests that governments themselves see a continuing role for non-departmental public bodies, particularly when faced with politically hostile local authorities and bureaucratically organized government departments which may frustrate central government policy priorities. As Hill (1983, p. 124) observes, the 'attacks on Quangos have obscured, rather than illuminated, the serious issue of how ministerial patronage might be replaced by alternative selection procedures, and how these bodies might be made more accountable, without losing that very semi-independence which was a major reason for establishing them in the first place'.

12 Administering public ownership and privatization

Quasi-government in Britain extends to public ownership. While some publicly owned commercial or industrial undertakings are administered through orthodox central and local government institutions, such enterprises often require greater managerial and financial flexibility than organizations of this kind normally allow. Consequently, the arm's length approach typical of quasi-government is an important feature of British public ownership. This is especially true of the nationalized industries with which this chapter is largely concerned.

Terminology and ambiguity of public ownership

Public ownership typifies the ambiguity and complexity inherent in British public administration. It exists in various forms, offers a bewildering range of relationships with the wider political and administrative system, and presents complex problems of accountability and control. The very term 'public ownership' is ambiguous. Technically a vast range of assets – roads, schools, hospitals, libraries and so forth – are in public ownership, and in this sense the boundaries of public ownership might be regarded as coterminous with the public sector, or even the state itself. Usually, however, in Britain the term 'public ownership' applies to commercial and industrial undertakings. Although this narrows the scope considerably, ambiguity nevertheless remains. Does public ownership, for example, include undertakings in which the state has only a minority holding (such as British Telecom at the time of writing) and what precisely is a 'commercial' or 'industrial' undertaking? The water industry (in 1988) is largely in public hands, as is Girobank, and yet – until the prospect of privatization appeared – neither was usually regarded as a nationalized industry or included in discussions of public ownership.

Some writers attempt to resolve these ambiguities by focusing on particular types of public ownership. The term 'nationalization' – 'a process in which private assets . . . are transferred into national ownership' (Steel, 1978, p. 110) – is, for example, quite widely used. Nevertheless, 'nationalization' itself presents major terminological problems. One is that it need not apply to purely industrial or commercial concerns: for example, it is technically 'correct to talk of the nationalisation of the hospitals' (Steel, 1978, p. 110). Secondly, some nationalized industries (such as the postal services) are 'not in fact the end-product of nationalisation' having never been privately owned. Thirdly, nationalization represents only part of public ownership: for example, it excludes bodies in municipal ownership. Nevertheless, despite these difficulties, the term 'nationalized industries' is capable of fairly precise definition, and considerable agreement exists about the industries to which it refers (see Table 12.1).

Another approach is to focus on perhaps the most important form of public ownership, the 'public corporation'. This, however, is also fraught with problems. Public corporations embrace an even smaller part of public ownership than 'nationalization' and, more problematically, there is 'little agreement as to the essential characteristics of a public corporation' (Steel, 1978, p. 110); hence, defining or describing one, other than in general terms, poses serious problems.

Terms such as 'public ownership', 'nationalization', and 'public corporations' must, therefore, be used with caution. Confusion is compounded, moreover, because different authorities use the terms, and draw the boundaries between them, differently. Thus Tivey (1973a, pp. 67–9), viewed atomic energy as a 'major nationalized industry', whilst the McIntosh Report (1976, app. vol., p. 4) and Pliatzky Report (1980, p. 182) excluded it. Similarly, McIntosh (app. vol., p. 5) included regional water authorities in its list of public corporations, whereas Pliatzky excluded them (p. 183), arguing that they were 'more in the nature of a public service of the kind provided by local authorities' (p. 31). Even when the matter was cleared up in statutory terms – by the 1983 Water Act which declared water authorities bodies corporate – one observer (Topham, 1983) argued that water was not 'really a Nationalised Industry' because, unlike other NIs, its product, water, was 'tax financed and not traded' (see also Million, 1983). Even where consistent definitions are used, undertakings may be reclassified. Thus the Royal Mint and the Property Services Agency (Supplies Division) were officially reclassified from central government to the public corporation sector in the mid-1970s on being 'established as trading funds under the Government Trading Funds Act 1973' (Briscoe, 1981). It is therefore far from clear, not only how different forms of public ownership can be delineated, but even where the boundary should be drawn between 'public ownership' and the wider machinery of central and local administration.

The extent of public ownership

Public ownership is not exclusively a modern phenomenon. The Post Office, for example, has been publicly owned for centuries, and during the nineteenth century municipal gas and water undertakings were widespread. During the twentieth century, however, public ownership (until 1979) underwent enormous expansion, mainly with regard to nationalization (where the state – as opposed to local authorities – owns the assets).

Until the Second World War nationalization was of only peripheral economic importance – the main nationalization undertakings being the Forestry Commission, the British Broadcasting Corporation (BBC), the Central Electricity Board, and the London Passenger Transport Board. After the war, however, the Attlee government massively extended public ownership by nationalizing several basic industries: coal, iron and steel, electricity, gas, road transport, rail, inland waterways, and civil aviation.

Until 1979 Conservative governments – although partially denationalizing iron and steel and road transport in the 1950s, and selling minor undertakings to private enterprise (such as Thomas Cook Ltd, and State Management Pubs and Breweries) in the 1970s – were generally disposed to leave Attlee's legacy intact. Indeed, in some respects they extended it: for example, the Heath government nationalized Rolls Royce and Upper Clyde Shipbuilders. There were also further acts of nationalization by Labour governments in the 1960s and 1970s. Iron and steel was renationalized in 1967, and shipbuilding and aerospace nationalized in the 1970s. Major instruments were also established to channel public money – usually in return for state shareholdings – into industrial companies, the most important being the Industrial Reorganization Corporation (1966–71) and the National Enterprise Board (established in 1975).

In the late 1970s, when the economic impact of public ownership was probably at its peak, a White Paper (*Nationalised Industries*, 1978, para. 52) stated:

> The nationalised industries . . . employ about 1,700,000 people, or 7% of the country's total labour force. Their total investment this year and next is about £3,500 million at 1977 prices, and in 1976 they accounted for 14% of total fixed investment. . . . In 1976 they contributed about 10% of the total output of the U.K. economy. They dominate four strategic sectors of economic activity: energy, public transport, communications and iron and steel.

Although the late 1970s probably marked the peak in the expansion of public ownership, a decade later – despite substantial privatization (see pp. 245–46) – its economic importance remains substantial. In 1987, for example, the nationalized industries alone accounted for 5.5 per cent of UK output, employed around 800,000 people (just under 4 per cent of the total workforce), and spent £4b on capital account. (*Economic Progress Report*, no. 193, December 1987, London: H.M. Treasury). While subsequent asset sales, to which the Thatcher government is committed, will undoubtedly alter the picture, at the time of writing (1988) there remains a substantial nationalized sector.

Reasons for public ownership

The relationship of publicly owned enterprises to the wider political and administrative system cannot easily be understood without reference to the arguments for public ownership. These are numerous, often being geared to the pragmatic needs of particular industries, although several seminal influences can be identified, as follows.

(i) Ideological influences

The main ideological thrust towards greater public ownership has come from the Labour Party, which is committed by clause IV of its constitution to securing

> for the workers by hand or by brain the full fruits of their industry and the most equitable distribution thereof that may be possible upon the basis of the common ownership of the means of production, distribution, and exchange, and the best obtainable system of popular administration and control of each industry or service.

Part of the wider socialist goal of a more egalitarian society, public ownership was to enable industry to serve the interests of workers and the community. To achieve this, industries would be placed under 'popular administration and control', a phrase generally taken to mean 'that public ownership was likely to . . . be State and municipal' – that is, administered by politicians and public administrators – rather than controlled by 'workers themselves' (Taylor, 1980, p. 10).

(ii) Monopoly arguments

In some industries (such as the postal services) competition is *arguably* wasteful and unnecessary. In such cases statutory monopolies have been created, albeit public (rather than private) monopolies where workers and consumers can be protected by democratic controls.

(iii) Modernization and industrial efficiency

Where industries require major capital or 'high risk' investment, or where costly industrial restructuring is necessary, private finance may not be available. In such cases governments may inject public money in return for a stake in the industry.

(iv) Industrial rescues
In the 1960s and 1970s successive governments used public ownership as a means of rescuing private companies facing liquidation. Such action was arguably justified by the need to save jobs, protect the balance of payments, and maintain vital industries. Notable examples included Rolls Royce (nationalized by a Conservative government in 1971) and British Leyland (rescued by Labour in 1975).

(v) Economic management
The postwar expansion of nationalization provided governments with a major economic tool for controlling wages, prices, investment, and so on, in strategic industries. Although in practice usually used more for crisis economic management than for planning, it is a tool of which Labour and Conservative postwar governments alike made frequent use.

The above are not the only reasons for public ownership, but all have been important influences. The thread linking them together is the concept of industry serving the community: that, while goods and services should be produced efficiently, the wider public interest must be considered. The non-socialist arguments have been particularly crucial, for they alone explain the expansion of public ownership during a period often dominated by Conservative governments. Until 1979, successive Conservative governments generally accepted the more pragmatic arguments for public ownership, although they have been vigorously challenged by the Thatcher government which has pursued instead an active policy of privatization.

Forms of public ownership

The aims of public ownership are reflected in the forms in which it exists. A common theme, as already observed, is that industries should operate in the public interest; consequently, it is generally accepted that public control mechanisms are necessary to ensure that the public interest is pursued. It is also generally accepted that, as elsewhere within the public sector, those running public industries should be accountable. At the same time, however, such industries are usually felt to require a measure of independence from politicians. In some cases (such as broadcasting) this is deemed necessary to ensure political neutrality. More generally, however, it is justified as conducive to efficient management. Although profit is not the overriding goal, public enterprises must be efficiently managed; indeed, precisely because the profit-and-loss 'discipline' is often absent, high priority must be given to appropriate business and management skills. Because civil servants and politicians rarely possess such skills, experienced managers often have to be employed, and usually need to be given some independence from political intervention. Hence the justification for some relaxation of traditional control and accountability mechanisms.

Of course, once traditional forms of accountability 'are abandoned, many degrees of control and many special relationships become possible' (Tivey, 1973a, p. 29). In fact, various forms of public ownership are discernible, each offering in different measure the twin desiderata of public control and accountability on the one hand, and managerial independence on the other. In particular, four main forms can be identified: a) central government trading bodies; b) local authority trading bodies; c) state shareholding; and d) public corporations.

CENTRAL GOVERNMENT TRADING BODIES

Some public commercial and industrial enterprises have been administered as part of central government. Although varying arrangements are found, the 'pure' form is administration by government department (along the lines of the Post Office which functioned – until 1969 – as a department of state with a minister directly responsible for its activities to Parliament). Before the twentieth century the application of the departmental model to the few state trading concerns which existed seemed logical; the advantage which it offered – full ministerial control and parliamentary accountability – squared well with traditional constitutional principles. However, being run by civil servants and ministers, and with the Treasury exercising financial control, it offered little managerial independence. Consequently, other forms of administration have been applied to most of the undertakings brought into public ownership in the twentieth century, while existing undertakings administered on orthodox departmental lines have mostly either been reconstituted as public corporations (the Post Office, for example), or, particularly in recent years, turned into public limited companies and privatized (such as the Royal Ordnance Factories). Today no major industrial or commercial undertakings are administered as part of central administration, suggesting that as the twentieth century has progressed managerial freedom has received increasing emphasis – albeit at the expense of public accountability and control – as a desirable feature of public ownership. As Curwen (1986, p. 36) comments, 'This form of organization is unlikely ever to be used again, if for no other reason than that it implies the unwelcome need for day-to-day supervision by Parliament acting through the relevant minister'.

LOCAL GOVERNMENT TRADING BODIES

With this form of public ownership, sometimes known as municipalization, services are provided by local authorities. Seen by early socialists as the best means of controlling public utilities, many gas, water and electricity services were developed under municipal control until well into the twentieth century. Subsequently, numerous municipal restaurants, theatres, transport undertakings and so forth appeared, as well as a host of less conventional enterprises including a racecourse (Doncaster), a bank (Birmingham), a telephone system (Hull), and – in the early 1980s in a small number of county councils – local enterprise boards (see Chapter 8; Stoker, 1988, p. 62). While many such enterprises are still thriving, municipalization has nevertheless declined since the 1930s, particularly as services such as gas and electricity were transferred to forms of public ownership capable of administering them on regional or national bases. Moreover, in the early 1980s a number of (particularly Conservative controlled) local authorities have contracted out particular services such as refuse collection (Ascher, 1987, especially ch. 7). This trend has been strongly encouraged by the Thatcher government, notably through the Local Government Act, 1988, which requires that local authorities must put a number of services out to competitive tender. The services specified in the Act are refuse collection, cleaning, street cleaning, catering, ground maintenance and vehicle maintenance. The Secretary of State also has the power to add to the list of services (see Stoker, 1988, especially ch. 8; Walsh, 1988). Municipal trading has also been diminished following the deregulation of bus services under the 1985 Transport Act, whilst in London the abolition of the GLC was accompanied by the establishment in 1984 of the London Regional Transport Board, a public corporation officially listed as a nationalized industry.

STATE SHAREHOLDING

An important form of public ownership is the limited company in which the state holds shares. This arrangement allows maximum managerial independence with companies operating effectively as a normal commercial company within the Companies Acts. Where the government has a majority holding it may appoint directors, lay down financial targets and so forth, although usually it does not intervene in commercial or managerial decisions. With British Petroleum, for example, in which there was a large government shareholding until 1987, it was claimed in 1968 that, although the government had a veto over company affairs, this had never been used. The government's relationship was identical to that with other oil companies except that it was notified whenever dividend declarations were imminent and held consultations with the company 'if new capital or new financial structures . . . [were] under consideration' (Tivey, 1973b, p. 180). Of course, the managerial independence which state shareholding allows can only be achieved at the expense of public control and accountability. Boards are responsible to shareholders, not to Parliament, and the government's position is essentially like that of any other shareholder.

An important phase of state shareholding occurred from about 1966 to the late 1970s, a major role in effecting investments being taken by such bodies as the Industrial Reorganisation Corporation (1966–71) and National Enterprise Board (1975–83). This form of public ownership was popular for three main reasons: (i) State share purchases do not usually require specific enabling legislation; hence, they are 'cheap' in parliamentary time, and present limited opportunities for parliamentary criticism; (ii) being relatively swift and simple to implement it was particularly appropriate for industrial rescues and restructuring. It enabled 'rescued' companies to maintain existing management structures, avoid excessive ministerial and civil service control and retain the goal of profitability; (iii) it enabled the government or its agencies to intervene directly at the level of the firm to try and improve industrial performance (Young with Lowe, 1976, especially pp. 29–31).

In the 1980s – although the emphasis has changed from industrial rescues to privatization, and many state holdings have been sold off – state shareholding has remained an important form of public ownership. One reason for this is that the privatization of many former public corporations has been achieved through conversion to public limited company status and subsequent share disposal. Sometimes the entire shareholding has been sold (as with British Airways in 1987), in other cases a minority shareholding has been disposed of (for example, 49 per cent of Associated British Ports in 1983), and in others still a majority (51 per cent of Britoil in 1982). In the latter two types of case *hybrid* companies – in which there is a mix of public and private ownership – have been created. Similarly with many sales of state shareholdings, sell-offs have involved, initially at least, only a partial sale of the equity. Although in most cases (including the two mentioned above), the government has subsequently sold the remaining shareholding, the role of hybrids in the Thatcher government's privatization programme has been to blur still further the boundary between the public and private sectors, and to leave what Steel (1984a) refers to as 'a trail of unanswered questions' about the government's rights as shareholder particularly where public policy issues are involved.

PUBLIC CORPORATIONS

Arguably the most significant form of public ownership is the public corporation. Public corporations are important to the study of quasi-government generally. Tivey (1973a, p. 29) has observed that 'there lies behind the public corporation a theory and a fairly definite set of principles; the other autonomous bodies have developed in a much more confused and pragmatic way, with little background of deliberate principle'. The theory referred to is the reconciliation, within a single institution, of the twin desiderata of public control and accountability on the one hand and managerial independence on the other. It is strongly associated with (Lord) Morrison whose view, expressed most clearly in *Socialisation and Transport* (1933), was that nationalized industries required considerable freedom from political control if they were to operate efficiently. Hence their running should be entrusted to industrialists (rather than civil servants) whose discretion would extend to managerial and commercial matters. Each corporation would be financially self-supporting, and thereby escape Treasury control. Ministers would be limited to appointing board members and chairmen, and to issuing directives on general matters. In exercising these powers (but not for commercial and managerial matters which were the boards' responsibility) ministers would be accountable to Parliament.

The main prototypes of the public corporation are the British Broadcasting Corporation and the Central Electricity Board (both formed in 1926). The former owed much to the Crawford Report on Broadcasting (1926) which, drawing heavily on the ideas of (Lord) Reith, recommended the administration of public broadcasting by a 'Public Commission operating in the national interest'. Although several other public corporations were created in the interwar years, it was only after the Second World War that the model became firmly established, being used by the Attlee government to administer such industries as coal, steel, gas, electricity, rail, road transport, waterways, and civil aviation (the latter having been partially nationalized in 1939). Subsequently the model was extended to the Post Office, aerospace, and shipbuilding. The National Enterprise Board was also a public corporation (once again illustrating the administrative complexity surrounding public ownership) as also are a host of regulatory and promotional non-departmental public bodies (see Chapter 11).

Because of its diversity of functions and forms the public corporation is difficult to define. However, according to Tivey (1973a, pp. 33–4), it has five main features:

(i) It is a 'corporate body' (that is, a legal entity which can trade, own property, sue and be sued, and so forth).

Table 12.1 Nationalized Industries 1987–8[1]

Corporation	*Sponsoring department*
British Coal Corporation	Energy
British Railways Board	Transport
British Shipbuilders (Merchant)	Trade and Industry
British Steel Corporation	Trade and Industry
British Waterways Board	Environment
Civil Aviation Authority	Transport
Electricity Council (plus Central Electricity Generating Board and area electricity boards for England and Wales)	Energy
London Regional Transport	Transport
North of Scotland Hydro-Electric Board	Scottish Office
Post Office[2]	Trade and Industry
Scottish Transport Group	Scottish Office
South of Scotland Electricity Board	Scottish Office
Water	Environment[3]

Notes:

1 Industries in the public sector at end of 1987–8 (including British Steel Corporation, scheduled for privatization in November, 1988).

2 Includes Girobank.

3 England only. Other departments have responsibility in Scotland and Wales.

Major Sources: Economic Progress Report, no. 193, December 1987 (London: H.M. Treasury); Cabinet Office, 1987; *Public Bodies, 1987* (London: HMSO); P. Jackson and F. Terry (1988), *Public Domain* (London: Public Finance Foundation/Peat Marwick).

(ii) 'It is a statutory body; its constitution, powers and duties are prescribed by law and can be modified only by legislation.'

(iii) 'It is publicly owned.'

(iv) 'There is some degree of Government control. This normally includes the appointment of a corporation's governing board, and may include by statute various policy and financial matters.'

(v) 'The corporation is independent in respect of its actual operations and management . . . . Its personnel are not civil servants, and its finances are separate from those of the Government.'

Not every public corporation with these features is concerned with public ownership, nor strictly is public control and composition of boards always a matter for central government. Passenger transport executives and port authorities both offer examples of public corporations with membership wholly or partially appointed by local authorities. Nevertheless, a group of the larger public corporations are normally regarded as constituting 'the nationalized industries'. Identified largely 'by the degree to which they are engaged in sale of goods and services and the extent to which revenue is derived directly from their customers' (McIntosh Report, 1976, app. vol., p. 3), those nationalized industries existing in 1988 are shown in Table 12.1.

Public corporations in action

While public corporations have developed from their interwar origins into a major form of public ownership, their postwar operations owe little to Reith's concept of public corporations acting as trustees for the public interest. Although considerable differences exist between corporations, several common problems can be identified which have made the Reith/Morrison concept largely unattainable.

Five main 'problem areas' have characterized postwar public corporations: (a) administrative structure; (b) financial arrangements; (c) ministerial control; (d) accountability to Parliament; (e) consumer representation and protection.

ADMINISTRATIVE STRUCTURE

Public corporations exhibit a variety of administrative structures. Until the 1950s centralized structures were normally preferred, being considered most likely to attract the best managers, and to maximize potential for national economic planning. In the light of experience, however, centralization was seen to present serious problems; industries were too large for effective management, and boards became remote and bureaucratic. Consequently, several industries (notably inland transport) underwent major decentralization. As this indicates, administrative structures do not remain static: they change in response to new circumstances and to experience of running the industries. Moreover, different industries require differing structures; for example, while electricity, like inland transport, experienced substantial postwar decentralization, the gas industry (before privatization in 1986) underwent a major centralizing reorganization in the 1970s to meet technological problems arising from North Sea gas discoveries.

Common to all public corporations is their management by a publicly appointed board, in the case of nationalized industries appointments being made by a 'sponsoring minister' designated by statute. This is a fundamental feature of public corporations: experienced industrialists manage the industries as public trustees and at arm's length from politicians. Each enabling Act confers upon the board management responsibilities, and usually also stipulates numbers and qualifications of appointees. Most boards have about ten members, some of whom may be part time, and most of whom have appropriate business or industrial experience. Normally neither the board nor its employees are civil servants; consequently, wages, conditions, and so forth can be geared to the industry's requirements.

In practice many of the anticipated advantages of this arrangement have not materialized. Partly this is because remuneration of board members and chairmen compares unfavourably with the private sector, which has sometimes inhibited recruitment. Partly also, however, it stems from the 'haphazard' method of appointment, whereby board members 'have limited terms of appointment and no promise of reappointment'. Thus of twenty-four chairmen in post in January 1978, fourteen had left within three years, only two through retirement. Some industries had as many as three chairmen during the period. While such insecurity 'destroys . . . continuity of experience, knowledge, and commitment' at board level (Barlow, 1981, pp. 31–2), it also reflects the boards' relationships with the wider political system and especially with sponsoring ministers.

FINANCIAL ARRANGEMENTS

Theoretically, public corporations enjoy financial autonomy. Expenditure is met from operating revenue; surpluses are retained (not surrendered to the Treasury) to finance investment and build reserves; and borrowing is permissible within statutory limits. Sponsoring ministers usually also have financial powers: to appoint auditors, approve capital investment programmes, and determine the form of the accounts. These powers are theoretically conferred on ministers to ensure that boards exercise proper stewardship of public assets, while having sufficient financial freedom to operate commercially.

These theoretical arrangements have not materialized. From the 1950s, government control over capital finance was imposed by requiring loans to nationalized industries to be raised from the Treasury. There have also been various government attempts to impose investment critieria: for example, in 1967 a test discount rate of 8 per cent was recommended for new investment projects (*Nationalised Industries: A Review of Economic and Financial Objectives*, 1967, para. 10); and in 1978 5 per cent was recommended as a real rate of return on new investment (*Nationalised Industries*, 1978, para. 61). While such targets have rarely been obtained, more stringent control has been achieved by the imposition since the late 1970s of external financing limits (EFLs). As Curwen (1986, p. 90) explains, 'An EFL controls the amount of external finance in the form of grants or borrowings which a public corporation can raise in any one financial year'. Allocated by sponsoring departments and the Treasury, EFLs are often influenced by short-term political and economic considerations – such as the size of the Public Sector Borrowing Requirement – and have had serious effects upon some industries disrupting 'investment planning' and causing delays in 'profitable investment projects' (Knight, 1982, p. 3).

With revenue finance, governments have also attempted to impose guidelines. The 1961 White Paper (*Financial and Economic Obligations of the Nationalised Industries*, para. 19) recommended that revenue surpluses 'should be at least sufficient to cover deficits on Revenue Account *over a 5-year period*' (italics in original). In 1967 another White Paper (*Nationalised Industries: a Review of Economic and Financial Objectives*) suggested that prices should be related to marginal costs, financial objectives geared to prices, and – where social considerations required departure from commercial principles – corporations should receive government compensation. While this latter provision had some influence in the case of British Rail (which subsequently received compensation for uneconomic passenger services) it was difficult to implement. In any event the long-run marginal cost rule proved largely unattainable, and in 1978 another White Paper (*Nationalised Industries*) was issued, requiring prices to be geared to financial targets set for each industry. These targets (which mostly applied to periods of three to five years ahead) were to be geared to 'general policy objectives, including considerations of social, sectoral and counter inflation policy, as well as the need to cover costs' (para. 67). In practice, however, these guidelines have proved hardly more successful than earlier ones. Prices, in practice, have often had to be manipulated to meet increasingly stringent EFLs – which apply only to a single year – whilst ministerial involvement in pricing decisions has also been apparent. As Dunleavy and Rhodes (1988, p. 135) observe, the nationalized gas, electricity, telephone and water industries were all during the 1980s pressurized into 'additional or unnecessary price increases . . . to pull more funds into the Exchequer [or to] . . . "fatten up" the industries for privatisation'.

It is clear from the above that the original 'break-even' concept of public corporations has now largely been abandoned. In practice many nationalized industries, particularly prior to the 1980s, made large losses and needed 'bailing out' by increased borrowing, deficit grants or debt write-offs (see Curwen, 1986, especially pp. 86–8). Others, increasingly in the 1980s, have made healthy profits. While this mixed record is partly due to differences in market and operating conditions, it also partly reflects different patterns of ministerial intervention. Sponsoring ministers intervene in nationalized industries' financial affairs far more than either theory or statute suggests. For example, prices, wages, and industrial relations are all technically board matters; however, ministers are usually consulted informally about significant price increases (*Financial and Economic Obligations*, para. 31) and some ministers deal directly with union leaders. Again, Treasury-determined EFLs seriously constrain the boards' commercial freedom, with shortfalls in external financing often necessitating plant closures, price increases, or wage restraint.

Such interventions not only prevent boards from pursuing their commercial judgement but also largely explain frequent failures to meet the government's own financial targets. Whatever the theory, government control of nationalized industry finance is extensive – so much so that it has totally undermined the concept of financially autonomous corporations operating at arm's length from ministers.

MINISTERIAL CONTROL

Each enabling Act creating a public corporation confers explicit powers on a designated sponsoring minister. The reasons for conferring such powers have long been controversial. The initial rationale was that ministers should be responsible for 'general policy' and boards for 'day-to-day administration', although this subsequently tended to be replaced by a distinction between 'national interest' and 'commercial responsibilities'. In fact, both distinctions are somewhat artificial and difficult to apply in practice. In 1968 the Select Committee on Nationalised Industries (SCNI) (1967/8, vol. I, para. 74) suggested a different rationale. Two basic purposes, it suggested, justified ministerial control: first, securing 'the wider public interest', and second, overseeing and 'if possible' ensuring 'the efficiency of the industries'. Although not universally accepted, this analysis nevertheless offers a useful starting point for examining the position of sponsoring ministers.

(i) In securing 'the wider public interest' the minister's role is to relate corporation activities to wider social and economic considerations. The main instrument provided by statute for discharging this function is the general directive, which may be issued to a board 'on the exercise and performance of its functions in relation to matters which appear to the Minister to affect the national interest'. Once issued, general directives must be obeyed.

(ii) The minister's efficiency powers involve both oversight and the laying down of performance standards. To this end ministers have extensive statutory powers: appointment and dismissal of board members; financial powers; approval of research programmes, training, education and pension schemes; and requiring returns of accounts and information.

In practice, the functional division between ministers and boards is far more ambiguous than the above might suggest, an ambiguity heightened by four main factors:

(i) There are several sponsoring departments

The thirteen nationalized industries listed in Table 12.1 were sponsored by five different departments, co-ordination between which has often been inadequate (see Select Committee on Nationalised Industries, 1967/8, vol. I, paras 335–43). The allocation of industries to departments, moreover, owes as much to haphazard political and departmental factors as to logic. These arrangements not only impair co-ordination within industrial sectors (such as transport), but – because board/sponsoring department relationships may vary – also produce inconsistency between Whitehall and the nationalized industries.

The situation is further confused because non-sponsoring departments, particularly the Treasury, are also frequently involved in nationalized industry affairs. The precise role of these departments is often obscure and, as the McIntosh Report (1976, p. 25) observed, 'opportunities' for boards to establish 'direct contact' with them have been 'limited'.

(ii) There are frequent changes of personnel

Not only boards, but also sponsoring ministers and departmental officials are subject to frequent changes of personnel. This prevents 'adequate understanding . . . and . . . essential personal relationships' from developing (McIntosh Report, 1976, p. 40), and means that board/department relationships are continually changing.

(iii) Statutory obligations vary between industries

The statutory obligations of ministers and boards vary from industry to industry. While these differences are usually unimportant, their existence further complicates ministerial/board relationships.

(iv) Ministers enjoy extra-statutory influence

In practice ministers have more control over nationalized industries than even the most liberal interpretation of enabling legislation would suggest. Usually there are regular monitoring meetings between a nationalized industry and its sponsoring department which occur monthly (Hyman, 1988, p. 18). One investigation (McIntosh Report, 1976, app. vol., p. 136) found that boards frequently complained of ministers acting 'without . . . statutory backing'. Ministers, in fact, have often intervened in commercial matters (such as prices, equipment purchases, and plant closures) and in managerial issues (wages, redundancies, liaison with unions and so forth). One dramatic example was the 1984–5 coal dispute when 'the Cabinet' virtually granted 'British Coal a blank cheque to outface the strike by over two-thirds of its workforce' (Dunleavy and Rhodes, 1988, p. 135). Usually they have been inspired not by a desire to lay down policy guidelines, but by short-term political or economic expediency. Consequently the theoretical position has largely been reversed, with ministers giving 'very little guidance in regard to . . . policies' but becoming 'closely involved in many aspects of management' (Select Committee on Nationalised Industries, 1967/8, vol. I, para. 877).

Significantly, ministerial interventions have rarely been effected by the statutory remedy, the general directive, which has been used only twice on major matters since the war (1951 to the Iron and Steel Corporation as a prelude to partial denationalization, and in 1952 to the British Transport Commission over rail fares). Instead there has appeared the 'lunch-table directive', a reference to the 'informal relationships between Ministers and board chairmen and between departmental officials and public corporation staff' which today exist in most industries (Johnson, 1978, p. 126). Often, of course, ministers appoint chairmen and members sympathetic to their policies – such as, arguably, Sir Ian MacGregor appointed as chairman of the British Steel Corporation and, subsequently, of the National Coal Board by Conservative ministers in the 1980s – in which case boards may need little persuasion to accept ministerial views.

Ministerial influence should not, of course, be exaggerated. Not only does information move in both directions during informal exchanges but sponsoring departments – with small supervisory units, insufficient technical assistance and a relative lack of business acumen (Garner, 1983) – cannot be perfectly informed about and respond to every aspect of corporation affairs. Ministers' powers to hire and fire board members, moreover, are seriously circumscribed in practice; chairmen usually have contracts, and their low remuneration relative to private industry often presents difficulties in finding replacements. Ministers themselves, moreover, are not unaware of the political dangers which may attend over-involvement in the management of nationalized industries; indeed, as Davies (1988, p. 16) argues, in this respect, 'contrary to conventional wisdom, considerable continuity exists between the policies adopted' by ministers in governments both 'before and after 1979'. Furthermore boards often contain high-calibre members, who are unlikely to meet ministerial interference simply with passive resistance. The British Gas chairman, Sir Denis Rooke, 'resisted fiercely and publicly' government attempts before privatization 'to circumscribe the industry's activities. With the help of trade unions . . . he succeeded in preventing the "hiving off" of gas showrooms to the private sector, but not in stopping the sale of the Corporation's oil exploration and off-shore gas interests' (Price, 1986, p. 13). In recent years boards have been prepared to ally with unions and/or consumer councils against perceived political threats, and even to organize with other industries. Particularly significant was the emergence in the 1970s of the Nationalised Industries Chairmen's

Group (NICG). Meeting regularly with ministers, to some extent it bypassed sponsoring departments by dealing direct with Treasury ministers, the 'real source' of many government initiatives affecting nationalized industries (see Tivey, 1982a).

Even so, while ministers have to accept 'give and take' when dealing with boards, in the final analysis they are usually able to prevail. Even without resort to directives, they possess considerable powers. Significantly these are powers technically concerned more with overseeing efficiency than with public-interest considerations. They include the ministers' financial powers – for example, the power to approve investment and borrowing – and the ultimate power of dismissal. The latter is not unknown, but happens rarely; boards usually realize that they are unlikely to prevail against determined ministers, while ministers prefer to work 'behind the scenes' – by encouragement, persuasion, even threats – in the knowledge that boards usually give way, and that the short-term nature of most board appointments will eventually provide an opportunity to rid themselves of 'uncooperative' members without resort to dismissal.

The extent of ministerial control, of course, has repercussions also for sponsoring departments, which sometimes become overburdened with what are nominally board functions, and for civil servants who arguably lack the 'education and training' necessary to 'get to grips with the problem of corporate planning, investment appraisal' and the like (Garner, 1983, pp. 32, 31). Equally significant are the implications for accountability, for where ministers intervene informally, responsibility to Parliament may be avoided.

ACCOUNTABILITY TO PARLIAMENT

Nationalized industry boards control sizeable public assets and should, therefore, be accountable for their actions. Early advocates of public corporations, however, feared that detailed parliamentary scrutiny might inhibit managerial freedom, and consequently normal conventions of ministerial responsibility do not apply to public corporations.

The theoretical position regarding accountability is described by Tivey (1973a, p. 139) as 'simple and logical'. He explains: 'The Minister had certain powers over the corporations. For the exercise of these powers he was answerable to Parliament, just as he was answerable for all his other powers. On those matters where the Minister exercised no powers, there was no accountability.' Thus a minister issuing a general directive, dismissing a chairman, withholding capital investment approval (or failing to do any of these things) could be held accountable. However, on matters within the board's jurisdiction the minister was not statutorily responsible, and was, therefore, not accountable to Parliament. The boards, for their own part, were required to present accounts and annual reports to ministers, who in turn placed them before Parliament. They also had to act within any general directives or other statutory controls imposed by ministers. Otherwise, however, they were to operate free from parliamentary scrutiny.

In practice this 'simple and logical' arrangement has not worked, partly because of the blurred division of responsibilities inherent in enabling Acts, and partly also owing to the growth of informal ministerial intervention. Not only can ministers technically deny responsibility for matters falling within the boards' jurisdiction, but the degree of accountability for informal intervention inevitably depends largely on whether ministerial actions are public knowledge. Nevertheless, parliamentary opportunities to call sponsoring ministers to account have increased since the 1940s. MPs have become adept at framing parliamentary questions which obtain answers (for instance, by asking if the minister *intends* to issue a general directive) while debates are frequently raised on matters for which ministers are not technically responsible. Since 1949, moreover, it has been customary to debate the reports and accounts which corporations submit annually to Parliament, while in addition any modification of enabling Acts, or any extension of borrowing limits, usually requires legislation. Generally, however, such debates are conducted along party lines and provide little opportunity for detailed scrutiny.

Partly to overcome these deficiencies the House of Commons in the mid-1950s established a Select Committee on Nationalised Industries (SCNI), which subsequently gained wide acceptance both within Parliament and the nationalized industries. Normally it investigated one or two industries each year, and its reports undoubtedly made MPs better informed about nationalized industries and even had some small influence on government policy. Nevertheless, it lacked the professional staff to perform financial or efficiency audits, or even to monitor particular industries continuously (see Coombes, 1966; 1971, pp. 79–84). In any event the SCNI disappeared in 1979 with the reorganization of Commons select committees (see Chapter 14), and the task of scrutinizing nationalized industries is now fragmented between several different specialist committees. Provision was also made in 1979 for the formation of a sub-committee – drawn from two or more appropriate select committees – to consider any matter affecting two or more NIs, but this was never acted upon during the first eight years of operation (Factsheet No. 6, House of Commons Library, revised edn, April 1987; see also Liaison Committee, 1982–3, paras 40–4). Although the new arrangements mean that NIs can now be investigated by specialist committees well versed in the work of sponsoring departments – and some committees, notably the Energy Committee, have given a high priority to monitoring NIs within their jurisdiction (Liaison Committee, 1984–5, especially pp. xxviii–xxx) –

the disappearance with the SCNI of 'a forum for discussion of common problems' and a 'group of MPs with considerable expertise' in nationalized industry matters may well, as Redwood and Hatch observed in 1982 (pp. 37–8), prove detrimental to the industries' long-term interests.

A further factor is that the expenditure of nationalized industries is outside the jurisdiction of the Comptroller and Auditor General, despite backbench attempts in 1983 to change the position (see Chapter 14)) and adverse comment from the Comptroller himself (see, for example, Downey, 1986). The public accountability of nationalized industries in fact remains problematical. Because they required substantial managerial independence, public corporations were initially given considerable freedom from both ministerial control and parliamentary accountability. In practice, ministers have acquired more control over the industries than was initially envisaged. The problem for Parliament is that there has not been a *commensurate* increase in ministerial accountability, with the result that ministers – by dealing informally with boards rather than using formal powers – can often escape full accountability for their actions.

CONSUMER REPRESENTATION AND PROTECTION

With many nationalized industries, provision for consumer representation exists in the form of nationalized industry consultative or consumer councils (NICCs). In 1981, forty-four NICCs, some with regional and local networks, were in existence and, although the number has subsequently declined, consumer councils are still an important feature of nationalized industries. In 1987 the most important were: Area Electricity Consumer Councils (twelve in all, the chairmen of which sat on the appropriate Area Electricity Board); Area Transport Users' Consultative Committees (eight); Central Transport Consultative Committee; Domestic Coal Consumers' Council; London Regional Passengers' Committee; Post Office Users' National Council; and similar bodies for Scotland, Wales and Northern Ireland. (See Cabinet Office, 1987, especially p. 69.) All are statutory bodies, their general function being 'to consider any matters raised by consumers, Ministers or the industries themselves concerning the service and facilities provided by their respective industries' (Department of Trade, 1981, p. 2) Traditionally two main roles have been distinguished: a consumer complaint-redressing role, and a policy-influencing role. While considerable differences exist from one NICC to another, the complaints role has become increasingly significant, with some 70,000 complaints annually being dealt with in the early 1980s.

NICCs, Tivey (1982b, p. 144) explains, 'originated as devices to check the impact of the monopoly status' of nationalized industries. Although their impact varies from industry to industry, dissatisfaction with their work has frequently been expressed. Three main criticisms have usually been levelled against them:

(i) NICCs are not widely enough known. One inquiry by the National Consumer Council (1976, pp. 31–2) found that 'the proportions of people who knew about [NICCs]', despite steps to publicize them, was 'still very low'.
(ii) NICCs are not sufficiently independent. As Tivey (1982b, p. 145) explains, 'the NICCs began in close association with the nationalised industries themselves, sometimes sharing premises and using the industries' own staff on secondment'. Moreover, although consisting largely of nominees from bodies deemed to represent consumers, actual appointments have usually been made by ministers. In 1984 ministers controversially failed to reappoint the chairman of the London Electricity Consultative Council which had vigorously opposed tariff increases by the London Electricity Board (Henney, 1984–5).
(iii) NICCs are largely ineffective. They have too few staff, too little money, and insufficient expertise to challenge boards. As the McIntosh Report (1976, app. vol., p. 86) observed, 'All the councils had powers to consider any matter affecting consumers, but very little authority to do anything about it'. The fragmentation of NICCs – one, and sometimes more per industry – rather than sectoral NICCs arguably also reduces effectiveness and increases complexity for the public. (For discussion see Birkinshaw, 1985, pp. 103–13; National Consumer Council, 1982.)

Such criticisms, while undoubtedly in many respects still valid (see Department of Trade, 1981, pp. 5–8), nevertheless have lost force over time. For example, while public awareness remains a problem, in some industries such as electricity NICCs appear to be quite widely known (Tivey, 1982b, p. 148). NICCs also appear to have developed greater independence: few NICC staff are now recruited or seconded from the industries, and financing now comes from the government rather than the industries themselves. Effectiveness has also improved: in a 'majority of cases', Tivey reported in 1982 (1982b, p. 146), NICCs have 'some success' in redressing consumer complaints, while on a number of policy matters their influence can be detected. Generally these have concerned 'medium'- rather than 'high'-level policy: codes of practice, tariff structures, trading practices and so on rather than, say, general price levels or investment policies. Occasionally, however, there have been spectacular successes: in 1982, for example, planned increases in telephone charges were deferred immediately following criticism from the Post Office Users' National Council (*The Times*, 1 September 1982).

NICCs, clearly, have developed greater independence and effectiveness than, even now, is sometimes realized. Even so, they still face substantial problems. Some of these – such as their responsiveness to, and representativeness of, clientele – are shared with consumer organizations generally; others – accountability, appointment and so on – are familiar quasi-governmental problems. NICCs, however, also suffer from the political framework within which nationalized industries operate. While their relationship is nominally with the corporations, the effective determinant of policy – and sometimes tariffs – is often the government. As observed, NICCs generally lack resources and authority to challenge boards effectively, let alone to challenge boards, sponsoring departments and the Treasury combined. In particular they often lack the expertise, the right to information, and also the time, to mount in-depth studies in complex policy areas (Tivey, 1982b, pp. 146–7). More crucially, these deficiencies are unlikely to be rectified so long as ministers wish to retain their dominant position over the industries. Consequently, while the NICCs appear likely to survive – the Department of Trade in 1982 (p. 8) pledged itself to retain 'the essentials' of their present structure – their basic position seems unlikely to be significantly strengthened.

In two other respects attempts have been made to enhance protection for NI consumers. Firstly, following recommendations in the 1978 White Paper (*Nationalised Industries*, para. 78), NIs now publish key performance indicators in annual reports. While many industries have made good use of these for internal evaluation, 'governments have tended to intervene (often arbitrarily) for short-term, political/economic objectives' (Woodward, 1986, p. 316). There have also been disagreements about the type of performance indicators which should be used, and the amount of information about them which should be published by the industries (National Consumer Council, 1981). Consequently performance indicators have never become the 'primary objectives' of either 'the industry, or of central government', while NICCs, for their part, have had insufficient 'power to see that ... targets are met' (Barnes, 1988, p. 45).

Secondly, NIs have been subjected during the 1980s to investigation by the Monopolies and Mergers Commission (MMC). The Competition Act 1980 authorizes the Trade and Industry Secretary to order the MMC to investigate an industry's efficiency, costs, service provided and potential abuse of monopoly position (Garner, 1982). Between 1980 and 1984 an average of three NI references per year was made, and while these were investigated independently by the MMC their value was arguably weakened because the MMC lacks direct access to the industry's books. Furthermore, powers of reference and implementation of recommendations rest with ministers (Collins and Wharton, 1984b), although the industry's reaction and progress reports are given publicity (*Hansard*, VI, vol. 105, cols 7–8, 14 November 1986). While sponsoring departments have found MMC reports useful, and NIs have accepted most recommendations, the fact remains, as the Public Accounts Committee (1986–7b, para. 15) suggests, that more could be done with MMC procedures for strengthening the 'nationalised industries' accountability to consumers, the Government [and] Parliament.' (See also National Audit Office, 1986c.)

Reforming public corporations

Several proposals for reforming public corporations have been made. In the 1960s two broad alternatives were suggested. The first, associated with Robson (1960 and 1969; Select Committee on Nationalised Industries, 1967–8, vol. II, pp. 531–7; and 1969), held that ministers should be prevented from operating informally and without statutory authority. Hanson (1961; SCNI, 1967–8, vol. II, pp. 526–31), by contrast, recommended the removal of formal limits upon ministerial powers. Neither view, however, was wholly convincing; the postwar expansion of nationalization had provided an impetus for ministerial intervention beyond the level originally intended by Parliament, while governments were unlikely to clarify the blurred functional division between ministers and boards so long as this worked to their advantage.

In 1967–8 the Select Committee on Nationalised Industries suggested that sponsoring departments should disappear, and a new Ministry of Nationalised Industries should be responsible for ensuring the efficiency of NIs. Public interest considerations would rest with other departmental ministers, who could negotiate for corporations to depart from commercial principles in return for compensation. To these proposals the government made a predictably negative response (*Ministerial Control of the Nationalised Industries*, 1969), and in the 1970s the debate continued. In 1976 the National Economic Development Office (McIntosh Report, 1976) proposed the establishment in each NI of a policy council. Chaired by an independent president, policy councils would include officials from sponsoring departments and the Treasury, and representatives of boards, unions and consumers. Some 'independent' members would also be appointed, and an 'open seat' provided for the minister. Policy councils would determine corporate aims, monitor performance, and appoint boards; consequently, ministers would lose the right to intervene directly in board affairs. They could seek changes by agreement with policy councils, or alternatively issue formal directives (for which they would be accountable to Parliament). In this way policy councils would provide a buffer between boards and ministers, would provide more clearly defined accountability, and would enable all parties connected with the industries to become involved in developing policy.

In 1978 the government rejected these proposals (*Nationalised Industries*, 1978). Boards had generally responded unenthusiastically – fearing that policy councils would become another bureaucratic layer – and the government was unwilling to divest itself of important powers. The White Paper did concede that minister/board relationships were unsatisfactory, and proposed giving ministers power to issue directives on 'specific' as well as 'general' matters (para. 20). Significantly, however, while disavowing that ministers should become involved in 'matters of day-to-day management', it also observed that on 'many issues' the government would 'continue to . . . reach agreement' with industries without issuing 'specific directions' (para. 22).

In 1984 the Treasury proposed further changes: a single statutory framework to replace the separate enabling acts for each industry. Although presented as a tidying-up operation, the consultation document proposed far-reaching measures:

(i) statutory backing for government-set financial targets;
(ii) clear-cut government powers to hire and fire board members without assigning cause;
(iii) government powers to restructure balance sheets including turning accumulated reserves into debt or equity;
(iv) powers for ministers to order privatization without requiring enabling legislation (H.M. Treasury, 1984).

These proposals, it was widely argued, threatened the very foundations of NIs. Statutory backing for government financial targets undermined the theoretical break-even concept, whilst the proposed power to sack board members without assigning cause would have weakened the arm's length relationship which supposedly underlay government–board relationships. The proposal to turn reserves into debt or equity would benefit government by enabling it to order 'loan repayments' or dividends to the Treasury. The proposed powers to order privatization were particularly sweeping and would have required industries to discontinue any activity, and set up or dispose of any subsidiary, at ministerial command. These draconian proposals were widely criticized by consumer groups and nationalized industry chiefs, (see Smith, 1985; Energy Select Committee 1985a; Environment, Trade and Industry, and Transport Select Committees, 1985), and were subsequently dropped by the government.

Table 12.2 Nationalized Industries: Major Asset Sales, 1979–88[1]

Industry	*Sale details*	
British Telecom	1984 (50.2%)	
British Gas Corporation	1986 (97%)	
Britoil[2]	1982 (51%)	1985 (49%)
British Airways	1987 (100%)	
British Airports Authority	1987 (100%)	
British Aerospace	1981 (51%)	1985 (49%)
British Shipbuilders (warship yards)[3]	1985 (piecemeal sales of yards)	
Associated British Ports	1983 (49%)	1984 (51%)
National Freight Company	1982 (100%)	
Enterprise Oil[4]	1984 (100%)	
National Bus Company	1986[5] (partial, piecemeal disposal)	

Notes:

1 Disposals to end of 1987–8. Excludes (a) partial disposals of assets of some remaining NIs (for example, British Rail Hotels (1983) and Hoverspeed (1984); (b) British Steel Corporation – scheduled for privatization, late 1988.

2 Britoil was separated from the British National Oil Corporation (BNOC) in 1982. BNOC itself was subsequently wound up.

3 Staggered, piecemeal disposal. See Curwen (1986), pp. 187–90.

4 Formed to control former oil-producing assets of British Gas Corporation.

5 Date of first disposal.

Sources: Economic Progress Report, No. 193, December 1987, p. 4; Curwen (1986), table 6.3, pp. 174–5; Dunleavy and Rhodes (1988), table 5.2, pp. 136–7.

Since 1979, of course, privatization has increasingly been seen as a possible solution to the control, accountability, and consumer-responsiveness problems of NIs. If public corporations are defective instruments for administering public ownership, one alternative is to sell assets to the private sector. At the time of writing eleven major industries (see Table 12.2) had been privatized, and plans announced for the privatization of others (notably steel, electricity and water). While the nationalized sector is still substantial, Veljanovski's conclusion (1988, p. xv) that the Thatcher government 'now appear determined to privatise the whole nationalised sector' is widely shared. Privatizing public enterprises, in short, has become one of the dominant themes of successive Thatcher administrations.

Privatizing public enterprise

Privatization since 1979 has developed apace in Britain. While the first Thatcher administration (1979–83) was *relatively* modest in its privatization programme, in its second (1983–7) and third (1987 on) terms public asset sales have been substantial. Veljanovski (1988, p. 49) writes: 'By the beginning of 1987, twelve major companies and a larger number of smaller ones have been privatised. This has transferred 20 per cent of the state sector and over 400,000 jobs to the private sector . . . and raised over £12 billion.'

It is important to note that privatization, to date, has affected almost every part of the public sector. Asset sales, for example, have included former central government trading bodies (such as Royal Ordnance), state shareholdings (such as Cable and Wireless, Rolls Royce, Jaguar and BP), and – most dramatically – former nationalized industries (see Table 12.2). In addition, privatization has encompassed many non-commercial/industrial fields of public activity – most notably council houses, of which over three-quarters of a million had been sold by 1987 raising £8bn – and has affected almost every part of the public sector. As Heald (1985, p. 7) puts it, 'the Conservative Government's privatisation programme has acquired such momentum that hardly any public enterprise is exempt from action or proposals'.

Forms of privatization

Much debate surrounds the meaning of privatization. As Wiltshire (1987, p. 2) notes, 'It is an all-embracing term for several actions, all of which shift activity from the so-called "public" sector to the "private" sector'. What is clear is that the concept – and in Britain also the practice – goes much further than transfer of ownership. In fact, it takes a number of forms, of which Young (1986, pp. 238–44) identifies seven:

1 selling off public-sector assets (for example, British Gas in 1986), thus exposing public sector organizations to increased competition;
2 relaxing state monopolies (for example, enabling Mercury to compete with British Telecom before the latter's privatization);
3 contracting services out (for example, contracting out refuse collection by local authorities);
4 private provision of services (for example, sponsorship or provision of public services – such as arts or leisure facilities – by private companies);
5 investment projects (for example, private investment in public projects such as advance-factory building or urban redevelopment);
6 extending private sector practices in the public sector (for example, secondment of businessmen into government to utilize their expertise);
7 reduced subsidies and increased charges for public sector services so that consumers pay a greater proportion of the real cost.

While some of these forms – particularly the first three – are more important than others, all are found in the Thatcher government's privatization programme; and while none is wholly new – examples of all can be found before 1979 – with the Thatcher government they have been promoted on a sustained basis. Nevertheless it is important to note that privatization in all these forms is likely to require a continuing, albeit reduced, role for public bodies. Of the seven listed forms of privatization two, types 6 and 7, do not necessarily diminish the public sector (although they may change its character). The same is true of type 2, which is essentially a *liberalization* approach, removing, through government action or legislative changes, barriers to competition. Types 4 and 5 envisage a partnership between the public and private sectors (albeit with a public sector-led approach) as also to a lesser extent does type 3 (which at the *very minimum* requires a continuing public agency role in awarding contracts and monitoring performance). Even with type 1 (asset sales) a governmental role will remain, particularly where ownership or commercial activity may give rise to public interest questions (such as with British Aerospace), or where regulation may be necessary to promote efficiency and competition. As Young (1986, p. 250) concludes 'All these changes add up. They do not seem to mean a greatly reduced role for government. There appears to have been a reduction in control, but an increase in influence'.

Reasons for privatization

The objectives of privatization have evolved gradually, with different goals being stressed at different times. As well as wider factors, such as the breakdown of political consensus, one can detect influences such as the Thatcher government's rejection of Keynesian economics (with its stress on physical controls), its belief in the inefficiency of public ownership, and its perceived need to create increased opportunities for private sector investment. In addition several more specific reasons for privatization have been advanced, the most important of these being summarized by Veljanovski (1988, p. 8) as follows: (see also *Privatisation of the Water Authorities*, para. 3):

(i) to reduce government involvement in the decision-making of industry;
(ii) to permit industry to raise funds from the capital market on commercial terms;
(iii) to raise revenue and reduce the public sector borrowing requirement;
(iv) to promote wider share ownership;
(v) to create an enterprise culture;
(vi) to encourage workers' share ownership in their own companies;

(vii) to increase competition and efficiency;
(viii) to replace ownership and financial controls with a more effective system of economic regulation designed to ensure that benefits of greater efficiency are passed on to consumers.

Whether this list is comprehensive and coherent, and the extent to which objectives have been met, is beyond the scope of this text. What, however, can be noted, again, is a continuing governmental role after privatization. Not only can some objectives be met by forms of privatization within a state-ownership framework (by liberalization, for example), but, even where full denationalization results, some objectives – such as ensuring that consumers benefit from greater efficiency – may require continuing state monitoring and regulation. In some cases (such as British Aerospace) industries will remain dependent on government contracts and subsidies, and will retain a significant role in such key policy fields as defence, energy and transport. In fact, Heald (1985, p. 9) notes, 'it is far from clear that', despite the rhetoric, the Thatcher 'Government's free-enterprise instincts are anything like as committed to competition as they are to private ownership'. While public ownership as a means of ensuring accountability, control and efficiency has been rejected, privatization, he argues, offers a possibility of securing public influence without public ownership. As he concludes (1985, pp. 21, 9), 'Balances will still have to be struck between public policy and private interests. . . . Relationships "just like those with any ordinary private enterprise" are unlikely to be feasible'.

Administering privatized enterprises

As already seen, the state will have a continuing role after the privatization of many enterprises. In this section we shall concentrate on the impact of the government's role in the post-privatization affairs of former nationalized industries and major state-shareholding enterprises. While for some such undertakings the state's role may virtually cease with privatization, and for others continue indirectly through dependancy on government contracts, in still others direct state involvement is likely to remain a permanent feature. Basically such industries fall into two main categories:

(i) where the public interest requires that the provision of essential or sensitive services (like oil or aerospace) should not be subject to undesirable ownership or takeover;
(ii) where the undertaking will remain the sole or dominant supplier of the service to the public (like British Telecom, British Gas).

While, thus far, consistent patterns have not emerged, three main approaches to these problems can be discerned. Firstly, as already observed, in some instances major government holdings have been retained after privatization, creating *hybrid* companies. This has occurred for various reasons, some of which (such as the size of the capital market) are unrelated to questions of control. In most such cases the government initially retained just under 50 per cent of the equity, enabling the industry's external financing limit (EFL) to be excluded from public sector borrowing requirement calculations (Heald, 1985, p. 13), whilst retaining for the government the largest, and in effect controlling, shareholding. Whilst the government's declared intention is not to intervene in such companies' affairs, as Steel (1984b, p. 106) notes, the fact that they have previously been in 'full public ownership has given rise to expectations among MPs and the media about access' which ministers might on occasions find difficult to resist. Again with some hybrids (although not all) the government has appointed directors to the board of the new body. While the government stresses that these directors owe loyalty to the company, not the government, it is widely argued that their role is ambiguous. Of course, for the industries these may be matters of only temporary importance. The government officially sees hybridity as a transitional stage to full denationalization, has already divested itself of many residual holdings, and in more recent privatizations has tended to sell the entire shareholding at once (see Table 12.2). Nevertheless the pace of the government's programme, and the dictates of the capital market, mean that Heald's comment in 1985 (p. 14) – that 'hybrids are likely to remain a feature of the industrial scene throughout the 1980s' – is probably not short of the mark.

Secondly, there are important ownership restrictions attached to many privatized undertakings, particularly those in aerospace and energy. In some cases articles of association contain limits, usually 15 per cent, on maximum individual shareholdings, while others (such as British Aerospace and British Airways) have restrictions on foreign ownership. In addition, with most major sales the government has retained – for an initial period at least – a 'golden share' which enables it to outvote all other shareholders on specified matters such as asset sales and takeovers. According to Veljanovski (1988, p. xxiii) of the major sales to 1988 'only two (Associated British Ports and BP) are entirely free of the reins of government', although as the exceptions indicate no consistent pattern has yet emerged. Indeed there is even no systematic pattern as to which department – the Treasury or sponsoring department – holds government shareholdings, although the latter invariably now has responsibility for golden shares. Taken together the golden share and ownership restrictions are of considerable potential significance. As Curwen (1986, pp. 216–7) notes, they 'effectively [allow] the government to dictate the structure of major privatised concerns, and to determine within fairly narrow limits who will own their shares'.

A third feature of the state's post-privatization role has been the emergence in some industries of regulatory agencies. This, it must be acknowledged, is not purely a feature of privatized industry: many private industries are subject to specific regulation and some are even supervised by regulatory agencies (the Independent Broadcasting Authority, for example). Nevertheless, where former public monopolies – such as gas and telecommunications – have retained all or some monopoly powers after privatization, a regulatory regime has been felt appropriate. Although, as with other post-privatization controls, development has been piecemeal, several key features can be observed. For some industries (notably British Telecom, British Gas, British Airports Authority and – possibly in the future – water and electricity) price controls have been introduced. These have normally taken the form of the 'RPI−X' formula, which ties price increases to the retail prices index (RPI) minus an arbitrary figure (X) designed to reflect changes in the industry. (For discussion, see Littlechild, 1983.) Application of this 'deceptively simple' formula (Helm, 1987) is one of the responsibilities of new regulatory agencies – notably the Office of Telecommunications (OFTEL) and Office of Gas Supply (OFGAS). The emergence of these agencies again reveals no consistent pattern. OFTEL, for example, employing 112 staff in 1987, is much larger, and has wider powers, than OFGAS (employing only nineteen staff). Both, however, are technically non-ministerial government departments, staffed by civil servants, and headed by a Director-General appointed by the sponsoring minister. Broadly their role is to assist ministers in monitoring the industries with the public interest in mind, to promote efficiency and economy and (where appropriate) competition, and to enforce licence terms. Veljanovski (1988, p. 169–70) sees them as part of 'a system of two-tiered and sometimes three-tiered regulation', having above them competition agencies such as the Office of Fair Trading (OFT) (to which alleged instances of monopoly abuse are reported) and the Monopolies and Mergers Commission (MMC) to which the OFT, in turn, has power to refer the industry. Above these, as the top tier, are sponsoring ministers who have power to license operators and, on advice from the MMC, to decide whether mergers should be permitted.

This growth of regulatory agencies raises important questions. One is whether separate regulatory bodies for each industry are preferable to a single utilities commission. The National Consumer Council in evidence to the Energy Select Committee (1985b, Memorandum and Annex 1) argues that they are not, partly because it would 'be easier' for a national body to resist 'capture' by the industry concerned. Although 'capture' is a quite familiar feature of regulatory agencies in the USA, the limited experience of British agencies to date would appear mixed. Veljanovski (1988, p. 186) suggests that, while telecommunications may be a special case, capture has not yet materialised' with OFTEL. With OFGAS, however, Hetherington and Price (1987, p. 18) argue that capture 'may well be continued in the unequal relationship between British Gas plc and OFGAS. . . . It is difficult to see how [OFGAS], with only about twenty employees, can satisfy itself that adequate information has been made available'. In any event regulatory 'capture' is not the only possible outcome. As Steel (1984b, p. 107) warns, 'it is just as likely' that regulatory agencies 'will be "leaned upon" by ministers'.

This latter point raises the implications for control and accountability of these developments. In one sense privatization has removed the blurring of control and accountability which beset public sector industries. Industries are now accountable to shareholders and controlled by a board of directors responding to market forces. Where, as in the case of (virtual) monopolies, market forces cannot apply, control is regulated by agencies such as OFTEL and OFGAS. These not only monitor pricing and service quality, but ensure that any social obligations built into licensing conditions – such as British Telecom's requirement to maintain telephone kiosks and '999' emergency calls – are honoured. In performing these functions regulatory agencies to date have had mixed success. British Telecom since privatization has been widely criticized for tariff structures and poor service, and OFTEL for its part 'has been highly critical of BT's ability to repair faults, install phones and maintain public telephone boxes' (Veljanovski, 1988, p. xxv). It has also required BT (by the so-called Interconnect decision) to allow its main competitor, Mercury, to interconnect with its own network (see OFTEL, 1985). At the same time, however, accountability is made more difficult as 'the privatised firm has a direct incentive to frustrate the regulator' (Veljanovski, 1978, p. 172), elements of which were apparent, both with BT over the Interconnect decision, and with OFGAS's widely publicized dispute with British Gas over access to accounting information necessary for its judgement of a tariff increase.

In another sense, too, accountability and control are blurred with privatization. As Webb (1984, p. 97) notes, 'regulation tends to spawn regulation', slows decision-taking, and 'leads to the growth of an associated bureaucracy'. Today a vast plethora of agencies – regulatory agencies, competition agencies, government departments (and in some cases consumer councils or similar bodies) – as well as boards, shareholders and Commons select committees all have some say in how privatized industries are run. A further issue is the wide discretion allowed to director-generals of the new agencies, and the question as to whom their accountability properly lies – to ministers, Parliament, consumers, shareholders or (where appropriate) competing companies. Some of these issues have simply not been addressed in the piecemeal development of regulatory agencies. While ministerial control and public accountability along lines enshrined in the archetypal model is disappearing, 'the regulation of privately-owned utilities', as Heald (1985, pp. 19, 21) observes, 'generates much the same dilemmas as establishing effective control over publicly-owned utilities. . . . What will be very different is the unexplored terrain over which such accommodations will have to be worked out'.

13 Regional administration

The context of regional administration

According to Jones (1982b, p. 772) there is 'between central and local government . . . a bewildering array of boards, corporations, commissions, councils, agencies, offices and associations, which constitute a tangled administrative jungle'. Elected regional *government* may be absent in Britain but regional *administration*, in a number of guises, is far from insignificant. It is difficult to be precise about numbers of regional bodies but the listing provided by Hogwood and Lindley (1982, pp. 48–9) gives a total of 523 different regional organizations in England alone – and that list was incomplete! As Hogwood (1982, p. 4) observes: 'there may not be a clearly identifiable "regional level of government" in England, but there is certainly a lot of government activity going on in the regions'. In part, the development of a large-scale regional tier of administration in Britain has coincided with the demise of elected local government.

The decline of local authority powers is well charted, going back to the 1930s when they lost their powers in respect of poor relief (1934) and trunk roads (1936). Subsequently their demise in areas such as supplementary benefits (1940), hospitals (1946), electricity supply (1947), gas undertakings (1948), water supply and sewage treatment (1974), and community health care (1974) has occurred. Many of their services were passed over to newly created regional bodies, remote from elected local government and directly accountable to nobody at the local level. As Saunders (1983, p. 2) observes, 'The result is that many key services are today administered through regional boards and authorities which are not only non-elected but which retain a remarkable degree of anonymity'. As a result, this extensive regional tier of administration has 'not been subject to the same analysis and investigation that the more familiar local and central tiers have' (Gray, 1985, p. 45). Yet this regional network is a significant component of British public administration (see Hogwood, 1987).

At the outset it is important to emphasize that much of British public administration is decentralized. Even the civil service, often presented as remote and Whitehall-based, is numerically highly decentralized, with some 75 per cent of civil servants working outside Greater London. Not only do many central government departments (such as Trade and Industry, Employment, Environment, Transport) maintain *regional* outposts but some (such as the DSS and the Inland Revenue) have an extensive network of *local* offices which have direct contact with the public. In addition, many nationalized industries (such as British Rail, British Coal) organize themselves regionally while many non-departmental public bodies (such as the Sports Council and the Tourist Board) have extensive regional structures.

There is, however, a lack of coherence in both the boundaries and size of such networks. Some regional networks incorporate the whole of the United Kingdom, some Great Britain, some England and Wales, while others cover only England. While, for example, the Inland Revenue divides England and Wales into twenty-three regions for valuation purposes, the Department of Trade and Industry has only three regional development grant offices throughout England. Other public bodies exhibit similar diversity: for example, the regional health authorities in England have fourteen regions; the water authorities in England and Wales have ten regions; British Rail in Great Britain has five regions. Not only is there diversity *between* regional public authorities but also *within* them. As Hogwood and Lindley show (1982, p. 48) the Department of the Environment in 1979 had six separate patterns of regional administration ranging from the DOE Ancient Monument Works Areas (GB) with seven English regions to the DOE Rent Assessment Panel Areas with fifteen. Diversity of boundaries both *between* and *within* the various agencies is a major characteristic of regional administration. As Jones (1982b, p. 772) observes, in Britain regions are essentially 'administrative inventions of the centre, not expressions of any political community'.

This diversity of regional structures reflects the pragmatic needs of different departments and organizations. While it might appear that standardization of boundaries would ensure greater inter-organizational co-ordination, it must be emphasized that structural diversity is paralleled by similar diversity in legal powers, lines of accountability, degrees of discretion and sources of finance. As Hogwood and Lindley (1982, p. 46) put it, 'the problems posed by differing degrees of discretion accorded to regional offices and the essentially vertical lines of control to London would still remain'.

While differences *between* regional organizations require emphasis, the distinctiveness of individual regional offices *within* a single public body needs to be explored. For example, Young (1982, p. 92) illustrates the importance of different operational styles within the DOE's regional structure: 'One of the clearest examples of the 1970s was the willingness of the DOE in Manchester or Birmingham to stretch the availability of Derelict Land Grants to the limit . . . In the North West this included the demolition of derelict textile mills. However, the Leeds DOE was more conventional and consistently refused to approve applications to demolish similar structures in West

Yorkshire'. Complexity, therefore, exists not only *between* but also *within* the different constitutent units operating regionally (see also Houlihan, 1984).

Although the UK lacks the natural regions found in many other countries, Scotland, Wales, and Northern Ireland do, however, offer distinctive territorial units as a basis for administrative organization. The *Scottish Office* consists of five departments covering Economic Planning, Development (housing and roads), Home and Health (hospitals, child care, police and education), Education, and Agriculture and Fisheries. Other central government functions in Scotland are administered by appropriate (UK) departments, which have offices in Scotland and work closely with the Scottish Office.

The *Welsh Office* has full responsibility in Wales for ministerial functions relating to health and personal social services, housing, local government, education (except universities), new towns, water and sewerage, roads and agriculture plus other minor functions. It works closely with UK government departments.

The *Northern Ireland Office* now exercises many of the executive powers which were vested in the Northern Ireland government before 1972. In addition there are twenty-six unitary district councils but these are not responsible for as many services as such councils in the rest of the UK. As Hampton (1987, p. 50) notes, the small size of the population in Northern Ireland, along with political and other difficulties, 'have led to many services being administered at a provincial level'. Services currently administered in this way include education, housing, libraries, personal health, planning, roads, water and sewage. Since the suspension of Stormont in 1972 many of these services have been administered via a network of largely nominated regional boards (for example, there are four regional health and social services boards and five education and library boards) responsible to the Northern Ireland Office.

As Keating, (1985, p. 111) observes, it is 'notoriously difficult in the United Kingdom to specify, for analytical purposes, what we mean by the region'. From an organizational perspective Self's definition (1964, p. 55) is helpful. He defined a region as: 'Some area intermediate between national and local government which is a focus for shared demands, common needs or important issues of decision-making'. Saunders (1983) views the region very differently, in terms of what he calls a 'dual-state' model, seeing the regional level as being dominated by corporate interests, as opposed to the producer or consumer interests which, he maintains, are articulated at either central or local levels. Keating (1985, p. 111), prefers to see the region as a political 'space' (understood in a functional as well as a territorial sense) 'in which a variety of types of intervention can occur, precisely because of the weakness of the region's political and institutional articulation'.

Whatever perspective is adopted it is clear that regional agencies invariably have a relatively low political profile. Additionally, there is little sense, at least in metropolitan England, of any regional identity, perhaps because none of the agencies operating at this level is subject to popular election. Despite the growth in the range and scope of regional administration it 'has remained immune to electoral control and divorced from pluralistic processes of political competition. Regional level decision-making appears curiously non-contentious and uniquely apolitical precisely because most of us have enjoyed precious little opportunity to make our voices heard' (Saunders, 1983, p. 19). It is this lack of direct accountability to the local population which has accounted for much of the uneasiness about the expansion of what Saunders calls the 'regional state'.

While regional administration in the UK lacks coherence, it is nevertheless crucially important. Inevitably a text such as this cannot give comprehensive treatment to the subject. As separate chapters deal with departments (Chapter 2), non-departmental public bodies (Chapter 11), and nationalized industries (Chapter 12), all of which exhibit some instances of regional administration, this chapter focuses upon two important services currently (in 1988) administered regionally which have not elsewhere been discussed. These services, water and health, are both extremely important in terms of their expenditure, manpower, and political significance.

The water industry

In 1986 the Conservative government announced plans for a £7bn privatization programme for the ten water authorities in England and Wales. Following its 1987 election victory the new Conservative government 'promised' a bill to effect such a change and in 1988 the Public Utility Transfers and Water Charges Act was passed, an enabling measure to allow the ten water authorities to become public limited companies and to establish a National Rivers Authority to be responsible for water quality and pollution control, land drainage and flood protection, conservation and recreation, fisheries and navigation.

Following privatization, scheduled for November 1989, the new companies will be responsible solely for providing water and sewerage services. After privatization has been effected the government plans to appoint a new Director General of Water Services, responsible for safeguarding customers from excessive charges and poor service (*The Times*, 12 May 1988).

The pre-privatization water industry, as the Pliatzky Report (1980, p. 31) noted, exhibits some of the 'features of a nationalized industry but in other respects it is more in the nature of a public service of the kind provided by local authorities'. Indeed, prior to 1974 many water-based services were provided by local authorities, as is still the case in Scotland.

The Water Act, 1973, established nine regional water authorities (RWAs) in England plus the Welsh Water Authority. These ten authorities currently have overall responsibility for every aspect of water usage in England and Wales: water resources; water treatment; distribution and supply; pollution control; sewerage and sewage treatment; river management; land drainage; sea defences; recreation; and fisheries. Prior to 1 April 1974 these functions had been divided amongst a number of organizations, both private and public: a) water was supplied by 187 separate water undertakings; b) sewerage and sewerage treatment was in the hands of 1,393 local authorities; c) water conservation and land drainage was the responsibility of twenty-one river authorities.

The official rationale for reorganization in 1974 was that water supply must be organized according to hydrological boundaries; such technical considerations were 'subordinated to the political criterion of rendering them democratically accountable . . . so the RWAs emerged essentially as technocratic agencies in the political space which was relatively free from central or local control' (Keating, 1985, p. 117).

Despite this 'rationalization' there were still major disparities between the ten new authorities in terms of size and resources. Thames, for example, has a population of some 11.5m; South West has only 1.4m customers. Likewise, revenue expenditure is six times greater in Thames than in the South West Region. Additionally, some twenty-eight private water companies (like the South Staffs Waterworks Co.) supply water to 25 per cent of the population as agents for the regional authorities. Confusion is compounded since *in Scotland* local authorities still carry out most water functions.

The Local Government (Scotland) Act, 1973, which came into force in May 1975, was the product not of a desire to reorganize water management but rather of a desire to reform local government. The Report of the Royal Commission on Local Government in Scotland (Wheatley Report, 1969) had called for the disbandment of river purification boards and water boards and for the return of their functions to local authorities. The report, in other words, argued that in terms of water management Scotland should move in a completely opposite direction to England and Wales. In the event, intensive opposition was aroused to the proposal to dispense with river purification boards, and it was ultimately agreed to retain a reduced number. However, similarly strong opposition could not be mounted in favour of the water boards; consequently the thirteen catchment-based regional boards were abolished and their functions returned to local government.

Why were two such clearly differing approaches to water management adopted? If the arguments for bringing all the functions of the water cycle in an entire river basin under one authority were so compelling, how did a system emerge in Scotland based on totally different principles? The availability of water supplies provides some clue. England and Wales are far more populous than Scotland and it became apparent in the early 1970s that careful planning and conservation of water resources was necessary to secure water supplies on a long-term basis. In this context technical arguments, advanced by professionals, prevailed in England and Wales. In Scotland, however, water is more plentiful; hence the focus of reform was on local government rather than on the water industry in particular.

ACCOUNTABILITY AND CONTROL

The regionalization of the water industry stemmed primarily from managerial motives. As the emphasis was upon technical efficiency rather than democratic participation, and as river catchment areas did not coincide with existing administrative units, the new structure was removed from direct local government control. However, both to represent consumer interests, and because in numerous policy fields close co-operation between the new water authorities and local government would be essential, some links with local government were retained. On each board a majority of members were local authority nominees, although the chairman and other members were to be appointed by the Secretary of State. The rationale for these ministerial appointees was to give representation to particular groups – such as industrialists and anglers – as well as to secure the appointment of members with knowledge and experience relevant to the efficient management of the industry.

These arrangements, Gray (1982, pp. 146, 151) observes, produced for the administration of water 'a form of quasi-nationalized industry'. The close links with local authorities were coupled with features similar to those of public corporations (see Chapter 12) – the appointment of chairmen and members of RWAs by ministers, and some important ministerial controls (for example over the industry's investment programme). For the most part, however, the RWAs created by the 1973 Act were intended to be 'autonomous and executive' with 'clearly defined statutory duties' including power to determine the level of water charges. In practice, as Gray (1982, pp. 159–60) notes, these arrangements were widely criticized 'as being neither adequately representative of the public, nor completely based upon the criteria of managerial expertise'. They also tended 'to confuse, and obscure, where their accountability [lay]'. RWAs, in fact, combined both local and ministerial forms of accountability. The Pliatzky Report (1980,

p. 32) observed of the system: 'It can be claimed . . . that it carries with it all the accountability to Ministers, and through them to Parliament, that exists in the case of nationalised industries; and that in addition the local authority nominees provide effective representation of local interests.' In fact, ministerial accountability to Parliament 'in the case of nationalised industries' poses many problems (see Chapter 12), while in practice local authority nominees – being drawn from only a few councils within the area – were generally regarded as remote and inaccessible. In addition, the extent of local authority representation to some extent counteracted the original intention which was to managerialize the industry. Gray (1982, p. 161) concluded:

> The seemingly innocuous question of WA membership thus raises serious questions concerning the extent of local authority involvement in policy-making, the role of members within the industry and whether the WAs are accountable to the local, political level or to the central, ministerial level, or whether they are accountable at all.

The 1973 Water Act also established an instrument of liaison between central government and the RWAs, namely, the National Water Council (NWC). This was intended to function as a central co-ordinating, consultative and advisory body, its major task being to advise ministers on national policy and to promote efficiency within the RWAs. The council also had responsibilities for training, industrial relations and superannuation. However, it had no *executive* powers over RWAs; indeed, neither the government nor the RWAs were obliged to accept its advice. The NWC nevertheless performed 'a vital buffer role between the WAs and the government' and provided 'a coherent voice for the water industry at the national level' (Gray, 1982, p. 152).

The Water Act, 1983, saw major changes to the industry. Water authorities, in effect, acquired a structure closely resembling that of nationalized industries, with all its inherent control and accountability problems. The previously automatic local authority representation on the boards of RWAs was abolished altogether. The Secretary of State now appoints a chairperson, designates a deputy chairperson and, together with ministerial colleagues, appoints all other members of each board. The boards are also far smaller than hitherto with between nine and fifteen members. Additionally, the NWC was abolished. The 1983 Water Act also saw the curtailing of the rights of the press and public to attend meetings despite the fact that water authorities levy rates from the local populace.

The final abolition of automatic local authority representation on the RWA boards in 1983 saw consumer representation largely pass to new 'consumer consultative committees' (consisting of representatives from local authorities, local industrialists, farmers, and so on) established along lines similar to other nationalized industry consumer councils (see Chapter 12). These committees have no executive power and appear to be marginalized in terms of policy influence. The water industry, therefore, now has no automatic local authority representation on its boards and nothing other than token consumer representation.

By 1988 privatization of the industry was firmly on the political agenda. As Keating notes (1985, p. 119) privatization would have the advantage for the government of taking the water authorities' investment out of the public sector borrowing requirement, and also of reducing the political fallout from increases in charges. 'It would not, given the authorities' status as a national monopoly, resolve the questions of control and accountability or how to balance the interests of commercial and domestic users, local planning requirements and shareholders'. Essentially, the 1983 Water Act continued the movement away from local accountability that was begun in 1973 (see Gray, 1984). The 'promised' privatization of the industry in late 1989 will be interpreted by some as completing the process.

The National Health Service

Like the water industry, the National Health Service (NHS) receives scant treatment in most public administration texts but it is, in fact, a major arm of British public administration. Some 981,000 people were employed by the NHS in 1986–7; and government spending plans for 1988–9 allocated £18.35bn for public expenditure on the NHS, some 11.7 per cent of total planned public expenditure (Cm 56, Table 14.1). While central government, mainly through the agencies of the Department of Health (DOH) and the Scottish and Welsh Offices, is responsible for overall policy and for allocating funds, the NHS has always maintained a regional tier of administration and, despite two recent reorganizations (1974 and 1982), this regional structure has survived. Indeed the regional tier was strengthened when in 1974, regional hospital boards broadened out to become regional health authorities (RHAs). The DOH and the RHAs are, however, only part of a much more extensive organizational structure which has evolved since the end of the Second World War.

THE ESTABLISHMENT OF THE NHS

The NHS is a primary ingredient of Britain's 'welfare state'. Although it came fully into existence in 1948, the National Health Service Act, 1946, which established it in fact amalgamated many services which formerly had been provided separately: its aim was to provide a free and comprehensive system of health care to the whole community. Under the Act a tripartite organizational structure was established which lasted until 1974. This consisted of:

(i) *Hospitals.* Regional Hospital Boards had strategic planning and resource allocation functions, and were accountable to the Minister of Health. Day-to-day running of hospitals was left to hospital management committees.
(ii) *Local authorities.* These had responsibility for health centres, district nursing, the school health service, the ambulance service, and environmental and public health.
(iii) *Executive councils.* Made up, approximately, of half from appointees of the minister and local authorities, and half from local practitioners, they administered local services provided by general practitioners, opticians, pharmacists, and dentists. Their existence reflected the resistance of many doctors and dentists, when the NHS was formed, to becoming salaried local authority or state employees.

In the late 1960s, the increasing difficulties associated with co-ordinating this tripartite service led to pressure for reorganization. According to Brown (1975, p. 142) three major defects weakened the old system: (i) The 'absence of any single body with overall responsibility for the provision of health services'; (ii) 'the difficulty of securing effective policy co-ordination below the level of the central department'; (iii) 'the lack of any proper machinery for local medical planning'.

RESTRUCTURING THE SERVICE: 1974

In 1974 the NHS was brought into a unified administrative structure (see Figure 13.1) based in England on fourteen RHAs, ninety area health authorities (AHAs) and 199 districts. This reorganization, however, did not extend to social services, which remained under local authority control. Given the need for an integrated health service, the retention by local authorities of responsibility for personal social services seemed illogical from a NHS standpoint. However, from a social services perspective it made more sense; not only does efficient social service provision require close links with other local authority services – such as housing and education – but the administration of personal social services had been comprehensively reorganized under local authority control in 1971 following the recommendations of the Seebohm Report (1968). Consequently, it became necessary as part of the 1974 reorganization to facilitate co-operation between health

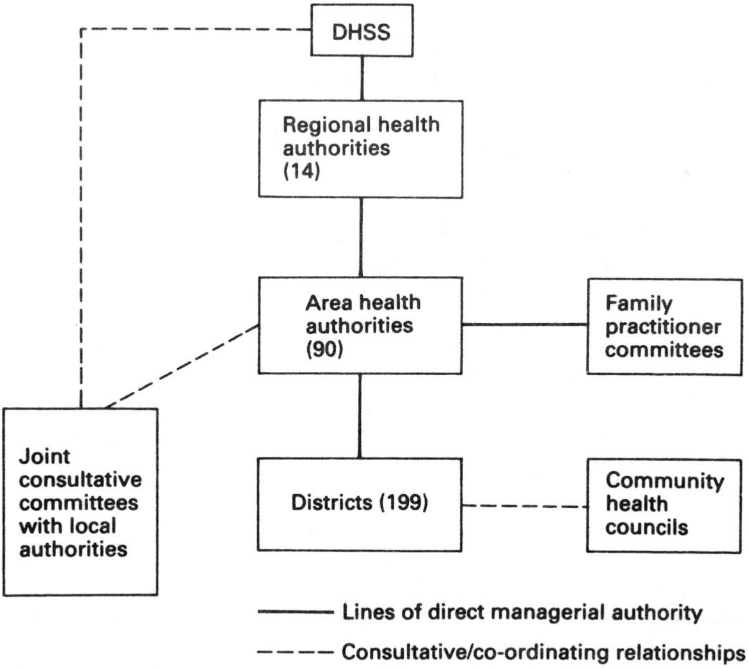

Figure 13.1 The NHS in England: organizational pattern established in 1974.

authorities responsible for health services and local authorities which retained responsibility for social services. As Wistow (1982, p. 44) has observed:

> So important was such collaboration considered that the boundaries of the new Area Health Authorities (AHAs) were not based upon the organisational requirements of health service administration alone. Instead, they were drawn coterminous with those of shire counties and metropolitan districts and personal social services in the restructured local government system.

The importance of collaboration, particularly in the context of *joint planning*, was emphasized in the 1973 NHS Reorganisation Act which 'provided for the establishment of formal collaboration machinery centred upon a member-level body – the Joint Consultative Committee . . . composed of representatives drawn from matching health and local authorities and supported by an officer working group' (Wistow, 1982, p. 45). Joint funding was an integral part of this arrangement.

The fourteen English RHAs established in 1974 were made responsible for determining regional priorities and for allocating resources to their respective AHAs. Generally they consist of around twenty members, appointed by the Secretary of State, who have been nominated by the three 'constituencies': the service itself (comprising hospital doctors, GPs, nurses); local authorities; lay members.

The ninety area health authorities (abolished in 1982) consisted of about twenty members, including doctors and nurses, appointed by the Secretary of State and had a 'management' rather than a 'representative' function. They were responsible for assessing health needs and for service provision – a task often involving a good deal of liaison with local authority social services and housing departments.

The ninety AHAs were divided, in turn, into 199 districts which were essentially management units and were usually organized round a district general hospital incorporating a population of between 100,000 and 500,000. District management teams, consisting of six members, were allocated responsibility for day-to-day service provision. As Figure 13.1 shows, the former executive councils were replaced in 1974 by family practitioner committees with similar functions and with DHA, local authority, and professional representation.

COMMUNITY HEALTH COUNCILS (CHCs)

These became operative from 1974 and survived the 1982 restructuring (albeit only against a background of DHSS pressure to abolish them), having been established as the 'representative' arm of the new-look NHS, but with the clear intention of keeping representation distinct from management. One CHC was normally established for each health district. CHCs generally have about thirty members: half from local authorities (who need not be councillors) and the remainder from local voluntary organizations and RHA nominees. Essentially, CHCs have the task of representing the public's view to those who administer the service but in practice few members of the public know of their existence, let alone attend meetings. Additionally, when they do recommend changes their suggestions do not *have* to be taken up.

It is sometimes suggested that CHCs have no representativeness or legitimacy because they are not elected. As Bates (1982, p. 94) notes, the argument put forward is generally 'that CHCs are appointed, not elected bodies and except for members who have been elected to a local authority, have no right to speak for the community or to regard themselves as representative'. The same author comments, however (p. 94), that 'representativeness in a democracy can be argued on the basis of representatives being authorized to act for someone else, or being accountable to someone, or being representative in the sense of being a microcosm of society as a whole. On none of these grounds do CHCs qualify.' On the other hand, some form of consumer voice is essential in the NHS; CHCs at least attempt to act in this capacity.

Bates (1982, pp. 97–8) concludes:

> Regardless of their legitimacy and representativeness, CHCs have clearly succeeded in turning the minds of administrators outwards to the community and to the hitherto neglected groups of patients . . . . [They] are performing successfully the function of giving a voice to groups for whom no exit is possible from the NHS.

CHCs, although lacking executive power, at least enable some local people to play (or appear to play) a part in running the service by conveying suggestions and complaints to managers, not unlike the consultative councils of the nationalized industries. It remains the public face of a relatively closed system of administration.

ACCOUNTABILITY AND CONTROL

The 1974 reorganization, coinciding with the 'reform' of local government, meant that local authorities lost their remaining health functions to the newly created, non-elected health authorities, raising similar questions about accountability and control to those in the water industry. Although the new arrangements were intended to retain sensitivity to local opinion, this has barely materialized. The real influence on decision-making rested mainly with the chairmen of RHAs who, as appointees of the Secretary of State, largely owed their security of tenure to retaining the confidence of ministers and senior personnel in the authority. In fact, ministers, through the chairmen of RHAs, have a *potential* for control over most aspects of the NHS. The NHS is funded almost totally by the Exchequer, and the Secretary of State for Health (and equivalent Welsh and Scottish ministers) have responsibility for policy developments, the allocation of funds, and general oversight.

In practice, however, ministers' ability to secure implementation of their policy objectives has been limited. According to Haywood and Elcock (1982, p. 139), RHAs have functioned 'as extensions of interests within the NHS rather than the representatives of central policy'. Decision-making is heavily dependent on expert opinion and upon the co-operation of powerful interests – consultants, teaching hospitals, and so forth – to an extent that 'diminishes the effective public accountability of Ministers'. The Royal Commission on the National Health Service (1979) Report (ch. 19) referred pointedly to 'the inconsistency between the theoretical responsibilities for the NHS carried by health ministers, permanent secretaries and health departments, and the practical realities.' However, its solution, that RHAs 'become accountable to Parliament for matters within their competence', was rejected by the government. Consequently, while ministers remain nominally responsible for most aspects of the NHS, their effective control over the RHAs is, in practice, somewhat limited.

While these arrangements mean that the NHS largely avoids effective public accountability or *direct* democratic control, it is not immune from scrutiny. In addition to CHCs, the 1973 Act (and the 1974 Scottish Act) established Health Service Commissioners empowered to investigate complaints within the NHS. However, in practice their value is limited as they cannot pass judgement in clinical matters (see Chapter 15 for fuller discussion). In addition, MPs are able to raise issues concerning the NHS in Parliament, and since 1979 a Social Services Select Committee has provided a useful means for further scrutiny of the health service.

It is also important to stress that, although democratic control might not be direct, as with local authority services, local politics in the wider sense does influence NHS decision-making. MPs, councillors, pressure groups and the media frequently take up cases; for example that of a hospital about to be closed, and might thereby have some indirect influence (albeit possibly a diminishing one now that decisions increasingly have to be made in the light of economic constraints).

SLIMMING DOWN: 1982

In 1982 a slimmed-down NHS came into being (see Figure 13.2), the major change being the replacement of the ninety AHAs and their 199 districts by a single structure of 192 district health authorities. The rationale behind the restructuring was the reduction of bureaucracy and costs, coupled with a desire to delegate more decisions to the local level.

Although the existing planning procedures had looked rational in theory, in practice planning passed through so many tiers that procedures had become discredited.

The Royal Commission on the National Health Service (1979) pointed to a number of defects in the service, notably the multiplicity of management tiers and administration and inefficiency in decision-making and use of resources. In its 1979 election manifesto, the Conservative Party had talked of simplifying, decentralizing and cutting back on bureaucracy, and in a consultative paper, *Patients First* (Department of Health and Social Security, 1979), the government asserted (p. 1): 'We have reached the firm conclusion that the structure and management arrangements of the Service introduced in 1974 do not provide the best framework for the effective delivery of care to the patients. The Royal Commission on the NHS . . . has confirmed us in our view.' The government, however, rejected any radical restructuring (such as transferring the NHS back to local government) in favour of incremental change. The main points of the government's proposals, which came into effect on 1 April 1982, were:

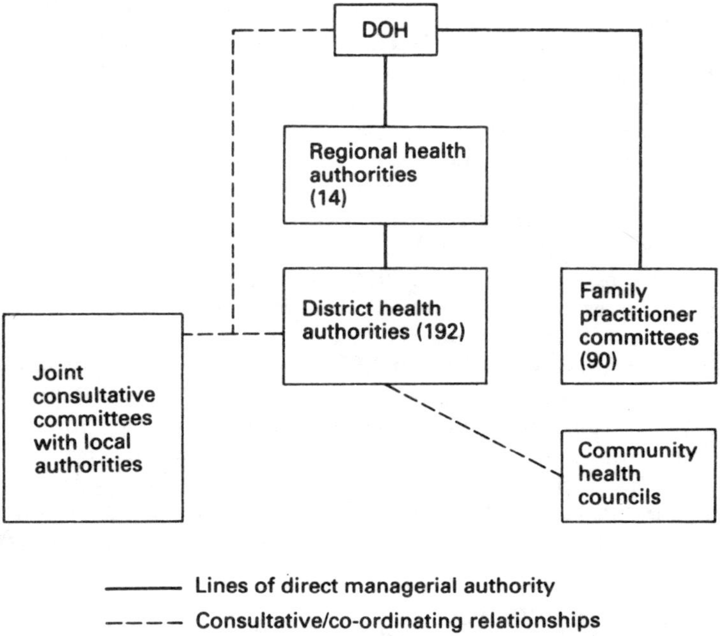

Note: see Ham (1987), ch. 1, for details about structural changes in the rest of Great Britain.

Figure 13.2 The NHS in England: the structure in 1988.

(i) Area health authorities were to be abolished. District health authorities (DHAs) were to be retained, following as far as possible the boundaries of existing health districts (thus the area tier was to be abolished). The aim was that the new district authorities should serve communities with populations up to 500,000.

(ii) The DHAs were to have, on average, sixteen members each, four of them nominated by local authorities (this was a reduction in local authority representation from 33 per cent of the total to 25 per cent). The chairman of a district authority was to be appointed by the Secretary of State and the other members (apart from local authority nominees) were to be appointed by the RHA, although the practice of having a consultant, a GP, a nurse, a university nominee and a trade union nominee was to continue.

(iii) Decision-making was to be brought as far as possible down to hospital and community level with a strengthening of management at that level. Each DHA was to appoint a team to co-ordinate all health service activities of the district, including policy implementation. The government also argued for the maximum delegation of resonsibility to those in the hospital and community services within policies determined by the DHA.

(iv) RHAs were to remain for strategic purposes, although the government promised a review of their functions at a future date. Some observers continue to feel that the regions have become too remote and (possibly) candidates for abolition or reform. RHAs themselves, however, stress their strategic importance and their value as buffers against the over-centralization of power.

(v) Community Health Councils were to remain (one for each new district authority), but again the government promised that they were to be subject to future review, arguing (Department of Health and Social Security, 1979, p. 14) that, as district authority members would 'be less remote from local services than . . . [area authority] members necessarily' had been, the need for separate consumer representation was less clear than in the past. In practice, however, some new district authorities are more remote from the consumer than they had been before the 1982 reorganization. In Leicestershire, for example, prior to 1982 there was an AHA and three districts, each with a CHC. Following restructuring there is only a single district authority (serving 836,000 people) with one CHC. Such a structure hardly facilitates administrators being 'more closely in touch with the needs of the community' as *Patients First* (p. 14) had suggested.

(vi) While the Royal Commission recommended that family practitioner committees (FPCs) should be abolished and their functions absorbed by health authorities, the government decided against this, largely because of the opposition of the medical professions. In the event, on 1 April 1985 the FPCs became independent bodies and were given the status of employing authorities in their own right, thereby confirming the effective position they had long enjoyed. From April 1985 FPCs have been directly accountable only to the Secretary of State, not (as previously) to the local health authority. The 1985 changes involved some new responsibilities including the need to consult the Community Health Council over any significant change in practitioner services, but in essence FPCs are now more directly under the control of the DOH.

THE POST-1982 STRUCTURE

In England there are three administrative tiers in the NHS: (i) DOH, (ii) RHAs and (iii) DHAs. Health care is still under a single organizational structure and, while the removal of a management tier has streamlined the system, much complexity remains. Indeed, so far as local government/health authority relationships are concerned, complexity has increased. Whereas previously AHA boundaries were coterminous with social service authority boundaries, under the new arrangements 'the boundaries of two or more DHAs are combined within that of a social services authority' (Wistow, 1982, p. 59). Coterminosity has largely disappeared.

The 1982 developments need to be seen as part of the Thatcher government's desire to streamline public sector administration. A leaner, more efficient structure, with the maximum delegation of responsibility for service provision to the DHAs, was the government's professed aim, but doubts have been expressed that the new structure has produced more central and regional direction since the DHAs are relatively small and thereby are unlikely to carry much political weight. In addition, local authority representation has been reduced: from 1976 one-third of the membership of each RHA and AHA had consisted of local authority nominees, but since 1982 this has been reduced 'so reversing the effect of Barbara Castle's decision in 1976 to increase the local democratic accountability of the NHS' (Elcock, 1986, p. 278). At the same time there has been some evidence of attempts to exert ministerial *control* over RHAs; for example, four chairmen were replaced in 1982 after they had criticized government handling of an NHS pay dispute, and in 1986 ministers were accused of trying to replace chairmen who had fought publicly for more resources with 'safe Conservative' supporters (*The Times*, 6 March 1986). However, these developments have not necessarily stimulated a commensurate move towards increased *accountability*; on the contrary, as Haywood and Elcock (1982, p. 141) comment, ministers could now 'argue that their responsibilities in practice do not extend to all activities but are confined to the minimal requirements of accountability – that money is spent honestly and properly, efficiently and with economy'.

The new simpler structure might help to streamline the NHS, but as Brown (1982, pp. 83–4) emphasizes, 'administrative reform cannot . . . solve all the problems involved in delivering medical care . . . [particularly] the crucial questions on objectives or priorities that medical care currently raises'. Structural change seems unlikely to be able to dislodge the medical profession from its dominance of every level within the NHS. Indeed, *Patients First* – which outlined the official rationale for the 1982 reorganization – can be criticized for not making patients the main consideration (Department of Health and Social Security, 1979). Many people concerned with preventative and community medicine argue that the evolving of districts around hospital units will merely perpetuate the emphasis on hospital care – in line with the interests of the medical profession and other established groups – which already absorbs what they see as too large a share of NHS resources. According to Elcock (1986, p. 283), decentralized administration 'has increased resistance to the implementation of policies that challenge established professional hierarchies and priorities within the NHS'. Public administration in the NHS is strongly influenced by a network of 'specialist' professional and managerialist elites whose dominance it is difficult to exaggerate.

According to Dearlove and Saunders (1984, pp. 398–9), the organization of the NHS is:

> remarkably immune to popular pressure or control. Within cash limits imposed by the centre, the RHAs can effectively determine their own health priorities without having to worry too much about consumer opinion, and this effectively lays them open to the sustained influence of the medical profession in general and the hospital consultants in particular.

As with the water industry, policy-making seems to be predominantly in the hands of professionals and managers. In both water and health authorities elected local control has been abolished and decision-making pushed to more remote structures 'which are inaccessible and non-accountable to the populations they administer'. In the NHS a regional system, then, has not only allowed the government to keep overall financial control but has also enabled the medical profession to perpetuate its long-standing dominance, given the lack of direct electoral accountability to the local population.

Saunders (1984), however, warns against exaggerating the dominance of professional interests (engineers in the water industry and hospital consultants in the NHS). Their influence, he argues, might have been exaggerated in some literature. While there is no doubt that such groups certainly retain some influence, Saunders argues that their dominance might have been eroded somewhat in recent years because of 'organisational innovations (which have made management structures stronger and more cohesive) and to tightening financial constraints (which have placed a check on their aspirations)'. The managerialist ethos increasingly prevails so that while the influence of professional groups is still considerable, 'the initiative today lies more with the administrators, chairmen and finance chiefs'.

Managing the NHS: the Griffiths Reports

One of the most influential pressures toward managerialism came about as a result of the first Griffiths Report in 1983 which, in line with thinking elsewhere within the public sector (see Chapters 1 and 7), encouraged selected managerial practices found in the private sector to be adopted within the NHS. Griffiths argued that, despite good work done by many lay members of health authorities and CHCs, management itself ought to play an active, not merely a reactive, role in relation to patients. To this end there needed to be more dynamism and direction: 'We believe that a small, strong general management body is necessary at the centre' (p. 2). As a result, within the DHSS (DOH from 1988) a Health Services Supervisory Board and a full-time NHS Management Board were established. The role of the former was to strengthen oversight of the NHS, being concerned with determination of purpose, objectives and direction, approval of the overall budget and resource allocations, strategic decisions and receiving reports on performance and other evaluations from within the service. Its composition was to be the Secretary of State (chair), the permanent secretary, the chief medical officer, the chairman of the NHS Management Board and two or three non-executive members with general management skills and experience.

Under this Board, and accountable to it, would be the small, multi-professional NHS Management Board whose membership included functions such as personnel, finance, procurement, property, scientific and high technology management and service planning. Its role was spelled out in the report (pp. 3–4) as follows: to plan implementation of the policies approved by the Supervisory Board; to give leadership to the management of the NHS; to control performance and to achieve consistency and drive over the long term. Its chairman would perform the general management function at national level and would 'be seen to be vested with executive authority derived from the Secretary of State'. He and other members of the board, it was argued, would need to have, 'considerable experience and skill in effecting change in a large, service-oriented organisation and . . . would initially almost certainly have to come from outside the NHS and the Civil Service'. The first chairman, Victor Paige (previously deputy chairman of the National Freight Consortium) resigned in 1986 after only sixteen months in office. Part of the 'problem' appeared to be that the civil servants were continuing to take a detailed interest in the running of the NHS and that ministers involved themselves in matters which Paige felt were the proper province of management. The distinction between management and political accountability proved hard to draw. This is perhaps reflected by the fact that the chairman of the Management Board has subsequently been a minister. There has also been some concern that the roles of the Supervisory and Management boards have in practice become blurred.

Griffiths also maintained that general managers should be appointed at regional, district and unit levels of the NHS with overall responsibility for management and performance. To date this proposal has made most impact at district and unit levels, although full acceptance of the 'spirit' of Griffiths has been patchy. It took about two years for all the general managers to be appointed down to unit level, a development marked by much staff movement and uncertainty as the appointees restructured their new domains. Several of the earlier appointments from outside the service proved to be short-lived, despite preferential employment packages being offered to attract them. The situation in 1988 is that the general management of the health service is still predominantly the responsibility of people who started off as administrators, clinicians or (occasionally) nurses. However, as many of these 'managers' are employed on fixed-term contracts, with remuneration linked to stringent performance targets, resolve to implement the intentions of ministers and health authorities has been sharpened. There has also been increased emphasis upon devolved budgeting, income generation, internal marketing and contracting-out of domestic and other services. More use of information technology has allowed improved sophistication in the collection of performance-indicator information (given particular impetus by the Körner Committee in 1982). In this climate the orientation has become increasingly entrepreneurial, and the management implications for staff – many of whom did not enter the service with such orientations – are not without their own resource implications. The position has been further complicated by a reallocation of resources from richer to less endowed regions (on the basis of RAWP – resource allocation working party – formulae), creating tensions both between regions and between regions and the centre.

Urgency concerning the need to integrate more closely the various wings of the health service, and of services related to it such as social services and housing, has continued during the 1980s, and in March 1988 there came a second Griffiths Report (*Community Care: Agenda for Action*). Its theme was that responsibility for care of groups such as the very elderly and those with physical and mental disabilities needed to be more firmly located with one authority and that much of the work currently being done by health authorities might with advantage be handed over to local authority social services departments. This has led to speculation as to what the future holds, speculation fuelled further by the government's review of the NHS being conducted (at the time of writing) in secret and probably unlikely to be made public until January 1989.

Conclusions

Water and health authorities are just two examples of the non-elected bodies which inhabit the 'regional state', the numbers of which have increased in some localities since the abolition of the GLC and the six 'mets' in 1986. There is no *direct* electoral check on bodies such as these, which spend vast amounts of public money and make 'politically crucial and contentious decisions' (Dearlove and Saunders, 1984, p. 402). Such bodies are, of course, relatively easily controlled by the centre compared with the resistance which central government often encounters from local authorities. According to Dearlove and Saunders (1984, p. 402) this potential for direction explains why regional agencies are so attractive to central government. While some degree of decentralization of service provision is invariably necessary to take account of different local circumstances it can also be dangerous 'since it opens up the possibility of resistance from below. The solution it seems, lies in the further extension of non-elected peripheral agencies which can be kept out of the reach of potentially troublesome opponents'. Regional agencies may, therefore, represent an ideal solution from a centralist perspective, despite the problems of inter-organizational co-ordination which their proliferation can create.

From time to time political parties (notably the Alliance in the 1987 general election) argue that an elected regional layer of government would represent a genuine devolution of power from the centre if it took over functions currently performed by government departments in the regions as well as those of single-purpose *ad hoc* agencies. In practice, of course, the reverse could be true: a regional administrative layer could increase centralization, since it would probably control elected local government at close quarters. In any event political regionalism remains unlikely. Untidy administrative regionalism is, however, very much a reality.

14 Parliament and Accountability

In a formal sense Parliament sets the parameters of British public administration. It lays down the functions of all public agencies and is the ultimate source of their authority. In practice, however, executive dominance over the last hundred years has severely restricted its role. Even allowing for changes which have occurred since 1970 – a more participative and independent attitude by many MPs, and structural changes such as the establishment of departmental select committees (see pp. 294–98) – Britain has, at best, 'a policy influencing legislature' (see Norton, 1985 and 1987). Indeed, some analyses see Parliament as of no great importance at all. As Ryle, for example, claimed in 1981 (p. 14) ministers and civil servants today 'implement their policies and act over the vast range of executive authority with little need to refer to Parliament at all'.

Four main aspects of Parliament nevertheless remain particularly relevant for students of public administration and are dealt with in this chapter. They are: legislation; parliament and public finance; ministerial responsibility; and parliamentary scrutiny and redress.

Legislation

Parliament's legislative work has increased enormously as the role of the state has expanded. In 1982 B. Jones (1982, p. 313) observed: 'Fifty years ago Parliament produced 450 pages of legislation; now, using largely the same methods, it processed 3,000 pages plus 10,000 [pages of] Statutory Instruments not to mention the EEC regulations and directives'. Broadly speaking, two main forms of legislation can be identified: a) primary legislation; and b) delegated legislation. Although the former is arguably the more important, delegated legislation tends to cause more confusion for students of public administration and consequently it is given fuller treatment in this chapter.

PRIMARY LEGISLATION OR STATUTE

This for the most part originates within government. In 1968 Walkland (p. 20) described the legislative process as comprising 'deliberative, Parliamentary and administrative stages, over all of which [the government was] predominant'. This predominance stems partly from the party system – in normal circumstances the government has a parliamentary majority – and partly also from the procedures of the House of Commons, the major legislative chamber. Commons procedures allow few opportunities for effective scrutiny by MPs. Detailed scrutiny of Bills is possible in the committee stage, but standing committees which deal with legislation are non-investigative and (although they may contain a nucleus of party spokesmen and 'experts') essentially non-specialist (for discussion see Silk with Walters, 1987, especially ch. 6). Commons procedure also enables the government to curtail discussion by MPs by utilizing such devices as the closure and the guillotine. Even so, parliamentary time is usually scarce: there is invariably only time to enact three or four *major* government bills per session. One consequence of this is the increasing use of delegated legislation, the process by which Parliament delegates its law-making powers to ministers and administrative agencies such as public corporations and local authorities.

DELEGATED LEGISLATION

This is also known as subordinate or secondary legislation and exists in several forms, of which the most common are ministerial and departmental regulations, public corporation and local authority bye-laws, and compulsory purchase orders. Of these various forms the most important is the first: ministerial or departmental regulations, which enable ministers or their officials to issue regulations which have legal force. Alternatively, ministers may be given power to issue rules by Order in Council, a procedure usually reserved for the more important or sensitive subjects of ministerial regulation. Whichever of these two forms is adopted, however, rules or orders issued under them are commonly known as 'statutory instruments'. While statutory instruments (SIs) are nothing new, the growth in the volume and complexity of government business has made them an increasingly important feature of the modern state. Today the annual total of SIs is usually around 1,000, and every year 'their length and complexity appears inexorably to have expanded' (Shell, 1988, p. 180).

Advantages and disadvantages

The increasing use of delegated legislation reflects its many advantages. The most important of these are:

(i) It relieves pressure on parliamentary time by leaving some subordinate matters for regulation by ministers, local authorities and so forth.

(ii) It offers technical advantages. In highly specialized fields regulation by statutory instrument – drawn up on the advice of experts – is often more appropriate than asking MPs to enact legislation.

(iii) It enables government to deal with unforeseen circumstances. When enacting legislation it is usually impossible to anticipate all the circumstances in which it will apply. Delegated legislation allows Parliament to lay down the broad framework of law, leaving ministers to fill in the details later as and when appropriate.

(iv) Speed is often necessary (to respond to outbreaks of disease, to change exchange controls, or to deal with war and emergencies, for example). Delegated legislation enables ministers (or other agencies) to issue regulations with immediate effect without waiting to pilot legislation through Parliament.

(v) Circumstances change and delegated legislation provides flexibility. It would be overbearing to have to produce new Bills whenever, for example, changes in hire purchase controls are required.

Despite these advantages concern is often expressed about delegated legislation. Many of its 'advantages' accrue only because normal safeguards and procedures are relaxed. For example, while the courts are able to inquire whether delegated legislation has been *intra vires*, this is not always the safeguard it might appear owing to the broad powers which (to allow maximum flexibility) have sometimes been conferred upon ministers. As Punnett (1980, p. 347) observes, 'some delegated powers are so wide as to justify almost any action by the executive, as with the wartime emergency powers, and the clause that was contained in some legislation, giving the Minister the power to make any changes necessary to put the legislation into effect'. Again, the fact that regulations can be issued with almost immediate effect, without parliamentary debate, and many years after the enabling legislation was passed, means that there is often little or no public awareness of changes in the law.

A particular problem is, that, while much secondary legislation is highly technical, some SIs are extremely important. In 1981 Beith claimed (pp. 166–7) that what was effectively taxation could be introduced by SI, as 0.25 per cent in the national insurance contribution of all employees could be levied in this way at any one time. Similarly, immigration rules, welfare benefit levels and employment protection procedures are all determined by SIs. Since direct rule was introduced in Northern Ireland in 1972 the majority of legislation for the province, covering all aspects of life except security, taxation and constitutional matters, has been in the form of SIs (Silk with Walters, 1987, p. 155). Matters of considerable significance, in other words, can be effected by delegated legislation, often with negligible parliamentary discussion, a fact not infrequently taken advantage of by governments desirous of introducing 'unpopular' measures with minimum public debate.

PARLIAMENTARY SCRUTINY OF DELEGATED LEGISLATION

The problem of maintaining effective parliamentary scrutiny of delegated legislation has long been recognized. It was one of the major concerns expressed by Hewart in *The New Despotism* (1929) and by the Donoughmore Report on ministers' powers (1932). Despite this, contemporary procedures for scrutiny are generally regarded as inadequate. With some forms of delegated legislation, notably local authority bye-laws, parliamentary scrutiny is virtually non-existent (although ministerial approval is normally a prerequisite for confirmation). Even where parliamentary scrutiny is provided for, however, as with ministerial regulations and European instruments, the position is still often unsatisfactory. This is the more disturbing because *ministerial* control over delegated legislation is generally far less effective than with primary legislation; indeed, because of the technical content of SIs, as well as their number and length, departmental civil servants, in consultation with client groups, have a largely free hand in preparing them.

The present scrutiny arrangements largely date from the end of the Second World War, when two important developments occurred. The first was in 1944, when a select committee (known after 1946 as the Select Committee on Statutory Instruments) was established. It had power to consider every Statutory Rule or Order laid before the Commons and to draw attention to any SIs making unusual or unexpected use of the powers conferred by the enabling statute. While performing a useful function, its lack of support staff, the immensity of its task, and the difficulty of finding parliamentary time to debate its reports, reduced its effectiveness. There was also a lack of co-ordination between this committee and the Special Orders Committee, which since 1925 had been responsible for examining affirmative instruments coming before the Lords.

The second development was the passing of the Statutory Instruments Act, 1946, which rationalized the diverse procedures governing the approval and publicizing of delegated legislation. Most instruments other than the least contentious and important, are now 'laid' before Parliament in one of two ways: *Affirmative Instruments*, normally the most important, which need to be approved by Parliament within a specified time (commonly twenty-eight or forty days); and *Negative Instruments*, the most numerous, which become effective automatically unless annulled by resolution (a motion to annul is called a 'prayer'). The 1946 Act provided that all negative instruments should be open to challenge by Parliament for forty days irrespective of the period mentioned in the parent statute. Notwithstanding this rationalization, however, major deficiencies, and some confusion, remain. Some instruments, for example, have to be laid in draft form before becoming effective; others must be complete before laying. Again most SIs have to be laid before both Houses, but some are laid only before the Commons. Most important of all, the failure by governments to allow time to debate prayers in the Commons within the forty days stipulated in the 1946 Act – or even at all – has meant that many negative instruments become effective without MPs obtaining a hearing. (In the Lords time is always found to debate prayers, but few are tabled.) Largely because of such deficiencies the Brooke Committee on Delegated Legislation in 1972 (Brooke Report, 1971/2) recommended the establishment of two new committees designed to strengthen parliamentary scrutiny.

(i) Joint Scrutiny Committee (JSC)

In February 1973 a Joint Committee on Statutory Instruments was developed out of the House of Commons Select Committee on SIs and the House of Lords Special Orders Committee. The JSC consists of seven members of each House (Commons members sit separately to deal with the few SIs laid before the Commons only) and is usually chaired by an opposition MP. It has power to investigate every instrument laid before both Houses and to draw attention to any SI on specified grounds: for example, if it imposes a charge on the public, excludes challenge in the courts, appears to be *ultra vires*, has retrospective effect, has been unduly delayed in publication, or makes unusual or unexpected use of the powers conferred by the enabling statute. As this list suggests, the committee is confined to *technical* scrutiny (that is, it is not able to debate the merits of instruments). Nevertheless its task is daunting, and it is able to issue substantive reports on only a tiny fraction of instruments. Even then, SIs are quite often debated in the Commons before the Joint Committee has had time to consider them properly, and there is no guarantee anyway that the government will act on an adverse report. (For discussion see Silk with Walters, 1987, especially pp. 153–5, and Shell, 1988, pp. 179–85).

(ii) Standing Committees on Statutory Instruments

In 1973 provision was made for one or more standing committees to be established to consider the *merits* of SIs. This was considered necessary because of the many prayers that were either not being debated or being debated out of time. The position at the moment is that prayers are debated in a standing committee unless twenty MPs oppose this (in which event they can be discussed in the House subject to a one-and-a-half hour time limit).

While standing committees have enabled more contentious negative instruments to be debated than hitherto, they have nevertheless attracted much criticism. Each committee meets only once, is limited to one and a half hours' debate and cannot reject an instrument or secure a debate in the Commons. Moreover, unless twenty MPs object, affirmative instruments can also be referred to a standing committee for consideration, following which a vote, without debate, is taken on the floor of the House. The main beneficiary of standing committees has therefore been the government which has increasingly 'used this arrangement as a useful method of saving time on the Floor' (Byrne, 1976, p. 373; see also Silk with Walters, 1987, pp. 152–3).

EUROPEAN SECONDARY LEGISLATION

In 1974, following British entry into the EEC, a Select Committee on European Legislation was established in the Commons. Possessing the usual powers of a select committee its main functions are: i) technical scrutiny of draft legislation emanating from the European Commission (prior to its submission to the Council of Ministers, the final EC law-making body); and ii), where appropriate, recommending items for debate in the house. Generally the government acts upon such recommendations by allowing a debate on the floor. As with domestic SIs, provision exists for such debates, unless twenty MPs object, to take place in an *ad hoc* Standing Committee on European Documents.

A Select Committee on the European Communities performs a similar function in the Lords, although it has wider powers – being able to comment on the *merits* of proposed EC instruments – and different procedures from its Commons counterpart (see Shell, 1988, pp .185–91). In addition, the post-1979 Commons specialist select committees (pp. 296–8) can discuss the merits of EEC documents in their respective areas. While these various committees are able to make ministers aware of Parliament's views about EEC proposals, usually in advance of their being considered by the Council of Ministers, it would be naive to see them as doing more than making minor inroads into an area where Parliament's influence is limited and indirect. Parliamentary opinion remains only one among very many influences upon EEC policy.

OVERVIEW

Despite these reforms parliamentary scrutiny of delegated legislation remains inadequate. Whereas about one-third of Commons time is spent debating government Bills, under one-tenth of its time is used to debate secondary legislation (Norton, 1981, p. 96). Such debates upon SIs as do take place in the House usually occur late at night within a one-and-a-half-hour time limit, and without any opportunity for line-by-line scrutiny or amendment (that is, they can only be rejected or approved). Of course, the vast majority of SIs receive no debate on the floor, being debated either in standing committee or, overwhelmingly, not at all. Even the JSC provides an inadequate safeguard; not only does it fail to examine the vast majority of SIs, but it often relies heavily on advice given by sponsoring government departments. As Alderman (1982, p. 99) observes, 'If a department is adamant that a particular instrument is necessary, and that no unexpected or unusual use has been made of the powers conferred by the parent Act, the Select Committee is unlikely to raise any objection'. There is also the problem that SIs, European legislation and the like by no means exhaust all the rule-making mechanisms. As Ganz (1987, p. 1) observes, recent years have seen 'an exponential growth . . . in a plethora of forms [of] Codes of practice, guidance, guidance notes, guidelines, circulars, White Papers . . . codes of conduct, codes of ethics and conventions', to name but some. This 'quasi-legislation' may or may not be statutory, may or may not be legally enforceable, and may – and often does – fall outside normal and systematic parliamentary control procedures.

While Parliament is now able to exercise greater scrutiny over delegated legislation than before the war, the volume of SIs is today so extensive that detailed scrutiny of all but the most politically contentious is out of the question. As Norton (1981, p. 99) comments, delegated legislation 'remains a much neglected form of legislation (except by affected interests groups and the Departments that promulgate it) . . . even more than primary legislation, [it] is the product of consultations between Government and outside interests, and is "made" before it reaches the House of Commons'. Perhaps it is the extent of such consultations which explains why, despite the inadequacy of parliamentary scrutiny, delegated legislation – the *vires* of which, unlike primary legislation, can be challenged in the courts – gives rise to relatively little litigation.

Parliament and public finance

Technically, Parliament holds the 'power of the purse'; parliamentary authorization is necessary both for raising taxation and for government spending. In reality, Parliament's role is far more limited, partly because the huge sums involved make effective scrutiny and control almost impossible. In the last decade public expenditure has usually been somewhere between 40 and 50 per cent of gross domestic product, and although much of this is actually spent by agencies with little or no accountability to Parliament – local authorities, public corporations, quangos and so forth – government departments, which are accountable to Parliament, nevertheless *control* the bulk of public spending. This, as Robinson (1981, p. 155) points out, means that 650 MPs 'of very different interests, backgrounds, training and aptitude for figures', and with 'many other functions to perform' may be responsible for 'detailed scrutiny [of] more than half the entire British economy'.

The inadequacy of parliamentary scrutiny of public finance stems not only from the size of the task, but also because Parliament's procedures have not adapted to the increasing demands of the job. For example, taxation and expenditure legislation is considered separately, and the huge sums involved are discussed and approved using more or less normal legislative procedures.

Essentially two main processes dominate Parliament's financial business: authorizing taxation; and authorizing and appropriating expenditure.

AUTHORIZING TAXATION

Here the main legislative instrument is the Finance Bill, which seeks statutory authority for raising taxation in accordance with the Chancellor's budget proposals. The procedure is the same as for other public Bills, except that the committee stage is conducted partly in standing committee and partly in Committee of the Whole House. In addition only ministers can move resolutions to increase or impose new taxes. Because the budget is usually prepared in secret without the consultations with interest groups that normally characterize the pre-legislative policy stage, attempts to alter the budget proposals are often channelled through Parliament (Silk with Walters, 1987, p. 177). While government reverses during Finance Bill proceedings are not unknown, they tend to be spasmodic, and a government's main tax proposals are usually immune from defeat. 'Government backbenchers', Norton (1981, p. 177) explains, are unlikely 'to defeat a Government on the central tenet of its economic policy . . . because economic policy is at the heart of a Government's programme', and defeat would probably precipitate resignation.

AUTHORIZING AND APPROPRIATING EXPENDITURE

This process also occurs annually. Each year departments present Parliament with their expenditure estimates for the following year, and these are subsequently approved by the annual Consolidated Fund and Appropriation Acts. Procedural requirements prevent MPs other than ministers from proposing expenditure and in any case Parliament usually approves the vast sums involved virtually 'on the nod'. Indeed most of the time nominally devoted to expenditure business has traditionally been allotted to either backbench MPs, who have frequently used it to raise constituency items, or to the opposition, who have invariably used these 'opposition days', as they came to be called, to initiate debates on issues of political rather than financial significance. These traditional proceedings on the Floor, however, have since 1979 been supplemented by those of Commons specialist committees, which are empowered to examine departmental expenditure and, in the case of the Treasury and Civil Service Committee, government financial and economic policy (Flegman, 1986). Since 1982, moreover, three days per session have been set aside to debate the estimates in the House, the subjects for debate being chosen by the Liaison Committee (see p. 295) after consultation with select committees. Even so, parliamentary scrutiny of future expenditure remains seriously deficient. Three days per session is totally inadequate to consider the estimates, given the huge sums involved, while the select committees' expenditure scrutiny function is blunted by resource constraints (see pp. 298) and their preoccupation with policy matters. In practice, the three Estimates Days have often been used to discuss general policy matters (Silk with Walters, 1987, p. 174), while select committees in the normal course of their work 'have, on average, spent [only] about 5 per cent of their time on public spending' (Likierman, 1988, p. 63).

This somewhat cursory scrutiny of government financial legislation is supplemented by other opportunities to consider public expenditure. In recent years these have consisted mainly of the *Autumn Statement* providing information, usually in November, on the outcome of the Public Expenditure Survey as soon as this has been agreed by the Cabinet (see Chapter 3) and the *Public Expenditure White Paper* (normally published in January), giving detailed plans in total and for departmental programmes. Although forming the initial plans upon which the estimates (normally published in March) are based, these three different sets of information published at different times of year often proved confusing, and from 1990 public expenditure information will be presented to Parliament in a new form. Broadly, this will involve (i) an expanded Autumn Statement, replacing the Public Expenditure White Paper, and (ii) departmental expenditure reports published in March at the same time as, and in a form reconcilable with, the estimates (*Financial Reporting to Parliament*, Cm 375). These arrangements 'should provide . . . select committees with a logical focus' for scrutinizing proposals at what Likierman (1988, pp. 62–3) describes as 'a logical time in the public spending cycle'. However if, as he adds, the select committees 'treat them with contempt, or go for sensation rather than investigation', they will miss the opportunity.

In addition to the above, the Public Accounts Committee (PAC) provides *post hoc* control of government spending through its examination of the reports of the Comptroller and Auditor General (CAG), whose department, the National Audit Office (NAO) annually audits the accounts of government departments. Workmanlike, useful and feared within Whitehall (Flegman, 1980; Latham, 1986), the PAC is nevertheless limited to being able to 'bolt the door after the horse has fled'. It is also limited because about half of British public expenditure – including that of local authorities and nationalized industries – is outside the Comptroller's jurisdiction (*Role of the Comptroller and Auditor General*, 1980). In 1983 a Private Member's Bill designed to increase jurisdiction, although watered down by the government (Garrett, 1986, p. 426), did extend the CAG's access to the books of certain other bodies in receipt of half their income from public funds. The final Act (National Audit Act, 1983) also made the CAG a servant of Parliament rather than, as formerly, of government. Appointed by the PAC chairman and the Prime Minister, the Act made the Comptroller responsible to a new Public Accounts *Commission*, consisting of senior MPs. It also conferred statutory powers to examine the economy, efficiency and effectiveness of departmental expenditure (as opposed to merely checking whether money has been spent as authorized by Parliament). Nevertheless, while the 1983 Act 'effects a welcome up-dating of the statutory basis of central audit', Britain, as Drewry and Butcher (1988, p. 209) observe 'still lags a long way behind countries such as the USA and Sweden in its arrangements for central audit, especially in its lack of emphasis on regular evaluation of the effectiveness of government programmes'. The new NAO, in fact, has been widely criticized for its 'gently, gently' approach to departments, its sometimes tentative and inexplicit findings, and its concern with economy rather than with the efficiency and effectiveness of departmental spending. The NAO is also restricted by the need to avoid judgements about the merits of policy and by limitations in the numbers, qualifications and experience of its staff. (For discussion see, *Public Money*, September 1984, pp. 67–9; Downey, 1984; Garrett, 1986.) As Garrett (1986, p. 433) concludes, the 1983 Act has given the Public Accounts Committee and the NAO 'a new charter', but they 'have yet to find a new direction. Far-reaching changes in the management of the civil service arising from the financial management . . . [initiatives]' – notably devolved budgeting and greater managerial accountability (see Chapter 7) – 'can provide them with new opportunities to develop parliamentary and public accountability'. Whether they will grasp them fully remains to be seen.

What is clear is that, even with relatively recent developments such as departmental select committees and the limited revamping of the CAG's powers, serious deficiencies in Parliament's financial control remain. As one former Treasury official (Pliatzky, 1985, p. 61) comments, 'The formal procedures of the House for approving expenditure and taxation play virtually no substantive part in the decision-making process'.

Minsterial responsibility

Ministerial responsibility to Parliament occupies a crucial role in governmental accountability in Britain. Not only is *legal* responsibility for departmental work vested in ministers, but by convention ministers have *political* and *constitutional* responsibility to Parliament for all the actions of government – including those of civil servants. The convention has two main strands: a) the *collective* responsibility of ministers for the actions of the government; and b) their *individual* responsibility to Parliament both for their personal behaviour and for the work of their departments. There is, of course, some inter-linkage between individual and collective responsibility. Sometimes a matter of collective responsibility is turned into individual responsibility so that the damage to a government's credibility is minimized – albeit at the expense of losing one or two ministers. An example is perhaps provided by Lord Carrington's resignation over the Falklands crisis in 1982. Conversely, individual responsibility is sometimes made a matter of collective responsibility; that is, the government throws the shield of collective responsibility around a minister to prevent his having to resign (as in the case of Strachey, for example, over the ground nuts fiasco in 1949 – see Birch, 1964, p. 143).

The convention of ministerial responsibility grew up in the nineteenth century in circumstances very different from today. This section examines its current usefulness as a vehicle of government accountability to Parliament.

COLLECTIVE RESPONSIBILITY

This has two main elements: i) if the Commons defeats the government on a motion of confidence the government should resign; and ii) all members of the government – not just those in the Cabinet – are responsible to Parliament for all the work of the government. (All ministers must, therefore, publicly support government decisions; if they feel they cannot, they should resign.)

In the mid-nineteenth century, prior to the rise of strongly disciplined parties, collective responsibility proved an effective means by which Parliament could call governments to account. Between 1832 and 1867 ten governments were obliged to resign through lack of parliamentary support, but as party government became entrenched this weapon for controlling the executive lost potency. Since 1900 only three governments have been forced to resign (or call a general election) following parliamentary defeats (the Baldwin and MacDonald governments in 1924, and Callaghan's in 1979). These circumstances were, however, exceptional: no single party had an overall majority in the Commons, so a combination of other parties was able to defeat the government. Normally modern governments have enjoyed the support of a highly organized party commanding a majority in the Commons. Consequently, even at times of major crisis, strong party discipline has usually been sufficient to secure the government's survival, however strident the opposition's calls to 'resign' might be.

It is also clear that the strand which states that all ministers share collective responsibility for all government decisions, and must defend them or else resign, is being eroded. Two points are particularly relevant in this context:

(i) *Agreements to differ.* Prime ministers, under pressure to avoid ministerial resignation, have occasionally allowed 'agreements to differ' on contentious issues. Three such examples are: a) the National government's 'agreement to differ' in 1932 over tariff policy; b) the Wilson government's 'agreement to differ' during the 1975 referendum over Britain's EEC membership; c) Callaghan's agreement in 1977 to allow ministers wishing to vote against the government's European Assembly Elections Bill to do so. Although 'agreements to differ' are rare, they nevertheless represent a breach of the convention of collective responsibility.

(ii) *Unattributable leaks.* Informal leaks to the media by disaffected ministers – whereby ministers make known to journalists their disagreement with government policy but do not resign – also weaken collective responsibility. In recent years such occurrences have been quite common.

In 1969, for example, widespread publicity was given to the opposition of the Home Secretary, James Callaghan, to the government's trade union reform proposals. Tony Benn's opposition to policies propounded by the Labour governments of 1974–9 was also widely documented as was Michael Heseltine's opposition, within the Cabinet, to decisions relating to Westland in 1986. Indeed, Shell (1981, p. 159) argues that during the Thatcher government the Prime Minister herself offended against collective responsibility with her public admission over the Employment Bill that 'some of us would have liked to have gone further'.

To what extent should collective responsibility be rigorously applied? In the early nineteenth century unity was relatively easy to attain – governments were smaller, policy was simpler and there was less of it – but today it is naive to assume anything other than differences on policy among senior ministers. Moreover, as Edmund Dell (1980, p. 28) has argued, many ministers, including Cabinet ministers, are often ignorant of many government decisions until they are announced. Indeed, some decisions of government which are not announced remain unknown to many members of the government, including Cabinet ministers. Dell's observations lead him to argue (p. 33) that collective responsibility 'is an enemy of open government'; it also confuses responsibility in that to 'make everyone responsible means in the end that no one feels responsible' (p. 39). An end to collective responsibility, he adds, would make government more open and ministers more free to speak their mind, subject only to constraints of collective purpose and tolerance. While greater discussion of the options open to ministers would clearly be welcome from a number of standpoints, it must nevertheless be recognized that governmental cohesiveness could become seriously eroded if there were too many 'agreements to differ' and ministers were even more free than at present to reveal their differences publicly.

Despite the erosion of collective responsibility, resignations have not totally disappeared from the scene. Rush (1981, p. 265) notes that between 1900 and 1976 there were sixty such resignations over specific issues or because of general disagreement with government policy. In fact, the convention provides prime ministers with a convenient way to remove dissidents and, likewise, allows dissidents who feel strongly to disassociate themselves publicly from the government. Nevertheless, ministerial differrences normally stop short of resignation (a recent exception being Michael Heseltine's resignation in January 1986 over the Westland affair – see pp. 289–91). Collective responsibility – by concealing ministerial differences behind a facade of unity – serves to strengthen the Prime Minister and government. The convention of collective responsibility therefore survives, its rationale being to deflect attack away from individual ministers and present a united front to the House. Essentially it is an instrument for artificially strengthening government against Parliament, and in the eyes of the public, by making it seem more united than often it really is.

INDIVIDUAL RESPONSIBILITY

There are two main elements to this doctrine: i) that the political head of a government department, and he or she alone, is answerable to Parliament for all the actions of that department; and ii) ministers must accept responsibility for their department, by explaining and defending their actions in Parliament and by resigning if serious errors are discovered.

While the constitutional principles are clear, their practical application is problematical. As with collective responsibility, the rise of strongly disciplined parties has largely eroded its punitive aspect – government party backbenchers invariably support ministers who are in difficulty rather than force their resignation. Additionally, the massive expansion and increased complexity of government makes it unjust to demand a ministers's resignation over an issue in his department about which he knows little or nothing.

Under the convention of individual responsibility ministers are obliged regularly to appear and answer questions in Parliament on the work of their departments. As such, individual responsibility has traditionally been regarded as a major instrument of accountability – the means by which any act or omission within any part of central administration could be called to account in Parliament. In practice, however, many ministers are past masters at producing generalized, evasive answers when necessary; sometimes they actually refuse to answer.

Government ministers not only deal with MPs' questions; they are also expected to participate in debates on government business concerning their own departments. Thus, when a department sponsors legislation, the minister pilots it through the various legislative stages. In this context ministers are deemed to be 'answerable' to Parliament for the work of their departments; they are not now generally held 'responsible' for departmental blunders.

The resignation of ministers following major policy errors is now rare; while errors are constantly being admitted resignations occur only infrequently. Finer (1956, pp. 377–96) found that between 1855 and 1955 only twenty ministers resigned as a result of parliamentary criticism of themselves or their departments. What distinguished these cases was not normally the gravity of the errors but the fact that ministers lost popularity within their own party. In a sense, therefore, ministers are now accountable to their party and the Prime Minister rather than to Parliament. Indeed, opposition criticism might actually help a minister to survive by rallying party support around him. Criticism from within his own party could, however, be fatal (as with Dugdale and Crichel Down in 1954, and Brittan and the Westland affair in 1986, for example: see pp. 287–91).

Resignations can be considered under two headings: (a) personal indiscretions; and (b) administrative and policy errors.

PERSONAL INDISCRETIONS

Personal indiscretion by a minister is the simplest cause of resignation. A number of examples are worthy of note:

(i) In 1947 Hugh Dalton resigned after giving budget details to a journalist before announcing them in Parliament, although he was readmitted to the government after an interval.

(ii) In 1962 John Profumo resigned from the War Office after admitting lying to the Commons about his relationship with Christine Keeler.
(iii) In 1973 both Lord Lambton and Lord Jellicoe resigned following disclosures that they had consorted with prostitutes.
(iv) In 1983 Cecil Parkinson resigned following disclosure of his relationship with Sarah Keays (although he was readmitted to the government in 1987).

Bromhead (1974, p. 68) argues that such cases present no difficulty, but even this category is not entirely straightforward, 'given that the dividing line between behaviour which is considered scandalous and that which is not is not always clear and changes over time' (Norton, 1981, p. 149).

ADMINISTRATIVE AND POLICY ERRORS

It is not the seriousness of an error which determines a minister's destiny, but rather whether the Prime Minister and party is prepared to support him or her. Birch (1980, p. 200) shows how blatant failures in British postwar policy 'have led to stormy debates in Parliament and to scathing comments in the press, but . . . not . . . to the resignation of the ministers concerned'. The failure of British policy in Palestine from 1945 to 1948; the groundnuts scheme fiasco in 1949; the 1956 Suez crisis are but three episodes cited by Birch to indicate that despite major policy errors the 'responsible' ministers were not forced to resign because they retained the support of their own party. More recently, in 1984, following the highly critical Hennessy Report on the security arrangements at the Maze Prison in Belfast, from which there had been a mass escape of prisoners, neither James Prior, the Secretary of State for Northern Ireland, nor Nicholas Scott, the parliamentary under secretary responsible for Northern Ireland's prison service, resigned. It was, at the time, politically preferable for the Prime Minister to retain them both in the government so, despite the seriousness of the break-out, both remained in office (see Drewry and Butcher, 1988, p. 154).

Until Lord Carrington in 1982, the major postwar example of resignation was that of Sir Thomas Dugdale, Minister of Agriculture, over the Crichel Down affair in 1954 – someone heavily criticized by his own party backbenchers. This case (see Birch, 1964, pp. 143–6) concerned land which had been acquired by the government during the war for use as a bombing range. After the war Ministry of Agriculture officials refused to honour an undertaking that the former owner should have a chance to repurchase the land. A subsequent inquiry found that civil servants had acted improperly. There was, Bromhead (1974, p. 69) notes, 'severe criticism in the press, and great indignation among Conservative [MPs]'. Dugdale resigned, largely as a result of criticism from the backbench Conservative Food and Agriculture Committee, although some accounts argue that he wanted to give the civil service a 'jolt'. Whatever the reason, Crichel Down was a relatively minor incident compared with the catalogue of errors committed by many Cabinet ministers since the war.

While resignations are very occasional, other less dramatic means of removing erring ministers exist: 'promotion' to the Lords, appointment to a public body, and reshuffling ministerial posts are all used by prime ministers to avoid dismissals or resignations. Indeed, reshuffles also serve to diffuse responsibility: which ministers, if any, were responsible? Today, individual responsibility no longer requires a minister to resign or accept total blame for any departmental error. While he is answerable to Parliament for his department's work, it is now widely recognized that he cannot be held *responsible* for decisions made in his name about which he could have had no knowledge and of which he would not have approved. The massive size of modern departments means that ministers can actually deal with relatively little departmental business.

The problems associated with size are well illustrated by the collapse of the Vehicle and General Insurance Company in 1971, which left many motorists without insurance (see Chapman, 1973). A subsequent inquiry, while criticizing named officials of the Department of Trade and Industry (which had responsibility for oversight of insurance companies), exonerated the relevant ministers who refused to resign. Evidence at the inquiry showed that the matter had been handled a considerable way down the departmental hierarchy over a period during which several departmental ministers had held office. The department also stated that less than 1 per cent of business was referred to ministers. To expect ministers to resign in such circumstances is clearly unreasonable. Interestingly, however, the same affair shows how difficult it can be to apportion culpability between ministers and civil servants. In some quarters the inquiry's verdict was heavily criticized, on the grounds that the Secretary of State, John Davies, had considerable business experience and contacts, and should have been in a position to anticipate and handle the crisis (Baker, 1972b).

Despite the problems it presents, the doctrine of individual responsibility survives, albeit in a diluted form, because it has benefits for both ministers and civil servants. The advantage for ministers is that they, and they alone, are the official mouthpiece of their department as well as the recipient of all departmental advice. As Mackintosh (1982, p. 169) argues:

> the public, the press and MPs are often starved of the material with which to make up a counter-argument. . . . If the doctrine was

> broken and officials could explain their views freely in public, then ministers would have the much more formidable task of making their case against men who are seized of the key counterpoints and who knew that their arguments were accepted by many in the ministry.

The major advantage for civil servants, it is often alleged, is that the doctrine generally protects their anonymity, leaving them publicly free of any repercussions arising from their advice, and this is held to greatly increase 'their freedom and power' (Mackintosh, 1982, p. 170). In practice, however, as observed in Chapter 5, recent years have seen a number of developments which have effectively diluted the anonymity of civil servants: investigation by the Ombudsman, testimony before select committees, and the development of devolved budgeting under the financial management initiative. Indeed, the Ibbs *Next Steps* proposals (1988), by advocating executive agencies managed by named individuals, threatens to further erode the 'anonymity' of civil servants (see Chapter 2). In all of these ways the personal responsibility of civil servants seems to be enhanced and the pure doctrine of ministerial responsibility eroded commensurably.

THE FALKLANDS CRISIS, 1982

This crisis saw the resignation of three Foreign Office ministers including Lord Carrington, the Foreign Secretary. The Defence Secretary John Nott also offered to resign, but subsequently agreed to the Prime Minister's request that he should remain in office. Criticism of the government's unpreparedness for the Argentine attack upon the Falkland Islands came not only from the opposition but from senior Conservative MPs. The three ministers resigned because of Parliament's loss of confidence in the Foreign Office, particularly in its handling of the situation prior to the invasion. In an interview Lord Carrington explained that it would have been wrong to 'behave as if nothing [had] happened' and that resignation was 'the honourable thing' (*The Times*, 6 April 1982). However, *The Times* itself described the resignation as an 'act of expiation' necessitated by parliamentary criticism of the government's unpreparedness – an interpretation suggesting that individual responsibility might have been a device to avoid involving the collective responsibility (and resignation) of the whole government (Pyper, 1983). The Falkland Islands Review (Franks Committee), 1983, provides a useful resource for those wanting to analyse this issue.

THE WESTLAND AFFAIR, 1986

The Westland affair, which came to a head in January 1986 and saw the resignation of two Cabinet ministers, had implications for both collective and individual responsibility. Westland was the only British firm manufacturing helicopters for military purposes but in 1985 faced financial difficulties. A rescue bid was necessary but two senior ministers, Michael Heseltine (Secretary of State for Defence) and Leon Brittan (Secretary of State for Trade and Industry) openly disagreed about strategy. As Shell (1987, p. 280) observes, the government's stated policy was neutrality between two rival consortia bids for the company, 'but the Secretary of State for Defence was not prepared to remain neutral. The press was full of accounts of his disagreements with colleagues and his backing for a European consortium's take-over of Westlands'. Given the disagreements, Mrs Thatcher insisted that all ministerial statements on the subject should be cleared by the Cabinet Office. This was, for Heseltine, the last straw; he walked out of a Cabinet meeting on 9 January 1986 and resigned from the government.

It could be argued that the failure of the Prime Minister to enforce the convention of collective responsibility at an earlier stage in the saga was curious. But 'leaks' have become part and parcel of the British political scene. In addition there was always the possibility of Heseltine being won over, thereby avoiding the political damage a government inevitably faces when a senior minister resigns. In the event, however, Heseltine did not change his position and given his isolation he resigned. There was much talk about the importance of collective responsibility but the difficulty about this convention in contemporary political life is the propensity of all governments and most ministers 'to conduct what by convention should be private arguments within government in a semi-public way in order to try and mobilise political support to their particular cause' (Shell, 1987, p. 280). Perhaps, at the end of the day, as Jordan and Richardson argue (1987b, p. 148), collective responsibility remains essentially 'a convenience for the Prime Minister, as it reinforces dominant opinion, usually defined by the P.M. in the Cabinet'.

The Westland affair illustrated the ambiguity of collective responsibility. On the one hand it can be argued that Heseltine breached the convention by openly disagreeing with his Cabinet colleagues and not accepting clearance on future statements by the Cabinet Office. On the other hand, Heseltine's argument is that the doctrine of collective responsibility requires more than just adhering to a policy, but requires also genuine collective decision-taking. He argued that Mrs Thatcher breached the convention by not allowing full discussion and collective judgement by colleagues to take place in Cabinet and committees (see especially Hennessy, 1986a, pp. 106–10; and 1986c). As Drewry and Butcher reflect (1988, p. 220), 'Does collective responsibility mean collective decision-making, or does it mean ministers closing ranks behind a Prime Minister, come what may – or does the truth lie somewhere between these positions?' The Westland affair did little to clarify the issue.

The Westland affair also had important implications for individual ministerial responsibility. As noted earlier, according to this doctrine ministers are accountable to Parliament for the actions of their civil servants, although the circumstances under which a minister might actually have to resign are not precisely defined. What is crucial, however, is the extent to which his colleagues in office and his party in Parliament are prepared to support him. On 24 January 1986 Leon Brittan resigned as Secretary of State for Trade and Industry following the leaking by Ms Colette Bowe, Director of Information at the DTI, of a letter from the Solicitor General to Michael Heseltine. On his resignation Leon Brittan agreed that his civil servants had acted according to his wishes and should not therefore be blamed.

A full Commons debate on the 'leak' had been arranged but backbench Conservative MPs expressed such unhappiness at Brittan's conduct that he resigned before the debate took place. Though Brittan appeared to retain Mrs Thatcher's support it seemed to many backbench Conservative MPs that her continued support, and the close involvement which it was revealed her office had had with the disclosure of the Solicitor General's letter, could endanger her position if Mr Brittan did not resign. Brittan's departure seems to fit the theory that resignations occur not so much where the minister's act has offended Parliament but where it has alienated a substantial part of his own party.

The day before Brittan's resignation the Prime Minister confirmed that the leak had been authorized by Brittan after he had obtained 'cover' from Bernard Ingham, the PM's press secretary, and Charles Powell, the PM's private secretary specializing in foreign and defence matters. Ministerial responsibility for the actions of her staff was not accepted by Mrs Thatcher. Indeed, later in 1986 the House of Commons and the Defence Committee were denied the opportunity to cross-examine these crucial witnesses on the grounds, outlined by her, that for private secretaries and personal staff to give evidence had major implications for the conduct of the government and for relations between ministers and their private offices. This provides an interesting example of how a more partisan civil service could soon blur conventional notions of responsibility. A subsequent report from the Select Committee on Defence (1985/6, HC 519), was critical of both Leon Brittan and the civil servants involved, and it is in this context that post-Westland attempts by the government to define the duties and responsibilities of civil servants in relation to ministers should be seen (see Chapter 5 and pp. 297–98).

OVERVIEW

In 1978 Dunsire (p. 41) suggested that being 'accountable' may mean, in the context of ministerial responsibility, 'no more than having to answer questions about what has happened or is happening within one's jurisdiction'. Since then the defeat of the Callaghan government, and the resignations over the Falklands crisis and Westland affair serve, however, as a reminder that loss of office remains a possibility under the conventions of both collective and individual responsibility. Nevertheless, in the sense of allocating blame and requiring resignation, both conventions are likely to remain weak so long as majority governments can rely on the party faithful to protect a minister, or ministry, in difficulties.

It was for reasons of *accountability* that collective and individual responsibility emerged, but they cannot really be considered entirely appropriate in this context today. Collective responsibility strengthens and shields the government in the face of parliamentary criticism, while individual responsibility presents a barrier between civil servant and MP. A civil servant, for example, may make serious errors but the ministers may shield him to prevent a storm. Even worse, the minister may be misled or misinformed by his officials, and yet MPs traditionally have been able to question only the minister and not the civil servants who really have the facts. It is for such reasons that in recent years the doctrine of individual responsibility has been relaxed somewhat: for example, by allowing civil servants increasing exposure to journalists and parliamentary select committees, and by making their actions investigable by the Ombudsman (Chapter 15). Even so, it may be premature to write off the doctrine as totally unimportant. Not only do ministers and civil servants both have vested interests in its retention, but as Johnson (1977, pp. 83–4) observes, it still serves to remind us 'about the manner in which powers are to be established and located: it defines who is responsible for what rather than who is responsible to whom'.

Scrutiny and redress

Parliament does not govern: its job is to scrutinize government actions and, if dissatisfied, seek redress. This role cannot be totally divorced from other parliamentary functions: debating government legislation, examining SIs, considering tax and expenditure proposals, for example, all provide opportunities for scrutiny. The government usually also provides further opportunities by initiating debates on policy proposals or matters of political moment. In addition, however, a number of specific instruments of scrutiny and redress are available to

MPs. These can be divided into three broad categories: (a) debates and questions; (b) private channels; (c) select committees.

DEBATES AND QUESTIONS

Both the opposition and individual MPs can raise matters in the House. The opposition, for example, may use one of its Opposition Days (see Norton, 1987, pp. 78–9), or table a motion of censure (which the government must find time to debate). Individual MPs also have opportunities to initiate business, notably by tabling parliamentary questions (for either oral or written answer) or initiating one of the daily half-hour adjournment debates (see Borthwick, 1979). In addition there has been a growing tendency in recent years for MPs to raise bogus points of order, request private notice questions and emergency debates (which are rarely granted by the Speaker), and even to commit minor acts of misbehaviour – many of which devices are, in reality, staged media events.

While these opportunities can sometimes be useful for focusing public attention on issues, for raising constituency problems, or for obtaining basic information, as instruments of scrutiny and redress they are seriously deficient. They provide no opportunities for impartial, expert, or in-depth investigation of government activity, and in many respects suffer from procedural limitations. For example, only a fixed number of Opposition Days are available; adjournment debates usually occur late at night and attract little media attention; and question time is usually insufficient to allow oral answers to all MPs requesting them. (Although there is no limit to the number of questions for *written* answer – of which currently 50,000 per session are tabled.) Nevertheless, despite increasing backbench independence since 1970 (Norton, 1985, ch. 2), many government supporters apparently believe 'that advancement to office is achieved by not creating difficulties for one's own Ministers' (Norton, 1981, p. 139) with the result that many members are reluctant even to use the limited means available for scrutinizing and influencing executive actions. As a result the 'scrutiny and influence' function, while widely acknowedged to be of vital importance, is generally conducted in a manner which many observers feel is ineffective, random, piecemeal, and unsystematic.

PRIVATE CHANNELS

The opportunities available for scrutiny and redress within the House are supplemented by private channels of communication between MPs and ministers. MPs, for example, may seek information or raise grievances through correspondence or discussion with ministers. The network of party committees within Parliament also provides a vehicle for liaison; government supporters, especially, often prefer to seek concessions in these committees rather than risk embarrassing ministers in the House. Sometimes, also, the opposition deals with government through private channels; securing information on privy councillor terms in sensitive policy areas; negotiating compromises when governments require inter-party support; and requesting concessions in return for co-operation with the parliamentary timetable. While much depends upon the issues concerned, and upon the number and standing of the MPs concerned, the efficiency of such channels is often contingent upon the extent to which, if necessary, they can be reinforced by formal proceedings in the House. Such proceedings, as already observed, are usually quite inadequate for exerting effective scrutiny and influence over a majority government which is unwilling to yield.

SELECT COMMITTEES

In recent decades, as the scale and complexity of government has grown, traditional parliamentary procedures of scrutiny and redress have become increasingly inadequate. Consequently, several important new developments have occurred. First, the traditional procedures for securing redress have been supplemented by the establishment of the Ombudsman (see Chapter 15). Secondly, the scrutiny function has been strengthened by the development of a comprehensive system of select committees.

House of Commons *select* committees should not be confused with the *standing* committees which deal with legislation; usually they are smaller, have a more permanent membership, and are empowered to appoint advisers and 'send for persons, papers and records'. Such committees are not new: for example, the Public Accounts Committee has existed since 1861, while between 1912 and 1979 an Estimates (later Expenditure) Committee was employed examining government expenditure proposals. From the late 1960s, however, there was considerable expansion of select committee activity. Some committees were established to scrutinize the work of particular departments: others to oversee specialized areas (such as race relations, science and technology). Although intended to improve the House's powers of scrutiny their record was generally disappointing, not least because ministers and civil servants often saw them as a threat to departmental power (for discussion see Baines, 1985; Johnson, 1981). In 1979, however, fourteen new committees were established, each having responsibility for 'shadowing' specified departments, as shown in Table 14.1.

With this reorganization the Expenditure Committee and the Select Committee on Nationalised Industries both disappeared, their work

Table 14.1 The Post-1979 Select Committee System in the House of Commons

Committee	*Government depts principally concerned*
Agriculture	Ministry of Agriculture, Fisheries and Food
Defence	Ministry of Defence
Education, Science and Arts	Dept of Education and Science
Employment	Dept of Employment
Energy	Dept of Energy
Environment	Dept of the Environment
Foreign Affairs	Foreign and Commonwealth Office
Home Affairs	Home Office
Trade and Industry	Dept of Trade and Industry
Social Services	Dept of Health and Dept of Social Security
Transport	Dept of Transport
Treasury and Civil Service	Treasury, Inland Revenue, Office of the Minister for the Civil Service, Customs and Excise
Welsh Affairs	Welsh Office
Scottish Affairs	Scottish Office

having largely been absorbed by new committees. Each committee has power 'to examine the expenditure, administration and policy of the [relevant] government departments . . . and associated public bodies' (*Hansard*, V, vol. 969, cols 33–4, 25 June 1979), terms of reference which include not only departments, but public corporations and other non-departmental agencies. Three committees have power to form sub-committees, while those shadowing 'sponsoring' departments of nationalized industries may set up sub-committees drawn from two or more parent committees to consider matters affecting more than one industry. The work of select committees is overseen by a liaison committee which includes the chairmen of the fourteen departmental committees.

In an attempt to protect the committees from arbitrary disbandment by government, each is appointed for the duration of a Parliament. Membership is small (normally eleven) to enable them to function as effective working groups. Empowered 'to send for persons, papers and records' and to appoint specialist advisers, each committee can receive written submissions and oral evidence not only from ministers but from civil servants, pressure groups, and outside experts. Membership is bi-partisan, and opposition members hold several chairs. Covering virtually the whole spectrum of government activity, these arrangements are of considerable significance. As Borthwick (1982, p. 9) observed, 'For the first time, perhaps, the House of Commons has a coherent *system* of select committees, rather than a haphazard assortment of pieces'.

Some advantages of the new committees are already apparent. Each committee chooses its own subjects for investigation and between 1979 and 1985 a total of 275 reports on a wide variety of subjects was produced (Liaison Committee, 1984–5, para. 17). Some of these were short investigations; others longer and more intensive. Some dealt with policy issues (such as government economic strategy, overseas students' fees, selling council houses); others with 'administrative' matters (deaths in police custody; the Welsh Office's role in developing job opportunities). One of the most notable successes was the Home Affairs Committee's inquiry into the 'sus' laws, which produced a firm recommendation favouring abolition, and a threat from committee members to introduce a repeal Bill if the government refused to act (Drewry, 1985, p. 199). (The government subsequently introduced its own repeal measure.) Another significant report followed the Defence Committee's investigation (1985–6, HC 519) of the Westland affair. This 'named and blamed' senior officials for their involvement in the disclosure of information and criticized the government for failing to take action against them (Pyper, 1987, p. 359). As these examples indicate, the new committees operate with some freedom from party discipline. There is also considerable enthusiasm among their members: fierce competition for places, good attendance, and low membership turnover (Lock, 1985). The media, moreover, show considerable interest in committee reports, and pressure groups use them increasingly as targets for their representations. The new committees, in short, have emerged as an important part of the policy community, capable of publicizing the less defensible aspects of governmental work. In the Liaison Committee's view (1984–5, para. 1), on the evidence of the first six years select committees 'can . . . be seen as a major, successful Parliamentary reform'.

Despite their promising start, however, there are several problems and deficiencies associated with the new committees. From the governmental perspective they are sometimes criticized for imposing 'excessive burdens on ministers and civil servants in the preparation of memorandums' (Riddell, 1982). An influential lobby argues also that the new committees divert MPs away from the Chamber into committees examining information which, Enoch Powell (1982, p. 175) claims, 'the rest of the House . . . cannot read and has no possibility of keeping up with'. In his view select committee members risk losing objectivity through over-exposure to departmental briefings and civil service advice. He adds also that committees have no 'effect except through the House' – a point reinforced by the government's failure to allocate a fixed number of days for debating committee reports. (During the first six years the House debated reports on substantive motions on only four occasions: Liaison Committee, 1984–5, para. 17). In Giddings' view (1985, p. 371), 'it would be difficult to argue . . . that the departmentally related committees have had a significant direct impact on [the House's] major activities, on legislation, debates, questions'. The committees' influence may also be diminished by their being 'pre-eminently the preserve of . . . younger and least experienced back-benchers' (Johnson, 1984, p. 64), while from time to time there have been allegations of attempts by the whips (not always successful) to influence selection of membership and chairmen (for examples see Drewry, 1985, p. 391). A further problem arose after the 1987 general election when the Conservatives were left with insufficient Scottish backbenchers to ensure a majority on the Scottish Affairs Committee and which (by mid-1988) had still not been empanelled.

The new committees have no legislative or executive powers: they can only investigate, recommend and report. Moreover, the power 'to send for persons, papers and records' does not extend to departmental files and records, and ministers and civil servants cannot be *required* to attend. Although attendance when requested is usual, only the House can compel this, an eventuality unlikely to happen on a whipped vote in the face of government opposition. During the Defence Committee's investigation of the Westland affair the government refused to allow several named civil servants to give evidence – although it did allow Sir Robert Armstrong, the Cabinet Secretary, to testify – and the committee failed to press the issue (Drewry, 1987; Kennon, 1988; Pyper 1987). Ministerial evidence, moreover, is sometimes less than frank, while civil servants appear before committees under restrictive conditions laid down in the so-called Osmotherly memorandum (CSD General Notice Gen 80/38, 16 May 1980). The convention that civil servants anonymously advise ministers who take the final decisions pervades this memorandum: for example, it precludes civil servants from giving evidence on advice given to ministers, inter-departmental exchanges, and Cabinet committees. As a result vast and ill-defined areas of government work are excluded from the matters which civil servants may discuss before select committees. Indeed, following the Westland affair the government proposed to limit civil service evidence still further by precluding testimony about their own conduct and that of their ministerial masters. Only an indignant all-party protest by MPs secured a retraction (Pyper, 1987, p .30) but in 1987 a further note of guidance was issued by the Cabinet Secretary. This explicitly stated that civil servants giving evidence to select committees did so 'as the representative of the Minister . . . and subject to the Minister's instructions . . . . [The] ultimate responsibility lies with Ministers, and not with civil servants, to decide what information should be made available, and how and when it should be released' (*Hansard*, VI, vol. 123, cols 572–5, Written Answers, 2 December 1987; see also Benyon, 1988, pp. 133–4).

The government alone cannot be blamed for the deficiencies of select committees. As Norton (1985, p. 143) states, 'The House enjoys the power', if it seeks to exercise it, 'to compel the government to concede reforms'; hence, greater backbench assertiveness might have weakened the government's resolve and ability to limit the committees' powers. It might also have increased the resources made available to employ specialist advisers. Although committee expenditure is controlled by the House of Commons Commission, not the Treasury, the sums allocated for specialist assistance are particularly meagre. On average in the 1979–83 Parliament each committee spent only just over £30,200 on specialist advice and under £45,000 on fact-finding visits (calculated from Lock, 1985, table 18.10): As Drewry (1985, p. 353) observes, these meagre resources, coupled with 'the constitutional realities which constrain all parliamentary activity in the executive-dominated system', mean that 'select committees are a small squad of Davids facing an army of departmental Goliaths'.

Despite these restrictions, much valuable information nevertheless flows between government departments and select committees. While the performance of committees has been uneven, 'many matters that would otherwise not be discussed in Parliament at all are comprehensively examined and opened to public attention' (Drewry, 1985, p. 392). Even so, further development is necessary if the new committees are to become more effective as instruments of scrutiny and influence: more time to debate reports in the Chamber, more specialist staff, and wider investigative powers. In the longer term, the new committees could usefully 'take over' the legislative work of standing committees, as well as more comprehensive and detailed examination of departmental estimates (see pp. 280–81). Indeed a limited further reform has already occurred, namely the experimentation with special standing committees 'which allows a standing committee to examine witnesses for a short time as if it were a select committee' (Downs, 1985, p. 67; see also Norton, 1985, pp. 164–5). Major reform along these lines, however, seems unlikely, and if the role and powers of select committees are to be developed further, old attitudes will have to disappear. Ministers and civil servants must become more responsive to demands for 'open government'; MPs more prepared, irrespective of party, to assert themselves against government; and the House generally to accept that under modern conditions sustained questioning of ministers and civil servants in committee is invariably a more searching and effective form of scrutiny than proceedings in the Chamber. Whether, given the understandable sensitivities of government to any increase in backbench assertiveness, such changes will occur remains to be seen.

15 Public administration and redress

The traditional democratic avenues of accountability through MPs and councillors have become increasingly inadequate with the growth of state activity. Not only has government bureaucracy expanded, so have the points of contact between citizen and state. For example, the welfare state has increased people's rights to benefits; planning and compulsory purchase procedures affect property rights; government intervention in industrial matters regulates employer and employee rights; and so on. Normally such matters do not give rise to disagreement; however, some disputes inevitably occur, and often on a scale and complexity which renders traditional avenues of redress largely inappropriate. To resolve such disputes there exist numerous mechanisms through which the decisions and actions of public authorities can be challenged. Four main avenues can be identified: the courts; statutory inquiries; administrative tribunals; ombudsmen.

The courts

Some countries, notably France, have a system of administrative law (*droit administratif*) and a separate administrative court (*Conseil d'Etat*) to deal specifically with disputes between citizen and state. In Britain this is not the case. All public bodies, however, derive their authority from statute (unless exceptionally they are created by prerogative powers), and thus public administrators and their political masters work within legally defined powers. Any action outside the scope of such power is *ultra vires* (beyond the powers) and may be declared unlawful by the courts. Indeed, there exists a number of judicial remedies by which public bodies can be required to fulfil their statutory obligations and unlawful decisions can be quashed or declared nullities. These remedies include injunctions, declarations, and three prerogative orders: *certiorari* (which removes decisions of administrative authorities, tribunals or inferior courts to the High Court for review); *prohibition* (which requires a public body to desist or refrain from unlawful – *ultra vires* – acts); and *mandamus* (issued by the High Court, and which compels public bodies to perform their statutory duties according to law).

In recent years judicial challenges to the *vires* of official acts have increased. The courts, for example, have made important contributions to defining both local authority powers (see Chapter 10) and the extent of ministerial discretion (see, for example, Griffith, 1985, especially pp. 129–49). Moreover, since *Ridge* v. *Baldwin*, [1964] AC 40, the courts have increasingly required public authorities to respect principles of natural justice. Thus, today, as Boynton (1986, p. 149) explains, the courts can 'intervene whenever it can be shown that an administrative decision was either (a) wrong in law, or illegal, or (b) was irrational or so unreasonable that no sensible person could have reached it, or (c) was procedurally improper, unfair or failed to observe the rules of natural justice'. In addition the provisions as to *locus standi* governing access to the courts have been relaxed and procedures for applications for judicial review simplified by the introduction in 1977 of new Order 53 of the Rules of the Supreme Court (see, also, Supreme Court Act, 1981). In effect this procedure *must* now be used (see *O'Reilly* v. *Mackman*, [1983] 2AC 237) in all applications for any type of remedy – including prerogative orders, declarations, injunctions or damages – whenever the issues involve any matter of public law. (This applies in England and Wales only, although in 1985 a special procedure for administrative law cases was introduced in Scotland.) As a result, Yardley (1986, p. 142), suggests we may have 'reached a position where the law has ceased to concern itself with procedural side issues, and where the courts will decide cases on administrative law according to . . . merit'. One report (Justice–All Souls, 1988, para. 7.3), suggests that 'in practice, though not in name, there is [now] . . . a functional segregation of administrative law cases . . . generally tried by specialist judges'; hence the introduction in Britain of 'anything on the lines of a Conseil d'Etat' or 'new Administrative Division of the High Court' would be unnecessary.

While the courts' role in supervising the fairness and legality of administrative actions is substantial and increasing it is important to stress that judicial review is concentrated upon a fairly limited range of administrative activity and that the number of cases overall is infinitesimal compared with the millions of decisions taken by public authorities (Harlow and Rawlings, 1984, p. 258; see also Sunkin, 1987, especially p. 465). Where it does occur, moreover, the judges' involvement raises fears that they 'are taking over the responsibilities of administrators . . . without the expertise to exercise [them] properly' (Feldman, 1988, p. 22). It may also, as Bridges *et al.* (1987, p. 144) suggest, have 'caused authorities to follow procedures ritualistically, prepare lengthier reports [and] . . . made decision-making less efficient'. Additionally, considerations of cost, formality, accessibility and delay makes litigation often a last resort, used only when other avenues have failed to secure redress. During the twentieth century, in fact, there has been a proliferation of alternative mechanisms for resolving disputes and it is upon these that the remainder of the chapter focuses.

Inquiries

Inquiries are an important feature of British public administration, although they exist in a number of forms and the term 'inquiry' lacks coherent usage. Most important, perhaps, are those *statutory inquiries* which have an appellate nature or which permit citizens to object to proposed administrative action. Many statutes, in fact, provide for public inquiries although they are used most widely in land use matters where certain ministerial decisions – notably those by the Environment Secretary on appeals against the decisions of local authorities on planning applications and in respect of compulsory purchase orders referred for confirmation where objections are made – are usually taken only after a public inquiry. Such inquiries are 'an everyday occurrence in British public administration' (Wraith and Lamb, 1971, p. 13). (In the mid-1980s there were some 16,000 planning appeals in England annually.) A full invstigation into the facts is conducted by an inspector, and parties are entitled to state their case. In these respects public inquiries resemble a judicial process. Indeed, since the Franks Report (1957), increasing judicialization has entered into the handling of inquiries: inspectors' reports, for example, must be published, reasons given for any decisions by virtue of the statutory procedural rules, and opportunities provided for reopening the inquiry or submission of fresh representation in some circumstances if the Secretary of State rejects his inspector's recommendation or wishes to take into account new considerations which were not considered at the inquiry.

In other respects, however, the process is more like an administrative exercise. Wraith and Lamb (1971, p. 13) write: 'Public Inquiries are . . . for the most part concerned only to establish facts and to make recommendations'. The inspector is, in fact, a civil servant appointed by the minister to ascertain facts on his behalf. Moreover, in an attempt to reduce delays, simplified procedures have been introduced: for example, since 1969 many cases (currently over 90 per cent) have been delegated to inspectors for decisions, whilst in around 85 per cent decisions are now made on the basis of written representations only. Additionally, in a small but growing number of cases, informal hearings are offered to parties as an alternative to full oral hearings. Consequently only the most complex and controversial cases are today subject to a full hearing and a final decision by the minister (although even then, *in practice*, the decision will usually be taken by departmental civil servants rather than the minister personally). From this perspective inspectors have a typically civil service role, assembling facts and recommending or taking decisions on their ministers' behalf. Thus appeals may be decided not solely on merits, but according to policy guidelines, and ministers have the same freedom to reject inspectors' recommendations (although it happens in only a tiny percentage of cases) as to reject civil service advice generally.

Although most planning inquiries are completed quickly – in less than one day – those which raise issues of national importance may take much longer (the Sizewell inquiry into Britain's first pressurized water reactor lasted 340 days). Such inquiries may arise through normal appeals procedures, although special statutory provisions sometimes also enable citizens to object to, and ministers to institute inquiries into, major development projects (such as motorways or the siting of nuclear power stations). Normally in such cases an eminent person, usually a lawyer, will act as inspector and may be assisted by an expert panel. Although special codes of practice usually apply, major inquiries can present considerable problems: for example, the duality of interest between developers (usually 'the government' in some guise) and the final decision-taker (the Secretary of State); and the disparity of resources available to developers on the one hand and objectors (usually local residents and interested groups) on the other, a position exacerbated by the absence of legal aid for inquiry proceedings. Another difficulty is that underlying specific proposals may be questions of national policy (such as the 'need' for nuclear energy) which may not be properly examined under normal procedural rules. (For discussion, see Outer Circle Policy Unit, 1979b; Select Committee on the Environment, 1985–6, HC 181–I, especially paras 193–4; the Governments' Response (1985–6), Cm 43; and Justice–All Souls, 1988, paras 10.64–87.)

Partly to avoid such problems governments in recent years have sometimes dispensed with normal procedures. Under the Local Government Planning and Land Act, 1980, for example, normal planning requirements do not apply in designated 'enterprise zones', whilst other devices such as special development orders and the promotion of hybrid and private Bills (used most controversially is the case of the Channel Tunnel) have sometimes been used instead of public inquiries. Although arguably a denial of objectors' rights, too many challenges to major projects could seriously overload the planning process. 'Government', moreover, is ultimately 'accountable to Parliament for policy, not to objectors' (Birkinshaw, 1985, p. 38), and as most major planning projects have policy implications it is arguably wasteful 'of time and money to [invoke] . . . elaborate adversarial procedures . . . in situations where the ultimate decision need not be tied to material presented to the adjudicator' (Cane, 1986, p. 299). As Ridley (1984, p. 4) suggests, 'the idea of "political" rather than "legal" protection of citizens against administration is deeply embedded in British political traditions' and recent governmental attempts to circumvent normal planning procedures for major projects – as well as the policy-based framework of planning inquiries themselves – offer a clear manifstation of this.

Administrative tribunals

Administrative tribunals also usually have both an administrative and judicial dimension to their work. Most tribunals contribute to the administrative process by determining the extent to which departmental policies apply in particular cases. The judicial aspect of their work normally arises because such cases involve the rights and obligations of individual citizens (or organizations) in the specialized fields of law under which such policies are administered. Although their work usually has both administrative and judicial dimensions, tribunals – as the Franks Report (1957, para. 40) stated – 'are not ordinary courts, but neither are they appendages of Government Departments'. Neither are they on all fours with statutory inquiries. Their respective functions, Wraith and Lamb claimed in 1971 (p. 13), were 'fundamentally different'. Whereas inquiries essentially established 'facts' and made 'recommendations' (*before* an administrative decision was taken) tribunals were responsible for 'deciding or adjudicating in disputes' (usually *after* an administrative decision had given rise to disagreement). In practice, today, this distinction is less clear cut, particularly from the citizen's standpoint, especially since most decisions at inquiries are now taken by inspectors.

However, another distinction drawn by Wraith and Lamb generally still holds good: 'Public inquiries are constituted *ad hoc* to inquire into particular matters' whereas tribunals usually have a more 'regular or permanent existence'. During the twentieth century tribunals have proliferated. Their development has been largely piecemeal, with particular tribunals being formed as and when necessary. One effect of this is that a precise count of tribunals is impossible. In some cases a single tribunal serves the whole country, but more usually there is a regional or local network. In other cases still tribunals are constituted on an *ad hoc* basis. Consequently it is safer to think less in terms of numbers of tribunals than in terms of tribunal systems or categories. Thus the Pliatzky Report (1980, p. 2) identified sixty-seven 'tribunal systems' in the UK in 1978/9; the Council on Tribunals in 1985/6 'some 60 kinds of Tribunal' within its jurisdiction in England and Wales and a further '20 or so' under its Scottish Committee (Annual Report, 1985/6, para. 2.18); and the Cabinet Office in 1987 (p. iv) sixty-four tribunals, 'including bodies with licensing and appeal functions'. Even these figures, however, are not definitive, for the distinction between tribunals and other non-departmental bodies is not always clear (for instance, the Monopolies and the Mergers Commission, an investigative body with many tribunal-like features, is excluded from the above 'counts'). Nevertheless, tribunal machinery is extensive, with cases heard running at about a quarter of a million annually or approximately six times the number of contested civil cases disposed of at trial before the High Court and county courts.

In 1957 Franks identified five main fields of public administration covered by tribunals: land and property, national insurance and assistance, NHS, military service, and transport. Today with subsequent growth, other fields might be added, notably immigration, employment and taxation. Indeed, with the possible future delegation of many functions currently performed by government departments to executive agencies in line with the Ibbs *Next Steps* strategy (see Chapter 2), tribunal mechanisms may well increase at the expense of conventional ministerial responsibility as a means of controlling actions of public officials.

Between them the various tribunal systems have two main functions:

(i) Resolving disputes between private individuals. The main fields involved here are land and property, and employment. Among the former are Rent Tribunals and Rent Assessment Committees, which arbitrate between landlord and tenant on rent and other matters; and, among the latter, Industrial Tribunals which determine disputes between employer and employee on issues such as unfair dismissal and entitlement to redundancy payments.

(ii) Resolving disputes between public bodies (usually government departments) and citizens. Among the most widely used in recent years have been local valuation courts, which hear appeals against rateable value assessments (over 150,000 cases received annually); social security appeal tribunals (70,000 cases in 1986); and general commissioners of income tax (who receive over half a million cases annually). These all have extensive local networks (for example, in 1986/7 some 5,000 general commissioners of income tax sat in 486 divisions in England and Wales).

As should be clear, 'administrative tribunal' is a general term, incorporating a variety of boards, courts, committees, tribunals and so forth. Each established by statute, as and when the need has arisen, British tribunals exhibit a wide variety of procedures and constitutions. However, the reason for their prolific development is clear. As the Pliatzky Report (1980, p. 25) explains, there are two main alternatives to their use; namely 'to make the Executive the final arbiter in disputes to most of which it is itself a party, or to transfer [their] jurisdiction . . . to the ordinary courts of law'. The former course is *relatively* rare in Britain. 'Unlike some countries, Britain has little in the way of formalised *internal* procedures for appeal; i.e. from one official to another within a particular authority (whether to a hierarchic superior or an independent complaints officer within the organisation)' (Ridley, 1984, p. 2). However, it is not unknown: the Education Secretary, for example, decides disputes about teachers' superannuation; and in some fields – notably taxation and social security – complaint to a departmental adjudication officer normally precedes appeal to some tribunals. Particular controversy was aroused by the Social Security Act, 1986, which requires appeals from DHSS officials against social fund discretionary grant and loan decisions to lie, not to social security appeal tribunals, but to internal social fund inspectors (Council on Tribunals, *Annual Report 1985–86*, pp. 31–3). Despite such instances, however, it is clearly undesirable in principle, as Pliatzky (1980, p. 3) observes, for a government department to be 'judge and jury . . . in dealing with . . . appeals against its administrative decisions'.

The other course identified by Pliatzky, jurisdiction through the courts, is also arguably undesirable. Not only would courts become overburdened, but tribunals offer several advantages over the courts:

(i) They are more specialized – many deal with technical matters where adjudication is best discharged by persons with specialist knowledge (such as trade union representatives on industrial tribunals).
(ii) They are more accessible and informal – people are more likely to utilize tribunals because the daunting atmosphere of the courts is absent.
(iii) They are more flexible – being less bound to legal precedent and procedures than courts, tribunals are better able to allow for local or special circumstances in arriving at decisions.
(iv) They are more expeditious – largely because of their greater specialization and flexibility.
(v) They are cheaper – panel members are usually part-time and local, and parties rarely have legal representation.

These advantages are particularly important because of the kinds of case typically brought before tribunals. 'Ordinary' individuals claiming benefit entitlement, or lower rents/rateable values and so on, require more informal, cheap, and speedy adjudication than the courts provide. These 'advantages', however, can become problems if they produce judicial safeguards significantly below the standards of the courts, or if independence from the executive is compromised. In fact on both these grounds, as well as on the more theoretical one that constitutional principles such as the rule of law and separation of powers are threatened (Hewart, 1929), administrative tribunals have been widely criticized. This is particularly evident in the main criticisms of tribunals made in the Franks Report (1957) (although see also the Donoughmore Report, 1932). Franks' main criticisms were:

(i) *Independence*. Franks felt that tribunals should be free 'from the influence, real or apparent, of Departments concerned with the subject-matter of their decisions' (para. 42). He expressed anxiety that this view was not always shared by departmental officials.
(ii) *Appointment*. Many tribunal chairmen and members were appointed by the minister concerned. While 'no significant evidence' was found that departments tried to influence tribunals, these arrangements were considered 'undesirable in principle', and a potential source of 'misunderstanding' (para. 45).
(iii) *Membership qualifications*. Although tribunal members were normally appointed from nominees of appropriate organizations (such as trade unions in the case of industrial tribunals), lack of legal qualifications was quite widespread.
(iv) *Procedural deficiencies*. Tribunal procedures varied widely. Most had 'a simple procedure usually without the oath and sometimes with a ban on legal representation' (para. 36). Some failed to give reasoned decisions, held hearings in secret, and provided no appeals machinery.

Most of these criticisms could be defended either from the administrative standpoint (that tribunals performed a primarily administrative function and hence close departmental links were desirable); or on the grounds that the advantages of tribunals over the courts inevitably required relaxation of normal judicial procedures. Franks' view, however, was that tribunals had been 'provided by Parliament for adjudication rather than as part of the machinery of administration' (para. 40) and that they should manifest three basic characteristics: openness, fairness and impartiality. To achieve these characteristics several recommendations were made. Reasoned decisions, public hearings, legal representation (with legal aid), and appeal to the courts on points of law, were to be the norm. Tribunal chairmen were ordinarily to have legal qualifications, and were to be appointed by the Lord Chancellor. Other members were to be appointed by a new body, the Council on Tribunals, which was also 'to keep the constitution and working of tribunals under continuous review' (para. 43).

Most of Franks' recommendations were implemented shortly afterwards, either by departmental circular or legislation. There was also a 'change in general attitude' by many tribunals 'which had not previously appreciated the full import' of the Franks 'characteristics' (Yardley, 1986, p. 207). As a result improvements have appeared in tribunal procedures: rights of legal representation are now generally recognized, public proceedings are the norm, and legally qualified chairmen – normally selected by appropriate ministers from panels appointed by the Lord Chancellor – are far more widespread. Many of Franks' criticisms are simply no longer valid. Indeed, the situation today is a developing one, as many of the post-Franks changes work their way through and fresh ones continue to be effected.

While these reforms have improved the fairness and impartiality of tribunals, they have also made their proceedings more legalistic. Not only has there been a trend towards legally qualified chairmen, and more parties with legal representation, but attitudes to evidence and points of law are more strict. Appellate tribunals, for example, now customarily publish selected decisions and consequently case law and precedent have assumed greater importance with some tribunals. As tribunals have become more legalistic, however, many of their professed advantages over the courts – informality, flexibility, cheapness, expedition and so forth have become less visible. This in fact illustrates the fundamental dilemma posed by administrative tribunals: how to reconcile the need for swifter, cheaper, more flexible justice with that for adequate judicial safeguards. A balance must be struck, and in the post-Franks era the point of balance has moved markedly towards judicialization.

Even so, the administrative view of tribunals – held mainly within departments – has not been abandoned, and several of Franks' more radical recommendations have been resisted by successive governments. Tribunal members, for example, are not appointed by the Council on Tribunals (departmental ministers – or in practice, their civil servants – still largely exercise this right); and 'interested' departments often still have a hand in appointing chairmen. Access to tribunals, moreover, has been seriously undermined by the non-availability of legal aid for most tribunal hearings (despite evidence that representation – by solicitors, social workers, union officials and so on – does increase appeal success rates), and by widespread lack of awareness of many tribunal remedies (see Justice–All Souls, 1988, paras 9.25–67). Delay is also now a serious problem for some tribunals, occasioned mainly through overloading and resource deficiencies. Tribunal procedures also vary widely and many exhibit controversial features – some, for example, allow evidence that would be inadmissible in court – leading to calls for a comprehensive review of tribunal procedures and adoption of model rules (ibid., paras 9.19–21; and Benson Report, 1979, recommendation R 15.1). In many cases, too, departments are responsible for finding tribunal staff and accommodation and for reimbursing members, features which 'sometimes creates an appearance if not the actuality of bias' (Cane, 1986, p. 285). As these examples show, the conflicting demands which underlie administrative tribunals (departmental convenience and administrative flexibility on one hand, and judicial rectitude and fairness on the other) remain problematical. As Sayers (1986, p. 45) puts it, 'It is easy for tribunals and inquiries to become either too court-like . . . or too much tied to departmental administration: the balance is difficult to achieve'. Despite advances since Franks, the haphazard pragmatic development of tribunals is still in evidence, and doubts remain about the standard of justice they dispense and about their independence from departmental influence.

Control of tribunals and inquiries

Control lies with the courts and partly with specially created machinery. Any unlawful or *ultra vires* act, or any failure to discharge statutory obligations, can be remedied through the courts by way of an application for judicial review (see p. 300). In addition, appeals and review may be allowed in respect of ministers' (or inspectors') decisions following statutory inquiries, and from some (but by no means all) tribunals, on points of law. Special appellate tribunals, which hear appeals from first-instance tribunals, also exist in some fields, sometimes with jurisdiction over facts, merit, and law, but in other cases only on points of law. Since Franks, judicial control of tribunals and inquiries has been strengthened substantially, although significantly not to the extent that Franks actually recommended (see Yardley, 1986, especially pp. 204–7). In fact, considerable confusion and inconsistency persists, reflecting once again the largely piecemeal development of British tribunal machinery.

Perhaps the most significant product of the Franks Report is the *Council on Tribunals*. Established in 1958, its current functions, specified in the Tribunals and Inquiries Act, 1971, are as follows:

(i) to keep under review the constitution and workings of the tribunals specified in Schedule 1 to the Act and, from time to time, to report on their constitution and working;

(ii) to consider and report on matters referred to the council under the Act with respect to tribunals other than ordinary courts of law;

(iii) to consider and report on these matters, or matters the council may consider to be of special importance, with respect to administrative procedures which involve or may involve the holding of a statutory inquiry by or on behalf of a Minister (*Annual Report, 1986–87*, app. A).

The council must also be consulted before new procedural rules are made for inquiries or scheduled tribunals, and may make general recommendations about membership of the latter. An independent body, the council consists of between ten and fifteen members appointed by the Lord Chancellor and Lord Advocate, plus the Parliamentary Commissioner who sits *ex-officio*. (Some of these, plus other persons appointed by the Lord Advocate, form the council's Scottish Committee).

The council's jurisdiction is generally regarded as somewhat limited. It excludes ministerial and other administrative jurisdiction beyond the scope of tribunals and inquiries, and does not extend to Northern Ireland. Its powers are essentially advisory and consultative: it cannot award compensation, overturn decisions or hear appeals, and several tribunals – or statutory bodies which form tribunal-type functions (such as the Gaming Board and Legal Aid Committees (see Birkinshaw, 1985, especially p. 31) – are outside its jurisdiction. Its membership, moreover, is part-time and mostly unpaid, and its tiny staff and limited budget (1986–7 expenditure was £309,860) are wholly inadequate for effective oversight of the several hundred thousand tribunal and inquiry proceedings occurring annually. The council also remains largely unknown to the public. Significantly, in 1980, the council issued a report (Council on Tribunals, 1980) calling for increased resources and powers, notably powers to call relevant papers from tribunals and government departments, and to attend private tribunal hearings. It also requested fuller consultation by ministers, and fuller jurisdiction across the whole field of administrative adjudication. These recommendations, however, were mostly ignored by the government, and the problem of effective supervision of tribunal and inquiry proceedings remains. As the Justice–All Souls Report (1988, para. 9.12) observed, 'The Council . . . do not have the resources to provide continuous and widespread oversight; the legal profession is not widely concerned with tribunals; the ombudsmen have no jurisdiction; the courts' supervision of tribunals is random; and few individual appellants are likely to have much experience on which to judge the performance of tribunals'.

Even so, the council has made some impact and has quietly 'endeavoured to secure improvements by persuasion' (ibid., para. 9.85). Being consulted about new or modified rules for tribunals and inquiries it has brought some uniformity and coherence to their procedures. Its investigations, moreover, have revealed numerous deficiencies which ministers have often proved willing to rectify. Surprisingly, perhaps, the council has had most impact upon statutory inquiries. Its reports into the Chalkpit case influenced 'a whole series' of subsequent inquiry procedure reforms (Yardley, 1986, p. 197); while its investigation into the proposed Stansted Airport development in the 1960s influenced the ordering of the Roskill Commission.

These successes, however, cannot conceal the remaining deficiencies. Notable among these is the lack of tribunal or inquiry machinery in several important fields (such as appeals against a local authority's decision regarding council house allocations or failure of a driving test). In 1961 the Whyatt Committee (Whyatt Report, 1961) proposed the establishment of a General Tribunal to hear appeals from discretionary decisions not covered by tribunals, but this has not been implemented. No less serious is the absence of a general right of appeal from tribunals, on fact and merits as well as law. In evidence to Franks, W. A. Robson suggested forming a general administrative appeals tribunal to hear appeals both from tribunals and against other administrative decisions where no tribunal existed. Franks itself recommended that appeals on law, fact and merits should be, in most cases, to appropriate appellate tribunals; and from the latter to the courts. In 1971 there was a further suggestion (Justice, 1971) for a general right of appeal from tribunals to a new administrative division of the High Court (although the force of this suggestion has arguably been weakened by the subsequent reform of the application for judicial review under the Order 53 procedure (see p. 300). In any event, while such arrangements might produce greater uniformity and stronger safeguards, there is an obvious objection to carrying appeals from specialist to non-specialist tribunals, whilst the potential jurisdiction of a general tribunal or similar body 'would be vast and the task of selection baffling' (Justice–All Souls, 1988, p. 255). For these reasons – and also, no doubt, because of bureaucratic opposition to increased judicial control of administrative discretion – comprehensive reform seems unlikely to materialize. The piecemeal pattern which has characterized the development of tribunal and inquiry mechanisms appears likely to continue.

Ombudsmen

Despite the powers of the courts and the growth of tribunals and inquiries, many administrative actions remain immune from impartial review. A decision, for example, may appear harsh, but unless it is in a field covered by a tribunal or similar mechanism, or unless a breach of law or natural justice is involved, no appeals machinery may be available. Traditionally in such cases the remedy for seeking redress has been an MP or councillor. Since 1967, however, they have been supplemented by a growing band of ombudsmen.

The term 'ombudsman' is Scandinavian in origin, and can be translated as 'grievance man' or 'complaints officer'. Such an official has existed in Sweden since 1809, but during the twentieth century ombudsmen have appeared in various other countries. The genesis of the British ombudsman is usually attributed to the Whyatt Report (1961), although the proposal was actually implemented by the Parliamentary Commissioner Act, 1967. This innovation proved to be only a first step, and by 1983 no less than five types of ombudsman machinery could be identified in the UK:

(i) Parliamentary Commissioner for Administration (created 1967);
(ii) Northern Ireland Parliamentary Commissioner (1969);
(iii) Commissioner for Complaints (N. Ireland) (1969);
(iv) Health service commissioners: England, Scotland, Wales (all 1973);
(v) Commission(er)s for local administration: England, Wales (both 1974) and Scotland (1976).

Of these, the most important for students of British public administration – the Parliamentary Commissioner for Administration, the health service commissioners, and the local commissioners – are examined below.

The Parliamentary Commissioner for Administration (PCA)

'Few new governmental agencies can have begun operations under a darker cloud of adverse publicity than the [PCA]' (Gwyn, 1982, p. 177). From the outset, there were claims that the PCA 'lacked teeth', particularly when compared with foreign ombudsmen. While these claims have sometimes been exaggerated, there are undoubtedly serious problems associated with the PCA, the most important of which are described in the following sections.

RELATIONS WITH PARLIAMENT

While the PCA exists to investigate citizens' grievances against central administration, he is a servant of Parliament. He works closely with a House of Commons committee, the Select Committee on the Parliamentary Commissioner for Administration, which receives his reports and oversees his work (Gregory, 1982). This relationship with MPs (peers have no access to the PCA) has several useful aspects. The select committee, for example, can reinforce the PCA's findings and recommendations, while its support – coupled with the provision that the PCA is removable from office only by addresses of both Houses of Parliament – offers protection from abuse or arbitrary dismissal by the executive. Nevertheless in one major respect this relationship has caused problems: namely the requirement that complaints to the PCA must be channelled through MPs. Of one hundred national ombudsmen the PCA is one of only two (the other is the French *médiateur*) who cannot receive complaints direct from the public (*PCA Annual Report*, 1983, introduction, paras 7 and 8).

This provision for 'filtering' complaints through MPs was introduced for two main reasons: (i) to prevent the PCA from being 'swamped' by complaints: and (ii) to reassure MPs that the PCA would supplement, not supplant, their own role as constituency 'grievance chasers'. The first reason, while probably appropriate at the outset, is less acceptable today. On average, the PCA in the mid-1980s receives around 750 complaints annually from MPs, and while direct access would generate more complaints the likely increase could probably be accommodated by simple organizational and procedural reforms (Widdicombe, 1977, paras 17–18) or by making available additional resources. At present the MP 'filter' produces serious under-utilization of the PCA: MPs vary widely in the use they make of him, and some never refer complaints. Moreover, every year many members of the public approach the PCA direct: in 1987 he received 1,137 letters (1,097 of which related to particular complaints) plus 1,619 telephone enquiries and thirty-two personal calls (*Annual Report*, 1987, para. 64). Initially such approaches were not acted upon. Since 1978, however, such complainants have been informed that, if they wish, their complaint will be forwarded to an MP for formal referral. While this represents a tentative move towards direct access, it occurs in only a few cases – only one in 1987 – and still leaves the PCA unable to investigate cases without an MP's agreement. It also affects his relationship with the public. To quote the Justice–All Souls Report (1988, paras 5–7), 'If direct access were allowed . . . the PCA would be able to project himself to the public in a far more positive way . . . [and] advertise . . . his services more vigorously'.

The second reason for the MP filter, the need to reassure MPs, is also unfounded today, for as Ridley (1984, p. 17) observes, the PCA receives 'infinitely fewer cases than . . . MPs themselves'. Nevertheless, although most authorities now support direct access, the select committee remains unconvinced. MPs, Gwyn (1982, p. 194) observes, have managed to restrict that aspect 'of the ombudsman institution that they believe to be harmful to themselves' by preventing the PCA from establishing a direct relationship with the citizens he exists to protect.

LIMITED JURISDICTION

The PCA's jurisdiction is limited in two main ways. First, several important fields of public administration are outside his terms of reference. Some initial exclusions – notably the actions of consular officials relating to UK citizens abroad – were later brought within the PCA's jurisdiction, while others (such as local government and the NHS) were later placed under other ombudsmen. Even so several controversial exceptions remain: nationalized industries, civil and criminal proceedings, civil service personnel complaints, and government commercial and contractual activities. Actions pursuable through the courts or tribunals are also excluded. Under the Parliamentary and Health Service Commissioner Act, 1987, the PCA's jurisidiction has now been extended to over fifty non-departmental public bodies, although again there are controversial exceptions (notably the BBC, the Monopolies and Mergers Commission, and the Civil Aviation Authority). While this leaves a jurisdiction narrower than that of many foreign ombudsmen, the PCA's jurisdiction nevertheless extends to administrative actions by both civil servants and ministers within all regular central government departments.

Secondly the PCA is restricted to investigating complaints of alleged *maladministration* causing injustice. Although not defined in the 1967 Act, Richard Crossman (the minister responsible for it) described maladministration as 'bias, neglect, inattention, delay, incompetence, ineptitude, perversity, turpitude, arbitrariness, and so on' (*Hansard*, V, vol. 734, col. 51, 18 October 1966). Essentially, maladministration concerns defects in administrative procedures, not the merits or substance of decisions. However, successive PCAs, encouraged by the select committee, have widened the interpretation to include 'bad decisions', the quality of which might reasonably suggest that maladministration had been involved in taking them. Nevertheless, technically the merits of administrative decisions (such as their fairness) cannot be challenged so long as appropriate procedures have been followed. This presents considerable jurisdictional ambiguity, for the distinction between the merits of decisions, and actions taken in their formulation and implementation, is hardly more precise than that between policy and administration (see Chapter 1). With at least one PCA investigation (Court Line, in 1974/5), controversy developed precisely because of such ambiguity: 'upon the question' of whether ministerial statements in Parliament were policy matters or actions 'taken in the exercise of administrative functions' (Gregory, 1977, p. 280).

The effect of these limitations is illustrated by the fact that the vast majority of complaints forwarded by MPs are usually not accepted for investigation, mostly because they are outside the PCA's jurisdiction. In 1987, for example, three-quarters of complaints were not accepted: 17 per cent of these were complaints against authorities outside his scope, 57 per cent did not concern administrative actions, and 7 per cent concerned public personnel matters (*PCA Annual Report*, 1987, para. 61). Jurisdictional limitations, therefore, prevent a high proportion of properly referred complaints from being investigated.

Numerous proposals have been made for extending the PCA's jurisdiction. In 1977, the Widdicombe Report (para. 67) recommended that the PCA should investigate complaints that actions, or omissions, by government departments are unreasonable, unjust or oppressive. The 1988 Justice–All Souls Report (paras 5.10–14), supporting an earlier call from the select committee, argued that, where particular complaints suggested that a department was not conducting its business properly, the PCA should be able to conduct 'a systematic investigation of the work of that branch'. Nevertheless, successive governments have failed to act. One factor is that ministers have probably been concerned to prevent the PCA from challenging policy decisions, and civil servants to limit the scope of the watchdog over their own departments. Like MPs over access, civil servants and ministers have restricted the PCA's jurisdiction to limits which present least threat to themselves.

APPOINTMENT AND STAFFING

Although a 'parliamentary commissioner', the PCA is appointed by government. The first three PCAs were all recruited from the civil service, as were all their investigative staff (who were seconded from various government departments). While a civil service background may be useful in discharging the PCA's functions, it inevitably arouses suspicion that too favourable a construction may be put on the way civil servants have acted. It may also explain the over-bureaucratic tendencies sometimes evident within the PCA's office: an unduly restricted interpretation (particularly by the first ombudsman) of the PCA's role, a cautious approach to the press, over-routinized investigations, and an over-reliance on the Treasury Solicitor (a government official) for legal advice. Moreover, while the PCA's salary is determined by the Commons and charged to the Consolidated Fund, the number – and conditions – of his staff require Treasury approval. The question of resourcing, moreover, is not unrelated to wider aspects, as additional resources would almost certainly be required if direct access and/or major jurisdictional extensions were allowed.

To rectify these deficiencies some changes have been made. For example, since 1979 the Select Committee has been consulted before the appointment of a new PCA and the choice is no longer limited to civil servants. Furthermore, since 1977 a small number of investigative staff have been recruited from outside the civil service, and legal advice obtained other than from the Treasury Solicitor. Nevertheless, scope clearly exists for allowing the PCA more independence, and more *appearance* of independence, from the executive whose activities he investigates and appraises.

INVESTIGATIONS

The PCA possesses wide investigative powers, including power to examine ministers and civil servants and to inspect departmental files. Information and documents relating to Cabinet or Cabinet committee proceedings can be withheld, but this is rarely an obstacle (although in the Court Line affair it did arouse controversy). In addition to formal powers he generally receives good co-operation from departments in answering queries and supplying records. Investigations are conducted with great thoroughness: in 90–95 per cent of investigations departmental files are examined, in 40–45 per cent officials are questioned, and in about 60 per cent complainants are interviewed at home (Gwyn, 1982, p. 181). Such thoroughness, while seemingly commendable, is perhaps unnecessary in routine cases. It arguably also makes inefficient use of resources and contributes to the long throughput time – averaging 10 months and 18 days in 1987 (*Annual Report*, para. 9) – taken to dispose of cases.

REMEDIAL POWERS

As successive PCAs have widened the interpretation of maladministration, the percentage of investigations producing findings of maladministration has increased. In 1968 and 1969 it was 10 and 16 per cent, throughout the 1970s it was consistently above 30 per cent, and in the 1980s it has often been above 40 per cent. Additionally in a number of cases (again, between 40 and 50 per cent in recent years) departmental actions are criticized though complaints are not upheld. All told in the mid-1980s around 75 complaints of maladministration giving rise to injustice have been upheld annually, and in a broadly similar number of rejected cases departmental actions have been criticized.

Following each investigation a report is issued to the referring MP, with a copy to the department concerned. But although the PCA may propose remedies, he cannot enforce them. In practice, however, the PCA's recommendations are usually accepted by departments, as failure to do so is likely to result in parliamentary criticism. The PCA, moreover, normally informs the select committee of any unremedied grievances and the committee, in turn, may examine the departmental permanent secretary. Such procedures have occasionally received striking results (Gregory, 1982, pp. 55–70) and, although there have been instances of non-compliance, departments do almost always 'comply and do carry out [the PCA's] recommendations' (Justice–All Souls, 1988, para. 5.37).

The select committee has powers to investigate all reports from the ombudsman, including annual reports and special reports which he is empowered to make on investigations of particular importance. Since

1972 the PCA has also published periodic reports containing anonymized details of investigations. Nevertheless, the PCA's recommendations are not binding – his ultimate weapon is a statutory right to lay before both Houses a special report in cases where injustice has not been remedied. While most authorities accept that Parliament must ultimately hold ministers accountable, it is nevertheless widely felt that the PCA could put more pressure on wayward departments: for example, by making more use of press conferences. To date, departmental intransigence has not presented major problems but, as a former PCA (Pugh, 1978, p. 133) observed, if 'recommendations for remedy were ignored on any significant scale . . . the credibility of my Office would be prejudiced'. If that were to happen there would be a strong case for extending to Britain the arrangement which applies to the Northern Ireland Commissioner for Complaints, whose reports can be used as grounds for an action for damages in the courts.

Any assessment of the PCA must take account of the above 'problem areas'. Undoubtedly, the limitations upon access and jurisidiction – limitations 'deliberately imposed because of constitutional sensitivities and political jealousies' (Birkinshaw, 1985, p. 139) – as well as the PCA's cautious approach to publicity, have resulted in underutilization; almost all foreign ombudsmen receive more complaints per citizen than the PCA. The nature, even the existence, of his office is not widely understood among the public, and consequently many complaints do not reach him or are outside his jurisdiction. In the period to 1986 the mean annual average of complaints referred by MPs was only 825 (*Annual Report*, 1986, para. 2), of which around only 10 per cent had been upheld. These limited results must be set against the extra workload – estimated at between one-and-a-half and five plus days per investigation (Gregory and Hutchesson, 1975, pp. 354–5) – which is created for government departments, particularly those (notably the Inland Revenue and DSS) which attract most complaints. Moreover, the PCA's existence has probably made civil servants more cautious, with consequent extra delays and administrative costs.

The PCA, however, has not been a total failure. Much of the first PCA's caution has subsequently been relaxed: later commissioners have interpreted their jurisdiction more liberally, have eased access and have discovered progressively higher incidences of maladministration. Moreover while numbers of cases received and upheld are low by international standards, this may reflect higher standards of administrative practice in Britain and the widespread use by MPs of other avenues for securing redress. In any event, by 1987 over 5,000 complaints had been investigated – many after all other channels had been exhausted. Of those upheld, moreover, almost all received appropriate recompense. Although many of the cases and remedies (an apology or small payment) have been relatively 'humdrum', for the complainant the outcome may nevertheless be important. There has also been the occasional *cause célèbre*, notably the 1968 Sachsenhausen case, where the PCA helped to secure compensation for survivors of Sachsenhausen concentraton camp, even though their claims had prevously been rejected by three Foreign Office ministers and the Prime Minister (see Gregory and Hutchesson, 1975, especially chs 11 and 12). Of course, even where complaints are not upheld, the PCA's investigation is not irrelevant. As the PCA observed in his 1979 *Annual Report* (p. 2): 'A grievance investigated is a resentment relieved, even if it be dismissed in the end.'

Many PCA investigations benefit more than just complainants. Some have brought important legislative changes: for example, the provisions in the 1974 and 1975 Finance Acts for interest to be paid on delayed tax repayments. Others have produced improved departmental practices. In 1975, for example, administrative changes introduced by the Driver and Vehicle Licensing Centre following an investigation were reported to have brought significantly reduced delays for driving licence applicants (see Gregory, 1982, pp. 57–9, 63–4). There have also been 'significant . . . changes in the attitudes of government departments to their dealings with . . . individual citizen[s]' (Pugh, 1978, p. 136). Indeed civil servants to some extent have also benefited; directly in the case of officials exonerated by the PCA, and indirectly in the sense that PCA investigations have undoubtedly improved the quality of central administration. It is important not to paint too antagonistic a picture of the PCA's relations with civil servants. His reports do more than simply keep them 'on their toes': in many cases they have done much to acquaint ministers and senior officials with problems experienced at lower departmental levels, while cumulatively they represent a sort of guide to good (and bad) administrative practice.

The PCA, therefore, has shortcomings, but has nevertheless been a qualified success. As Gwyn (1982, p. 193) observes, 'many thousands of taxpayers, recipients of social services, property owners, automobile licensees etc. have been helped by changes in administrative practices and procedures resulting . . . from the Commissioner's investigations'.

The Health service commissioner

In 1973 three health service commissioners were established with responsibility for investigating complaints against health authorities in, respectively, England, Scotland and Wales. Although in law separate from the PCA, all three posts have been vested in the person holding that office. Usually a single annual report is published containing information relevant to all three posts, and this is received by the Select Committee on the PCA.

Although exhibiting many common features with the PCA, three significant differences can be discerned:

(i) the MP 'filter' does not apply. Complainants may approach the commissioner direct provided they have first complained to the appropriate health authority;
(ii) the commissioner reports to the appropriate Secretary of State rather than to Parliament though his reports are laid before both Houses;
(iii) the commissioner's jurisdiction extends beyond investigating complaints of maladministration to those alleging injustice, or hardship, as a result of failure in a service provided by a health authority, or failure to provide a service which it was its duty to provide.

The Health Service Commissioner – like the PCA – suffers from important jurisdictional exclusions. The most significant are complaints about general medical and dental practitioners and opticians (which normally go to family practitioner committees or, if professional negligence is alleged, to the courts) and complaints about clinical judgements of health service staff (for discussion see Birkinshaw, 1985, pp. 147–51). Both exclusions are highly controversial and owe much to pressure from professional bodies such as the British Medical Association. Significantly, several authorities have suggested that the commissioner should investigate clinical complaints with the help of medical assessors (the practice adopted by the PCA, who has jurisdiction over top security hospitals controlled by government departments).

Normally, the commissioner receives about 700 complaints annually from England, Scotland and Wales (the highest total, 926, was in 1985/6). However, a high proportion usually cannot be investigated: in 1986/7 36 per cent were referred back (mainly through not having first been put to a health authority) and 48 per cent discontinued or rejected (mainly because they concerned clinical judgement, family practitioners, or other bodies outside the commissioner's jurisdiction). Only 16 per cent of cases were formally investigated and reported on. Clearly, as with the PCA, there is considerable underutilization of health service commissioners, and until their jurisdiction is widened NHS complaints procedures seem likely to remain a source of concern.

Local Commissioners for Administration

In 1974, coincident with local government reorganization, two Commissions for Local Administration (CLAs) were established, one each for England and Wales. The English commission consists of three local commissioners, each of whom investigates complaints in a particular part of the country, plus the PCA who sits *ex officio* but has no investigative powers; the Welsh commission consists of one local commissioner plus the PCA *ex officio*. (In Scotland a single commissioner – established in 1976 – investigates complaints with PCA involvement.) All three institutions have similar jurisdiction, namely to investigate complaints of injustice caused by maladministration by local authorities, water authorities, joint planning boards, police authorities (except the Metropolitan Police which is responsible to the Home Secretary), and housing and town and country planning functions of new town authorities and urban development corporations. Until 1988 complaints had to be directed through members of the authority concerned, although they could be accepted direct if commissioners were satisfied that a councillor/member had declined to forward them. From the outset concern was expressed that many complaints were sent direct to local ombudsmen without councillors first being approached – around 2,000 per annum in England alone in the 1980s – and that (despite procedures introduced in 1984 for encouraging formal re-referral via the civic head of the authority concerned) many were not subsequently passed back for investigation. Consequently a modified referral procedure was introduced in 1988 under which complainants can now approach the local ombudsman direct (or through a councillor as before).

The investigative powers of local commissioners are broadly similar to those of the PCA and health service commissioners. Like these other ombudsmen, however, they suffer from serious limitations.

JURISDICTIONAL LIMITATIONS

Not only are local commissioners limited to investigating complaints of maladministration, but several fields of local administration are outside their jurisdiction. The most significant of these are: (i) contractual and commercial activity; (ii) internal school and college matters (curricula, conduct, discipline, and so forth; (iii) actions taken in connection with the investigation or prevention of a crime by a police authority; (iv) the commencement or conduct of civil or criminal proceedings before any court; (v) personnel matters; and (vi) actions affecting 'all or most of the inhabitants of the authority concerned' (such as rate levels). The existence of what Lewis, Seneviratne and Cracknell (1986, p. 25) describe as these 'no-go areas' makes the system 'utterly confusing to complainants' and 'undermines confidence in the ombudsman system itself'.

NO REMEDIAL POWERS

Like the PCA, local commissioners have no remedial powers. Their only course, following a finding of injustice through maladministration, is to lay a report before the authority concerned. This report must be published and considered by the authority, and the commissioner notified of remedial action proposed or taken. If the commissioner is dissatisfied with the authority's response the only remaining power is to issue a further report stating the grounds of dissatisfaction, and requiring this also to be considered and published.

Unfortunately, unlike the PCA, local commissioners have experienced a significant minority of cases where authorities have failed to comply with recommendations. Between 1974 and 1986 second reports were issued in 9 per cent of English cases, and in 6.5 per cent further reports failed to produce satisfactory remedies. Even more disturbing, to May 1984 no less than 19 per cent of English local authorities had failed at least once to provide a remedy required by a local commissioner (Justice–All Souls, 1988, para. 5.63). Even where satisfactory outcomes were obtained, long periods often elapsed between the first report and the remedy being provided: in the first ten years, for example, delays of six months or more were experienced in 25 per cent of English cases (*Annual Report*, 1984, para. 75).

Inevitably lack of co-operation and delay on this scale arouses concern. The Widdicombe Report (*Conduct of Local Authority Business*, 1986, para. 9.69) recommended that findings of local commissioners should be enforceable through the courts (as already applies with Northern Ireland's Commissioner of Complaints), a proposal which now commands widespread support (see also Justice, 1980, para. 24, and Justice–All Souls, 1988, paras 5.76–99). Nevertheless it has been rejected by the government who propose instead legislative amendments to ensure in future that non-compliance decisions are taken by the full council and reasons stated publicly in the local press (Department of Environment *et al.*, 1988, paras 6.21–26). Although maintaining one of the basic principles of British ombudsman systems – that remedies should be applied through political rather than judicial processes – serious doubts must exist that these measures will produce more than minimal improvement. In any event, some non-compliance will still occur, which complainants will remain powerless to remedy.

THE REPRESENTATIVE BODY

The English and Welsh commissions report to a representative body consisting of nominees of water authorities and local authority associations. (Different arrangements apply in Scotland – see Bratton, 1984; Stacey, 1978, pp. 210–12.) Thus the English representative body receives the annual report of the English commission as well as its annual estimates (which, if it considers them excessive, it may refer to the Secretary of State). The object of these arrangements is to make local commissioners report to bodies representative of the authorities over whom they have jurisdiction. The effect, however, has been to give the commissions a constitutional relationship, not with an independent body such as the Select Committee on the PCA, but with one representing authorities against whom they investigate complaints (and who meet their expenses). Not surprisingly, the English representative body 'has consistently refused to support requests by the CLA to extend their jurisdiction' (Birkinshaw, 1985, p. 141) and has taken 'a negative view of proposals from the Commission for modifications to their procedures' (Widdicombe Report, 1986, para. 9.82). In 1988 the government (Department of Environment *et al.*, paras. 6.28–33), responding to these criticisms, proposed abolition of the representative body and the funding of the English and Welsh commissions by deductions from the rate support grant. It also proposed enlarging the commissions by the addition of external members, and legislation to enable local ombudsmen to comment and advise on local administrative procedures as a means of spreading good practice.

Notwithstanding its limitations, the CLA's achievements should not be ignored. Around 4,000 complaints are now being received annually in England (4,059 in 1986/7) plus over 200 in Wales and around 600 in Scotland. (Most relate to housing and planning.) About 200 cases of maladministration and injustice are uncovered each year (in England), the vast majority resulting in satisfactory settlements. (Additionally local authorities often settle complaints amicably without a formal report.) The CLA has also been influential in causing authorities to improve their administrative practices and procedures. As Lewis, Seneviratne and Cracknell (1986, vol. 1, p. 226) conclude, 'On almost any index the LO has been a force for the good'. Indeed with the government's proposed abolition of the Representative Body, coupled with an enlarged commission, increased concern with the quality of local administration and the already implemented provision of direct access, local ombudsmen in future may 'bulk [somewhat] larger in the world of local government' (Greenwood, 1989, p. 8).

The defects surrounding the system are, nevertheless, considerable. Although one of the major initial deficiencies – lack of direct access – has now been removed, and the government plans to legislate on others, problems still remain. Only a small proportion of complaints (around 10 per cent), for example, are fully investigated; the remainder either have their investigations prematurely terminated or are outside the commissioner's jurisdiction. Several reports (Justice, 1980, paras

200–25; Lewis, Seneviratne and Cracknell, 1986, vol. II, pp. 78–80) suggest that, even when investigations are concluded, many complainants remain dissatisfied either with the conduct of investigations (one factor being the time taken to complete these – on average 51 weeks in 1986–7) or with the remedy obtained. Public awareness of local ombudsmen also remains disturbingly low. Clearly, there remains substantial scope for improvement.

Too many avenues?

Ombudsman machinery has been extended gradually since 1967 to cover the main layers of British public administration: central government, local government, and NHS. That development, however, has been largely piecemeal. Not only have important fields of public administration escaped the ombudsman phenomenon, but where ombudsmen do exist the varying provisions relating to access and jurisdiction are bewildering. The fragmentation of machinery also weakens its overall impact. A single centralized ombudsman would carry more authority within Whitehall, and become more prominent in the public eye, than the various individual commissioners who now operate separately.

Despite piecemeal development some co-operation between ombudsmen does occur. The PCA is an *ex officio* member of the English and Welsh CLAs, and the same person serves as Health Service Commissioner for England, Scotland, and Wales. (At various times the person holding office as PCA has concurrently served as the Northern Ireland PCA or as the Northern Ireland Commissioner for Complaints.) Occasionally, too, composite investigations are conducted on matters involving two or more of the ombudsman systems. In addition, the English CLA regularly invites the Welsh and Scottish local commissioner to its meetings. Such arrangements, however, are of little direct advantage to aggrieved citizens. Indeed, it is difficult to avoid the conclusion that, while the establishment of ombudsmen in Britain has extended citizens' opportunities for securing redress, it has not only failed to simplify the machinery and procedures available, but has actually made them confusing and complex.

Access could be simplified and standardized, notably by allowing direct access to all ombudsmen, or by allowing MPs to refer complaints to any commissioner. However the select committee is unwilling to allow direct access to the PCA, and local authority opinion is unlikely to welcome the prospect of MPs concerning themselves with local authority matters.

A more comprehensive reform would be the establishment of a single ombudsman. In 1975, the then PCA, Sir Alan Marre, observed:

'In the long term it . . . will be important to consider how a more co-ordinated total system, more directly related to the interests of members of the public, can be brought about' (*Annual Report*, 1975, para. 55). Subsequently one of his successors, Cecil Clothier, observed: 'Possibly the only way to remove all potential inconvenience to Members and the Public . . . would be to have a single central "Ombudsman" organisation to which everything could be addressed' (Select Committee on the Parliamentary Commissioner, 1979/80, p. 2). While Clothier appears to be advocating little more than a central collection point for complaints, the idea could be applied to a single official performing investigative functions across the jurisdictional field of all existing ombudsmen. Such an arrangement would not only be tidier, but would make the ombudsman more accessible and probably more effective in securing redress.

Of course, with many fields of public administration, redress lies not with an ombudsman but with other agencies. Indeed, from the citizen's standpoint, the multiplicity of agencies is a major source of confusion. In addition to agencies covered in this chapter, the following further channels can, in 1988, also be identified: MPs; councillors ('county', 'district', or 'parish', depending on service and area concerned); nationalized industry consumer councils (see Chapter 12); Police Complaints Authority – a lay body which supervises investigations (conducted by police officers) of complaints against the police; Equal Opportunities Commission (which deals with sex discrimination complaints); Commission for Racial Equality; family practitioner committees and community health councils (see Chapter 13); Office of Fair Trading (complaints about unfair trading practices and individual consumer rights); National Consumer Council (representing consumer viewpoints); European Commission and Court on Human Rights (in cases where public authorities breach the European Convention on Human Rights). Even this list is not exhaustive, and alternative remedies may apply in some cases. The Justice–All Souls Report (1988, ch. 4), criticizing the *ad hoc* nature of existing arrangements, argued for the establishment of a standing 'watchdog' Administrative Review Commission, independent of government, to draw attention to deficiencies in redress mechanisms, comment on pending legislation, and propose reforms.

There are today a multitude of channels through which to challenge the actions or decisions of public officials. The proliferation of agencies, however, obscures rather than clarifies the opportunities for redress available to ordinary citizens. To some extent the problems can be overcome by channelling grievances through pressure groups or the media, although to the man in the street these may not be particularly accessible. Alternatively, assistance may be provided by Citizens Advice Bureaux, or consumer/legal/housing advice centres, which in many localities function almost as clearing houses for grievances emanating from within the local community. Such bodies, however, are only advisory, and whether redress is obtained still depends upon the efficacy of official channels.

The machinery for the redress of grievance lacks coherence. Some fields of public administration are well endowed with complaints machinery but others are not. The multitude of agencies reveals a plethora of procedures, investigative methods, remedial powers, and jurisdictional exclusions which reflects the piecemeal, haphazard pattern of their development. Proposals for rationalization abound: the creation of something similar to the French *droit administratif*; Whyatt's proposed general tribunal; Clothier's single ombudsman; an Administrative Review Commission; and so on. Such proposals, however, are unlikely to be implemented. A host of obstacles – the conservatism of the English legal profession, the vested interests of public officials, the threat to established institutions and so on – bar the way to wholesale reform. The essentially piecemeal development of the past, with all its attendant complexity for citizens seeking redress, seems likely to continue into the foreseeable future.

REFERENCES

Alderman, G. (1982), 'Jews and Sunday trading: the use and abuse of delegated legislation', *Public Administration*, vol. 60, no. 1, pp. 99–104.

Alderman, R. K., and Cross, J. A. (1981), 'Patterns of ministerial turnover in two Labour Cabinets', *Political Studies*, vol. XXIX, no. 3, pp. 425–30.

Alexander, A. (1982a), *Local Government in Britain since Reorganisation* (London: Allen & Unwin).

Alexander, A. (1982b), *The Politics of Local Government in the United Kingdom* (London: Longman).

Allen, D., Harley, M., and Mackinson, G. T. (1987), 'Performance indicators in the National Health Service', *Social Policy and Administration*, vol. 21, no. 1, pp. 70–84.

Alt, J. (1971), 'Some social and political correlates of county borough expenditure', *British Journal of Political Science*, vol. 1, no. 1, pp. 49–62.

Alternatives to Domestic Rates (1981), Cmnd 8449 (London: HMSO).

Ascher, K. (1987), *The Politics of Privatisation: Contracting out Public Services* (London: Macmillan).

Assheton Report (1944), *Report of the Committee on Training of Civil Servants*, Cmd. 6525 (London: HMSO).

Atkinson Report (1983), *Selection of Fast-Stream Graduate Entrants to the Home Civil Service, the Diplomatic Service and the Tax Inspectorate; and of Candidates from within the Service* (London: Management and Personnel Office).

Audit Commission (1984a), *Improving Economy, Efficiency and Effectiveness in Local Government in England and Wales* (London: HMSO).

Audit Commission (1984b), *The Impact on Local Authorities' Economy, Efficiency and Effectiveness of the Block Grant Distribution System* (London: HMSO).

Audit Commission (1985a), *Obtaining Better Value from Further Education* (London: HMSO).

Audit Commission (1985b), *Capital Expenditure Controls* (London: HMSO).

Audit Commission (1986), *Performance Review in Local Government* (London: HMSO).

Bagehot, W. (1963 edn), *The English Constitution* (London: Fontana).

Baines, P. (1985), 'History and rationale of the reforms', in G. Drewry, (ed.), *The New Select Committees: A Study of the 1979 Reforms* (Oxford: Clarendon Press).

Bains Report (1972), *The Local Authorities: Management and Structure* (London: HMSO).

Baker, R. J. S. (1972a), *Administrative Theory and Public Administration* (London: Hutchinson).

Baker, R. J. S. (1972b), 'The V and G affair and ministerial responsibility', *Political Quarterly*, vol. 43, no. 3, pp. 340–5.

Barker, A. (1982), *Quangos in Britain* (London: Macmillan).

Barlow, Sir W. (1981), 'The problems of managing nationalized industries', in *Allies or Adversaries?* (London: RIPA), pp. 29–42.

Barnes, F. (1988), 'Regulation and quality in monopoly industries', *Public Money and Management*, vol. 8, nos 1 and 2, pp. 45–9.

Barrett, S., and Fudge, C. (eds) (1981), *Policy and Action* (London: Methuen).
Bates, E. (1982), 'Can the public's voice influence bureaucracy? The case of the community health councils', *Public Administration*, vol. 60, no. 1, pp. 92–8.
Beard, W. (1988), 'Information technology in the public service', in P. Jackson and F. Terry (eds), *Public Domain 1988* (London: Public Finance Foundation with Peat, Marwick, McLintock).
Beesley, I. (1983), 'The Rayner scrutinies', in A. Gray and W. I. Jenkins (eds), *Policy Analysis and Evaluation in British Government* (London: RIPA), pp. 31–6.
Beeton, D. (1987), 'Measuring departmental performance', in A. Harrison and J. Gretton (eds), *Reshaping Central Government* (Oxford: Policy Journals), pp. 77–89.
Beith, A. (1981), 'Prayers unanswered: a jaundiced view of the parliamentary scrutiny of statutory instruments', *Parliamentary Affairs*, vol. XXXIV, no. 2, pp. 165–73.
Bellamy, C., and Franklin, B. (1985), 'BTEC's educational policy and public administration', *Teaching Politics*, vol. 14, no. 2, pp. 160–74.
Benn, T. (1982), *Arguments for Democracy* (Harmondsworth: Penguin).
Benn, T. (1982), 'Manifestos and mandarins', in *Policy and Practice: the Experience of Government* (London: RIPA), pp. 57–78.
Benson Report (1979), *Final Report of the Royal Commission on Legal Services*, Cmnd. 7648 (London: HMSO).
Benyon, J. (1988), 'Civil servants and ministers: accountability and responsibility', *Social Studies Review*, vol. 3, no. 4, pp. 132–3.
Berrill, Sir K. (1985), 'Strength at the centre – the case for a Prime Ministers' Department', in A. King (ed.), *The British Prime Minister* (London: Macmillan).
Binder, B. J. A. (1982), 'Relations between central and local government since 1975 – are the associations failing?' *Local Government Studies*, vol. 8, no. 1, pp. 35–44.
Birch, A. H. (1964), *Representative and Responsible Government* (London: Allen & Unwin).
Birch, A. H. (1980), *The British System of Government* (London: Allen & Unwin).
Birkinshaw, P. (1985), *Grievances, Remedies and the State* (London: Sweet & Maxwell).
Boaden, N. (1971), *Urban Policy Making* (Cambridge: Cambridge University Press).
Bogdanor, V. (ed.) (1987), *Blackwell Encyclopedia of Political Institutions* (Oxford: Blackwell).
Booth, S., and Pitt, D. C. (1984), 'Continuity and discontinuity: I.T. as a force for organisational change', in D. C. Pitt and B. C. Smith (eds), pp. 17–38.
Borthwick, R. L. (1979), 'Questions and debates', in S. A. Walkland (ed.), *The House of Commons in the Twentieth Century* (Oxford: Oxford University Press), pp. 476–526.
Borthwick, R. L. (1982), 'Recent changes in House of Commons committees', in Robins, op. cit., pp. 1–14.
Bourn, J. (1979), *Management in Central and Local Government* (London: Pitman).
Bowen, G. (1978), *Survey of Fringe Bodies* (London: Civil Service Department).

Boyle, G., and Crosland, A. (1971), *The Politics of Education* (Harmondsworth: Penguin).
Boynton, Sir J. (1982), 'Local councils in confrontation: the current conflict with the centre', *Policy Studies*, vol. 2, pt 4, pp. 199–216.
Boynton, Sir J. (1986), 'Judicial review of administrative decisions – a background paper', *Public Administration*, vol. 64, no. 2, pp. 147–61.
Bradley, D. (1983), 'Management in government', in A. Gray and W. I. Jenkins (eds), *Policy Analysis and Evaluation in British Government* (London: RIPA), pp. 37–45.
Bratton, K. (1984), *The Work of the Commissioner for Local Administration in Scotland 1975–83*, I.O.I. Occasional Paper No. 25 (Alberta: I.O.I.).
Bray, A. J. M. (1988), *The Clandestine Reformer: A Study of the Rayner Scrutinies*, Strathclyde Paper on Government and Politics No. 55 (Glasgow: University of Strathclyde).
Bridges, Lord (1964), *The Treasury* (London: Allen & Unwin).
Bridges, L., Game, C., Lomas, O., McBride, J., and Ranson, S. (1987), *Legality and Local Politics* (Aldershot: Avebury).
Briscoe, S. (1981), 'Employment in the public and private sectors 1975–1981', *Economic Trends*, no. 338, pp. 94–102.
Bromhead, P. (1974), *Britain's Developing Constitution* (London: Allen & Unwin).
Brooke Report (1971/2), *Report of the Joint Committee on Delegated Legislation*, HL 184 and HC 475 (London: HMSO).
Brown, G. (1972), *In My Way* (Harmondsworth: Penguin).
Brown, M. (1982), *Introduction to Social Administration in Britain*, 5th edn (London: Hutchinson).
Brown, R. G. S. (1970), *The Administrative Process in Britain* (London: Methuen).
Brown, R. G. S. (1975), *The Management of Welfare* (London: Fontana).
Brown, R. G. S., and Steel, D. (1979), *The Administrative Process in Britain* (London: Methuen).
Bruce-Gardyne, J., and Lawson, N. (1976), *The Power Game* (London: Macmillan).
Bulpitt, J. (1967), *Party Politics in English Local Government* (London: Longman).
Burch, M. (1987), 'The demise of Cabinet government', in L. Robins (ed.), *Political Institutions in Britain* (London: Longman/Politics Association), pp. 19–38.
Byrne, P. (1976), 'Parliamentary control of delegated legislation', *Parliamentary Affairs*, vol. XXIX, no. 4, pp. 366–77.
Byrne, T. (1986), *Local Government in Britain: Everyone's Guide to How it all Works* (Harmondsworth: Penguin).

Cabinet Office (1987), *Public Bodies 1987* (London: HMSO).
Cabinet Office (MPO)/Treasury (FMU) (1984a), *Financial Management Initiative: Non-Departmental Public Bodies* (London).
Cabinet Office (MPO)/Treasury (FMU) (1984b), *Budgetary Control Systems* (London: HMSO).
Cabinet Office (MPO)/Treasury (FMU) (1985a), *Top Management Systems* (London: HMSO).

Cabinet Office (MPO)/Treasury (FMU) (1985b), *Policy Work and the FMI* (London: HMSO).

Cabinet Office (MPO)/Treasury (1985c), *Non-departmental Public Bodies: A Guide for Departments* (London).

Cane, P. (1986), *An Introduction to Administrative Law* (Oxford: Clarendon).

Cassels Report (1983), *Review of Personnel Work in the Civil Service: Report to the Prime Minister* (London: HMSO).

Cassels, J. (1985), 'Financial accountability', in *Developing the FMI Principles: Changes in Process and Culture* (London: RIPA/Peat Marwick).

Castle, B. (1980), *The Castle Diaries 1974–76* (London: Weidenfeld & Nicolson).

Central Policy Review Staff (CPRS) (1977), *Relations Between Central Government and Local Authorities* (London: HMSO).

Chandler, J. A. (1988a), *Public Policy-Making for Local Government* (London: Croom Helm).

Chandler, J. A., (1988b), 'Public administration or public management?' *Teaching Public Administration*, vol. VII, no. 1, pp. 1–10.

Chapman, R. A. (1973), 'The Vehicle and General affair: some reflections for public administration in Britain', *Public Administration*, vol. 51, no. 3, pp. 273–90.

Chapman, R. A. (1982), 'Civil service recruitment – bias against external candidates', *Public Administration*, vol. 60, no. 1, pp. 77–83.

Chapman, R. A. (1983), 'The rise and fall of the CSD', *Policy and Politics*, vol. 11, no. 1, pp. 41–61.

Chapman, R. A. (1984a), *Leadership in the British Civil Service: A Study of Sir Percival Waterfield and the Creation of the Civil Service Selection Board* (London: Croom Helm).

Chapman, R. A. (1984b), 'Administrative culture and personnel management: the British civil service in the 1980s', *Teaching Public Administration*, vol. IV, no. 1, pp. 1–14.

Chapman, R. A. (1988a), 'Editorial – The British civil service: inward secondments: cause for concern', *Public Policy and Administration*, vol. 3, no. 2, 1988, pp. 1–3.

Chapman, R. A. (1988b), *Ethics in the British Civil Service* (London: Routledge).

Chapman, R. A., and Greenaway, J. R. (1980), *The Dynamics of Administrative Reform* (London: Croom Helm).

Chapman, R. G. (1987), 'Public administration as a useful discipline: a rejoiner to John Kingdom', *Teaching Public Administration*, vol. VII, no. 1, pp. 15–30.

Chester, Sir N. (1979), 'Fringe bodies, quangos and all that', *Public Administration*, vol. 57, no. 1, pp. 51–4.

CIPFA (Chartered Institute of Public Finance and Accounting), *Performance indicators in the education service: a consultative document* (London: CIPFA).

Civil Servants and Ministers: Duties and Responsibilities: Government Responses to the Seventh Report from the Treasury and Civil Service Select Committee, Session 1985–86, HC 92, Cmnd 9841 (London: HMSO).

Civil Service Commission (1979), *Report of the Committee on the Selection Procedure for the Recruitment of Administrative Trainees* (London: Civil Service Commission).

Civil Service Department (1978), *Report of the Administration Trainee Review Committee* (London: CSD).
Civil Service Department (1980), *The Civil Service: Introductory Factual Memorandum Submitted to the House of Commons Treasury and Civil Service Committee* (London: CSD).
Clarke, A. (1977), 'Ministerial supervision and the size of the Department of the Environment, *Public Administration*, vol. 55, no. 2, pp. 197–204.
Clarke, Sir R. (1971), *New Trends in Government*, (London: HMSO).
Clarke, Sir R. (1975), 'The machinery of government', in Thornhill, op. cit., pp. 63–95.
Cockburn, C. (1977), *The Local State* (London: Pluto).
Cockerell, M., Hennessy, P., and Walker, D. (1984), *Sources Close to the Prime Minister* (London: Macmillan).
Collins, B. (1987), 'The Rayner Scrutinies', in A. M. Harrison and J. Gretton (eds), *Reshaping Central Government* (Oxford: Policy Journals).
Collins, B., and Wharton, B. (1984a), 'Investigating public industries: how has the Monopolies and Mergers Commission performed?', *Public Money*, vol. 4, no. 2, pp. 15–23.
Collins, B., and Wharton, B. (1984b), 'Nationalised industry responses to the Monopolies and Mergers Commisson', *Public Money*, vol. 4, no. 3, pp. 30–2.
Collins, C. A., Hinings, C. R., and Walsh, K. (1978), 'The officer and the councillor in local government', *Public Administration Bulletin*, no. 28, pp. 34–50.
Committee of Vice Chancellors and Principals (1986), *Performance Indicators in Universities* (London: Committee of Vice Chancellors and Principals).
Comptroller and Auditor General (1985), *Operation of the Rate Support Grant System* (London: HMSO).
Conservative Central Office (1983), *The Conservative Manifesto 1983* (London: CCO).
Coombes, D. (1966), *The Member of Parliament and the Administration* (London: Allen & Unwin).
Coombes, D. (1971), *State Enterprise: Business or Politics* (London: Allen & Unwin).
Coombes, D. (1981), 'Parliament and the European Community', in Walkland and Ryle, op. cit., pp. 236–59.
Council on Tribunals (1980), *Special Report, The Functions of the Council on Tribunals*, Cmnd 7805 (London: HMSO).
Cousins, P. F. (1982), 'Quasi-official bodies in local government', in Barker, op. cit., pp. 152–63.
Cousins, P. F. (1983), 'Local quangos – or how to make local government more confusing', *Teaching Public Administration*, vol. III, no. 1, pp. 1–16.
Craig, J. A. (1984), 'Review of J. Greenwood and D. Wilson *Public Administration in Britain*', in *Teaching Public Administration*, vol. 10, no. 2, pp. 67–9.
Crawford Report (1926), *Report of the Broadcasting Committee*, Cmd 2599 (London: HMSO).
Crossman, R. H. S. (1963), 'Introduction', in W. Bagehot, *The English Constitution* (London: Fontana).
Crossman, R. H. S. (1975), *The Diaries of a Cabinet Minister*, vol. 1 (London: Hamilton and Cape).

Curwen, P. J. (1986), *Public Enterprise: A Modern Approach* (Brighton: Wheatsheaf).

Daalder, H. (1975), 'Cabinet reform since 1914: Major Trends', in Herman and Alt, op. cit., pp. 242–76.

Davies, B. P. (1968), *Social Needs and Resources in Local Services* (London: Michael Joseph).

Davies, B. P. (1972), *Variations in Children's Services among British Urban Authorities* (London: Bell).

Davies, T. (1979), 'Employment policy in one London borough', in G. Craig *et al.* (eds), *Jobs and Community Action* (London: Routledge & Kegan Paul).

Davies, T. (1981), 'Implementing employment policies in a district authority', in S. Barrett and C. Fudge (eds), *Policy and Action* (London: Methuen), pp. 105–21.

Davies, P. (1988), 'Nationalized industries under Thatcher', *Politics*, vol. 8, no. 2, pp. 16–21.

De Smith, S. A. (1981), *Constitutional and Administrative Law* (Harmondsworth: Penguin).

Dearlove, J. (1973), *The Politics of Policy in Local Government* (Cambridge: Cambridge University Press).

Dearlove, J. (1979), *The Reorganisation of British Local Government* (Cambridge: Cambridge University Press).

Dearlove, J., and Saunders, P. (1984), *Introduction to British Politics* (Cambridge: Polity Press).

Delafons, J. (1982), 'Working in Whitehall: changes in public administration 1952–1982', *Public Administration*, vol. 60, no. 3, pp. 253–72.

Dell, E. (1980), 'Collective responsibility: fact, fiction or facade?' *Policy and Practice*, pp. 27–48 (London: RIPA).

Department of Environment *et al.* (1988), *The Conduct of Local Authority Business: the Government response to the Report of the Widdicombe Committee of Inquiry*, Cm. 433 (London: HMSO).

Department of Health and Social Security (1979), *Patients First* (London: HMSO).

Department of Trade (1981), *Consumers' Interests in the Nationalised Industries: A Consultative Document* (London: Department of Trade).

Department of Trade (1982), *The Nationalised Industry Consumer Councils: A Strategy for Reform* (London: Department of Trade).

Derbyshire, J. D., with Patterson, D. T. (1979), *An Introduction to Public Administration* (Maidenhead: McGraw Hill).

DHSS (1983), *Performance Indicators for the NHS* (London: DHSS).

DHSS (1985), *Performance Indicators for the NHS* (London: DHSS).

Doig, A. (1979), 'The machinery of government and the growth of governmental bodies', *Public Administration*, vol. 57 (Autumn), pp. 309–31.

Donoughmore Report (1932), *Report of the Committee on Ministers' Powers*, Cmd 4060 (London: HMSO).

Downey, Sir G. (1984), 'National Audit Office reports', *Public Money*, vol. 4, no. 3, pp. 10–11.

Downey, Sir G. (1986), 'Public accountability: fact or myth', *Public Money*, vol. 6, no. 1, pp. 35–9.

Downs, S. J. (1985), 'Structural changes: select committees: experiment and establishment', in Norton, op. cit., pp. 48–68.

Draper, P. (1977), *Creation of the DOE* (London: HMSO).
Drewry, G. (1983), 'Lord Haldane's Ministry of Justice – stillborn or strangled at birth?', *Public Administration*, vol. 61, no. 4, pp. 396–414.
Drewry, G. (1984), 'Review of J. Greenwood and D. Wilson *Public Administration in Britain*', in *Public Law*, Autumn, pp. 503–4.
Drewry, G. (ed.) (1985), *The New Select Committees: A Study of the 1979 Reforms* (Oxford: Clarendon Press).
Drewry, G. (1987), 'The Defence Committee on Westland', *Political Quarterly*, vol. 58, no. 3, pp. 82–7.
Drewry, G., and Butcher, T. (1988), *The Civil Service Today* (London: Blackwell).
Dugdale, W. (1982), 'The ten-month chairman', *Water Bulletin*, no. 37, 10 December, pp. 5–6.
Duke, V., and Edgell, S. (1981), 'Politics of the cuts', paper presented at PSA Urban Politics Group.
Dunleavy, P. (1980a), *Urban Political Analysis* (London: Macmillan).
Dunleavy, P. (1980b), 'Social and political theory and the issues in central–local relations', in G. W. Jones (ed.), *New Approaches to the Study of Central–Local Government Relationships* (Farnborough: Gower), pp. 116–36.
Dunleavy, P. (1982), 'Is there a radical approach to public administration?', *Public Administration*, vol. 60, no. 2, pp. 215–25.
Dunleavy, P., and Rhodes, R. A. W. (1987), 'The Conservatives and sub-central government', *Social Studies Review*, vol. 2, no. 5, pp. 19–26.
Dunleavy, P., and Rhodes, R. (1988), 'Government beyond Whitehall', in H. Drucker *et al.* (eds), *Developments in British Politics 2* (London: Macmillan), pp. 107–43.
Dunsire, A. (1956), 'Accountability in local government', *Administration*, vol. 4, pp. 80–8 (Dublin).
Dunsire, A. (1973), *Public Administration: The Word and the Science* (London: Martin Robertson).
Dunsire, A. (1978), *Control in a Bureaucracy* (Oxford: Martin Robertson).
Dunsire, A. (1982), 'Challenges to public administration in the 1980s', *Public Administration Bulletin*, no. 39 (August), pp. 8–21.

Eckstein, H. (1960), *Pressure Group Politics* (London: Allen & Unwin).
Efficiency and Effectiveness in the Civil Service, Government Observations on the Third Report from the Treasury and Civil Service Select Committee, HC 236 (1982), Cmnd 8616 (London: HMSO).
Efficiency in the Civil Service (1981), Cmnd 8293 (London: HMSO).
Efficiency Unit (1988), *Improving Management in Government: The Next Steps* (London: HMSO).
Elcock, H. (1985), 'Cutting chiefs as well as Indians: the Wardale review of the open structure', *Teaching Public Administration*, vol. 5, no. 1, pp. 11–20.
Elcock, H. (1986), *Local Government* (London: Methuen).
Energy Select Committee (1985a), *H. M. Treasury's Consultation Proposals for Legislation in Respect of the Nationalised Industries*, Sixth Report, 1984–5, HC 302 (London: HMSO).
Energy Select Committee (1985b), *Regulation of the Gas Industry: Memoranda* 1985–6, HC 15 i (London: HMSO).
Environment Select Committee (1985), *H. M. Treasury's Consultation Proposals*

for Legislation in Respect of the Nationalised Industries, First Special Report, 1984–5, HC 372 (London: HMSO).

Expenditure Committee (1977), *The Civil Service, Eleventh Report, and Volumes of Evidence, 1976–7*, vols. I–III, HC 535 (London: HMSO).

Feldman, D. (1988), 'Judicial review: a way of controlling government?', *Public Administration*, vol. 66, no. 1, pp. 21–34.

Financial and Economic Obligations of the Nationalised Industries (1961), Cmnd 1337 (London: HMSO).

Financial Management in Government Departments (1983), Cmnd 9058 (London: HMSO).

Financial Reporting to Parliament (1988), Cm 375 (London: HMSO).

Finer, S. E. (1956), 'The individual responsibility of ministers', *Public Administration*, vol. 36, no. 4, pp. 377–96.

Flegman, V. (1980), *Called to Account: The Public Accounts Committee of the House of Commons 1965–6/1977–8* (London: Gower).

Flegman, V. (1986), *Public Expenditure and the Select Committees of the House of Commons* (Aldershot: Gower).

Fletcher, P. J. (1967), 'Public administration', in H. V. Wiseman (ed.), *Political Science* (London: Routledge & Kegan Paul), pp. 51–77.

Flynn, N. (1986), 'Performance measurement in public sector services', *Policy and Politics*, vol. 14, no. 3, pp. 389–404.

Flynn, R., and Walsh, K. (1987), *Competitive Tendering* (University of Birmingham: INLOGOV).

Franks Report (1957), *Report of the Committee on Administrative Tribunals and Inquiries*, Cmnd 218 (London: HMSO).

Franks Report (1983), *Falkland Islands Review: Report of a Committee of Privy Counsellors*, Cmnd 8787 (London: HMSO).

Friend, J. K., Power, J. M., and Yewlett, C. J. L. (1974), *Public Planning: The Intercorporate Dimension* (London: Tavistock).

Fry, G. K. (1984), 'The development of the Thatcher government's "grand strategy" for the civil service: a public policy perspective', *Public Administration*, vol. 62, no. 3, pp. 322–35.

Fry, G. K. (1985), *The Changing Civil Service* (London: Allen & Unwin).

Fry, G. K. (1986a), 'Government and the civil service: a view of recent developments', *Parliamentary Affairs*, vol. 41, no. 2, pp. 267–83.

Fry, G. K. (1986b), 'The British civil service under challenge', *Political Studies*, vol. 24, pp. 533–55.

Fry, G. K. (1988a), 'The Thatcher government, the financial management initiative and the "new civil service"', *Public Administration*, vol. 66, no. 1, pp. 1–20.

Fry, G. K. (1988b), 'Inside Whitehall', in H. Drucker *et al.* (eds), *Developments in British Politics, 2*, revised edn (London: Macmillan), pp. 88–106.

Fulton Report (1968), *The Civil Service, Vol. I: Report of the Committee*, Cmnd 3638 (London: HMSO).

Ganz, G. (1987), *Quasi-Legislation* (London: Sweet & Maxwell).

Garner, M. R. (1979), 'The White Paper on nationalised industries: some criticisms', *Public Administration*, vol. 57 (Spring), pp. 7–20.

Garner, M. R. (1982), 'Auditing the efficiency of nationalised industries: enter the Monopolies and Mergers Commission', *Public Administration*, vol. 60, no. 4, pp. 409–28.

Garner, M. R. (1983), 'Nationalised industries and sponsoring departments', *Public Money*, vol. 3, no. 2, pp. 29–32.

Garrett, J. (1972), *The Management of Government* (Harmondsworth: Penguin).

Garrett, J. (1980), *Managing the Civil Service* (London: Heinemann).

Garrett, J. (1986), 'Developing state audit in Britain', *Public Administration*, vol. 64, no. 4, pp. 421–33.

Giddings, P. (1985), 'What has been achieved?', in Drewry, op. cit., pp. 367–81.

Goddard, J. (1988), 'Regional and local economic development', in P. Jackson and F. Terry (eds), *Public Domain* (London: Peat Marwick McLintock/Public Finance Foundation), pp. 150–8.

Goldsmith, M. (1986), *New Research in Central–Local Relations* (Aldershot: Gower).

Goldsmith, M., and Newton, K. (1986), 'Central–local government relations; a bibliographical summary', *Public Administration*, vol. 64, no. 1, pp. 102–8.

Goodin, R. E. (1982), 'Rational politicians and rational bureaucrats in Washingon and Whitehall', *Public Administration*, vol. 60, no. 1, pp. 23–41.

Gordon Walker, P. (1972), *The Cabinet* (London: Fontana).

Gorst, A. (1987), 'Suez 1956: a consumer's guide to papers at the Public Record Office', *Contemporary Record*, vol. 1, no. 1, pp. 9–11.

Government Observations on the Eleventh Report of the Expenditure Committee (1978), Cm 7117 (London: HMSO).

Government Purchasing: A Review of Government Contract and Procurement Procedures (1984) (London: HMSO).

The Government Response to the Fifth Report from the Environment Committee, 1985–86, Planning: Appeals, Call-in and Major Public Inquiries (1985/6), Cm 43 (London: HMSO).

Grant, M. (1986), 'The role of the courts in central–local relations' in M. Goldsmith (ed.), *New Research in Central–Local Relations* (Aldershot: Gower), pp. 191–206.

Gray, A. (1986), 'The background', in *Policy Management and Policy Assessment* (London: RIPA), pp. 11–19.

Gray, A., and Jenkins, W. I. (1982), 'Policy analysis in British central government: the experience of PAR', *Public Administration*, vol. 60, no. 4, pp. 429–50.

Gray, A., and Jenkins, W. I. (1984), 'Lasting reforms in civil service management?', *Political Quarterly*, vol. 55, no. 4, pp. 418–27.

Gray, A., and Jenkins, W. I. (1985), *Administrative Politics in British Government* (Brighton: Harvester Press).

Gray, A., and Jenkins, W. I. (1986), 'Accountable management in British government: some reflections on the financial management initiative', *Financial Accountability and Management*, vol. 2, no. 3, pp. 171–87.

Gray, A., and Jenkins, W. I. (1987), 'Public administration and government in 1986', *Parliamentary Affairs*, vol. 40, no. 3, pp. 299–318.

Gray, C. (1982), 'Regional water authorities', in Hogwood and Keating, op. cit., pp. 143–67.

Gray, C. (1984), 'Values and change in intergovernmental relations', *Public Administration Bulletin*, no. 44, pp. 2–18.

Gray, C. (1985), 'Analysing the regional state', *Public Administration Bulletin*, no. 49, pp. 45–64.

Green, D. G. (1981), *Power and Party in an English City* (London: Allen & Unwin).

Greenaway, J. R. (1987), 'The higher civil service at the crossroads: the impact of the Thatcher government', in L. Robins (ed.), *Political Institutions in Britain* (London: Longman/Politics Association), pp. 38–57.

Greenwood, J. R. (1988a), 'Mrs Thatcher's Whitehall revolution: public administration or public management?' *Teaching Politics*, vol. 17, no. 2, pp. 208–29.

Greenwood, J. R. (1988b), 'Understanding local government finance; a simple explanation of a complex subject', *Teaching Politics*, vol. 17, no. 1, pp. 94–110.

Greenwood, J. R. (1989) 'Facing up to the local ombudsmen: Are internal complaints procedures adequate?' *Local Government Studies*, vol. 15, no. 1.

Greenwood, J. R., and Wilson, D. J. (1982) 'Councillor/officer relationships: case material for simulation', *Teaching Politics*, vol. 11, no. 3, pp. 263–71.

Greenwood, J.R., and Wilson, D. J. (1986), 'The changing world of chief officers', *District Councils Review*, March, p. 15 and May, pp. 4–5.

Greenwood, J. R., and Wilson, D. J. (1987a), 'Training and the elected member', *Local Government Policy Making*, vol. 13, no. 4, pp. 19–22.

Greenwood, J. R., and Wilson, D. J. (1987b), 'More training is vital for elected members', *District Councils Review*, November, p. 7.

Greenwood, J. R., and Wilson, D. J. (1988), 'British public administration: the beginning of the end?', *Teaching Politics*, vol. 17, no. 3, pp. 346–51.

Greenwood, J. R., and Woodhead, N. (1988), 'Public administration in Britain: Acquiring knowledge through skills', *Teaching Public Administration*, vol. viii, no. 1, Spring, pp. 42–6.

Greenwood, R. (1982), 'The politics of central–local relations in England and Wales, 1974–81', *West European Politics*, vol. 5, no. 3, pp. 253–69.

Greenwood, R., Walsh, K., Hinings, C. R., and Ranson, S. (1980), *Patterns of Management in Local Government* (Oxford: Martin Robertson).

Gregory, R. (1977), 'Court Line, Mr. Benn and the ombudsman', *Parliamentary Affairs*, vol. 30, no. 3, pp. 269–92.

Gregory, R. (1982), 'The Select Committee on the Parliamentary Commissioner for Administration, 1967–1980', *Public Law*, no. 1 (Spring), pp. 49–88.

Gregory, R., and Hutchesson, P. G. (1975), *The Parliamentary Ombudsman* (London: Allen & Unwin).

Gretton, J., Harrison, A., and Beeton, D. (1987), 'How far have the frontiers of the state been rolled back between 1979 and 1987?', *Public Money*, vol. 7, no. 3, pp. 17–25.

Griffith, J. A. G. (1966), *Central Departments and Local Authorities* (London: Allen & Unwin).

Griffith, J. A. G. (1973), *Parliamentary Scrutiny of Government Bills* (London: Allen & Unwin).

Griffith, J. A. G. (1985), *The Policies of the Judiciary* (London: Fontana).

Griffiths Report (1983), *National Health Service Management Inquiry Report* (London: HMSO).

Griffiths Report (1988), *Community Care: Agenda for Action* (London: HMSO).

Griffiths, Sir R. (1988), 'Does the public service serve? The consumer dimension', *Public Administration*, vol. 66, no. 2, pp. 195–204.

Gwyn, W. B. (1982), 'The ombudsman in Britain: a qualified success in government reform', *Public Administration*, vol. 60, no. 2, pp. 177–95.
Gyford, J. (1976), *Local Politics in Britain* (London: Croom Helm).

HM Treasury (1984), *Nationalised Industries Legislation: Consultation Proposals* (London: HM Treasury).
HM Treasury (1985), *Multi-departmental Review of Budgeting, Phase I, Central Report* (London: HM Treasury).
HM Treasury (1986a), *Multi-departmental Review of Budgeting, Final Central Report* (London: HM Treasury).
HM Treasury (1986b), (ed. S. Lewis), *Output and Performance Measurement in Central Government Departments: Progress in Departments*, Treasury Working Paper No. 38 (London: HM Treasury).
HM Treasury (1987), *Output and Performance Measurement in Central Government Departments: Some Practical Achievements*, Treasury Working Paper No. 45 (London: HM Treasury).
Hague, D. C., Mackenzie, W. J. M., and Barker, A. (1975), *Public Policy and Private Interests* (London: Macmillan).
Haines, J. (1977), *The Politics of Power* (London: Cape).
Haldane Report (1918), *Report of the Machinery of Government Committee*, Cd 9230 (London: HMSO).
Hall, R., and Green, D. (1984), 'Ministers' Private Offices', *Teaching Politics*, vol. 13, no. 1, pp. 105–14.
Ham, C. (1987), *Health Policy in Britain* (London: Macmillan).
Hambleton, R. (1988), 'Consumerism, decentralisation and local democracy', *Public Administration*, vol. 66, no. 2, pp. 125–47.
Hampton, W. (1987), *Local Government and Urban Politics* (London: Longman).
Hanson, A. H. (1961), *Parliament and Public Ownership* (London: Cassells).
Hanson, A. H., and Walles, M. (1984), *Governing Britain* (London: Fontana).
Harlow, C., and Rawlings, R. (1984), *Law and Administration* (London: Weidenfeld & Nicolson).
Hawke, N. (1982), 'Administrative justice and the protection of individual rights', in Robins, op. cit., pp. 141–51.
Haynes, R. J. (1980), *Organisation Theory and Local Government* (London: Allen & Unwin).
Haywood, S. C., and Elcock, H. J. (1982), Regional health authorities: regional government or central agencies?', in Hogwood and Keating, op. cit., pp. 119–42.
Headey, B. (1974), *British Cabinet Ministers* (London: Allen & Unwin).
Headey, B. (1975), 'Cabinet ministers and senior civil servants: mutual requirements and expectations', in Herman and Alt, op. cit., pp. 121–39.
Heald, D. (1983), *Public Expenditure* (Oxford: Martin Robertson).
Heald, D. (1985), 'Will the privatisation of public enterprises solve the problem of control?', *Public Administration*, vol. 63, no. 1, pp. 7–22.
Heath, E., and Barker, A. (1978), 'Heath on Whitehall reform', *Parliamentary Affairs*, vol. 31, no. 4, pp. 363–90.
Heaton/Williams Report (1974), *Report on Civil Service Training* (London: CSD).
Heclo, H., and Wildavsky, A. (1981), *The Private Government of Public Money* (London: Macmillan).

Helm, D. (1987), 'RPI minus X and the newly privatised industries – a deceptively simple regulatory role', *Public Money*, vol. 7, no. 1, pp. 47–51.

Hennessy, P. (1985), 'The quality of Cabinet government in Britain', *Policy Studies*, vol. 6, pt 2, pp. 15–45.

Hennessy, P. (1986a), *Cabinet* (London: Blackwell).

Hennessy, P. (1986b), 'Michael Heseltine: Mottram's Law and the efficiency of Cabinet', *Political Quarterly*, vol. 57, no. 2, pp. 137–43.

Hennessy, P. (1986c), 'Helicopter crashes into Cabinet: Prime Minister and constitution hurt', *Journal of Law and Society*, vol. 13, no. 3, pp. 423–32.

Hennessy, P., Morrison, S., and Townsend, R. (1985), *Routine Punctuated by Orgies: The Central Policy Review Staff 1970–83*, Glasgow Strathclyde Paper on Government and Policy No. 31 (Glasgow: Dept of Politics, University of Strathclyde).

Henney, A. (1985), 'Three bags full: how the London Electricity Board fixed tariffs for 1984/85', *Public Money*, vol. 4, no. 4, pp. 39–42.

Herbert Report (1960), *Report of the Royal Commission on Local Government in Greater London*, Cmnd. 1164 (London: HMSO).

Herman, V., and Alt, J. E. (eds) (1975), *Cabinet Studies: A Reader* (London: Macmillan).

Heseltine, M. (1987), *Where there's a Will* (London: Hutchinson).

Hetherington, P., and Price, C. (1987), *What Price Private Water?* (London: Public Finance Foundation).

Hewart, Lord (1929), *The New Despotism* (London: Benn).

Hill, D. M. (1967), 'Leeds', in L. J. Sharpe (ed.), *Voting in Cities* (London: Macmillan), pp. 132–64.

Hill, D. M. (1983), 'Decisions, decisions . . .', *Parliamentary Affairs*, vol. 36, no .1, pp. 121–5.

Hogwood, B. W. (1982), 'Introduction', in Hogwood and Keating, op. cit., pp. 1–20.

Hogwood, B. W. (1987), *Recent Developments in British Regional Policy*, Strathclyde Paper on Government and Policy No. 51 (Glasgow: Dept of Politics, University of Strathclyde).

Hogwood, B. W., and Mackie, T. T. (1985), 'The United Kingdom: decision sifting in a secret garden', in T. T. Mackie and B. W. Hogwood (eds) (1985), *Unlocking the Cabinet: Cabinet Structure in Comparative Perspective* (London: Sage), pp. 36–60.

Hogwood, B. W., and Keating, M. (eds) (1982), *Regional Government in England* (Oxford: Clarendon).

Hogwood, B. W., and Lindley, P. D. (1982), 'Variations in regional boundaries', in Hogwood and Keating, op. cit., pp. 21–49.

Holland, P. (1979), *Quango, Quango, Quango* (London: Adam Smith Institute).

Holland, P. (1982), 'Shooting sitting quangos', *Daily Telegraph*, 11 March.

Holland, P., and Fallon, M. (1978), *The Quango Explosion* (London: Conservative Political Centre).

Hood, C. (1978), 'Keeping the centre small: explanations of agency type', *Political Studies*, vol. 26, no. 1, pp. 30–46.

Hood, C. (1979), 'The world of quasi-government', paper presented to PSA Annual Conference.

Hood, C. (1981), 'Axeperson spare that quango', in Hood and Wright, op. cit., pp. 100–22.

Hood, C. (1988), 'PGOs in the United Kingdom', in C. Hood and G. F. Schuppert (eds), *Delivering Public Services in Western Europe* (London: Sage), pp. 75–93.
Hood, C., and Dunsire, A. (1981), *Bureaumetrics* (Farmborough: Gower).
Hood, C., and Wright, M. (eds) (1981), *Big Government in Hard Times* (Oxford: Martin Robertson).
Hood, C., Dunsire, A., and Thompson, K. S. (1978), 'So you think you know what government departments are . . .', *Public Administration Bulletin*, no. 27, pp. 20–32.
Hoskyns, Sir J. (1983), 'Whitehall and Westminster: an outsider's view', *Parliamentary Affairs*, vol. 36, no. 2, pp. 137–47.
Houlihan, B. (1984), 'The regional offices of the DOE – policemen or mediators? A study of local housing policy', *Public Administration*, vol. 62, no. 4, pp. 401–21.
Howell, D. A. (1988), 'The future of local government under the Conservatives: the education service', *Local Government Policy Making*, vol. 14, no. 4, pp. 31–7.
Howells, D. (1981), 'Marks and Spencer and the civil service: a comparison of culture and methods', *Public Administration*, vol. 59, no. 3, pp. 337–52.
Hyman, H. (1988), *The Implications of Privatisation for Nationalised Industries* (London: Public Finance Foundation).

Isaac-Henry, K. (1984), 'Taking stock of the local authority associations', *Public Administration*, vol. 62, no. 2, pp. 129–46.
Isserlis, A. R. (1984), 'The CPRS and after', *Policy Studies*, vol. 4, no. 3, pp. 22–35.

James, S. (1986), 'The Central Policy Review Staff, 1970–1983', *Political Studies*, vol. 34, no. 3, pp. 423–40.
Jarrett Report (1985), *Report of the Steering Committee for Efficiency Studies in Universities* (London: Committee of Vice Chancellors and Principals).
Jenkins, S. (1985), 'The Star Chamber, PESC and the Cabinet', *Political Quarterly*, vol. 56, no. 2, pp. 113–21.
Jennings, R. E. (1982), 'The changing representational roles of local councillors in England', *Local Government Studies*, vol. 8, no. 5, pp. 67–86.
Johnson, N. (1971), 'The reorganizing action of central government', *Public Administration*, vol. 49, no. 1, pp. 3–6.
Johnson, N. (1977), *In Search of the Constitution* (Oxford: Pergamon).
Johnson, N. (1978), 'The public corporation: an ambiguous species', in D. E. Butler and A. H. Halsey (eds), *Policy and Politics* (London: Macmillan), pp. 122–39.
Johnson, N. (1979), 'Editorial: quangos and the structure of British government', *Public Administration*, vol. 57 (Winter), pp. 379–95.
Johnson, N. (1981), 'Select committees as tools of parliamentary reform: some further reflections', in Walkland and Ryle, op. cit., pp. 203–36.
Johnson, N. (1982), 'Accountability, control and complexity: moving beyond ministerial responsibility', in Barker, op. cit., pp. 206–18.
Johnson, N. (1984), 'An academic view' in D. Englefield (ed.), *Commons Select Committees: Catalysts for Progress* (London: Longman), pp. 60–5.
Johnson, N. (1985), 'Change in the civil service: retrospect and prospects', *Public Administration*, vol. 63, no. 4, pp. 415–34.

Jones, B. (1982), 'Select committees and the floor of the House: Du Cann vs. Kilroy-Silk', *Teaching Politics*, vol. 11, no. 3, pp. 312–20.
Jones, G. (1983), 'Prime Ministers' Departments really create problems: a rejoinder to Patrick Weller', *Public Administration*, vol. 61, no. 1, pp. 79–84.
Jones, G. W. (1965), 'The Prime Minister's powers', *Parliamentary Affairs*, vol. 18, no. 2, pp. 167–85.
Jones, G. W. (1969), *Borough Politics* (London: Macmillan).
Jones, G. W. (1973), 'The functions and organisation of councillors', *Public Administration*, vol. 51, pp. 135–46.
Jones, G. W. (1975), 'Development of the Cabinet', in Thornhill, op. cit., pp. 31–62.
Jones, G. W. (1976), 'The Prime Minister's secretaries', in J. A. G. Griffith (ed.), *From Policy to Administration* (London: Allen & Unwin).
Jones, G. W. (1980), *The Prime Minister's Aides*, University of Hull Occasional Papers in Politics No. 6 (Hull: University of Hull).
Jones, G. W. (1982a), 'Running those mysterious quangos to ground', *Local Government Chronicle*, no. 6013 (20 August).
Jones, G. W. (1982b), 'The regional threat', *Local Government Chronicle*, 9 July, p. 772.
Jones, G. W. (1985), 'The Prime Minister's aides: the prime minister's office under Margaret Thatcher 1979–84', in A. King (ed.), *The British Prime Minister* (London: Macmillan), pp. 72–95.
Jones, G. W., and Stewart, J. D. (1982), 'The Layfield analysis applied to central–local relations under the Conservative Government', *Local Government Studies*, vol. 8, no. 3, pp. 47–59.
Jordan, A. G., and Richardson, J. J. (1987a), *Government and Pressure Groups in Britain* (Oxford: Clarendon).
Jordan, A. G., and Richardson, J. J. (1987b), *British Politics and The Policy Process* (London: Allen & Unwin).
Jordan, G. (1976), 'Hiving-off and departmental agencies', *Public Administration Bulletin*, no. 22, pp. 35–51.
Jordan, G. (1978), 'Central co-ordination: Crossman and the Inner Cabinet', *Political Quarterly*, vol. 49, no. 2, pp. 171–80.
Justice (1971), *Administration Under Law* (London: Justice).
Justice (1980), *The Local Ombudsmen: A Review of the first five Years* (London: Justice).
Justice–All Souls (1988), *Administrative Justice: Some Necessary Reforms: Report of the Committee of the Justice – All Souls Review of Administrative Law in the United Kingdom* (Oxford: Clarendon).

Kavanagh, D. (1987a), 'Margaret Thatcher: a case of prime ministerial power?', in L. Robins (ed.), *Political Institutions in Britain* (London: Longman/Politics Associaton), pp. 9–18.
Kavanagh, D. (1987b), *Thatcherism and British Politics: The End of Consensus?* (Oxford: Oxford University Press).
Keating, M. (1985), 'Whatever happened to regional government?', *Local Government Studies*, vol. II, no. 6, pp. 111–22.
Kellner, P., and Crowther-Hunt, Lord (1980), *The Civil Servants: An Inquiry into Britain's Ruling Class* (London: MacDonald).
Kennon, A. (1988), 'Westminster and Westland', *Social Studies Review*, vol. 3, no. 3, pp. 88–91.

Kimber, R., and Richardson, J. J. (eds) (1974), *Campaigning for the Environment* (London: Routledge & Kegan Paul).
King, A. (1985), 'Margaret Thatcher: the style of a prime minister', in A. King (ed.), *The British Prime Minister* (London: Macmillan), pp. 96–140.
Kingdom, J. E. (1986a), 'Public administration: defining the discipline – Part 1', *Teaching Public Administration*, vol. IV, no. 1, pp. 1–13.
Kingdom, J. E. (1986b), 'Public administration: defining the discipline – Part II', *Teaching Public Administration*, vol. VI, no. 1, pp. 1–21.
Kingdom, J. E. (1987), 'Public administration: is it a useful discipline?', *Teaching Public Administration*, vol. VII, no. 2, pp. 1–9.
Knight, Sir A. (1982), 'The control of nationalised industries', *Political Quarterly*, vol. 53, no. 1, pp. 24–34.
Körner, E. (1982), *Report of the NHS/DHSS Steering Group on Health Service Information* (London: HMSO).

Laffin, M. (1986), *Professionalism and Policy* (Aldershot: Gower).
Laffin, M., and Young, K. (1985), 'The changing roles and responsibilities of local authority chief officers', *Public Administration*, vol. 63, no. 1, pp. 41–59.
Latham, M. (1986), 'A watchdog with teeth: the committee of public accounts', *Social Studies Review*, vol. 1, no. 4.
Layfield Report (1976), *Local Government Finance: Report of the Committee of Enquiry*, Cmnd 6453 (London: HMSO).
Lee, J. M. (1982), 'Epitaph for the CSD', *Public Administration*, vol. 60, no. 1, pp. 3–9.
Lee, J. M. (1984), 'Financial management and career service', *Public Administration*, vol. 62, no. 1, pp. 1–6.
Lee, M. (1981), 'Whitehall and retrenchment', in Hood and Wright, op. cit., pp. 35–55.
Levitt, M. (1986), 'Central government' in F. Terry and P. Jackson (eds), *Public Domain* (London: Peat Marwick), pp. 81–93.
Lewis, N., and Gateshill, B. (1978), *The Commission for Local Administration* (London: RIPA).
Lewis, N., Seneviratne, M., and Cracknell, S. (1986), *Complaints Procedures in Local Government*, 2 vols (Sheffield: Centre for Criminological and Socio-Legal Studies, University of Sheffield).
Liaison Committee (1982–3), *The Select Committee System*, First Report HC 92 (London: HMSO).
Liaison Committee (1984–5), *First Report, the Select Committee System*, HC 363 (London: HMSO).
Likierman, A. (1982), 'Management Information for Ministers: the MINIS in the Department of the Environment', *Public Administration*, vol. 60, no. 2, pp. 127–42.
Likierman, A. (1985), 'A framework for strategic management', *Developing the FMI Principles: Changes in Process and Culture* (London: RIPA/Peat Marwick), pp. 11–19.
Likierman, A. (1988), 'Parliament and public spending', *Public Money and Management*, vol. 8, no. 1, 2, pp. 61–3.
Littlechild, S. C. (1983), *Regulation of British Telecommunications' Profitability* (London: HMSO).

Local Government Finance (1977), Cmnd 6813 (London: HMSO).
Local Government in England: Government Plans for Reorganisation (1971), Cmnd 4854 (London: HMSO).
Local Government Reform in England (1970), Cmnd 4276 (London: HMSO).
Local Government Training Board (1987), *Getting Closer to the Public* (Luton: LGTB).
Lock, G. (1985), 'Resources and operation of select committees. A survey of statistics', in Drewry, op. cit., pp. 319–47.
Lowe, P., and Goyder, J. (1983), *Environmental Groups in Politics* (London: Allen & Unwin).

MacDonald, J., and Fry, G. K. (1980), 'Policy-planning units – ten years on', *Public Administration*, vol. 58, no. 4, pp. 421–37.
McGill, R. (1984), 'Evaluating organisational performance in public administration', *Public Administration Bulletin*, no. 46, pp. 15–38.
McIntosh Report (1976), *NEDO. A Study of UK Nationalised Industries* (London: HMSO).
Mackenzie, W. J. M., and Grove, J. W. (1957), *Central Administration in Britain* (London: Longman).
Mackintosh, J. P. (1977), *The British Cabinet* (London: Stevens).
Mackintosh, J. P. (1982), *The Government and Politics of Britain* (London: Hutchinson).
Mair, R. (1977), 'Civil service training and the Civil Service College', in Rhodes, op. cit., pp. 41–9.
Making Things Happen: A Report on the Implementation of Government Efficiency Scrutinies (1985) (London: HMSO).
Maud Report (1967), *Committee on the Management of Local Government*, vol. I: *Report* (London: HMSO).
Megaw Report (1982), *Report of an Inquiry into the Principles and the System by which the renumeration of the non-industrial Civil Service should be determined*, Cmnd 8590 (London: HMSO).
Metcalfe, L., and Richards, S. (1984), 'The impact of the efficiency strategy: political clout or cultural change?', *Public Administration*, vol. 62, no. 4, pp. 439–54.
Metcalfe, L., and Richards, S. (1987), *Improving Public Management* (London: Sage).
Michael, J. (1982), *The Politics of Secrecy* (Harmondsworth: Penguin).
Middlemas, R. K. (1979), *Politics in Industrial Society: The Experience of British Society since 1911* (London: Deutsch).
Miliband, R. (1973), *The State in Capitalist Society* (London: Quartet).
Million, G. (1983), 'Is water really a nationalised industry?', *Public Money*, vol. 3, no. 2, p. 12.
Ministerial Control of the Nationalised Industries (1969), Cmnd 4027 (London: HMSO).
Mitchell, D. (1982), 'Intervention, control and accountability: the National Enterprise Board', *Public Administration Bulletin*, vol. 38, pp. 40–65.
Monopolies and Mergers Commission (1981), *A Report on Water Services Supplied by the Severn Trent Water Authority and its Companies* (London: HMSO).
Moore, C., and Booth, S. (1987), 'Hunting the QUARC: an institution without a role', *Public Administration*, vol. 65, no. 4, pp. 455–66.

Moore, N. E. A. (1984), 'The Civil Service College: what it is and what it is not', *Management in Government*, vol. 39, no. 2, pp. 96–103.
Morris, C. (1988), 'Consumerism – lessons from community work', *Public Administration*, vol. 66, no. 2, pp. 205–13.
Morrison, H. (1933), *Socialisation and Transport* (London: HMSO).
Morrison, H. (1959), *Government and Parliament*, 2nd edn (Oxford: Oxford University Press).
Moseley, G. (1985), 'Managing a department', in *Developing the FMI Principles: Changes in Process and Culture* (London: RIPA), pp. 26–32.

National Audit Office (1986a), *The Rayner Scrutiny Programme 1979–83*, HC 322 (London: HMSO).
National Audit Office (1986b), *The Financial Management Initiative*, HC 588 (London: HMSO).
National Audit Office (1986c), *Report by the Comptroller and Auditor General; Efficiency of Nationalised Industries: References to the Monopolies and Mergers Commission*, HC 574 (London: HMSO).
National Consumer Council (1976), *Consumers and the Nationalised Industries* (London: HMSO).
National Consumer Council (1981), *Performance Indicators for the Nationalised Industries* (London: NCC).
National Consumer Council (1982), *Response to Consumers' Interests and the NIs* (London: NCC).
National Consumer Council (1987), *Performance Measurement and the Consumer* (London: NCC).
Nationalised Industries (1978), Cmnd 7131 (London: HMSO).
Nationalised Industries: A Review of Economic and Financial Objectives (1967), Cmnd 3437 (London: HMSO).
Neustadt, R. E. (1966), 'White House and Whitehall', *Public Interest*, vol. 2, pp. 55–69.
Newman, O. (1981), *The Challenge of Corporatism* (London: Macmillan).
Newton, K., and Karran, T. S. (1985), *The Politics of Local Expenditure* (London: Macmillan).
Newton, K. (1976), *Second City Politics* (Oxford: Clarendon).
Newton, K. (1979), 'The local political elite in England and Wales', in J. Lagroye and V. Wright (eds), *Local Government in Britain and France* (London: Allen & Unwin), pp. 105–13.
Newton, K., and Karran, T. J. (1985). *The Politics of Local Expenditure* (London: Macmillan).
Nigro, F. A., and Nigro, L. G. (1973), *Modern Public Administration* (New York: Harper & Row).
Non-Departmental Public Bodies: A Guide for Departments (1981) (London: HMSO).
Norton, P. (1979), 'The organisation of parliamentary parties', in S. A. Walkland (ed.), *The House of Commons in the Twentieth Century* (London: Oxford University Press), pp. 7–68.
Norton, P. (1981), *The Commons in Perspective* (Oxford: Martin Robertson).
Norton, P. (1982), *The Constitution in Flux* (Oxford: Martin Robertson).
Norton, P. (1983), 'Party committees in the House of Commons', *Parliamentary Affairs*, vol. 36, no. 1, pp. 7–27.

Norton, P. (ed.) (1985), *Parliament in the 1980s* (Oxford: Blackwell).
Norton, P. (1987), 'Independence, scrutiny and rationalisation: a decade of changes in the House of Commons', in L. Robins (ed.), *Political Institutions in Britain: Development and Change* (London: Longman), pp. 58–86.

OFTEL (1985) *Determination of Terms and Conditions for the Purpose of an Agreement on the Interconnection of the BT Telephone System and the Mercury Communications System under Condition 13 of the Licence Granted to BT under Section 7 of the Telecommunications Act (1954).*
Oliver, D., and Austin, R. (1987), 'Political and constitutional aspects of the Westland Affair', *Parliamentary Affairs*, vol. 40, no. 1, pp. 20–40.
Oliver, I. (1987), *Police, Government and Accountability* (London: Macmillan).
Omand, D. (1983), 'MINIS in MOD', *Management in Government*, vol. 38, no. 4, pp. 261–73.
Outer Circle Policy Unit (1979a), *What's Wrong with Quangos?* (London: OCPU).
Outer Circle Policy Unit (1979b), *The Big Public Inquiry* (London: OCPU).

Page, B. (1979), 'Labour's culture of illusions', *New Statesman*, 29 September, pp. 446–8.
Pahl, R., and Winkler, J. (1974), 'The coming corporatism', *New Society*, 10 October, pp. 72–6.
Painter, M. J. (1980), 'Policy co-ordination in the Department of the Environment, 1970–1976', *Public Administration*, vol. 58, no. 2, pp. 135–54.
Parkinson, M. (1985), *Liverpool on the Brink* (Hermitage: Policy Journals).
Parkinson, M., and Duffy, J. (1984), 'Governments' response to inner city riots: the Minister for Merseyside and the Task Force', *Parliamentary Affairs*, vol. 37, no. 1, pp. 76–96.
Parris, H. (1969), *Constitutional Bureaucracy* (London: Allen & Unwin).
Paterson Report (1973), *The New Scottish Local Authorities: Organisation and Management Structures* (London: HMSO).
Paying for Local Government (1986), Cmnd 9714 (London: HMSO).
Peat Marwick (1986), *Current Issues in Public Sector Management* (London: Peat Marwick).
Peden, G. C. (1983), 'The Treasury as the central department of government 1919–1939', *Public Administration*, vol. 61, no. 4, pp. 371–85.
Peele, G. (1983), 'Government at the centre', in H. Drucker, P. Dunleavy, A. Gamble and G. Peele (eds), *Developments in British Politics* (London: Macmillan), pp. 83–105.
Pitt, D., and Smith, B. (1981), *Government Departments* (London: Routledge & Kegan Paul).
Pitt, D. C., and Smith, B. (1984), *The Computer Revolution in Public Administration* (Brighton: Harvester Press).
Pliatzky Report (1980), *Report on Non-Departmental Public Bodies*, Cmnd 7797 (London: HMSO).
Pliatzky, L. (1982), *Getting and Spending: Public Expenditure Employment and Inflation* (Oxford: Blackwell).
Pliatzky, Sir L. (1984), 'Mandarins, ministers and the management of Britain', *Political Quarterly*, vol. 66, no. 1, pp. 23–8.
Pliatzky, Sir L. (1985), *Paying and Choosing* (Oxford: Blackwell).

Plowden Committee (1961), *The Control of Public Expenditure*, Cmnd 1432 (London: HMSO).

Plowden, W. (1981), 'The British Central Policy Review Staff', in P. R. Baehr, and B. Wittrock (eds), *Policy Analysis and Policy Innovation: Patterns, Problems and Potentials* (London and Beverly Hills: Sage), pp. 61–91.

Plowden, W. (1985), 'What prospects for the civil service?', *Public Administration*, vol. 63, no. 4, pp. 393–414.

Pollitt, C. (1974), 'The Central Policy Review Staff, 1970–1974', *Public Administration*, vol. 52 (Winter), pp. 375–92.

Pollitt, C. (1980), 'Rationalising the machinery of government: the Conservatives 1970–1974', *Political Studies*, vol. 28, no. 1, pp. 84–98.

Pollitt, C. (1982), 'The CSD: a normal death?', *Public Administration*, vol. 60, no. 1, pp. 73–6.

Pollitt, C. (1984), *Manipulating the Machine* (London: Allen & Unwin).

Pollitt, C. (1985), 'Measuring performance: a new System for the National Health Service', *Policy and Politics*, vol. 13, no. 1, pp. 1–15.

Pollitt, C. (1986a), 'Beyond the managerial model: the case for broadening performance assessment in government and the public services', *Financial Accountability and Management*, vol. 12, no. 3, pp. 115–70.

Pollitt, C. (1986b), 'Performance measurement in the public services: some political implications', *Parliamentary Affairs*, vol. 39, no. 3, pp. 315–29.

Pollitt, C. (1987), 'The politics of performance assessment: lessons for higher education?', *Studies in Higher Education*, vol. 12, no. 1, pp. 87–98.

Pollitt, C. (1988a), 'Bringing consumers into performance measurement: concepts, consequences and constraints', *Policy and Politics*, vol. 16, no. 2, pp. 1–11.

Pollitt, C. (1988b), 'Consumerism and beyond', *Public Administration*, vol. 66, no. 2, pp. 121–4.

Poole, K. P. (1978), *The Local Government Service* (London: Allen & Unwin).

Potter, T. (1988), 'Consumerism and the public sector: how well does the coat fit?', *Public Administration*, vol. 66, no. 2, pp. 149–64.

Powell, E. (1982), 'Parliament and the question of reform', *Teaching Politics*, vol. 11, no. 2, pp. 167–76.

Price, C. (1986), 'Privatising British Gas: is the regulatory framework adequate?', *Public Money*, vol. 6, no. 1, pp. 13–19.

Prince, M. J. (1983), *Policy Planning Units and Organisational Survival* (Aldershot: Gower).

Privatisation of the Water Authorities in England and Wales (1986), Cm 9734 (London: HMSO).

Progress in Financial Management in Government Departments (1984) Cmnd. 9297 (London: HMSO).

Promoting Better Health: The Government's Programme for Improving Primary Health Care (1987), Cm 249 (London: HMSO).

Public Accounts Committee (1985–6), 'Thirty-ninth Report', *The Rayner Scrutiny Programme 1979 to 1983*, HC 365 (London: HMSO).

Public Accounts Committee (1986–7a), 'Fifteenth Report', *Sponsorship of Non-Departmental Public Bodies: Department of the Environment: Welsh Office*, HC 38 (London: HMSO).

Public Accounts Committee (1986–7b), 'Fourth Report', *Efficiency of Nationalised Industries: References to the Monopolies and Mergers Commission*, HC 26 (London: HMSO).

Public Accounts Committee (1986–7c), 'Thirteenth Report', *The Financial Management Initiative*, HC 61 (London: HMSO).
Pugh, Sir I. (1978), 'The ombudsman – jurisdiction, powers and practice', *Public Administration*, vol. 56, no. 2, pp. 127–38.
Punnett, R. M. (1980), *British Government and Politics* (London: Heinemann).
Pyper, R. (1983), 'The F. O. resignations: individual minsterial responsibility revived?', *Teaching Politics*, vol. 12, no. 2, pp. 200–10.
Pyper, R. (1987), 'The Westland affair', *Teaching Politics*, vol. 16, no. 3, pp. 346–63.

Rates: Proposals for Rate Limitation and Reform of the Rating System, White Paper (1983), Cmnd 9008 (London: HMSO).
Rayner, Sir D. (1982), *The Scrutiny Programme – a note of guidance* (revised) (London: Management and Personnel Office).
Redwood, J., and Hatch, J. (1982), *Controlling Public Industries* (Oxford: Blackwell).
Regan, D. E. (1977), *Local Government and Education* (London: Allen & Unwin).
Regan, D. E. (1983), 'Central–local relationships in Britain: applying the power-dependence model', *Teaching Politics*, vol. 12, no. 1, pp. 44–53.
Reorganisation of Central Government, White Paper (1970), Cmnd 4506 (London: HMSO).
Rhodes, R. A. W. (1979), 'Research into central–local relations in Britain: a framework for analysis', unpublished paper, Department of Government, University of Essex.
Rhodes, R. A. W. (1981), *Control and Power in Central–Local Government Relations* (Farnborough: Gower).
Rhodes, R. A. W. (1984), 'Continuity and change in British central–local relations: the "Conservative threat", 1979–83', *British Journal of Political Science*, vol. 14, pp. 261–83.
Rhodes, R. A. W. (1988), *Beyond Westminster and Whitehall* (London: Unwin Hyman).
Rhodes, R. A. W. (ed.) (1977), *Training in the Civil Service* (London: Joint University Council for Public and Social Administration).
Rhodes, R. A. W., Hardy, B., and Pudney, K. (1981), 'Public interest groups in central–local relations in England and Wales', *Public Administration Bulletin*, no. 36, pp. 17–36.
Richards, S. (1987), 'The Financial Management Initiative', in A. Harrison and J. Gretton (eds), *Reshaping Central Government* (Policy Journals).
Richardson, J. J., and Jordan, A. G. (1979), *Governing Under Pressure* (Oxford: Martin Robertson).
Riddell, P. (1982), 'Select committees two years on', *Financial Times*, 16 February.
Ridley, F. F. (ed.) (1979), *Government and Administration in Western Europe* (Oxford: Martin Robertson).
Ridley, F. F. (1984), 'The citizen against authority in Britain', *Parliamentary Affairs*, vol. 37, no. 1, pp. 3–32.
Ridley, F. F. (1985), 'Political neutrality and the British civil service', *Politics, Ethics and Public Service* (London: RIPA), pp. 32–42.
Ridley, F. F. (1986), 'Political neutrality in the civil service', *Social Studies Review*, vol .1, no. 4, pp. 23–8.

Ridley, F. F. (1987), 'What are the duties and responsibilities of civil servants?', in Symposium on Ministerial Responsibility, *Public Administration*, vol. 65, no. 1, pp. 79–87.
Robins, L. (ed.) (1982), *Topics in British Politics* (London: Politics Association).
Robinson Report (1977), *Remuneration of Councillors* vol. 1: *Report*, Cmnd 7010; vol. 2: *The Surveys of Councillors and Local Authorities* (London: HMSO).
Robinson, A. (1981), 'The House of Commons and public expenditure', in Walkland and Ryle, op. cit., pp. 154–74.
Robinson, A. (1985), 'The FMI and Parliament', in *Developing the FMI Principles: Changes in Process and Culture* (London: RIPA/Peat Marwick), pp. 39–45.
Robinson, A. (1987), 'What are the implications of devolved budgeting for ministerial responsibility?', *Public Administration*, vol. 65, no. 1, pp. 62–8.
Robinson, A. *et al.* (1987), 'Symposium on ministerial responsibility', *Public Administration*, vol. 65, no. 1, pp. 61–91.
Robson, W. A. (1960), *Nationalised Industry and Public Ownership* (London: Allen & Unwin).
Robson, W. A. (1966), *Local Government in Crisis* London: Allen & Unwin).
Robson, W. A. (1969), 'Ministerial control of nationalised industries', *Political Quarterly*, vol. 39, no. 1, pp. 103–12.
Role of the Comptroller and Auditor General (1980), Cmnd 7845 (London: HMSO).
Rose, R. (1980) contributions in R. Rose and E. Suleiman (eds), *Presidents and Prime Ministers* (Washington DC: American Enterprise for Public Policy Research).
Rose, R., and Suleiman, E. (1980), *Presidents and Prime Ministers* (Washington, D.C.: American Enterprise for Public Policy Research).
Rose, R. (1987), *Ministers and Ministries: A Functional Analysis* (Oxford: Clarendon).
Royal Commission on the National Health Service (1979), *Report*, Cmnd 7615 (London: HMSO).
Rush, M. (1981), *Parliamentary Government in Britain* (London: Pitman).
Rush, M. (1984), *The Cabinet and Policy Formulation* (London: Longman).
Ryle, M. (1981), 'The Commons today – a general survey', in Walkland and Ryle, op. cit., pp. 11–38.

Saunders, P. (1980), *Urban Politics* (Harmondsworth: Penguin).
Saunders, P. (1981), 'The crisis of central–local relations in Britain', unpublished paper given to the Issues in Contemporary Planning Seminar, University of Melbourne.
Saunders, P. (1982), 'Why study central–local relations?', *Local Government Studies*, vol. 8, no. 2, pp. 55–66.
Saunders, P. (1983), *The Regional State. A Review of the Literature and Agenda for research*, Urban and Regional Studies Working Paper No. 35 (Brighton: University of Sussex).
Saunders, P. (1984), *We Can't Afford Democracy Too Much: Findings from a Study of Regional State Institutions in South East England*, Urban and Regional Studies Working Paper No. 43 (Brighton: University of Sussex).

Sayers, M. (1986), 'The Council on Tribunals', *Social Policy and Administration*, vol. 20, no. 1, pp. 39–46.
Schmitter, P. (1979), 'Still the century of corporatism?', in P. Schmitter and G. Lehmbruch (eds), *Trends Towards Corporatist Intermediation* (London: Sage), pp. 7–52.
Sedgemore, B. (1980), *The Secret Constitution* (London: Hodder & Stoughton).
Seebohm Report (1968), *Report of the Committee on Local Authority and Allied Personal Social Services*, Cmnd 3703 (London: HMSO).
Select Committee on Defence (1985–6), *Fourth Report, Westland plc: the Government's Decision Making*, HC 519.
Select Committee on the Environment (1985–6), *Fifth Report, Planning: Appeals, Call-in and Major Public Inquiries*, HC 181–I (London: HMSO).
Select Committee on the Parliamentary Commissioner for Administration (1979–80), *Second Report, The System of Ombudsmen in the United Kingdom*, HC 254.
Select Committee on Nationalised Industries (SCNI) (1967–8), *Ministerial Control of the Nationalised Industries*, First Report, HC 371 (3 vols).
Self, P. (1964), 'Regional planning in Britain', *Urban Studies*, vol. 1, pp. 55–70.
Seneviratne, M., and Cracknell, S. (1988), 'Consumer complaints in public sector services', *Public Administration*, vol. 66, no. 2, pp. 181–93.
Seymour-Ure, C. (1974), *The Political Impact of Mass Media* (London: Constable).
Seymour-Ure, C. (1984), 'British War Cabinets in limited wars: Korea, Suez and the Falklands', *Public Administration*, vol. 62, no. 2, pp. 181–200.
Sharpe, L. J. (1970), 'Theories and values of local government', *Political Studies*, vol. 18, no. 2, pp. 153–74.
Sharpe, L. J. (ed.) (1981), *The Local Fiscal Crisis in Western Europe, Myths and Realities* (London: Sage).
Shell, D. R. (1981), 'The British constitution in 1980', *Parliamentary Affairs*, vol. XXXIV, no. 2, pp. 149–64.
Shell, D. R. (1982), 'The British constitution in 1981', *Parliamentary Affairs*, vol. XXXV, no. 2, pp. 118–35.
Shell, D. (1987), 'The British constitution in 1986', *Parliamentary Affairs*, vol. 40, no. 3, pp. 279–98.
Shell, D. (1988), *The House of Lords* (Oxford: Philip Allen).
Silk, P., with Walters, R. (1987), *How Parliament Works* (London: Longman).
Simon, H. A., Smithburg, D. W., and Thompson, V. A. (1971), *Public Administration* (New York: Knopf).
Skelcher, C. (1983), 'Towards salaried councillors? – the special responsibility allowances', *Local Government Studies*, vol. 9, no. 3, pp. 10–15.
Smith, B. (1985), *Decentralisation: The Territorial Dimension of the State* (London: Allen & Unwin).
Smith, B. L. (1969), 'The justification of local government', in L. D. Feldman and M. D. Goldrick (eds), *Politics and Government of Urban Canada: Selected Readings* (Toronto: Methuen), pp. 332–47.
Smith, B. L. (1976), *Policy Making in British Government* (London: Martin Robertson).
Smith, B. L. (1977), 'The development of central training in the civil service', in Rhodes, op. cit., pp. 30–40.

Smith, J. G. (1985), 'Nationalised industries: Damocles' sword', *Public Money*, vol. 4, no. 4, pp. 8–9.

Stacey, F. (1978), *Ombudsmen Compared* (Oxford: Oxford University Press).

Stanyer, J. (1976), *Understanding Local Government* (London: Fontana).

Stanyer, J., and Smith, B. (1976), *Administering Britain* (London: Fontana/Collins).

Steel, D. (1984a), 'Government and the new hybrids: a trail of unanswered questions', *Fiscal Studies*, vol. 5, no. 1, pp. 87–97.

Steel, D. (1984b), 'Government and the new hybrids', in D. Steel and D. Heald, *Privatising Public Enterprises* (London: RIPA), pp. 101–12.

Steel, D. R. (1978), 'Nationalisation and public ownership', in C. Cook and J. Ramsden (eds), *Trends in British Politics since 1945* (London: Macmillan), pp. 109–31.

Steel, D. R. (1979), 'Britain' in Ridley, op. cit., pp. 18–66.

Steel, D. R., and Heald, D. A. (1982), 'Privatising public enterprise: an analysis of the government's case', *Political Quarterly*, vol. 53, no. 3, pp. 333–49.

Stephenson, H. (1980), *Mrs Thatcher's First Year* (London: Jill Norman).

Stevens, A. (1978), 'The role of the Ecole Nationale d'Administration', *Public Administration*, vol. 56, no. 3, pp. 283–97.

Stewart, J. D. (1974), 'The politics of local government reorganisation', in K. Jones (ed.), *The Year Book of Social Policy 1973* (London: Routledge).

Stoker, G. (1988), *The Politics of Local Government* (London: Macmillan).

Stoker, G., and Wilson, D. J. (1986), 'Intra-organisational politics in local authorities: towards a new approach', *Public Administration*, vol. 64, no. 3, pp. 285–302.

Strauss, A., Schatzman, L., Ehrlich, D., Bucher, R., and Sabshin, M. (1971), 'The hospital and its negotiated order', reprinted in F. G. Castles, D. J. Murray and D. C. Potter, *Decisions, Organisations and Society* (Harmondsworth: Penguin, in association with Open University Press), pp. 103–23.

Sunkin, N. (1987), 'What is happening to applications for judicial review?', *Modern Law Review*, vol. 50, no .4, pp. 432–67.

Taylor, I. (1980), 'Ideology and policy', in C. Cook and I. Taylor (eds), *The Labour Party* (London: Longman), pp. 1–31.

Theakston, K. (1987), *Junior Ministers in British Government* (Oxford: Blackwell).

Thompson, J. W. (1984), 'Fast stream training at the Civil Service College', *Management in Government*, vol. 39, no. 1, pp. 48–54.

Thornhill (1975), *The Modernisation of British Government* (London: Pitman).

Thorpe-Tracey, S. F. (1987), 'The Financial Management Initiative in practice: Newcastle Central Office', *Public Administration*, vol. 65, no. 3, pp. 331–7.

Tivey, L. (1973a), *Nationalisation in British Industry* (London: Cape).

Tivey, L. (1973b), *The Nationalised Industries Since 1960* (London: Allen & Unwin).

Tivey, L. (1982a), 'Nationalised industries as organised interests', *Public Administration*, vol. 60, no. 1, pp. 42–55.

Tivey, L. (1982b), 'Quasi-government for consumers', in Barker, op. cit., pp. 137–51.

Topham, N. (1983), 'Is water really a nationalised industry?', *Public Money*, vol. 3, no. 1, pp. 12–13.

Trade and Industry Select Committee (1985), Third Special Report, Session 1984–85, *H. M. Treasury's Consultation Proposals for Legislation in Respect of the Nationalised Industries*, HC 334 (London: HMSO).

Transport Select Committee (1985), Third Report, Session 1984–85, *H. M. Treasury's Consultation Proposals for Legislation in Respect of the Nationalised Industries*, HC 354 (London: HMSO).

Travers, T. (1986), *The Politics of Local Government Finance* (London: Allen & Unwin).

Treasury and Civil Service Committee Report (1980), *The Future of the Civil Service Department*, First Report, 1980–81, HC 54 (London: HMSO).

Treasury and Civil Service Select Committee (1982), 'Third Report', *Efficiency and Effectiveness in the Civil Service*, HC 236–I, II, III (London: HMSO).

Treasury and Civil Service Select Committee (1986), *Seventh Report, 1985–86, Civil Servants and Ministers: Duties and Responsibilities*, HC 92 (London: HMSO).

Treasury and Civil Service Select Committee (1988), 'Eighth Report', Session 1987–88, *Civil Service Management Reform: The Next Steps, Minutes of Evidence and Appendices*, vol. II, HC 494–II (London: HMSO).

Tyson, S. (1987), 'Personnel management', in J. Harrison and J. Gretton (eds), *Reshaping Central Government* (Oxford: Policy Journals), pp. 57–76.

Veljanovski, C. (1988), *Selling the State: Privatisation in Britain* (London: Weidenfeld & Nicolson).

Wade, H. W. R. (1982), *Administrative Law* (Oxford: Oxford University Press).

Waldo, D. (1955), *The Study of Public Administration* (Garden City: Doubleday).

Walker, S. D. (1982), 'Managing a government department', *Management in Government*, vol. 37, no. 4, pp. 251–9.

Walkland, S. A., and Ryle, M. (eds) (1981), *The Commons Today* (London: Fontana).

Walkland, S. A. (1968), *The Legislative Process in Great Britain* (London: Allen & Unwin).

Walsh, K. (1988), 'Tendering and trading: the organisational implications of competition', *Local Government Policy Making*, vol. 14, no. 4, pp. 24–30.

Wardale Report (1981), *Chain of Command Review: The Open Structure* (London: Civil Service Department).

Wass, Sir D. (1983), 'The public service in modern society', *Public Administration*, vol. 61, no. 1, pp. 8–20.

Wass, Sir D. (1984), *Government and the Governed* (London: Routledge).

Webb, M. (1984), 'Privatisation of the electricity and gas industries', in D. Steel and D. Heald, *Privatising Public Enterprises* (London: RIPA), pp. 87–100.

Weller, P. (1983), 'Do prime ministers' departments really create problems?', *Public Administration*, vol. 61, no. 1, pp. 59–78.

Weller, P. (1985), *First Among Equals: Prime Ministers in Westminster Systems* (London: Allen & Unwin).

Wheatley Report (1969), *Report of the Royal Commission on Local Government in Scotland*, Cmnd 4150 (London: HMSO).
Whitbread, M. (1987), 'Department of the Environment', in A. Harrison and J. Gretton (eds), *Reshaping Central Government* (Oxford: Policy Journals).
Whyatt Report (1961), *The Citizen and the Administration* (London: Justice).
Widdicombe Report (1977), *Our Fettered Ombudsmen* (London: Justice).
Widdicombe Report (1986), *The Conduct of Local Authority Business: Report of the Committee of Inquiry into the Conduct of Local Authority Business* (London: HMSO), Cmnd. 9797.
Willetts, D. (1987), 'The role of the Prime Minister's Policy Unit', *Public Administration*, vol. 65, no. 4, pp. 443–54.
Williams Report (1987), *Top Jobs in Whitehall: Appointments and Promotions in the Senior Civil Service* (London: RIPA).
Williams, D. G. T. (1982), 'The Donoughmore Report in retrospect', *Public Administration*, vol. 60, no. 3, pp. 273–92.
Williams, M. (1972), *Inside Number 10* (London: Weidenfeld & Nicolson).
Williams, S. (1980), 'The decision makers', *Policy and Practice: The Experience of Government* (London: RIPA), pp. 79–102.
Wilson, D. J. (1988), 'Inside local authorities: sources of policy making', *Social Studies Review*, vol. 3, no. 4 (March), pp. 135–9.
Wilson, D. J., and Woodhead, N. (1982), 'Public administration', *Teaching Politics*, vol. 11, no. 2, pp. 210–20.
Wilson, Sir H. (1977), *The Governance of Britain* (London: Sphere).
Wilson, T. (1986), 'Paying for local government', *Policy Studies*, vol. 7, part 2, pp. 45–68.
Wiltshire, K. (1987), *Privatisation: The British Experience – An Australian Perspective* (Melbourne: Longman Cheshire).
Wiseman, H. V. (1963), 'The working of local government in Leeds', *Public Administration*, vol. 41, pp. 51–69 and 137–55.
Wistow, G. (1982), 'Collaboration between health and local authorities: why is it necessary?', *Social Policy and Administration*, vol. 16, no. 1, pp. 44–62.
Wood, G. (1981), 'Examining statistics on the higher civil service', *Public Administration*, vol. 59, no. 3, pp. 473–80.
Woodward, S. N. (1986), 'Performance indicators in nationalised industries', *Public Administration*, vol. 64, no. 3, pp. 303–17.
Wraith, R. E., and Lamb, G. B. (1971), *Public Inquiries as Instruments of Government* (London: Allen & Unwin).
Wright, B. M. (1984), 'Auditing the efficiency of nationalised industries: exit the Comptroller and Auditor General', *Public Administration*, vol. 62, no. 1, pp. 95–100.
Wright, M. (1977), 'Public expenditure in Britain: the crisis of control', *Public Administration*, vol. 55 (Summer), pp. 143–70.
Wright, M. (1980), 'From planning to control: PESC in the 1970s', in M. Wright (ed.), *Public Spending Decisions – Growth and Restraint in the 1970s* (London: Allen & Unwin).
Wright, M. (ed.) (1980), *Public Spending Decisions* (London: Allen & Unwin).

Yardley, D. C. M. (1986), *Principles of Administrative Law* (London: Butterworth).

Young, H., and Sloman, A. (1982), *No, Minister* (London: BBC Publications).
Young, S. (1982), 'Regional offices of the Department of the Environment: their roles and influence in the 1970s', in Hogwood and Keating, op. cit., pp. 75–95.
Young, S. (1986), 'The nature of privatisation in Britain 1979–85', *West European Politics*, vol. 9, no. 2, pp. 235–52.
Young, S., with Lowe, A. V. (1976), *Intervention in the Mixed Economy* (London: Croom Helm).

INDEX

References in *italics* are to figures. References in **bold** denote chapters that are wholly concerned with the subjects to which they refer.

ACC *see* Association of County Councils
accountability, public 9, 14, 16, 25, 32, 84, 153, 156, 177, 242, 246, 299
  central government 46, 55, 139–41
  local 148–9, 160, 162, 205, 258, 260
  NHS 264–5, 268–70
  parliamentary **273–98**
  privatized industries 251–2
  public corporations 222, 226–7, 229–30, 238–40, 243–4, 248
  quangos 209–10, 214–17, 220–1
  water industry 258–60
accountable units 10–11, 19, 29–30, 120–1, 127, 139
ad hoc authorities 29, 149, 151, 172
ad hoc committees 54, 71–3
ad hoc ministerial meetings 72, 74, 77, 79
ADC *see* Association of District Councils
administration group of civil service 111–13, *6.1*
Administration Trainee (AT) 115, 117–19
administrative class of civil service 103–5, 111–12, 114–15, 117, *6.1*
administrative counties *8.1*
administrative expenditure 132–3, 135
administrative law 299–300
Administrative Review Commission 323–4
advisory committees/councils 8, 33–4, 66, 211, 220
Advisory, Conciliation and Arbitration Service (ACAS) 29
agency
  clientele-based 36–7
  departmental 19, 22, 28–30, 32
  executive 30–3, 113–14, 220, 289, 304
  non-departmental/autonomous 22, 29, 30–3, 142, 212
  semi-autonomous 21–2, 30–1, 131, 141
agency agreements, local authority 153
agency model of central-local government relationships 185–7, 205–6, 208
Agriculture, Ministry of 41, 55, 210, 287
Agriculture Committee 72, Table 14.1
Agriculture, Fisheries and Food, Ministry of 35, Tables 2.1, 14.1
Alternatives to Domestic Rates (Green Paper 1981) 161
AMA *see* Association of Metropolitan Authorities
anonymity of civil servants 87, 175, 289, 297
appeals' procedures 192–3, 301–6, 308, 310
appelate tribunals 307–8, 310
Apple and Pear Development Council 7, 209
area health authorities (AHAs) 261–3, 265–8, *13.1*
armed forces 6, 110, Table 1.1
Armstrong, Sir Robert 88, 110, 297
Armstrong, Sir William 87, 96
art galleries 151, *8.4*
Arts Council 149, 209
arts graduates in civil service 105, 118–19
asset sales 225, 245–6, 249, Table 12.2
Assheton Report (1944) 104
Assistant Secretary 27, *6.1*
Associated British Ports 29, 249, Table 12.2
Association of County Councils (ACC) 154, 195
Association of District Councils (ADC) 154, 195
Association of Metropolitan Authorities (AMA) 154, 195
atom bomb 71, 74
Atomic Energy Authority 209
attendance allowances 172, 179–80
Attlee, PM Clement/Attlee government 71–2, 74, 96, 224, 230
audit, central 282
Audit Commission 151–2
auditors, district 193
Autumn Statement 281

Bains Report (1972) 168–9, 176
Balogh, Thomas 97
BBC *see* British Broadcasting Corporation
Benn, Tony 85, 96–7, 284
Berrill, Sir Kenneth 58
block grant 162–3, 199–200, 203, 205

borrowing 164–5, 201, 223–4, 239
Bowe, Colette 291
Bridges, Edward 95–6
British Aerospace 248–9, Table 12.2
British Airports Authority 250, Table 12.2
British Airways 229, 249, Table 12.2
British Broadcasting Corporation (BBC) 209, 224, 230, 313
British Coal 236, 254, Table 12.1
British Gas 246, 248, 250–1, Table 12.2
British Leyland 8, 226
British Medical Association 33, 318
British Petroleum (BP) 228–9, 246, 249
British Rail 234, 254, Table 12.1
British Shipbuilders Tables 12.1–2
British Steel 237, Table 12.1
British Telecom 222, 246, 248, 250–1, Table 12.2
British Waterways Board Table 12.1
Britoil 229, Table 12.2
Brittan, Leon 88, 286, 290–1
Brooke Committee on Delegated Legislation (1972) 277
budget 65, 280
budgetary decentralization 130–1, 135–6
bureaucracy 16, 24–7, 84, 94, 122, 131, 299, 314
  partisan 97–9
  reforming **101–20**
Butler, Sir Robin 110
bye-laws 274, 276

Cabinet 18–19, 38–9, 43, 55, 57, 59–60, 62, **63–83**, 93, 108, 170, 281, 315
  composition 69–71
  functions 63–6
  inner 64, 70, 74
  partial 64, 71, 74
Cabinet committees 53–7, 59, 64–5, 71–5, 80, 85, 93, 315
  composition 72
  functions 73
Cabinet Office 12, 53, 55, 58–62, 71–3, 75–9, 81, 109–10, 128, 212, 290, 303
Cabinet Secretariat 59, 70, 75–7, 80–1
Cabinet Secretary 59–60, 64, 72, 75, 77, 107–10, 297
Callaghan, PM James/Callaghan government 60, 72, 284, 292
capital finance 164–5, 200–1, 233
Carrington, Lord 283, 287, 289
Cassels Report (1983) 136–7
Castle, Barbara 43, 95–6, 268
censure motion 293
central administration/government 5–6, 11, 13, 15, 17, **44–62**, 247–8, 322
  relationship with local government 5, 158–9, 163, 183, **184–208**
  see also government departments
Central Electricity Board 224, 230
Central Office of Information 52
Central Policy Review Staff (CPRS) 56, 58–62, 79–81, 121–2, 169, 195
centralization 16, 21, 149, 203, 232, 272
Centre for Administrative Studies 105
Centre for Policy Studies 79
Chalkpit case 309
charges, local authority 159–60, 163–4
Chartered Institute of Public Finance and Accounting (CIPFA) 196
chief executive, local authority 168–70, 174, 176, 181–2
chief officer, local authority 175–6, 179–82
Churchill, Winston 54, 95
circulars 190–1
citizen's advice bureaux 323
City Action Teams 54
City of London Corporation 145, *8.1*
Civil Aviation Authority 313, Table 12.1
Civil Contingencies Unit 72
civil service/servants 5, 7, 19, 51, 53, 60–1, 71–2, 78, 82, **84–100**, 137, 238, 253, 270, 273, 276, 295–8, 313–15, 317
  classes 103–4, 106–8, 110–14
  definition 86
  Fulton Report 10–11, 28–30, 94, 102–20
  generalists/specialists 27–8, 41, 50, 59, 102–4, 107–8, 111–14, 118–19
  grades 27–8, 47, 103, 107, 110–13, 116, *6.1*
  Northcote-Trevelyan Report 101–3
  reform **101–20**
  relationship with ministers 19, 41, 84, 86, 88–100, 119, 140, 180, 217, 283, 288–9, 291–2
  see also employment, public
Civil Service, Minister for the 75–6
Civil Service College 107–8, 114–16, 136
Civil Service Commission 102, 105, 108, 118
Civil Service Department 43, 53, 60, 80, 107–11, 114, 119–20, 211
Civil Service Selection Board 105, 118
Clay Cross 189, 191–2
clerical class, civil service 103, 111–12
clientele-based agencies 36–8

clientelism 34
Clothier, Cecil 323–4
Colonial Office 34–5, 37
Commission for Racial Equality 323
Commissions for Local Administration 311, 319–22
committees
inter-departmental 53–4, 59, 64, 71, 85
local authority 166–70, 173–4, 178–80
party 293–4
see also select committees; standing committees
common service divisions 48
common service organizations 52–3
Commonwealth Relations Office 35
Community Care (Griffiths Report, 1988) 271
community charge 161–2
community councils 146–7, *8.3*
community health councils (CHCs) 263–4, 267, 270, 323, *13.1–2*
competition 12, 246–8
Competition Act (1980) 13, 242
competition agencies 250–1
complaints procedures **299–324**
Comptroller and Auditor General 140, 215–16, 240, 282
concurrent powers, local authority 153
Conservative party/governments 90, 145–9, 157, 172–3, 186, 189–90, 192, 199–200, 203–4, 208, 221, 224, 226, 228, 246, 256, 265, 297
see also individual administrations
consultative committees 8, 259–60
Consultative Council on Local Government Finance (CCLGF) 162, 197–8
consumer councils 237, 240, 251, 260, 323
consumer protection 240–3, *8.4–5*
contracting-out of services 13–14, 122, 151, 207, 228, 246, 271
control of public bodies 9, 32, 213–14, 222, 226–7, 229–31, 235–8, 240–1, 251–2
NHS 258–60, 269
tribunals 308–10
water industry 258–60, 269
Control of Public Expenditure (Plowden Report, 1961) 49
co-ordinating departments 55–6, 75–6
co-ordinating ministers 54–5, 70
co-ordination **44–62**, 236, 261
by Cabinet 63–6, 70, 73, 76–7, 109
informal 47–8, 106
inter-departmental 44–8, 51–7, 59
intra-departmental 48–51, 59
local government 144, 149, 153–4, 166–70, 176, 195
of policy 44–6, 49–50, 52–3, 77, 168
by Prime Minister 78, 80–1
regional 254, 259, 272
Co-ordination of Defence, Minister for the 54
corporate planning 167–70, 176, 182, 238
corporatism 69
cost centres 127, 130–2, 136, 139
council meetings 166, 174
Council on Tribunals 303, 306–10
councillors 143, 155, 157, 167–8, 171–3, 265, 299, 319, 323
and officers 172, 177–83
county boroughs 144, 146, 153, *8.1*
county councils 142, 144, 146–7, 153–4, *8.2*
Court Line affair 313, 315
Court on Human Rights 323
CPRS *see* Central Policy Review Staff
Crawford Report on Broadcasting 230
creative accountancy 204
Crichel Down affair 287–8
Crosland, Anthony 90–1
Crossman, Richard 42, 74, 91–2, 313
Crown Suppliers 29
culture, departmental 122, 125, 137–8, 141
Customs and Excise, Board of 21, 24, 34, 103, Table 14.1

Dalton, Hugh 286
Davies, John 288
debates 292–3
decentralization 16, 127, 144, 149, 221, 232, 253, 272
budgetary 130–1, 135–6, 139
functional 24, 28
territorial 24–5
default powers 191–2
Defence Committee 88, 291, 296–7, Table 14.1
Defence, Ministry of (MOD) 22, 29, 35, 38–9, 55–6, 125, 136, Tables 2.1, 14.1
Defence Procurement Executive 22, 37, 137
delegated budgeting 130–1, 139, 282, 289
delegated legislation 274–9
democracy 149–50, 153–9
denationalization 224, 248–9
Denning, Lord 192

departmental agencies 19, 22, 28–30
departmental and specialist classes, civil service 103–4
departmental pattern 34–40, 51, 53, 66, 121, 167
departments *see* government departments
Deputy Secretary 27, 105,111, 124, *6.1*
deregulation 228
DES *see* Education and Science, Department of
DHSS *see* Health and Social Security Department of
Director General of Water Services 256
disputes, redress of **299–324**
district authorities 145
district councils 142–3, 146–8, 153–4, 169, *8.2–3*
district health authorities (DHAs) 265–7, *13.2*
districts, health 261, 263, 265, *13.1*
DOE *see* Environment, Department of
Donoghue, Lord Bernard 60, 98
Donoughmore Report on Ministers' Powers (1932) 276, 306
Driver and Vehicle Licensing Directorate 31, 317
Dugdale, Sir Thomas 287–8

Ecole Nationale d'Administration 116
Economic Affairs, Department of 35, 42, 53, 55–6
economic matters 25, 53, 108, 152, 226
economy 12–14, 123, 132, 134, 169, 282
Eden, PM Sir Anthony 74
education 1–2, 13, 16–18, 46, 94, 144–5, 148, 151, 153, 158–9, 166–7, 169–70, 175, 186–7, 190, 192, 196, 201, Table 10.1, *8.4–5*
Education Act (1944) 158, 190
Education and Science, Department of (DES) 24, 35, 46, 94, 194, Tables 2.1, 14.1
effectiveness 12–13, 120, 123, 132, 134, 138, 282
efficiency 12–13, 120, 132, 134, 138, 141, 225–7, 235, 238, 247–8, 258, 282
  PM's Special Adviser on 123
Efficiency Unit 30, 75, 123, 135
elections 66, 155–6
electricity industry 142, 224, 228, 230, 232, 234, 240–1, 245, 250, 253, Table 12.1
Employment, Department of 24, 26, 29, 42–3, 55, 253, Tables 2.1, 14.1
employment, public 6, 15, 17, 53, 143, 224–5, 260, Tables 1.1, 2.1, 11.1
  civil service 86, 109, 126, 131
Energy, Department of 35, 39, 96, Tables 2.1, 12.1, 14.1
Energy Committee 239, Table 14.1
enterprise zones 208, 219, 302
environment 4–5, 66, 101, 170
Environment, Department of the (DOE) 25, 29, 38–9, 41, 46, 54, 125–7, 129, 142, 149, 197, 199, 205, 214, 253–5, Tables 2.1, 12.1, 14.1
environmental health 194–5, Table 10.1, *8.4–5*
Equal Opportunities Commission 323
equity 9–10, 14, 16, 26, 46, 139, 141
European Commission 323
European Community (EC) 66, 76, 100, 284
  secondary legislation 273, 276, 279
executive bodies 30–3, 113–14, 212–13, 218, 220, 289, 304, Table 11.1
executive class, civil service 103, 111, 113, *6.1*
executive councils (NHS) 261, 263
Expenditure Committee 86, 95–6, 109–11, 113, 117–18, 294
expenditure, public 17, 49–50, 53, 56–7, 64, 115, 128, 133, 240, 260, 279–83, 292, 294, Table 11.1
  local 159–64, 186, 197–205, Table 10.1
  restraint 12, 32, 120, 126, 162–3, 218
expertise of ministers and civil servants 90–2, 95
external financing limits (EFLs) 233–5, 249

Falklands crisis 64, 71, 156, 283, 289, 292
family practitioner committees 263, 267, 318, 323, *13.1–2*
field offices 24–6, 46, 52, 135, 176
Finance Bills/Acts 280, 317
finance, public 279–83
  local government 159–65, 183–5, 193–4
  public corporations 233–5
  quangos 216–17
  see also expenditure, public
Financial and Economic Obligations of the Nationalised Industries (White Paper, 1961), 234
financial control by Treasury 52–3
financial management initiative (FMI) 13, 87, 122, 128–41, 216, 282, 289
Financial Management Unit 128, 132–4
fire service 149, 192, 196, 219, *8.4–5*

Food, Ministry of 35, 55
Foreign and Commonwealth Office (FCO) 24, 34–5, 38, 46, 65, 289, 317, Tables 2.1, 14.1
Forestry Commission 224
France 98, 104, 115–16, 299, 312
Franks Report (1957) 301, 303–4, 306–8, 310
Fuel and Power, Ministry of 35, 55
Fulton Report on the Civil Service (1968) 10–11, 28–30, 49–50, 94, 102–22, 127, 213
functions, allocation of 36–9, 49, 167

gas industry 224, 228, 230, 232, 234, 237, 250, 253
general category, civil service 111
general directives 235, 237–9, 244
general service classes, civil service 103–4
Girobank 222, Table 12.1
GLC *see* Greater London Council
goal-setting 129–30
government departments 7, 11, 18–19, 21–43, 78, 142, 210, 227–8, 251, 279, 283, 285–6, 288
  and Cabinet 63–4
  co-ordination 48–57
  departmental pattern 34–40, 51, 53, 66, 78, 121
  departmental select committees 215, 273, 282, 294–8, Table 14.1
  giant 38–9, 51, 56
  and local government 151, 183, **184–208**
  and nationalized industries 236, 238, 243, 249, Table 12.1
  and ombudsmen 315–17
  organization of 23–30, 33
  and public spending 280–2
  and regional administration 253, 260–1, 264
  size 6, 23–4, 38–9, 41, 45–67, 92–3, Tables 1.1, 2.1
  and tribunals 302–7
  types of 21–2
  see also civil service/servants
Government Purchasing 124
Government Trading Funds Act (1973) 223
Government's Chief Scientific Officer 75
grades, civil service 27–8, 47, 103, 107, 110–13, 116, *6.1*
graduates in civil service 101–2, 105, 107–8, 115–17
grant related expenditure assessment (GREA) 199–200, 202, 204
grants, government 159–64, 185, 197, 199–200, 233–4
Greater London Council (GLC) 145–6, 191, 206, *8.1*
  abolition 148–50, 189, 202, 208, 219, 228, 271
Griffiths Report (1983) 269–71 (1988) 271

Haldane Report (1918) 36–40, 43
Healey, Denis 91
Health, Department of 33, 35, 39, 41–2, 260, 267, Tables 2.1, 14.1
health authorities 13, 142, 148, 153, 176, 212, 260–71, 317–18
Health, Ministry of 194
Health and Safety Commission 29, 209
Health and Social Security, Department of (DHSS) 13, 23, 38–9, 131, 263, 270, 305, *13.1–2*
  Resettlement Units 31
Health Service Commissioners 265, 311, 317–19, 322
Health Services Supervisory Board 270
Heath, PM Edward/Heath government 57–60, 87, 96, 224
Hennessy Report (1984) 287
Herbert Report (1960) 145
Heseltine, Michael 55, 65, 74, 82, 85, 96–7, 125, 284–5, 290–1
hierarchy 16, 20, 24–6, 28, 41, 49, 51, 102–3, 106, 129, 131, 139
  integrated 28–9
  parallel 28–9, 104, 112
  specialist 104
Higher Executive Officer (HEO) 117–19, *6.1*
hiving-off 19, 22, 29–30, 32–3, 211, 213, 237
Home Affairs Committee 296, Table 14.1
Home Civil Service, Head of, *see* Cabinet Secretary
Home Office 34–5, 41, 135, 194, Tables 2.1, 14.1
Home Secretary 72, 145
Hoskyns, Sir John 62, 81, 98–9
hospitals 255, 261, 268
House of Commons Commission 298
housing 16–18, 148, 151–3, 166–7, 186, 192, 194–5, 198, 201, 246, 263, 271, 319, Table 10.1, *8.4–5*
Housing Act (1980) 192

Housing and Local Government, Ministry of 41
Housing Finance Act (1972) 191–2
hybrid companies 229, 249

Ibbs, Sir Robin 30, 58, 123
Ibbs Report (1988) 30–3, 110, 113–14, 120, 141, 220, 289, 304
ideology, political 225
ILEA *see* Inner London Education Authority
income tax 161, 304
Independent councillors 156
Industrial Reorganization Corporation 224, 229
industrial rescues 226, 229
industrial tribunals 304
Industry, Department of 39, 42–3, 51
information system, top management 128–9, 132, 135, 139, 141
information technology 15–16, 85, 115, 271
informational resources 93–5, 178
Ingham, Bernard 79, 291
Inland Revenue, Department of 21, 34, 103, 111, 254, 316, Table 14.1
inner Cabinet 64, 70, 74
inner cities 54, 208
Inner London Education Authority (ILEA) 145, 149, 190, 202, *8.4*
inquiries, public 66, 301–3
inspectors, departmental 192
inter-authority relationships 152–4
inter-departmental committees 53–4, 59, 64, 71, 85
inter-departmental co-ordination 44–8, 51–7, 59
intervention, government 33, 35, 53
intra-departmental co-ordination 48–51, 59
investment, government 211, 224–5, 233–4
  private sector 246–7
Irish Office 34–5, 37
island authorities (Scotland) 147, *8.3*

Jellicoe, Lord 230
joint boards 149, 182, 202, 219, *8.4*
joint consultative committees (district councils) 154
  (NHS) 262, *13.1–2*
Joint Management Unit 135
joint planning boards 319
Joint Scrutiny Committee 277, 279
Joubert Study 125, 127
judicial control 191, 215–16, 275, 277, 299–301, 305, 308, 310
junior ministers 85
Justice-All Souls Report (1988) 309–10, 312, 314–15, 323

Labour, Ministry of 35
Labour party/governments 94–5, 97, 145, 157, 164, 171–4, 186, 189–92, 198, 202–3, 206, 224, 225–6, 284
  see also individual administrations
Lambton, Lord 287
Law Officers' Department Table 2.1
Layfield Report (1976) 161
leaks of information 5, 43, 61, 79, 88, 284, 286, 290–1
Leathers, Lord 55
Legal Aid committees 309
legality *see ultra vires* doctrine
legislation 229, 239, 273–9
  delegated 274–9
  local government 189–90
  primary (statute) 273–4, 276, 279
leisure services 151, 246, *8.4–5*
Levene, Peter 137
liaison, local authority 152–4, 176
Liaison Committee 281, 295–6
Liberal party 157
libraries *8.4*
local authorities 5–6, 9–10, 13, 17–18, 53, 127, **142–65**, 221, 228, 253, 282, 313, 319, 322, Table 1.1
  associations 154, 195, 320
  and central government 5, 158–9, 163, **184–208**
  development and structure 143–50, **166–83**, *8.1–3*
  finance 159–65, 183–5, 193–4
  inter-authority relationships 152–4
  and NHS 261–6, 268, 271
  reorganization 145–50, 153–4, 156, 174, 257, 319
  services 150–2, 155, *8.4–5*
  and water industry 257–60
local education authorities 158
local enterprise boards 228
Local Government Act (1888) 143
  (1894) 142
  (1972) 143, 145–6, 152–3, 193
  (1985) 143, 146, 148–9, 189
  (1986) 203, 207
  (1988) 146, 149, 190, 207–8, 228
Local Government and Planning Department 35

Local Government Finance (Green Paper, 1977) 161
Local Government Finance (Layfield Report, 1976) 161
Local Government Finance Act (1982) 193, 201–2
(1988) 161–2
Local Government in England, Royal Commission on (1966) 145–6
Local Government in England (White Paper, 1971) 153
Local Government in Greater London, Royal Commission on (1957) 145
Local Government in Scotland, Royal Commission on (1966) 145, 147, 257
Local Government (Miscellaneous Provisions) (Scotland) Act (1981) 202
Local Government, Planning and Land Act (1980) 153–4, 180, 198–201, 302
Local Government (Scotland) Act (1973) 147, 257
local offices of central government 142, 253–4
'local state' theory 205–7, 256
local valuation courts 304
London boroughs 145–6, 149, 152, 161, *8.1*, *8.4*
London Boroughs Grant Scheme 149
London County Council 145
London Government Act (1899) 143
(1963) 145
London Passenger Transport Board 224
London Regional Transport Board 219, 228, Table 12.1
Lord Chancellor's Department/Office 34, 42, Table 2.1

MacGregor, Sir Ian 237
Machinery of Government Committee (1918) 36
McIntosh Report (1976) 223, 236, 241, 243
Macmillan, Sir Harold 64
maladministration 313, 315–16, 319–21
management accounting 11, 128
Management and Personnel Office 109–10, 123, 135–6
Management Information Systems for Ministers (MINIS) 13, 50, 122, 125–8
management skills in civil service 104–5, 107–8
management systems 128–9, 132, 135, 139
managerialism 2, 10–15, 50, 113, 120, **121–41**, 169, 269
manpower *see* employment, public
Manpower Services Commission (MSC) 29, 54, 86, 209, 218
Marre, Sir Alan 322
Maud Committee on the Management of Local Government 167–8
MAXIS 127
media 19, 66–8, 78, 82, 178, 203, 249, 265, 293, 296, 323
mergers, departmental 38–9, 51
Merits Committee *see* Standing Committee on Statutory Instruments
metropolitan county councils 145–6
abolition 148–50, 190, 202, 208, 272
metropolitan district councils 146, 152, 175, *8.4*
Metropolitan Police 145, 319
Middleton, Peter 89
MINIS *see* Management Information Systems for Ministers
Ministerial Control of the Nationalised Industries 243
ministerial departments 21–2, 25, Table 2.1
ministerial policy units 99
ministerial responsibility 9, 25, 32, 34, 87, 139–40, 214–17
collective 46, 283–5, 289–90, 292
individual 283, 285–92
ministers 5, 21–2, 27, 58, 61, **84–100**, 122, 124, 126, 129, 136, 192–3, 197–8, 214, 250, 273, 280, 293–4, 296–8, 301, 308–9, 313, 315
Cabinet **63–83**
co-ordinating 54–5
and NHS 264, 266, 268, 270
patronage 217–18, 220–1
and public corporations 230, 232–4, 235–9, 241–4
and quangos 214–15
relationships with civil servants 19, 41, 84, 86, 88–100, 103–4, 119, 283, 288–9, 291–2
roles 85, 89
and RWAs 258–9
and statutory instruments 274–6
MISC committees 72
MOD *see* Ministry of Defence
monetarism 97, 189
monopolies, statutory 225, 246, 250
Monopolies and Mergers Commission (MMC) 13, 242–3, 250, 304, 313

Morrison, Lord 230, 232
MPs 67, 84, 140, 203, 215, 239–40, 249, 265, **273–98**, 299, 311–12, 315–16, 322–3
see also Parliament
municipal boroughs 144, 146, *8.1*
Municipal Corporations Act (1835) 143
municipalization 228

National Audit Act (1983) 282
National Audit Office 52, 135, 243, 282
National Consumer Council 209, 241, 250, 323
National Economic Development Office 243
National Enterprise Board 224, 229–30
National Health Service (NHS) 6, 13, 17, 42, 212, 260–71, 304, 313, 322, Table 1.1
Management Board 270
Royal Commission on (1979) 264–5, 267
National Health Service Act (1946) 260–1
National Health Service Reorganization Act (1973) 262, 265
National Insurance, Department of 35
National Research Development Organization 210
National Rivers Authority 256
National Water Council 259
Nationalised Industries (White Paper, 1967) 233–4
(1978) 224, 233–4, 242, 244
Nationalised Industries Chairmen's Group (NICG) 237
nationalization 96, 222–4, 226, 243
nationalized industries 6, 8, 13, 16, 32, 53, 210, 212, 222–5, 228, 230–46, 254, 256, 258–9, 282, 295, 313, Tables 1.1, 12.1, 12.2
select committee on 235–7, 239–40, 243, 294
nationalized industry consultative or consumer councils (NICCs) 240–3
NATO 66, 94, 100
NEB *see* National Enterprise Board
negotiated order model 48
neighbourhood councils 146
Next Steps see Ibbs Report
NHS *see* National Health Service
non-departmental agencies 22, 29, 295
non-departmental public bodies 142, **209–21**, 230, 254, 313
advisory 212–13, 218, Table 11.1
Non-Departmental Public Bodies 216
non-metropolitan county councils 169, 175, *8.4*
non-metropolitan district councils 204, *8.4*
non-ministerial departments 21, 250
Northcote-Trevelyan Report (1854) 101–3
Northern Ireland 255, 274, 287, 309, 311, 322
Commissioner for Complaints 311, 316, 320, 323
Northern Ireland Office 24–5, 35, 37, 46, 255
Nott, John 289

objectives, statement of 129–30, 135
Office of Fair Trading 250, 323
Office of Gas Supplies (OFGAS) 250–1
Office of Telecommunications (OFTEL) 250–1
Office of the Minister for the Civil Service 75–6, 110, Table 14.1
officers, local government 157, 167–70, 172, 174–6
chief 175–6
and councillors 172, 177–83
Official Secrets Act 67–8
Official Steering Group 197
officials, dictatorship of 96, 177, 179
ombudsmen 19, 87, 89, 215, 289, 292, 294, 309–24
open structure in civil service 111, 113, 117–18, 120, *6.1*
opposition days 281, 293
opting out 208
Ordnance Board 34–5
organization, departmental 23–30, **101–20**
see also bureaucracy
organizational learning 121
Osmotherly memorandum 297
Overlords 54–5

Paige, Victor 270
PAR *see* Programme Analysis and Review
parish councils 6, 146–7, *8.1*
Parkinson, Cecil 287
Parliament 9, 19, 25, 32, 65, 67, 78, 93, 115, 140, 151, 184–5, 189, 203, 208, 214–15, 228, 230, 238–40, 259, 264–5, **273–98**, 311–12, 316
see also MPs
Parliamentary and Health Service Commissioner Act (1987) 313

Parliamentary Commissioner Act (1967) 311
Parliamentary Commissioner for Administration 311–17, 322
select committee on 311, 314–15, 318, 320, 322
Parliamentary Committee of the Cabinet 70
parliamentary private secretary 85
Parsons, Sir Anthony 79
partial Cabinet 64, 71, 74
participation in local government 155–6
partnership model of central-local government relationships 187–8
party committees 293–4
party leader 82
party politics 217, 274, 284
local government 156–8, 166, 169–70, 173–5, 181–2, 185–6, 196
party pressure on Cabinet 66–7, 70, 78
Paterson Report (1973) 168
Patients First 265, 267–8
patronage 101
ministerial 217–18, 220–1
PM's 70, 82
Paying for Local Government (Green Paper, 1986) 161, 200–1
payment of councillors 172, 179–80
performance indicators 10–15, 121, 125–6, 128, 131–5, 141, 242, 271
permanence of civil service 87, 95
local government 178
permament secretary 27, 54, 89, 92, 105, 107–11, 123–4, 270, 315, *6.1*
personnel management 106, 136
PESC *see* Public Expenditure Survey Committee
Pile, Sir William 94–5
planning 41, 44, 49–51, 53, 55, 57, 152–4, 159, 262, 265, Tables 8.4–5
corporate 167–70, 176, 182, 238
planning inquiries 301–3
planning units 49
Pliatzky Report (1980) 212–13, 216, 218, 223, 256, 258–9, 303–5
Plowden Report (1961) 49
police 110, 145, 149, 164, 177, 186, 192, 319, *8.4–5*
Police Boards 149
police committees 166, 170
Police Complaints Authority 323
policy/administration dichotomy 3–4, 138–9
policy and resources committees 168, 170
policy communities 8, 196
policy councils, nationalized industries 243–4
policy making 21, 24, 33–4, 40–1, 43, 48, 58–61, 64–5, 77, 85, 89, 93, 97–8, 100, 102–4, 134, 141, 196, 220, 241, 243, 267, 269, 296
co-ordination 44–6, 49–50, 52–3
implementation 94–5, 178–9, 195
local 142, 159, 173–5, 177, 179, 182–3, 188
policy networks 154
policy units 58–61, 74, 79–80, 97, 99
Political Office, PM's 78
political regionalism 272
political system 4–5, 8, 18–19, 21, 35–6, 46–7
and civil service 87–9, 95, 97–9
Ponting, Clive 88
Post Office 22, 34, 224, 227, 230, Table 12.1
Post Office Users' National Council 240, 242
Powell, Charles 291
power-dependence model of central-local government relationships 187–9, 205, 207
press office, PM's 67, 78
pressure groups 5, 8, 19, 33, 66, 68–9, 100, 142, 157–8, 176, 178, 211–12, 218, 265, 295–6, 323
preventative co-ordination 44, 66
prices 234–6, 241, 246, 250
Prices and Consumer Protection, Department of 35, 39
Prime Minister 34, 54–5, 57–65, 67, 70–4, 77–83, 91, 107–10, 137, 284–7, 289–90, 317
prime ministerial government 63, 74, 81–3
Prime Minister's Department 62, 77–83
Prime Minister's Office 11, 22, 53, 62, 78, 81, 97, 123
Prime Minister's Special Adviser on Efficiency 123
Principal level in civil service 27, 111, *6.1*
Prior, James 287
Prison Service 111
private sector 7–12, 14–15, 17–18, 30, 94, 105, 122, 138–41, 233, 246, 269
privatization 12–14, 17–18, 122, 155, 193, 207, 224, 226–7, 229, 232, 234, 244–52, 256, 260
privy councillors 294
Privy Council Office 22, 34–5, 76
professionalism 178

Profumo, John 287
Programme Analysis and Review (PAR) 19, 49–51, 56–7, 59, 121–2
programme expenditure 132–3, 135
Property Services Agency 29, 52, 223
public accountability *see* accountability
Public Accounts Commission 282
Public Accounts Committee (PAC) 129, 131, 135, 214–16, 243, 281–2, 294
Public Buildings and Works, Ministry of 29
public corporations 5, 18, 66, 142, 212, 223, 230–45, 258, 279, 295
Public Expenditure Survey 281
Public Expenditure Survey Committee (PESC) 19, 49–51, 54, 56–7, 121
Public Expenditure White Paper 132, 281
public ownership **222–52**
  see also nationalized industries; public corporations
Public Record Office 37
Public Utility Transfers and Water Charges Act (1988) 256
purchasing unit, central 124

quangos 13, 19, 66, 132, **209–21**, 280
quasi-government 7, **209–21**, 222–9
  see also nationalized industries; public corporations
quasi-elected local government organizations (QUELGOs) 219
questions, parliamentary 293

rate-capping 202–5
rate support grant 162, 199, 321, Table 8.1
rates 152, 159–62, 165, 201–3, 205, 207
Rates Act (1984) 202–5
Rates: Proposals for Rate Limitation (White Paper, 1983) 161, 202
Rayner, Lord Derek 122–3
Rayner Scrutiny Programme 13, 50, 57, 122–5, 127–8, 135
recruitment, civil service 101–2, 105, 107–8, 110, 116–19, 141
Redcliffe-Maud Commission 145, 155
redress 292–8, **299–324**
refuse services 208, 219, 228, 246, *8.4*
regional agencies **253–72**
regional councils (Scotland) 147, *8.3*
regional government 272
regional health authorities (RHAs) 254, 260–4, 267, 269, *13.1–2*
regional hospital boards 260–1
regional water authorities (RWAs) 257
regions 255–6
regulatory agencies 250–2
Reith, Lord 230, 232
Rent Assessment Panels 254, 304
Rent Tribunals 304
Reorganisation of Central Government (White Paper, 1970) 38, 58
representative bodies 320–2
research councils 209
're-shuffles', ministerial 36, 90, 288
resignation, government 283–4
  ministers 283–92
resource allocation/management 120–1, 125–6, 133, 138–9, 141, 271
revenue finance 234
Ridge v. Baldwin (1964) 300
roads 153, 185, 253, *8.4–5*
Robson, W. A. 310
Rolls Royce 224, 226, 246
Rooke, Sir Denis 237
Roskill Commission 310
Rothschild, Lord 58, 60
Royal Commissions 66
  Local Government in England 145–6
  Local Government in Greater London 145
  Local Government in Scotland 145, 147, 257
  National Health Service 264–5, 267
Royal Ordnance Factories 227, 246
'RPI–X' formula 250
rural district councils 144, 146, *8.1*

Sachsenhausen case (1968) 317
Scientific and Industrial Research department 35
Scotland 145, 147–8, 161, 168, 202, 204, 255, 257, 297, 300, 303, 309, 317, 319, 321–2, *8.3*
Scott, Nicholas 287
Scottish Affairs Committee 297, Table 14.1
Scottish Office 24–5, 35, 37, 46, 204, 255, 260, Tables 2.1, 12.1, 14.1
Scottish Transport Group Table 12.1
scrutiny, parliamentary 276–81, 292–8
Secretary of State 84–5
Seebohm Report (1968) 261
select committees 32, 87, 89, 140, 239, 244, 251, 294–8, Table 14.1
  Defence 88, 291, 296–7
  departmental 215, 273, 282, 294–8
  Energy 239, 250
  Expenditure 86, 95–6, 109–11, 113, 117–18, 294

Home Affairs 296
on Nationalized Industries 235–7, 239–40, 243, 294
on the Parliamentary Commissioner for Administration 311, 314–15, 318, 320, 322
Public Accounts 129, 131, 135, 214–16, 243, 281–2, 294
Social Services 265
specialist 281, 294
on Statutory Instruments 276–7
Treasury and Civil Service 12, 32, 99, 110, 127, 140, 281
selection, civil service 105, 110, 118
semi-autonomous agencies 21–2, 30, 131, 141–2, 209, 212
Senior, Derek 146
senior policy advisers 49–50
service divisions 48, 52
sewerage 148, 253, 256–7
shareholding, state 228–9, 246, 249
Sharp, Dame Evelyn 91
size of public administration 5–6, 16–17, 23–4, 45–6, 92–3, 144, Tables 1.1, 2.1
Sizewell inquiry 302
Social Security, Department of (DSS) 24–5, 39, 92, 94, 142, 194, 254, 316, Tables 2.1, 14.1
Social Security Act (1986) 305
social security appeal tribunals 304
social services 16, 144, 148, 151–3, 164, 167, 169, 175, 186, 201, 261–3, 268, 271, Table 10.1, *8.4–5*
Social Services Select Committee 265, Table 14.1
social spectrum of civil service 105–6, 116–17
Socialisation and Transport (Morrison) 230
Society of Local Authority Chief Executives (SOLACE) 154, 196
Sparrow, John 58
special advisers 79–80, 87, 97–8, 123
Special Orders Committee 276–7
special responsibility allowances (SRAs) 172, 180
specialists, government departments 28, 41, 102–4, 107, 111–14, 118
local government 175–6, 179
NHS 269
specialization in departmental organisation 26
Standing Advisory Commission on Administrative Organization 221
standing committees 71–3, 274, 280, 298
Star Chamber 57
state, role of 34–5, 63
statute legislation 273–4
statutory inquiries 301, 309
statutory instruments 273–8, 292
Statutory Instruments Act (1946) 276–7
Stansted Airport investigation 309–10
steel industry 237, 245, Table 12.1
stewardship model of central-local government relationships 188–9
strategic co-ordination 44–5, 49, 58–9, 66, 80–1
strategic planning 145, *8.5*
Streamlining the Cities (White Paper, 1983) 148
subordinate legislation 274–9
Suez 71, 74, 287
Supply, Ministry of 35
surcharging 192, 203
'Sus' laws 296

Tameside dispute (1976) 190
target mechanism 199–202, 234
taxation 9, 275, 279–80, 292, 304, 317
local 161
Technology, Ministry of (1964–70) 28, 35
tenants' liaison committees 142
tendering 13, 18, 208, 228
tenure of office, civil service 90
Thames Water Authority 149
Thatcher, PM Margaret/Thatcher government 11–12, 14, 17, 30, 50, 60–2, 65, 69, 72–4, 79, 82, 89, 92, 95, 97, 113, 117, 119, 120–2, 125, 138, 141, 148, 161, 164, 188, 193–4, 198, 205, 207, 210, 218, 220, 225–6, 228–9, 245–8, 268, 284, 290–1
Think Tank *see* Central Policy Review Staff
Tisdall, Sarah 88
Trade, Board of 34
Trade, Department of 39, 43, 51, 55, 242
Trade and Industry, Department of 38–9, 54, 132, 242, 253–4, 288, Tables 2.1, 12.1, 14.1
trade unions 68, 109, 120, 126, 136, 158, 234, 237, 306
trading activities 152, 227–8, 246, *8.5*
trading funds 223
training 101, 104–5, 107, 114–16, 119, 128, 136, 141, 172
Training Agency 22, 216
Transition to War Committee 72

transport 149, 196, 201, 224, 228, 230, 232, 240, 304, *8.4–5*
Transport, Department of 35, 39, 55, 96, 149, 185, 253, Tables 2.1, 12.1, 14.1
Transport Act (1985) 228
Transport Boards 149
Treasury, H.M. 12, 24, 32, 34–5, 42–3, 52–3, 55–6, 60, 77, 80, 84, 105–6, 108–10, 119, 128, 135–6, 163, 197, 227, 230, 233, 236, 238, 243–4, 249, 314
Treasury and Civil Service Select Committee 12, 32, 99, 110, 127, 140, 281, Table 14.1
Treasury/Cabinet Office Joint Management Unit 128
Treasury Pay and Management Group 106, 108
Treasury Solicitor 314
tribunals 212, 218, 303–10, Table 11.1
two-tier system of local authorities 146, 152, *8.2*

ultra vires doctrine 10, 151, 191, 277, 299, 308
Under Secretary 27, 84–5, 105, 110–11, 114, 117, *6.1*
unification of civil service 101
unitary authorities 145
United Kingdom Atomic Energy Authority 7
United States 85, 87, 99, 104, 110, 251, 282
University Grants Committee 209
Upper Clyde Shipbuilders 224
urban development corporations 208, 219, 319
urban district councils 144, 146, 152, *8.1*

value-for-money 11–14, 121–2, 128, 131–2, 139, 220
Vehicle and General Insurance Company 288
Vehicle Inspectorate 31
voluntary organizations 151, 263

Wales 143, 146–8, 161, 163–4, 168, 211, 255, 317, 319, 321–2, *8.1–3*
Walters, Sir Alan 79
War Office Ordnance Board 34–5
War Pensions, Department of 35
Wass, Sir Douglas 98–9
Water Act (1973) 148, 257–9 (1983) 223, 259–60
water authorities 127, 142, 148, 153, 176, 212, 223, 254, 269, 271, 319–20
water industry 222, 224, 228, 234, 245, 250, 253, 256–60
Welsh Office 24–5, 35–7, 46, 214, 255, 260, 296, Tables 2.1, 14.1
Welsh Water Authority 257
Westland affair 43, 65, 74, 79, 82, 88, 284–6, 289–92, 296–7
Wheatley Commission on Scotland 146–7, 257
whips, government 67
White Papers 65
  Financial and Economic Obligations of the Nationalised Industries (1961) 234
  Local Government in England (1971) 153
  Nationalised Industries (1967) 233–4 (1978) 224, 233–4, 242, 244
  post-Widdicombe (1988) 152, 157, 169–70, 174, 176, 180–2, 193
  Public Expenditure 132, 281
  Rates: Proposals for Rate Limitation (1983) 161, 202
  Reorganisation of Central Government (1970) 38, 58
  Streamlining the Cities (1983) 148
Whitmore, Clive 89
Whyatt Committee 310–11, 324
Widdicombe Report 143, 154, 156–7, 166, 169–71, 173–4, 179–81, 314, 320
Williams, Marcia (Lady Falkender) 78, 95
Williams, Shirley 94–5
Wilson, PM Harold/Wilson government 60, 70, 74–5, 78–9, 81, 90, 96, 284
Women's Royal Voluntary Service (WRVS) 158, 209
Woolton, Lord 55
Works, Ministry of 35

youth service advisory councils 142